YEARS OF GLORY

1 9 4 2 1 9 6 7

YEARS OF GLORY
1 9 4 2 · NHL · 1 9 6 7

The National Hockey League's Official Book of
THE SIX-TEAM ERA

M&S

EDITED BY DAN DIAMOND

Canadian Cataloguing in Publication Data

Main entry under title:
Years of glory, 1942-1967 : the National Hockey League's
      official book of the six-team era

Includes index.
ISBN 0-7710-2817-2

1. National Hockey League – History. I. Diamond, Dan.

GV847.8.N3Y4 1994   796.962'06   C94-931891-4

Editor: Dan Diamond
Photo Editor: Ralph Dinger
Main Text and Captions: James Duplacey
Sidebars: Stu Hackel
Index: Elliotte Friedman
Coordinating Editor: Pat Kennedy for McClelland & Stewart
Production Editor: Peter Buck for McClelland & Stewart
Design: M&S
Design Assistant: Trish Lyon

Printed and bound in Canada on acid-free paper.

McClelland & Stewart Inc.
The Canadian Publishers
481 University Avenue
Toronto, Ontario
M5G 2E9

1   2   3   4   5   98   97   96   95   94

For everyone who cares for the game

Contents

Les Canadiens sont là: The Birth of a Dynasty, 1956-1960

Punch Time: Lord Stanley Returns to Toronto, 1961-1964

Prime Tickets: Big Jean and the Golden Jet, 1965-1967

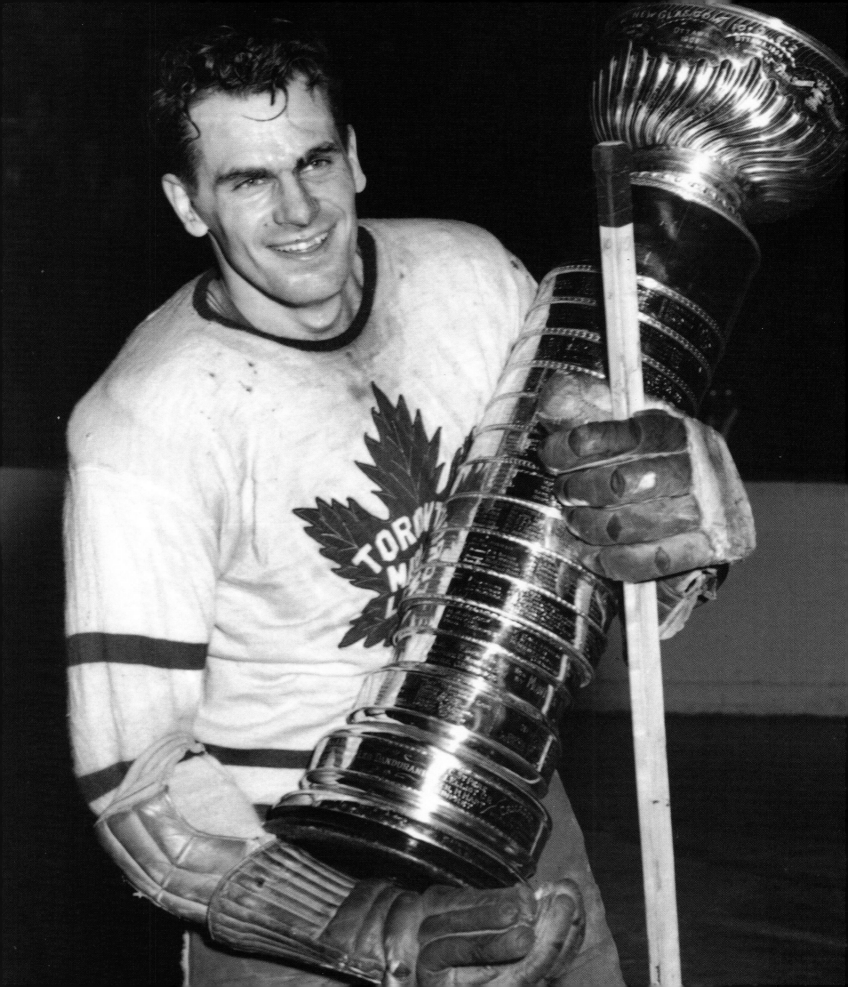

Introduction

by Trent Frayne

THE STUBBORN NATURE OF THREE MEN COMBINED TO MAKE THE QUARTER-CENTURY of 1942 through 1967 one of the most significant, and certainly the most parochial, in the history of the National Hockey League. For this, take a bow Jacques Plante, Frank Boucher, and Conn Smythe, Hall-of-Famers one and all.

It was a six-team quarter-century of dominant teams and great stars. In that twenty-five-year span the Montreal Canadiens finished in first place twelve times, the Detroit Red Wings ten times. In a stretch of seven seasons from 1948-49 through 1954-55, the Red Wings were first every time. In there, too, were the Toronto Maple Leafs, who rarely topped the standings, but who won the Stanley Cup on nine occasions. And the Canadiens, from the spring of 1956 through the spring of 1960, set a record still unmatched: five straight Stanley Cup championships.

And what a following they had, those hurtling Habitants. The gentlemanly Herbert Warren Wind, writing in the *New Yorker* magazine in the fall of 1954, was to say:

> It is doubtful if there is any group of sports addicts anywhere which year in and year out supports its team with quite the super-charged emotion and lavish pride expended so prodigally by the citizens of bilingual Montreal on their hockey team, *les Canadiens* . . . the Canadians. . . . It is not uncommon for crowds seeking standing room to run into several thousands and to swarm over Ste. Catherine Street and beyond onto Atwater Park. Hockey is deep in the Montrealer's blood.

Opposite: In addition to his considerable skills on the ice, Syl Apps was a renowned track and field star. The gold-medal winner in the pole vault at the British Empire Games in 1934, Apps represented Canada in the event at the 1936 Berlin Olympics, finishing sixth. Only weeks before, Apps made his debut as a Maple Leaf during the Totem Trophy exhibition series between Toronto and the Chicago Black Hawks, held after the conclusion of the 1935-36 season.

Bobby Hull's speed, blistering shot, and blond locks made him the NHL's marquee player of the 1960s and the first skater to break the 50-goal barrier.

Frank "Raffles" Boucher (center), spent twenty-nine seasons in the New York Rangers organization as a player, coach, and general manager. After a year in retirement, Boucher replaced legendary Lester Patrick behind the Rangers' bench prior to the 1939-40 season, and led the Broadway Blueshirts to a Stanley Cup championship in his first season as coach.

In that era, Maurice "Rocket" Richard was a veritable Napoleon on the Forum ice. When the Rocket scored, thunder and lightning erupted. As Wind was to write: "There is no sound quite like it in the whole world of sport."

Back in that memorable quarter-century, an advantage enjoyed by NHL fans was that they could tell the players without a program. Throughout this long period, through the influence of Conn Smythe and club owners like him, there were only six teams, a hundred or so players, parading into visiting rinks six or seven times a season, their faces and styles growing as familiar to the people laying down their money as were those of next-door neighbors.

What a parade of stars: Gordie Howe and the Production Line of Detroit, the dazzling Rocket and the Punch Line in Montreal, the Bentley brothers on the Pony Line in Chicago. Similarly, what goaltenders: Turk Broda, Frank Brimsek, Bill Durnan, Johnny Bower, a maskless (and soon stitched like a baseball) Terry Sawchuk, and the aforementioned Jacques Plante, of whom more later. Also, there were the cool defenders: Doug Harvey, Red Kelly, Bill Quackenbush, and Tim Horton. Putting the puck in the net were wingmen such as the blazing Bobby Hull and the Big M, the stylish Frank Mahovlich. And then, of course, down center there was the institution himself, Jean Béliveau.

But, as mentioned, there were those three whose contribution to the quarter-century stood out, significant and seemingly timeless. Frank Boucher spent twenty-nine years with the New York Rangers as a superlatively talented player, then as their coach and general manager. It was Boucher's persistence that brought the center red line to hockey; it was virtually the game's salvation when it was introduced for the 1943-44 season.

The Bouchers of Ottawa were a colorful family, which verged on eccentricity. Frank had five brothers and two sisters. Their father was half French and half Irish. Their mother was Irish. Four of the brothers, Frank, George, Billy, and Bobby, played in the NHL. The oldest boy, Carroll, was a circus buff. One night his wife sent him down to the corner store to buy a loaf of bread. Carroll didn't return for seven years. When he finally showed up, he was dutifully carrying a loaf of bread under each arm. He had spent the seven years traveling with the circus of Ringling Brothers, Barnum & Bailey.

And then there was Grandpa Antoine Boucher. When he was eighty, he decided that, since four of his grandsons were in the NHL, he should learn to play hockey himself. He wrote to a mail-order store for a pair of skates, a hockey stick, and a puck. He ventured onto a pond back of his farmhouse, where his daughter Sybil watched him through the kitchen window. He skated on thin ice and crashed through.

"Jack, Jack, come quick!" Sybil cried to her brother in another part of the house. "Pa's in the creek and the water's way up to his knees."

"Well, he can walk out, can't he?" snorted her brother.

"No, no, he can't!" she cried. "He's in head first."

Frank played on the Rangers' first great line, the centerman for the Cook brothers, Bill and Bun. He became the team's coach in 1939-40, and led the Rangers to their third Stanley Cup.

By 1942, Frank's third season of running the Rangers, a new system of defensive play had evolved, in which defensemen, who had always played about halfway between the goaltender and the blueline, moved out ahead of the blueline to break up the passing patterns of incoming forwards.

To combat this, forwards began shooting the puck past the defensemen and chasing in after it. When their own defensemen followed them in, there were eleven men inside the blueline, milling about. The defenders couldn't get the puck out for long periods, because forward passing was not permitted beyond the defending team's blueline. And so there developed seemingly endless periods of jamming at the puck with little result, first in one end of the rink, then in the other.

So Boucher, who had been busy fulfilling an assignment from NHL president Red Dutton to rewrite the league's rulebook, searched for a solution. He consulted other team leaders such as Art Ross in Boston and Toronto's Hap Day, and worked with Cecil Duncan, the president of the Canadian Amateur Hockey Association. Then one night he came up with a solution and called Duncan. "If one team's blueline is too near, and the other team's blueline too far, what about halfway between?" he proposed. "We can put a line at center ice, and we'll paint it red to avoid confusion."

And that's how the center red line, a staple in the game for fifty years (and counting), arrived to revolutionize hockey.

Fifteen years slipped past following the Boucher inspiration before there was another lasting and significant revolution: Jacques Plante's determination on a November night in 1959 to defy his coach, Toe Blake, and adorn his handsome kisser with a mask. If Jacques hadn't persisted, God knows where the game would be today. Without masks, the goaltending species would have long since grown extinct.

Plante played until he was forty-four. He provided noble service in Montreal, New York, St. Louis, Toronto, and Boston. To prolong his hockey life, Jacques followed a quirky set of preparation and training rituals as inflexible as the fiberglass mask he invented. In ten years with the Canadiens, he won the Vezina Trophy six times and drove everybody crazy. His employers called him a hypochondriac. But Jacques said, no, he really did get those funny itches and rashes and plugged noses from clothing and mysterious pollutants in the air.

Hockey has had few personalities as intriguing as Jacques. I visited

Jacques Plante's approach to goaltending combined rigorous conditioning, psychological preparation, and technical innovation. An inspiration to generations of goaltenders to come, Plante's NHL career began in the mid-1950s and extended beyond the six-team era. He is best remembered as a member of the Canadiens' dynasty teams of the late 1950s. He wore the facemask shown in this photo in an NHL game for the first time in November 1959.

Conn Smythe's famous battle cry, "If you can't beat 'em in the alley, you can't beat 'em on the ice," perfectly described the teams he iced during his three decades at the helm of the Toronto Maple Leafs.

him one time in his apartment in North Toronto. He was sitting on a couch with one leg on an ottoman. Strapped to his shoe was a sixteen-pound lead weight, in his lap a book. He would read three pages of the book, then pause to raise the leg three times, then three more pages of the book, then three more raises. Then he would switch the weight to the other foot and, if necessary, he'd switch the book. This day he was reading two books alternately, Jean-Jacques Marie's biography of Stalin in French and Mary Barelli Callaghan's biography of Jacqueline Kennedy Onassis in English.

Jacques was lifting the leg to strengthen the thigh muscles and ward off hamstring pulls. He was reading the books to strengthen his mind, which was razor sharp. He preferred biography. He had read the lives of Eisenhower, Churchill, Kennedy, Lenin, Khrushchev, Marx, Canada's hockey-playing prime minister Lester Pearson – anyone who'd had a book written about him or her, perhaps including Conn Smythe.

For more than three decades, as the boss of Maple Leaf Gardens, Smythe was the most bombastic and controversial figure in hockey. His was the loudest voice among the league's governors, a sort of George Steinbrenner in a dazzling white Borcelino. During his years of influence he was opposed to expansion, perfectly happy with the tight little six-team monopoly. Smythe had been the driving force behind the building of Maple Leaf Gardens in 1931 at the height of the Great Depression, and, for thirty years under his stewardship, ensured that it was the cleanest, brightest arena on the continent.

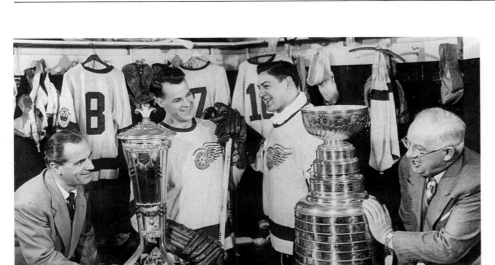

Left to right: Tommy Ivan, Gordie Howe, Alex Delvecchio, and Jack Adams gather around the Prince of Wales Trophy and the Stanley Cup after the Detroit Red Wings completed the two-trophy sweep during the 1953-54 season. During Adams's thirty-five-year reign as Detroit's general manager, the Red Wings finished first twelve times and won seven Stanley Cup titles.

Even in 1967, six years after his retirement, when economic forces and changing demographics combined to end the six-team era, Smythe remained outspokenly opposed to NHL expansion. "I'm for perfection," he clarioned during an interview in a typical uncompromising monlogue.

> We had the best players in the world split between six teams, and hockey was always worth the money. In the old days there were just as many players [who] could handle Gordie Howe as he could handle. In his last few years . . . nobody could get near him. Hockey today is like everything else; what are the cars like, what are the shoes like, what are the shirts like compared with before when the rule was the customer is always right? They are not made as tough and they haven't the same class. Maybe more people see hockey than before and more players get employed, but nobody will ever see again the brand of hockey we produced.

Even long before he retired, Smythe never hesitated to sound off on this topic. One night, along about 1953 or so, I remember him facing a panel on a CBC television program. A group from Cleveland was vainly seeking an NHL franchise, and I asked him why it wouldn't be good for the fans to relieve the monotony of the same six teams. Why not bring in Cleveland?

"Monotony!" he cried. "Monotony! This is the greatest game in the world and these are the greatest teams. Only a moron would want to change it."

That Smythe, so passionate about the six-team NHL that he'd call you a moron and you'd agree with him.

Years of Glory

1942-1967

IN THE FIRST TWENTY-FIVE YEARS OF ITS EXISTENCE, THE NATIONAL HOCKEY League evolved from a four-team league based in Ontario and Quebec to a ten-member organization that included cities as diverse as New York, Chicago, and Detroit. The talents of some of hockey's finest players were displayed in this era, from the on-ice brilliance of Howie Morenz and Aurel Joliat to the innovative artistry of Eddie Shore and Nels Stewart. However, the favorable economic conditions that spurred the league's growth in the 1920s were followed by a decade-long depression that severely tested its strength. Franchises in smaller cities, such as Ottawa and Pittsburgh, could no longer operate in this economic climate, despite attempts to stay afloat by relocating. The Montreal Maroons, the league's first expansion team, struggled on the ice and at the box-office, and eventually was granted a leave of absence from the league following the 1937-38 season.

By the early 1940s, the New York Americans, who had joined the league in 1926 and had managed to survive for fifteen seasons, despite limited on-ice success, were also facing financial difficulties. Forced to compete for fan support and newspaper coverage with the Stanley Cup-winning Rangers, as well as with baseball's Yankees, Giants, and Dodgers, the club changed its name to the Brooklyn Americans in 1941-42 in a last-ditch effort to spark local interest. Unfortunately, this didn't work, and the Amerks were forced to fold, leaving the NHL a six-team operation.

This six-club configuration remained unaltered for the twenty-five seasons from 1942-43 to 1966-67. Until the league's mammoth expansion of 1967, when six new teams were added, the 120 or so players on the rosters of the six NHL clubs were the game's elite, and the product of player-development systems that embraced everything from excellent minor pro leagues to playground rinks from coast to coast. It's an era that is frequently nominated as hockey's "Golden Age," and just as frequently – and erroneously – known as the years of the "Original Six." But by any name, the six-team years from 1942 to 1967 produced some of the game's greatest players, bitterest rivalries, and most enduring memories.

MONTREAL
FORUM

15¢

1909 ~ CELERITAS · AETERNAQUE · AUCTORITAS ~ 1946

The Red Line and the Rocket's Red Glare

1942-43 to 1945-46

| 61 PTS. | 57 PTS. | 53 PTS. | 50 PTS. | 49 PTS. | 30 PTS. |

1942-43
Birth of the Six-Team League

THE NATIONAL HOCKEY LEAGUE OPENED ITS TWENTY-SIXTH SEASON WITH SIX teams – the Montreal Canadiens, the Toronto Maple Leafs, the Detroit Red Wings, the Chicago Black Hawks, the New York Rangers, and the Boston Bruins – the smallest number of clubs since 1924-25. But although the number of clubs was down, each franchise was strong.

All four American franchises had tasted champagne from the Stanley Cup in the 1930s. In fact, in the four-year period from 1937 to 1940, each of the U.S.-based teams took a turn winning the championship. The Maple Leafs reached the Stanley Cup finals seven times in ten years, and were the defending champions as training camps opened in September of 1942. The Montreal Canadiens, who had come perilously close to folding in the mid-1930s, before a league ruling gave the team first rights to francophone talent, were gradually being rebuilt into a competitive unit. Although they had missed the post-season in four of the previous six campaigns, the Habs had an exciting crop of young, gifted forwards.

The major concern of the NHL, as teams gathered for the start of the 1942-43 campaign, was the war in Europe. Many fans were convinced the league would suspend operations, but all fears were put to rest when league president, Frank Calder, issued a statement on September 28 that concluded "authorities have recognized the place which the operations of the league hold in the public interest and have, after lengthy deliberation, agreed that in the interest of public morale, the league should carry on."

Although the immediate future of the league was secure, officials were still uneasy about the quality of hockey that was being played. At least eighty players were already serving in the armed forces, and every team was affected by the player shortage. The Boston Bruins were

Opposite: Three famous faces from three decades in the history of the Montreal Canadiens are featured on the cover of this Montreal Forum program. Newsy Lalonde, Howie Morenz, and Toe Blake each enjoyed an outstanding NHL career wearing the tricolore *of the Canadiens. Each is immortalized in the Hockey Hall of Fame.*

Sport News

Boston Garden 35¢

Bill Cowley, who set an NHL record with 45 assists during the 1940-41 season, captured his second Hart Trophy as league MVP in 1942-43, when he collected a career-high 72 points.

Three of a Kind

Hawks coach Paul Thompson united the three Bentley Brothers – Max, Doug, and Reg – to form a complete line for the 1943 New Year's Day game against the Rangers at Chicago Stadium. It was the first time three brothers were NHL linemates, a feat not duplicated until Quebec played Peter, Anton, and Marian Stastny as a unit in 1981.

missing their main offensive unit, the "Kraut Line" of Milt Schmidt, Bobby Bauer, and Woody Dumart, leaving the Beantowners with a cast of unproven youngsters and aging veterans.

Yet, Boston's weaknesses were minor compared to the troubles that confronted the New York Rangers, who lost the mainstays of their roster to the war effort, including Neil and Mac Colville, Alex Shibicky, Jim Henry, and Art Coulter. The impact of this personnel shortage would be felt all season long, as the Rangers fell from first place to the basement, winning a franchise-low 11 games during the 1942-43 campaign.

The Leafs lost seven players to the army, but compensated by acquiring Walter "Babe" Pratt from the Rangers and promoting rookies Ted Kennedy, Gaye Stewart, and Bud Poile. Detroit's roster escaped virtually untouched, appearing even stronger with the addition of Harry Watson from the defunct New York/Brooklyn Americans. Montreal lost Ken and Terry Reardon, but added a promising newcomer by the name of Maurice Richard.

In order to balance these player losses with the limited talent available, the league passed new legislation that abolished the rule requiring teams to dress at least twelve players, and reduced the size of each club's roster of players under NHL contract from fifteen to fourteen. A shortage of capable on-ice officials was avoided when four former players – Francis "King" Clancy, Archie Wilcox, Art Chapman, and Charley McVeigh – were hired to serve as referees for the season.

On November 21, three weeks after the start of the schedule, the league announced that regular-season overtime was being discontinued due to wartime travel restrictions. This made it impossible to delay trains that, in previous years, were routinely held to accommodate players, coaches, and reporters who were involved in overtime games. Overtime had been a feature of NHL play since 1917-18. The New York Rangers and Chicago Black Hawks were the last two teams to play a regular-season overtime game (until 1983-84, when regular-season overtime was reinstated), with the Rangers downing the Hawks 5–3 on November 10, 1942.

President Calder's verdict on the elimination of overtime was the last major decision he would make. On January 25, 1943, at a league meeting in Toronto, Calder suffered a coronary, eventually succumbing to heart failure on February 4. Mervyn "Red" Dutton, a former player, coach, general manager, and club executive, was chosen to replace Calder on an interim basis, becoming only the second president in the league's history.

With so many prominent players missing due to military service, defensive play suffered. For the first time, every team scored at least 150 times. Doug Bentley, the flashy Chicago forward who finished with 73 points, tied Ralph "Cooney" Weiland's single-season record, established in 1929-30. The two players tied for seventh place among the season's leading scorers, Montreal's Buddy O'Connor and Elmer Lach, each

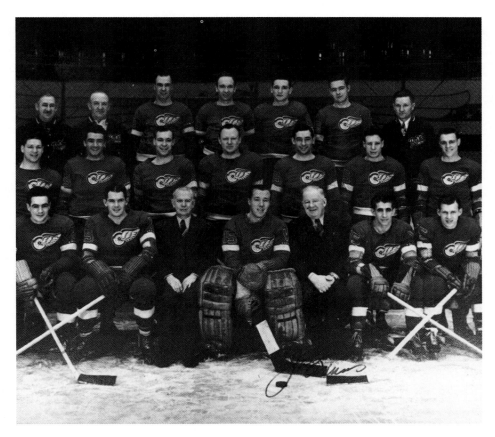

Johnny Mowers (front row, middle) led the Detroit Red Wings to the 1943 Stanley Cup championship, winning eight games in the playoffs while recording a 1.94 goals-against average and a pair of shutouts. He joined the army the following season and played only seven more games in his NHL career.

compiled 58 points, which would have been enough to win the scoring title in the previous season. Despite scoring a team-record 161 goals, the Rangers finished last in points, wins, goals-for, and goals-against, becoming the first NHL team to allow over two hundred goals in a season. Chicago went winless in its last seven games, enabling the Canadiens, who went undefeated in their final six contests, to nail down the final playoff spot by a single point. Despite being the only team without a scorer among the top ten, the Red Wings finished in first place, thanks in large part to their excellent defensive play.

One playoff format was employed throughout the six-team era: the league's top four clubs qualified for post-season play. In the best-of-seven semi-final round, the team finishing in first place in the regular season played the team that finished third, while the second-place club played the fourth-place finisher. The two semi-final winners would then meet in a best-of-seven Stanley Cup final.

The Detroit Red Wings' fine defensive play carried them through the post-season. Having lost to Toronto after leading three games to none in the 1942 Cup finals, Detroit exacted a measure of revenge by downing the Leafs in a six-game semi-final. Boston needed five games to eliminate Montreal in the other semi-final match-up. The Red Wings captured their third Stanley Cup title, outscoring the Bruins 16–5 en route to a four-game final-series sweep.

JOHNNY MOWERS RECORDS LEAGUE-LEADING SIXTH SHUTOUT

Mowers finished the season with six shutouts, surpassing the total number of shutouts – five – recorded by all other goaltenders in the NHL in 1942-43.

**March 6, 1943
at Detroit Olympia
Detroit 5, Chicago 0**

FIRST PERIOD

No Scoring

SECOND PERIOD

1) DET Watson (Bruneteau) 6:17
2) DET Carveth (Watson, Douglas) 17:54

THIRD PERIOD

3) DET Wares (Grosso) 3:42
4) DET Grosso (Wares, Jackson) 4:03
5) DET Abel 13:04

PENALTIES - Wiebe CHI (1 minor); Allen CHI (1 minor); Mitchell CHI (1 minor).

GOALTENDERS	TIME	GA	ENG	DEC
CHI Gardiner	60:00	5	0	L
DET Mowers	60:00	0	0	W

PP CONVERSIONS CHI 0/0 DET 0/3

| 83 PTS. | 58 PTS. | 50 PTS. | 49 PTS. | 43 PTS. | 17 PTS. |

1943-44
Center Red Line Ushers in Hockey's Modern Era

HOCKEY'S MODERN ERA BEGAN AT AN NHL BOARD OF GOVERNORS MEETING IN September 1943. At this gathering, league officials added a center red line to the ice surface, in an attempt to speed up the game and reduce off-sides. Prior to this innovation, forward passing was permitted in each of the defensive, neutral, and offensive zones, but the puck had to be carried over both bluelines. Teams with strong forechecking could pin their opponents in their own end of the ice, making it extremely difficult for the defending team to get out of its own zone. This resulted in numerous offside infractions and, at times, a plodding style of play.

Under the new rules, a player could pass from his own zone right up to the new center-ice red line. This gave the defending team greater ability to counter-attack. It forced forecheckers to cover more territory, and it opened up the game by placing emphasis on speed and passing. Although purists argued that the changes would result in a "too-liberalized" game, the fans took to the changes immediately. For the owners, suffering through wartime player and cash shortages, full seats and full tills took precedence over the art of stickhandling in close quarters.

A second rule change affected the position of players taking faceoffs. Under the old rules, players taking a faceoff would line up with their backs to the side boards. Many coaches employed a strategy that required the players taking the faceoff to ignore the puck and tie each other up, so that a second player could skate in and pick up the puck. Under the new rule, the position of players taking the faceoff was rotated ninety degrees. Now, players taking faceoffs would stand with their backs toward their own goals. The intent of the new rule was to speed up play by placing greater emphasis on cleanly winning the draw.

Military obligations continued to drain the rosters of the league's six franchises. The Red Wings, virtually untouched in 1942-43, lost nine of their starters, including Sid Abel, Jack Stewart, and Ebbie Goodfellow. The New York Rangers, already down to a threadbare lineup, lost another five skaters, including top scorer Lynn Patrick. Manager Lester Patrick suggested that the team suspend operations for the duration of the war, but the club continued to function and to struggle.

A Big Win

On January 23, 1944, the Red Wings crushed the New York Rangers, 15–0, in the most lopsided game in NHL history. Rangers goal-tender, Ken "Tubby" McAuley, was Detroit's unfortunate victim, as the club set an NHL record for most consecutive goals scored by one team. This record still stands. The Wings also set a mark for most goals by one team in a period with eight in the third. This record stood until the Buffalo Sabres scored nine times in a period in 1981.

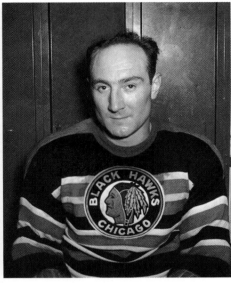

Left: Rangers right-winger Bryan Hextall scored 21 goals in 1943-44, giving him six consecutive seasons with 20 or more. A four-time All-Star, Hextall was also the league's top scorer in 1941-42.

Right: Defenseman Earl Seibert, who played fifteen seasons with the New York Rangers, Chicago, and Detroit, was selected to either the First or Second All-Star teams in ten consecutive seasons.

The top club in the first part of the season was the Montreal Canadiens, winners of twenty of their first twenty-five games. Rookie goaltender Bill Durnan was one of the league's outstanding freshman, but most of the attention was focused on a new forward unit put together by coach Dick Irvin. In the opening days of the schedule, Irvin put feisty right-winger Maurice Richard, who had missed most of the previous season with a broken leg, on a line with Elmer Lach and Hector "Toe" Blake, adding instant punch to the Habs' attack. The combination soon became the team's most consistent offensive unit.

Durnan's outstanding play notwithstanding, the greatest concern in the league was the lack of NHL-caliber goaltenders. Detroit employed seventeen-year-old rookie Harry Lumley, who appeared in two games for the Wings. The Leafs were forced to try three goalies, while the Bruins had five different men between the pipes during the season. The Rangers, who during the 1942-43 season became the first NHL team to have three goaltenders play at least nine games apiece, continued to struggle defensively. As a team, they allowed 310 goals, the most in league history to that point. Ken McAuley, whose nickname was "Tubby," set a record of dubious distinction by posting 39 losses in the 50-game schedule. In addition, McAuley's 6.20 goals-against average is still the NHL's highest single-season mark for a goalie who appeared in thirty or more games. The Rangers' plight only got worse as the schedule wore on. After defeating Toronto 5–1 on January 22 for their sixth victory, they were trounced 15–0 by Detroit the following evening and failed to win another game during the rest of the season.

As expected, the new rules sparked an offensive surge. Not only did four different teams reach the 200-goal plateau for the first time, but three different skaters, led by Boston's Herb Cain, surpassed the single-season mark of 73 points. Detroit's Syd Howe also earned a spot in the

ROCKET NETS ALL FIVE GOALS IN HABS' SEMI-FINAL WIN

Since Richard accomplished the feat, three players have scored five goals in one playoff game: Darryl Sittler (Toronto, 1976), Reggie Leach (Philadelphia, 1976), and Mario Lemieux (Pittsburgh, 1989).

**March 23, 1944
at Montreal Forum
Montreal 5, Toronto 1**

FIRST PERIOD
No Scoring
PENALTIES — Lamoureux MTL 6:43.

SECOND PERIOD
1) MTL Richard 1 (Blake, McMahon) 1:48
2) MTL Richard 2 (Blake, Lach) 2:05
3) TOR R. Hamilton 1 (Carr, Morris) PPG 8:50
4) MTL Richard 3 (Lach, Blake) 16:46
PENALTIES — Richard MTL 8:34; Richard MTL, Webster TOR 12:20; Morris TOR 19:24.

THIRD PERIOD
5) MTL Richard 4 (Blake, Lach) PPG 1:00
6) MTL Richard 5 (Blake, Lach) 8:54
PENALTIES — Heffernan MTL 14:57.

GOALTENDERS	TIME	GA	ENG	DEC
MTL Durnan	60:00	1	0	W
TOR Bibeault	60:00	5	0	L

PP CONVERSIONS   MTL 1/1   TOR 1/3

No Rush

Indicative of the "stay-at-home" style of defense played in the six-team era, Maple Leaf Walter "Babe" Pratt's 1943-44 record for points in a season by a defenseman (57 in 50 games) remained on the books for 21 seasons. Pierre Pilote of Chicago scored 59 points in the 70-game schedule of 1964-65, finally surpassing Pratt's mark. Similarly, Red Wing Frank "Flash" Hollett scored 20 goals in 1944-45, a mark for defensemen that stood until Bobby Orr's 21 goals for Boston in 1968-69.

NHL record book, becoming the first player since Cy Denneny to record six goals in a game, reaching the milestone on February 3, 1944. Toronto blueliner Babe Pratt, who became the first defenseman to record six assists in a single game on January 8, 1944, was awarded the Hart Trophy as the league's MVP. He joined Cain (top scorer), Clint Smith (Lady Byng Trophy – gentlemanly conduct), Bill Durnan (Vezina Trophy – top goaltender), and Gus Bodnar (Calder Trophy – top rookie) on the awards podium.

The Montreal Canadiens, who led the league in goals-for and goals-against, easily won the regular-season championship, finishing a record 25 points ahead of the second-place Detroit Red Wings. Led by the "Punch Line" of Richard, Blake, and Lach, and bolstered by the stalwart defensive pairing of Emile "Butch" Bouchard and Leo Lamoureux, the Habs motored through the playoffs, easily disposing of the Leafs and the Black Hawks in nine games. Maurice Richard, who had been dubbed "Rocket" by sportswriter Baz O'Meara during the season, became the first player since Bernie Morris in 1917 to score five goals in a playoff game, accounting for all the scoring in the Canadiens' 5–1 win over Toronto in game two of their semi-final match-up. In total, the Rocket exploded for 12 goals in the post-season to lead the Habs to their first Stanley Cup triumph in thirteen years.

| 80 PTS. | 67 PTS. | 52 PTS. | 36 PTS. | 33 PTS. | 32 PTS. |

1944-45
Rocket Scores 50 in 50, but McCool Ices Cup Win for Leafs

THE MONTREAL CANADIENS OUTDISTANCED THE DETROIT RED WINGS IN the second half of the 1944-45 campaign to win their second consecutive regular-season crown. As the war in Europe wound down, players began returning to active duty on the ice, although most rosters were still thinly stocked. An impressive crop of rookies was showcased, including Detroit's Ted Lindsay and Harry Lumley, Toronto's Frank McCool, and the Rangers' Bill Moe.

Although his convalescence from war wounds prevented Conn Smythe from being actively involved in the daily running of the Toronto Maple Leafs, he was still in the news, first for refusing the job of NHL

president, and then for offering thousands of dollars to the Bruins and Canadiens for Milt Schmidt and Rocket Richard. Smythe's offer for Richard was quickly dismissed, for the Rocket was emerging as the league's foremost marksman, averaging a goal a game throughout the season. Richard became the first player in league history to compile eight points in a single game when he scored five goals and added three assists in Montreal's 9–1 victory over Detroit on December 28. Later in the season, on February 25, he scored his 45th goal of the season, breaking Joe Malone's record set in 1917-18, the league's first year. The Rocket finished with 50 goals in 50 games. Although Richard was the first player in league history to reach the 50-goal plateau, he was only the fifteenth to average a goal per game over an entire season. Prior to 1942-43, teams played fewer than 50 games. When Malone scored 44 goals for the Canadiens in 1917-18, he did so over a 22-game regular-season schedule.

Richard shared the spotlight with a pair of notable NHL veterans during the 1944-45 campaign. Syd Howe became the league's all-time leading

Twenty-six-year-old Leaf rookie Frank McCool (top row, second from left) captured headlines during the 1944-45 season by winning the Calder Trophy and posting three consecutive shutouts in the Stanley Cup finals against Detroit.

During the 1944-45 season, Montreal's Maurice "Rocket" Richard eclipsed Joe Malone's single-season record of 44 goals by scoring 50 times in 50 games. The 50-goal season became the ultimate scoring achievement of the six-team era and remained unequalled for 16 seasons and unsurpassed until 1965-66.

Patience Rewarded

A well-behaved crowd of 7,687 fans waited almost three hours in their seats on January 18, 1945, for the New York Rangers, who were delayed by the weather, to arrive at the Detroit Olympia. The game started at 11:13 p.m. and ended at 12:56 a.m. The Red Wings rewarded their fans with a 7–3 win. Later that same season, the Rangers' train from Detroit was delayed, and the New York fans waited almost 2½ hours for a Rangers–Black Hawks game. New York won that game, 6–2.

scorer on March 8, compiling his 515th point to surpass the record set by Nels Stewart, while Boston's durable Aubrey "Dit" Clapper became the first NHLer to play eighteen seasons. In Detroit, veteran rearguard William "Flash" Hollett became the first defenseman to score 20 goals in a single campaign. Bill Durnan won his second consecutive Vezina

Trophy, Elmer Lach captured the scoring title with 80 points, and Toronto's Frank McCool was selected as the top rookie, appearing in all 50 games for the Leafs and posting four shutouts.

The Canadiens, favored in many circles to repeat as Stanley Cup champions, were eliminated by the Leafs in six games, despite a six-goal effort from Richard. Led by McCool's outstanding performance in goal, Toronto went on to defeat the Detroit Red Wings in the finals to capture its third Stanley Cup title, although the Wings came remarkably close to matching the Leafs' comeback of 1942. McCool established a new NHL post-season record by registering shutouts in the first three matches of the final to stake the Leafs to a 3–0 lead in games. The Red Wings, who didn't score a goal until the 8:35 mark of the first period of game four, reversed the tables on the Leafs by winning the next three contests to force a seventh game. McCool, who had a history of stomach ailments and was known as "Ulcers," played solidly, helping the Leafs regroup and defeat Detroit 2–1 in the decisive game to win the Cup.

FRANK MCCOOL POSTS THIRD CONSECUTIVE SHUTOUT IN '45 FINAL

McCool blanked the opposition for 188 minutes and 35 seconds, the longest shutout streak ever recorded in the Stanley Cup finals.

April 12, 1945
at Maple Leaf Gardens
Toronto 1, Detroit 0

FIRST PERIOD
No Scoring
PENALTIES – None

SECOND PERIOD
No Scoring
PENALTIES – None

THIRD PERIOD
1) TOR Bodnar 1 (Stanowski) 3:01
PENALTIES – Jackson DET 10:52.

GOALTENDERS		TIME	GA	ENG	DEC
DET	Lumley	60:00	1	0	L
TOR	McCool	60:00	0	0	W

PP CONVERSIONS DET 0/0 TOR 0/1

61 PTS.	56 PTS.	53 PTS.	50 PTS.	45 PTS.	35 PTS.

1945-46
The Punch Line Hammers Out Post-War Cup Win for Habs

A mainstay on the Boston blueline for thirteen seasons, Jack Crawford earned a berth on the NHL's First All-Star Team in 1945-46, helping the Bruins finish second in both points and goals-against.

DURING THE OFF-SEASON, THE CONFLICT IN EUROPE WAS FORMALLY SETTLED, returning more than forty players to the league for the start of training camp. There was also renewed interest in the future of the Montreal Maroons franchise, which had been held in abeyance since operations were suspended in 1936. A transfer of the team to Philadelphia was discussed, but league officials judged that the prospective owners did not have their finances in order.

One of the game's great architects, Art Ross, announced he would be relinquishing the coaching reins of the Boston Bruins to Dit Clapper, who became the team's first playing coach. Ross, who had served as coach and general manager of the Bruins since the team's inception, remained in the general manager's chair. In addition to Clapper, the Bruins were strengthened by the return of Frank Brimsek in net and the reappearance of Schmidt, Bauer, and Dumart. Although the trio had served in the armed forces, they had kept their hockey skills sharp by playing with the Ottawa Commandos, an armed-forces club that won the Allan Cup

Detroit goaltender Harry "Apple Cheeks" Lumley, who made his NHL debut as a seventeen-year-old in 1943-44, was the only goaltender to appear in all fifty games during the 1945-46 season. He compiled a 3.18 goals-against average for the fourth-place Red Wings.

Hall of Fame

In June 1945, the NHL's Board of Governors approved the establishment of a Hockey Hall of Fame. Members were first inducted in 1945. The first Hall-of-Fame building opened in August 1961 on the grounds of the Canadian National Exhibition in Toronto. The Hall moved to a new home in downtown Toronto in June 1993.

as Canada's senior amateur champions in 1943. With the Kraut Line and second-unit center Don Gallinger leading the way, the Bruins challenged for top spot much of the season before finishing five points behind the Canadiens in second place.

In Toronto, the Leafs were unable to sign Cup hero Frank McCool and decided to try Aldege "Baz" Bastien and Gordie Bell in goal. However, when the tandem combined to win just three of their first thirteen games, McCool's contract demands were met, and he returned to the fold. However, even Walter "Turk" Broda's return from overseas in January couldn't reverse the Leafs' 8–17–3 start. Adding to the Leafs' woes was a suspension handed out to All-Star defenseman Babe Pratt on January 30 for betting on hockey games. Although Pratt was reinstated after nine games, the team dropped out of the playoff picture when they won only two games in his absence. By finishing in fifth spot, Toronto became only the second team to miss the playoffs after winning the Stanley Cup in the previous campaign.

Prospects appeared brighter for the New York Rangers, who were reinforced by the return of Lynn and Murray "Muzz" Patrick, Neil Colville, and goalie Chuck Rayner. Unfortunately, the players were not in game shape and the Rangers' on-ice troubles continued. Rookie Edgar Laprade and veteran Ab DeMarco were the team's top performers, but the club finished last in every major statistical category for the third successive year.

The Montreal Canadiens continued their strong play, although they struggled for five weeks after Bill Durnan broke his hand. Replacement

During the mid-1940s, Maurice Richard was the fire in the Montreal Canadiens lineup, while Toe Blake was the club's heart and soul. In the 1945-46 season, Blake led the Habs in scoring with 29 goals and 50 points and added six goals in Montreal's four-game sweep of the Chicago Black Hawks in the semi-finals.

Paul Bibeault, who started the season with the Bruins, lost six of the ten games he played for the Habs, and the club fell to third place before rebounding to finish first for the third consecutive year. Much of the media attention was focused on the slumping Punch Line. Maurice Richard fell to 27 goals after clicking for 50 in 1944-45, while defending scoring leader Elmer Lach dropped to 47 points.

After missing the playoffs in two of the previous three seasons, the Chicago Black Hawks were considerably stronger, thanks to the "Pony Line" of Max Bentley centering his brother, Doug, and Bill Mosienko, which combined for 68 goals. Clint Smith and Alex Kaleta joined Mosienko and Max Bentley in the top-ten list of scorers to lead the Hawks to a third-place finish. Bentley's 61 points led the league, matching his brother Doug, who had topped all other scorers in 1942-43. The Bentleys were the first brother combination in NHL history to each lead the league in scoring.

Bill Durnan, who despite his injury led the league in goals-against average and shutouts, captured his third consecutive Vezina Trophy, while Toe Blake took Lady Byng Trophy honors. Edgar Laprade was the league's top freshman with 34 points, and Max Bentley was selected as the NHL's MVP.

In the playoffs, the Punch Line recovered its scoring touch to lead the Canadiens to their second Cup triumph in three years. Lach, Blake, and Richard finished 1–2–3 in post-season scoring, as the Habs swept past Chicago in the semi-finals, outscoring the punchless Hawks, 26–7, before outlasting the Boston Bruins in a five-game final. Maurice Richard, whose playoff performances would make him one of sports' greatest post-season competitors, scored the first overtime goal of his career in game one of the finals.

RECORD CROWD IN CHICAGO STADIUM LAUNCHES POST-WAR ERA IN NHL

A total of 49 players returned to the NHL in 1945-46 after spending part of the preceding seasons in the armed forces. In addition, 23 players began their NHL careers in 1945-46. This influx of old and new talent strengthened the league and promised increasingly competitive post-war hockey.

October 31, 1945 at Chicago Stadium Chicago 5, New York 1

FIRST PERIOD
1) CHI Hamill 3 (Grosso) 6:43
2) CHI M. Bentley 4 10:56
3) CHI Johnston 3 (D. Bentley) 13:56
4) NY Goldup 1 (Warwick) 17:21
PENALTIES – Horeck CHI 1:17; D. Bentley CHI; Brown NY 14:15.

SECOND PERIOD
No Scoring
PENALTIES – Moe NY 9:03.

THIRD PERIOD
5) CHI Johnston 4 (Kaleta) SHG 2:48
6) CHI Mosienko 1 (Wares) 5:32
PENALTIES – Wares CHI 1:02.

GOALTENDERS		TIME	GA	ENG	DEC
NY	Henry	60:00	5	0	L
CHI	Karakas	60:00	1	0	W

PP CONVERSIONS NY 0/3 CHI 0/2
ATTENDANCE – 18,877

Beating 'Em in the Alley: Maple Leaf Magic
1946-47 to 1950-51

78 PTS.   72 PTS.   63 PTS.   55 PTS.   50 PTS.   42 PTS

1946-47
Chicago's Dipsy-Doodle Dandy Tops Scoring

POST-WAR RECONSTRUCTION OF THE NHL BEGAN IN EARNEST DURING THE OFF-season, with the appointment of Clarence Campbell as the league's third president. A former amateur player and professional referee, in addition to being a Rhodes scholar and a lawyer, Campbell understood the on-ice and off-ice business of hockey.

It was also during this period that the groundwork was laid for the NHL's annual All-Star Game, when a journalist from Chicago suggested that an annual game be played between the defending Stanley Cup champions and a group of All-Stars. A percentage of the proceeds from these exhibition contests would be forwarded to the newly established players' pension fund. The first such game was scheduled to be held prior to the start of the 1947-48 season at the home of the Stanley Cup champion. In another off-ice development, the regular-season schedule was increased from fifty to sixty games.

On the ice, every team was replenishing its roster with returning veterans, with the possible exception of the defending-champion Montreal Canadiens, who had been least affected by the war. However, the Canadiens were strengthened by the addition of Frank Selke, who was appointed as the Habs' new general manager. Selke, a guiding force in the success of the Toronto Maple Leafs during Conn Smythe's absence overseas, lost a power struggle with Smythe and the Leafs' board of directors, which prompted his move to the Canadiens' front office.

In addition to the loss of Selke, the Leafs made numerous other personnel changes, and nine players from the previous year's squad were missing when Toronto opened training camp to prepare for the 1946-47 season. Babe Pratt, a former All-Star and Hart Trophy recipient, was traded

Opposite: Bill Barilko's victory salute in the Leafs' dressing room after scoring the Stanley Cup-winning goal in the 1951 finals was the final moment of glory in his brief NHL career. After his disappearance in the summer of 1951, Conn Smythe vowed that no player would wear Barilko's number (5) until his body was found. Although Barilko's downed plane was discovered in 1962, no Toronto Maple Leaf player has ever worn "Bashin' Billy's" number again.

Phil Watson (7) and Neil Colville (6) serenade New York Rangers goal-tender Chuck Rayner after the smiling Scot blanked the Boston Bruins, 6–0, on February 19, 1947. Rayner led the league with five shutouts during the 1946-47 campaign, although the Rangers finished out of the play-off picture in fifth place.

to Boston. Lorne Carr, Dave "Sweeney" Schriner, Mel Hill, and Bob Davidson, all of whom played key roles on the championship teams of 1942 and 1945, were asked to retire. As replacements, Smythe and coach Clarence "Hap" Day brought up a number of rookies, including Bill Barilko, Sid Smith, Howie Meeker, and Garth Boesch, the first musta-chioed player in the league since Andy Blair in the 1930s.

The Boston Bruins, Stanley Cup finalists in 1946, were basically intact, the only major addition being Joe Carveth, who was replacing the retired Herb Cain. Although Dit Clapper would have been content to remain behind the bench, an injury to Jack Crawford in the early weeks of the season forced him to take a six-game shift on defense. It marked

Clapper's twentieth NHL season, making him the first player to reach that plateau. Detroit, still guided by Jack Adams, was bolstered by the arrival of Roy Conacher, Billy Taylor, and a good-looking rookie named Gordon Howe. In Chicago, coach Johnny Gottselig was optimistic, despite the Hawks' poor showing in the 1946 playoffs. The Pony Line was still one of the league's top forward units, and the defense was greatly improved with the addition of rookie rearguard Bill Gadsby. Only the New York Rangers appeared weak. Three straight finishes in the league basement and the retirements of Ott Heller, Muzz and Lynn Patrick, and Alex Shibicky pointed to another year of rebuilding on Broadway.

The season's early surprise was the play of the Toronto Maple Leafs. Despite a rookie-laden roster, the squad was playing a determined brand of hockey. The Leafs' new-found toughness elicited the famous "If you can't beat 'em in the alley, you can't beat 'em on the ice" quote from Conn

The Montreal Canadiens allowed only 138 goals during the 1946-47 season, thanks to a solid defense, anchored by Ken Reardon and Butch Bouchard, who flank goaltender Bill Durnan in this photo. All three Hab heroes earned berths on the NHL's First All-Star Team.

After a disappointing return to NHL action in 1945-46, Boston's Kraut Line of Milt Schmidt (15), Bobby Bauer (17), and Woody Dumart (14) regained their famous on-ice flair in 1946-47. Schmidt finished fourth in scoring with 62 points, Bauer tied for second with 30 goals, while Dumart posted a career-high 52 points.

Smythe. In the early going, the Leafs proved they could do both, posting a 20–7–4 record through their first 31 games. One of the highlights for the club was the play of Howie Meeker, who set a rookie record by scoring five goals in the Leafs' 10–4 win over Chicago on January 8, 1947.

Although they started out slowly, winning only two of their first six games, the Canadiens were soon back in the title hunt, thanks to a return to form by Rocket Richard. Richard, who finished with 45 goals to lead all marksmen, led the league in scoring throughout much of the season, before a late-season swoon allowed Chicago's Max Bentley to secure the scoring title by a single point. The Habs, who were without the services of Elmer Lach for much of the campaign after the big centerman suffered a fractured skull, moved into first place on February 1, and eventually

Max Bentley, who joined his brother Doug as an Art Ross Trophy-winner in 1945-46, defended his scoring crown during the 1946-47 campaign, collecting 29 goals and 43 assists for the cellar-dwelling Chicago Black Hawks.

captured their fourth consecutive regular-season crown, finishing six points ahead of the second-place Leafs.

A rash of injuries hampered the Bruins for much of the season, forcing general manager Art Ross to adjust the roster. Babe Pratt was dispatched to the minors only thirty-one games into the season, marking the end of the rearguard's NHL career. He was replaced by rookie Fern Flaman, who had made his debut with the Bruins at the age of seventeen in 1944. Milt Schmidt led the squad in scoring, with 62 points, while his Kraut Line teammates, Bobby Bauer and Woody Dumart, each finished among the league's top-ten scorers. The Krauts did have to share the limelight with Chicago's Pony Line of the Bentley brothers and Bill Mosienko, all of whom finished in the top ten as well. Max Bentley captured his second consecutive scoring title, with 72 points. Unfortunately, his effort couldn't salvage the season for the Black Hawks, who fell into the league basement with 42 points.

Detroit lost only three games in the final month of the season to secure the final playoff spot, although their 22–27–11 record was their poorest showing since 1941-42. In their first game of the season, the

First Signals

At the start of the 1946-47 season, the NHL adopted the first set of hand signals for linesmen to indicate intentional offside, delayed offside, icing, and icing washed out.

LEAF ROOKIE HOWIE MEEKER SCORES FIVE GOALS VS. HAWKS

Meeker's record performance was equaled 29 years later by New York Rangers rookie Don Murdoch, who scored five goals in only his fourth game in the NHL.

January 8, 1947
at Maple Leaf Gardens
Toronto 10, Chicago 4

FIRST PERIOD
1) CHI M. Bentley 11 (Mosienko) 1:47
2) **TOR Meeker 12 (Stanowski) 3:41**
PENALTIES – Mariucci CHI (hooking) 6:59; Mortson TOR (tripping) 14:01; Fowler CHI (roughing), Klukay TOR (roughing) 16:55; Thomson TOR (tripping) 18:20.

SECOND PERIOD
3) CHI Smith 4 (Gee, Gadsby) 5:15
4) TOR D. Metz 4 (Poile, Stanowski) 8:44
5) **TOR Meeker 13 (Stanowski, Kennedy) 15:28**
6) **TOR Meeker 14 (Klukay, Kennedy) 16:48**
PENALTIES – Kaleta CHI (highsticking) 10:10.

THIRD PERIOD
7) TOR N. Metz 6 (Ezinicki) 1:51
8) **TOR Meeker 15 (Klukay, Kennedy) 2:12**
9) CHI Mosienko 10 (M. Bentley, D. Bentley) 3:46
10) TOR N. Metz 7 (Apps) 8:34
11) **TOR Meeker 16 (Kennedy, Klukay) 9:31**
12) TOR Poile 9 (Stewart) 12:14
13) TOR Stewart 9 (Poile, D. Metz) 12:41
14) CHI Gadsby 2 (M. Bentley, D. Bentley) 14:46
PENALTIES – None

GOALTENDERS	TIME	GA	ENG	DEC
CHI Bibeault	60:00	10	0	L
TOR Broda	60:00	4	0	W

PP CONVERSIONS CHI 0/2 TOR 0/2

Break It Up

Spurred by a prolonged but one-sided bout between Boston's Terry Reardon and Montreal's Butch Bouchard that occurred during his first year as NHL president, Clarence Campbell gave NHL linesmen the added responsibility of breaking up on-ice fights between players.

Wings were down 3–2 to the Leafs in the final minute, when coach Jack Adams pulled his goaltender and sent out an extra forward. Sid Abel scored to tie the game, and the innovation became a popular coaching ploy throughout the season. Although Chicago coach Paul Thompson had tried the maneuver in the early 1940s, it wasn't until Adams's success that other coaches utilized the new technique. The "empty net" strategy did create some headaches for officials, however. Defending players started throwing their sticks at the puck to try to stop scoring attempts on the vacated goal, forcing the league to draft new rules prohibiting this activity.

Both of the Red Wings' major acquisitions in the off-season, Billy Taylor and Roy Conacher, paid instant dividends. Taylor, who set an NHL record with seven assists on March 16, 1947, in a game against the Black Hawks, led the Wings in scoring, with 63 points, followed by Conacher, who chipped in with 30 goals and 24 assists. Ambidextrous rookie Gordie Howe, who scored a goal in his first NHL game, finished with 22 points.

It was another season of frustration in New York after the Rangers dropped six of their last seven games, including 2–0 and 4–2 losses to Detroit, to finish five points behind the Red Wings in fifth spot. Goaltender Chuck Rayner, who led the league with five shutouts, was also the league's finest entertainer, electrifying fans with a series of rink-long dashes in an attempt to become the first NHL goalie to score a goal. Howie Meeker of the Leafs was the top freshman, Bill Durnan captured his fourth straight Vezina Trophy, Bobby Bauer was the league's most gentlemanly player, and Maurice Richard won his first, and only, Hart Trophy as league MVP.

In the playoffs, the Canadiens survived a tough five-game series against Boston to return to the finals for the second consecutive year. The Habs, who needed a pair of overtime victories to defeat the Bruins, met the revitalized Toronto Maple Leafs in the finals and quickly took a one-game lead with a 6–0 victory in the series opener. Following the game, Montreal goalie Bill Durnan told the media that, from his viewpoint, the Leafs didn't deserve to be on the same ice surface as the Canadiens. Leafs' coach Hap Day posted Durnan's comments in the Toronto dressing-room, and his charges responded by winning four of the next five games to dethrone the Habs and return the Cup to Toronto. The Leafs connected for a quartet of power-play goals to win the second game, 4–0, then squeezed out 4–2, 2–1, and 2–1 victories to win the franchise's fourth Stanley Cup title. After the 1947 playoffs, the Stanley Cup trophy was rebuilt to accommodate the names of more winning teams. The silver bands that made up the stove-pipe-sized barrel of the old Cup were mounted on a hardwood frame to form a much broader base. The Cup's bowl, collars, and shoulders were then fitted on top of the new base. The resulting two-piece trophy was used for ten seasons.

| 77 PTS. | 72 PTS. | 59 PTS. | 55 PTS. | 51 PTS. | 46 PTS. |

1947-48
Deal of the Century
Brings Scoring Champ to Toronto

IT WAS A BUSY OFF-SEASON FOR THE LEAGUE GOVERNORS. ONCE AGAIN, A MOTION was forwarded to transfer the dormant Montreal Maroons franchise to Philadelphia. However, the prospective owner, Len Peto, could not meet the conditions required by the league. In December, two representatives from an ownership group in Los Angeles met with President Campbell to discuss an expansion franchise for California. Their application was also dismissed because traveling requirements would be problematic.

At a September 4, 1947, meeting, plans concerning the NHL pension fund were finalized. Each player would donate $900 to the fund, and the league would ante up $500 for each player, with additional monies coming from the All-Star Game and a special surcharge on playoff tickets. Players could start receiving their pensions at the age of forty-five.

A new rule stated that a defender throwing his stick to prevent an empty-net goal would result in a goal being credited to the attacking player who had been denied the scoring chance. As well, plans were finalized for the All-Star Game, which was held in Toronto on October 13. The All-Stars, coached by Dick Irvin, defeated the Leafs, 4–3, in a spirited game that was marred by an injury to Bill Mosienko, who suffered a fractured ankle.

Two of the game's greatest forward units were dismantled during the 1947-48 season. Bobby Bauer, who had his finest season during the 1946-47 campaign, retired after nine NHL seasons to take a coaching position with the Guelph juniors. His absence brought an end to the famed Kraut Line. The Bruins, who were also without Terry Reardon, Bill Shill, and Jack McGill, still had one of the league's toughest defenses, with Frank Brimsek in goal and Jack Crawford and Fernie Flaman on the blueline. Rookie Pete Babando was chosen to replace the departed Bauer on the top forward unit with Schmidt and Dumart. The Bruins, who had trouble all season mounting an effective offensive attack, finished in third place with a 23–24–13 record.

In Montreal, a fractured ankle brought the career of Toe Blake to a close, ending the reign of the Punch Line as well. Blake, who had begun in 1934-35 with the Montreal Maroons and came to the Canadiens in a trade for Lorne Chabot, was enjoying one of his finest seasons, with 24

Stick Up

Enthusiastic players had long celebrated goals with raised sticks, but, in 1947, the league attempted to make the act official. Acting on hockey pioneer Frank Patrick's suggestion, a player scoring a goal was to skate with an upraised stick for thirty or forty feet, so fans and the press could more easily identify the scorer. The experiment was initiated on November 13, and Montreal's Billy Reay became the first player to follow the procedure, but when Toe Blake later scored while being tied up by a Chicago defender, he forgot. Later, the Hawks' Roy Conacher raised his stick, but his goal was disallowed on an offside.

Ted Lindsay was very good during the 1947-48 season, leading all NHL sharpshooters with 33 goals in 60 games, the highest total of his seventeen-year career.

points in 32 games, before sustaining the ankle injury on January 11. While still recuperating from the injury, Blake joined Rudy Pilous in Houston, Texas, helping Pilous coach the Huskies to the United States Hockey League championship.

The loss of Blake was only one in a series of events that hampered the Habs. Maurice Richard missed seven games and saw his goal production drop from 45 to 28. Jimmy Peters was traded after scoring only one goal in 22 games, Leo Lamoureux retired, and his replacement, Doug Harvey, appeared in only 35 games. Even though Harvey was the only newcomer on the Habs' blueline, the team faltered defensively, falling to fourth in goals-against, after leading the NHL for four consecutive seasons. Elmer Lach won the scoring title with 61 points, but only two other Canadiens (Richard and defenseman Glen Harmon) reached double figures in goals, and the team fell to fifth place with a 20–29–11 record.

Although the league had lost two of its high-profile forward lines, another powerful trio was formed in Detroit, where Tommy Ivan had

Ted Kennedy provided the fireworks and the dramatics in the Toronto Maple Leafs' Stanley Cup run in 1948, scoring four goals in a 5–3 semi-final victory over Boston, and leading all post-season scorers with eight goals and 14 points.

taken over the coaching duties from Jack Adams. Ivan placed sophomore forward Gordie Howe on a line with Sid Abel and Ted Lindsay, bringing the "Production Line" to life. The Howe–Abel–Lindsay line appeared in all 60 games, combining for 63 goals. The emergence of the Production Line compensated for the loss of the Wings' two top scorers from the previous season. Billy Taylor was traded to Boston for Armand "Bep" Guidolin, while Roy Conacher, who couldn't come to terms on a contract and refused to report, was traded to Chicago.

Still, it was defense that allowed the Wings to fly. Harry Lumley led the league with seven shutouts, while Detroit's blueline corps of Jack Stewart, Bill Quackenbush, Leo Reise, and rookie Leonard "Red" Kelly were considered the league's best. The Wings rose to second place, only five points behind the Toronto Maple Leafs, who finished at the top of the league standings for the first time since the NHL was realigned into one division in 1938.

The Leafs entered the season with one of the league's most talented rosters, but Conn Smythe was not satisfied with the team's depth. In Smythe's eyes, the team was lacking a third center to complement Syl Apps and Ted "Teeder" Kennedy. Smythe was also aware that Apps was talking about retirement, making the search for the missing piece of the

Wally Wowed 'Em

During the 1940s and early 1950s, Wally Stanowski, first of Toronto and later New York, occasionally put on impromptu skating exhibitions, imitating popular "fancy" figure skaters for appreciative arena crowds. Stanowski's performances usually took place when an injured goalie left the ice to receive medical attention.

Toronto puzzle more desperate. The team stood pat to open the season, and went undefeated in its first six outings. However, following a 7–2 loss to New York on November 2, Smythe orchestrated the biggest trade in NHL history, sending five players – Bud Poile, Bob Goldham, Ernie Dickens, Gaye Stewart, and Gus Bodnar – to Chicago for perennial All-Star Max Bentley and rookie Cy Thomas. Clearly, the key to the deal was Bentley, who was a two-time scoring champion and a true "dipsy-doodler" as a puck handler. The Hawks, who had lost six games in a row before making the deal, received five talented players, who were immediately inserted into their everyday lineup. Unfortunately for Chicago, one big trade was not enough to turn around the fortunes of the team. Although they led the league in offense, they were last in defense and, consequently, last in the National Hockey League.

With Bentley aboard, the Leafs soared, compiling a 32–15–13 record to win the regular-season crown. Turk Broda led the league in victories and captured the Vezina Trophy with a 2.38 goals-against average, breaking off Bill Durnan's four-year hold on the award.

Perhaps the most surprising aspect of the season was the play of the New York Rangers, who made the playoffs for the first time since the NHL became a six-team league. The Rangers' resurgence was led by sophomore Edgar Laprade, "Tough" Tony Leswick, and Buddy O'Connor,

Although he was nearing the end of his brilliant career, Boston's Frank Brimsek appeared in all sixty games for the Bruins in 1947-48, recording three shutouts and posting a 2.80 goals-against average.

who was obtained from the Montreal Canadiens for Hal Laycoe. The Rangers' recovery was accomplished without Chuck Rayner, who spent much of the season on the sidelines recovering from a broken cheekbone. Rayner became one of the first goaltenders to use a facemask, wearing a plexiglass model in practices only.

The season was not without controversy. Two of the league's finest play-makers, Billy Taylor and Don Gallinger, were suspended for life for gambling on hockey games. Since this ban was also enforced by minor professional leagues, such as the American Hockey League and the USHL, neither Taylor nor Gallinger ever played again at any level.

Detroit rookie Jim McFadden, who scored 24 goals and added an equal number of assists, was awarded the Calder Trophy. Buddy O'Connor captured both the Hart and Lady Byng awards, while Montreal's Elmer Lach was the first winner of the new Art Ross Trophy awarded to the league's scoring leader.

The Toronto Maple Leafs rolled through the playoffs, downing the Bruins in five games before sweeping the Red Wings in the finals. Ted Kennedy led all post-season performers with eight goals, and Max Bentley tied for the playoff lead with seven assists. Syl Apps's goal in the second period of game four of the finals proved to be the last the talented centerman would score in his career. Apps, who rarely set personal goals for himself, had stated his intention to retire after reaching the 200-goal plateau. He scored three goals in the final game of the 1947-48 schedule, giving him 201 for his career, and he stood firm on his retirement plans, despite setting career highs for goals and points during the season.

(continued on p. 38)

LEAFS OPEN CUP DEFENSE WITH OT WIN VS. BOSTON

Toronto went on to defeat Boston and Detroit to become the first team to win consecutive Stanley Cup titles since the Red Wings in 1935-36 and 1936-37.

March 24, 1948
at Maple Leaf Gardens
Toronto 5, Boston 4

FIRST PERIOD
1) BOS Henderson 1 (Schmidt) 1:18
2) TOR Ezinicki 1 (Watson, Apps) 11:29
PENALTIES – Martin BOS (charging) 16:13.

SECOND PERIOD
3) BOS Harrison 1 (Babando, Warwick) 8:39
4) TOR Bentley 1 17:33
PENALTIES – Thomson TOR (holding) 11:11.

THIRD PERIOD
5) BOS Egan 1 (Peters, Schmidt) 2:35
6) BOS Smith 1 (Peirson, Ronty) 8:38
7) TOR Apps 1 (Stanowski) 12:03
8) TOR Thomson 1 (Kennedy, Meeker) 15:34
PENALTIES – None

FIRST OVERTIME PERIOD
9) TOR N. Metz 1 (Bentley) 17:03
PENALTIES – None

GOALTENDERS		TIME	GA	ENG	DEC
BOS	Brimsek	77:03	5	0	L
TOR	Broda	77:03	4	0	W

PP CONVERSIONS BOS 0/1 TOR 0/1

The Sun Room

by Bob Hesketh

The late, great sports columnist Ted Reeve of the Toronto *Telegram* and the *Toronto Sun* used to refer to newspaper sports departments as the "Sun Rooms of the Fourth Estate."

When I joined the sports department of the *Telegram* in 1947, it was indeed that, a place of Runyon-esque characters, journalistic freedom, and pride in producing sports pages in a time when athletes were lauded for how they performed and not for what they were paid.

Applying for an opening as a junior (read "go-fer") in the *Telegram* sports department and being accepted was, as it turned out, a happy turn of fate for me. I had been hired as a junior reporter after the war, mostly because I could type (maybe twenty-five words a minute), and I was sent to the City Hall police courts to cover the appearance in the halls of justice of prostitutes, pimps, pushers, wife-beaters, child-molesters, and various other human dregs whose fates never got in the paper anyway.

Being allowed into the Sun Room to join Reeve and associates opened up a whole new world for me, and also began that enjoyable sensation of at least some semblance of financial solvency.

When I started there, sorting mail, getting coffee, cleaning baskets, and watching how things were done, I was paid the same salary at which I'd been hired, fifteen dollars a week. The big plus – and it was one that I knew was not granted to many – was the opportunity to really learn the business.

My weekly pay envelope grew to twenty-five dollars, and things took an even better turn a while later, when George McCullagh, who owned the *Globe and Mail*, bought the *Telegram*. By that time, I was writing about the Maple Leafs on the road and was in the Detroit Olympia at a Red Wings practice, when a message came that I was wanted on the phone. McCullagh, the new owner, was calling long distance.

On the way upstairs to the Red Wings' head office, I was making plans about where I might work next and wondering why, if I was going to get fired, the publisher felt he had to do it personally.

A secretary put McCullagh on the line, and he asked me to verify that I was making twenty-five dollars a week. I verified it.

"That's disgraceful," I still remember his exact words. "If you are good enough to cover the Leafs, you are good enough to make forty-five dollars a week, starting now!"

Regrettably, McCullagh died an untimely death not long after.

Fortunately, the *Telegram* was bought by John Bassett, who also liked sports and generally treated sportswriters as though they were real people. He later became, among other things, a director of Maple Leaf Gardens, one of the high-rolling "Silver Seven" that included Jack Amell, Stafford Smythe, Bill Hatch, George Gardiner, George Mara, and Harold Ballard.

During the eight years I wrote about the Leafs, both on the beat and as a columnist, I was aware that Bassett was not only the publisher and director, but was also a rabid Maple Leaf fan. But only once was I asked if I would reconsider a comment I had written. I said I would rather not, and that was the last I heard about it.

I left the *Tely* Sun Room in 1957 to take a job with an advertising agency, working on the Dunlop Tire account, managing promotion for the Senior A champion Whitby Dunlops in their quest for the IIHF World Championship, which ended successfully in Oslo, Norway.

Journalist Jacques Beauchamp (second from left), sports editor of Montréal-Matin, *doubled as the Montreal Canadiens' practice goalie on the road during the late 1950s.*

Though he had no reason to feel kindly to me, Bassett nevertheless granted my request to write a weekend column in the *Telegram*, which I did for a couple of years.

So in the early days I was blessed with good bosses.

But, if I may go back a bit . . .

Working in the Sun Room was a dream job if you were a writer and hockey nut. I fancied myself as the former and, like all Canadian kids worth their salt, I was addicted . . . mesmerized . . . when on Saturday nights I would be with my dad, Joe, helping him make his home brew in the kitchen (the door closed because my mother gagged on the smell), imagining what it would be like to actually be there at Maple Leaf Gardens watching the Kid Line, Babe Pratt, Red Horner, Gordie Drillon, and all those legends whose pictures you got with chewing gum. But those years were not the best of times for my family, and paying to see the Leafs play at the Gardens was not as high on the priority list as buying milk and bread.

So it was not until the 1947-48 season that I saw my first live Leaf action, with the assignment many young reporters would kill for – covering the Leafs on the road in places to which, with the exception of Montreal, I had never been: Boston, Chicago, New York, and Detroit.

If anybody should ask (and nobody does this far down the road), Bill Barilko's goal against Gerry McNeil that won the Stanley Cup for Joe Primeau's Leafs in 1951 was probably the highlight of the years I spent writing about the Leafs.

The second most memorable event came after I had left the paper. It was the final game of the 1958 World Championships in Oslo. In this game, Canada, represented by Wren Blair's Whitby Dunlops, played the Soviets, and it still stands among the greatest moments I was privileged to witness from a press box.

Unlike the final game of the 1972 Summit series, when Paul Henderson became an instant national hero with a last-minute goal, the gold-medal game in 1958 was not televised, so the country did not go as gaga. The radio play-by-play for CBC was done by Foster Hewitt, with Wes McKnight doing color. The game was dramatic, as the underdogs from Ontario, who had been given little chance to beat the Soviets, temporarily re-established Canada's claim on the World Championship two years after the Kitchener–Waterloo Dutchmen had lost to the Soviets at the Winter Olympics in Cortina D'Ampezzo, Italy.

The Whitby Dunlops, IIHF World Hockey Champions in 1958. The "Dunnies" roster included former Maple Leaf star Sid Smith (front row, middle), who was reinstated as an amateur to play for Whitby. Until the early 1960s, Canada's top senior amateur club represented the country in international play each year.

New York Rangers goaltender "Bonnie Prince Charlie" Rayner entertains New York Herald-Tribune *scribe Norm Petrie with some tall tales after a Broadway Blueshirts practice.*

I can still picture, and almost hear, Foster Hewitt in a four-by-six broadcast booth, freezing his buns off with the rest of us in the press box and the stands at the outdoor arena that cold Sunday afternoon. The Dunnies, in a breathtaking burst, with Bobby Attersley and Bus Gagnon scoring fifteen seconds apart, beat the Soviets, 5–2.

In the six-team era, the Maple Leafs were the only club in the NHL that sent its writers on the road to cover the team throughout the season. Two Montreal writers – Baz O'Meara and Elmer Ferguson – occasionally made trips with the Canadiens, most often to Toronto, and hockey writers from Boston and Detroit would cover road games during the playoffs. In Chicago, the Black Hawks never got much play in the media because, under manager Bill Tobin, the club was a perennial doormat. Neither were the Rangers given all that much attention in New York papers that had two baseball teams, football, basketball, horse racing, golf, and lots of college sports to eat up space.

Major Conn Smythe, the Leafs' boss, was a very important influence in the life of any aspiring hockey writer in Toronto. One knew that if one offended him grievously by writing something nasty about the club, he could order one's press pass taken away. It's tough to cover the team from the street.

There had been precedents . . .

Gordon Sinclair, who at that time was one of Canada's best-known newscasters, was partaking of refreshments between periods in the Gardens' press room when Smythe made a comment about "freeloading." Sinclair was reported to have placed the half-eaten sandwich back on the serving plate, turned on his heel, and left without a word, a snub guaranteed to rankle Smythe.

Before the start of the next game, Sinclair was passing Smythe's box and, in his usual caustic manner, asked the Major what was wrong with his hockey team, which was in a slump at the time. Embarrassed in front of his guests, Smythe, whose manner could go from caustic to snarly in an instant, yanked Sinclair's press pass. Sensing a good story, Sinclair relinquished his pass without a fuss and immediately phoned his broker and bought some shares of Maple Leaf Gardens stock. Then, on his nightly newscast on radio station CFRB (to which, he said, he was sure the Major was tuned), he said that he could not be refused admission to the Gardens because, as a shareholder, he had a right to inspect his investment whenever he chose.

The Leaf training camp, during my time on the beat, was in St. Catharines, and the team was quartered at the old Welland House Hotel, where the means of escape, in the event of a fire, was a stout rope coiled and anchored to the floor near each room's window. Fortunately, there were no fires. Which is not to say that the ropes, on lower floors at least, were not used for some post-curfew nocturnal exits.

One writer from each of the Toronto papers, the *Star*, the *Globe and Mail*, and the *Telegram*, went to the training camp and on the road. Al Nickleson covered the majority of road games for the *Globe and Mail*, Red Burnett for the *Star*.

This was before television. Even after television coverage started in the mid-1950s, Saturday-night home games were carried, but out-of-town games were not, so, for a period of time, there was no coverage of out-of-

Maurice Richard and Butch Bouchard share the "peace-pipe" with Chief "Poking Fire" of the Caughnawaga Reserve in a promotional event held in the Montreal suburb of Verdun on March 4, 1947.

town games except in the newspapers. Well, this was not quite true.

Joe Crysdale, a great play-by-play baseball announcer for Jack Kent Cooke's radio station CKEY in Toronto, reconstructed play-by-play coverage for Leafs out-of-town games, much to the displeasure of Hewitt, who owned radio rights to Leaf games but was not yet broadcasting road games. Using just the bare information – goals, assists, penalties, and the times – that was provided by the wire service, and sometimes assisted by contacts whom he would call long distance and who would let him listen to local play-by-play on the phone, Joe would describe events that often never happened.

Once, returning from a particularly dull waltz in

New York, I was greeted by Tiny, who ran the only elevator in the old *Telegram* building and listened to Joe's broadcasts. The paper with my story wasn't out yet, and he demanded I tell him about the big fight – "Gloves and sticks all over . . . blood on the ice . . . guys coming over the boards . . . the fans into it . . . a real donnybrook." When I told him it hadn't happened, he said, "So I suppose you are going to tell me that Crysdale made the whole thing up!"

One of the few times I was at a loss for words was a Sunday I had taken off. Hal Kelly, who did between-periods fill for Crysdale's broadcast, phoned to ask me to come down to CKEY and be a guest. It paid ten bucks, if I remember correctly, and in those times that was hard to turn down.

After Joe had gone through his dramatics for the first period, his voice rising in crescendo to match the excitement of the play we could not see, it came time for Kelly to interview me.

"Well, Hesky," he opened, "tell us what you thought of the first period."

Then he walked away to the other end of the big studio, opened a Coke, and lit a cigarette.

Train travel was part of the adventure in the six-team years. Air travel was still considered unreliable due to winter weather conditions, and there was a story that Smythe feared if there was a plane crash, the team could be wiped out. Smythe reasoned this wouldn't happen in a train disaster. I was never able to confirm this, but it had about it Smythe's air of tough-minded logic.

But train travel had its risks. Even getting aboard could be a close shave for the traveling scribes. Many departures would be delayed from Toronto's Union Station just to accommodate the Leafs if a game was running late.

Usually the writers could get a head start by leaving the Gardens early, but this certainly wasn't the case coming home. Except for occasional extended road trips, out-of-town games in the six-team years were one-night stands. For players, it was a quick shower and then head for the bus to the railway station. For the trainers and equipment men, it was throw the stuff into trunks and get to the baggage car by truck. For the writers, it was ten minutes, maybe fifteen, to write and file the epic, grab a cab, and get to the station.

A cold after-the-game beer was out of the question.

A wide variety of goods was transported across the border on the trains, as customs officers, often hockey fans themselves, relaxed their vigilance. Golf clubs were a popular purchase, sometimes in complete sets with bags. An outboard motor was brought back on one occasion. But the most impressive haul that I can recall was the front bumper and grille for a Buick.

One day, at the end of a particularly long snowstorm-delayed trip from Chicago, Leafs coach Joe Primeau, looking through the window, saw a rookie defenseman, carrying a television, get off the train at a suburban station. This was in the early days of TV, when sets were about as big as a refrigerator.

"Look at that," said the coach. "Somehow I don't think he is ever going to make it as a Maple Leaf."

Joe was usually right, but not this time. The TV set's owner played for the Leafs for eight years, and played in an NHL All-Star Game.

Smythe seldom made trips with the team, but on one occasion he traveled with the club and, as was customary during those years, took a couple of bottles of fine Canadian spirits to a friend in New York. He asked Tim Daly, the Leafs' veteran trainer, to look after them. Daly put Smythe's two bottles with the pair he himself was taking across, packed in with the club's equipment. Customs men, perhaps not above taking a taste themselves the odd time, found and confiscated two of the bottles.

Daly, with the two remaining jars, knocked on the drawing-room door as the train pulled into Grand Central Station. When Smythe appeared, he said, "Really sorry, Mr. Smythe, but the customs men took your two bottles."

"No, Tim," said the Major, plucking one from the kindly old trainer's hands. "They actually got one of yours and one of mine."

Tim looked hurt, but offered no argument.

As mentioned, writers had little time to write deathless prose. One way to write was to do a summary of the first two periods in the second intermission, and then, after the game ended, bang out a short lead and give it to the Western Union man in the press box. Boston was particularly tight for time, but the train made a brief stop at Worcester, Massachusetts, about an hour out, and copy could be dropped there.

The best way to handle it was to get on the train and immediately commandeer the ladies' powder room on the Pullman. (The men's was reserved by the players for a game of penny-ante poker.) Ladies' rooms on the old sleeper cars had a counter running the length of the mirrored wall. This was big enough to hold two portable typewriters, with the writers sitting on two small benches. As there were three Toronto papers and three writers, the person who would sit on the only remaining seat was decided by a coin toss, odd man out . . . or on.

Perched on the can in a closed cubicle, balancing a typewriter on your knee, trying to read scribbled notes on a swaying railway coach was enough to give the heaves to the strongest stomach.

One day after a trip from Boston in which I had lost the tosses – of both coins and cookies – I met Annis Stukus of the *Star* at a Leaf practice.

"Did you write that piece on the can?" he asked.

I said I had.

"I knew," he said. "It read like it."

Happily I can claim, with some modesty, not all of them did.

And, in retrospect, I reckon the years I spent in the

Long-time Leaf trainer Tim Daly, who retired in 1960 at the age of seventy-six, was also the trainer and equipment manager of the New York Giants, Detroit Tigers, and Toronto Maple Leafs baseball clubs.

Sun Room at the old *Telegram* were the best of my fifty years in the media business.

'Til now anyway.

| 75 PTS. | 66 PTS. | 65 PTS. | 57 PTS. | 50 PTS. | 47 PTS. |

1948-49
Leafs Sweep Wings for Third Straight Stanley Cup

The 1948-49 New York Rangers media guide book featured Buddy O'Connor on its cover after the former member of the Canadiens won the Hart Trophy as league MVP in 1947-48. O'Connor established career highs in goals (24) and points (60) in helping to lead the Rangers into the playoffs for the first time since 1942.

THERE WAS FURTHER DEBATE CONCERNING THE EXPANSION PROPOSALS FROM Philadelphia and Los Angeles at the annual league meetings in June. The Los Angeles bid was once again refused, as the prospective owners had no facility available to house an NHL franchise. In a related order of business, league officials finally terminated the Montreal Maroons franchise after ten years in abeyance. It was also decided to forbid players and officials from endorsing alcohol and tobacco products.

The 1948-49 season opened on a sour note when five Ranger players were injured in a car accident. The Rangers, who were enjoying a productive training camp, were forced to start the season without Bill Moe, Edgar Laprade, Buddy O'Connor, Frank Eddolls, and Tony Leswick. Although three of the five sustained only minor injuries, O'Connor, the team's leading scorer, and Eddolls, the club's highest-scoring rearguard, would both be lost for at least two months. Frank Boucher was relieved as coach after a 6–11–6 start, with Lynn Patrick assuming bench duties for the first time. The Broadway Blues won only one of their last ten games and fell to the basement, missing the playoffs by ten points.

The Rangers were joined on the sidelines by the Chicago Black Hawks, who, despite having the league's two top scorers, could not nail down a playoff spot. Roy Conacher, who retired briefly during the 1947-48 season, led the league in scoring and won the Art Ross Trophy, with teammate Doug Bentley finishing in the runner-up position.

For most of the campaign, it appeared that the Toronto Maple Leafs would miss the post-season as well. The Leafs, without the services of retired veterans Nick Metz and Syl Apps, were besieged by injuries and languished in fifth spot throughout much of the season. Only a late-season collapse by both the Hawks and the Rangers allowed the Leafs, who themselves lost five of their last six games, to finish in fourth place, eight points behind the Canadiens. Montreal's weak offense was counterbalanced by the defensive foursome of Doug Harvey, Kenny Reardon, Glen Harmon, and Roger Léger, and the Habs finished with a 28–23–9 mark. Bill Durnan, the league's dominant goaltender, recorded ten shutouts, the most since Frankie Brimsek reached double figures in 1939. Durnan also

The lovable fat man, Turk Broda, was the consummate playoff performer, compiling a career post-season goals-against average of 1.98. In the 1948-49 playoffs, Broda won eight games, while losing only one, with a goals-against average of 1.67.

challenged Alex Connell's milestone for consecutive scoreless minutes, shutting out the opposition four games in a row before allowing a goal to Chicago's Gaye Stewart.

In Boston, the Bruins' productive line of Johnny Peirson, Kenny Smith, and Paul Ronty helped the club to climb to second place, but the top squad in the league was the Detroit Red Wings, who captured their first regular-season title since 1942-43. The Wings led the league in goals, despite losing the services of Gordie Howe for twenty games due to a knee injury. Bill Quackenbush, the robust rearguard best known for his bruising-but-clean bodychecks, became the first defenseman to play a full season without registering a penalty. Selected as the Lady Byng Trophy winner, he was the first blueliner to win the award. Sid Abel, who led the league in goals, was awarded the Hart Trophy as league MVP, while Bill Durnan regained possession of the Vezina Trophy. Pentti Lund, who was born in Finland but learned to play hockey in Canada, won the Calder Trophy as the league's top freshman.

In the playoffs, the Toronto Maple Leafs, healthy for the first time all season, easily defended their Stanley Cup title. The Leafs downed the Boston Bruins in five games, then swept past the Detroit Red Wings for the second straight year to become the first fourth-place team to win the Cup. In each of the Leafs' wins in the playoffs, they scored at least three goals, combining opportunistic offense with airtight defense, to become the first team in NHL history to capture three consecutive Stanley Cup championships.

DURNAN RECORDS FOURTH STRAIGHT SHUTOUT FOR MONTREAL

Durnan's shutout streak ended one game later on March 9, 1949, at the 5:36 mark of the second period during a 2–2 tie with the Chicago Black Hawks.

March 6, 1949
at Boston Garden
Montreal 1, Boston 0

FIRST PERIOD

1) MTL Richard 20 (Lach) 19:32
PENALTIES – Sandford BOS (crosschecking) 16:44.

SECOND PERIOD

No Scoring
PENALTIES – Carveth BOS (holding) 6:01; Schmidt BOS (boarding) 15:28; Harvey MTL (boarding) 19:30.

THIRD PERIOD

No Scoring
PENALTIES – Richard MTL (roughing), Schmidt BOS (roughing) 3:10; Plamondon MTL (hooking) 5:50; Mosdell MTL (hooking) 7:00; Egan BOS (crosschecking) 9:15; Reay MTL (interference) 12:24; Babando BOS (slashing) 15:31.

GOALTENDERS	TIME	GA	ENG	DEC
MTL Durnan	60:00	0	0	W
BOS Brimsek	60:00	1	0	L

PP CONVERSIONS   MTL 0/5   BOS 0/4

88 PTS. 77 PTS. 74 PTS. 67 PTS. 60 PTS. 54 PTS.

1949-50
Wings Work Overtime in Superb Seven-Game Stanley Cup Final

ACROSS MUCH OF NORTH AMERICA, THE ERA OF TELEVISION WAS BEGINNING, AND the NHL took steps to modify the look of the game to suit the new medium. Although games would not be broadcast across Canada for another two seasons, the Chicago Black Hawks had been televising their games locally since 1948. In an effort to make games easier to watch, the league required that all ice surfaces be tinted white, an alteration that was greeted enthusiastically throughout the NHL. In previous seasons, ice surfaces were not colored, resulting in a grey, mottled look that was the result of the fact that the arena's concrete or sand floor could be seen through the transparent ice. Midway through a game, the combination of grey ice and white snow and scratches on the surface of the rink made the puck difficult to follow for both fans and players.

Another interesting rule change was also proposed. In the past, if a goaltender received a major penalty, a penalty shot would be awarded instead of having the goalie serve the penalty. The revised rule dispensed with the penalty shot. Instead, the penalized team would select a substitute, who would sit in the penalty box until the goalie's penalty had expired. Although Bill Durnan and Mike Karakas had been the only goalies to receive major penalties since 1942, a dispute between Kenny Reardon and Harry Lumley during the 1949 playoffs warranted the rule revision. The scuffle occurred in sudden-death overtime and Lumley went unpunished because the referee was hesitant to invoke the major penalty-shot rule in overtime. However, he did tag Reardon with a two-minute hooking penalty, and Detroit won the game on the ensuing power play.

The Detroit Red Wings were favorites early in the season, and they quickly established themselves as the league's strongest unit, winning eight of their first ten games. In a surprising roster shuffle, the Wings traded All-Star defenseman Bill Quackenbush to Boston in return for four players, including Pete Babando and Jim Peters, who would each play important roles in the Wings' championship season.

That Detroit could afford to move their All-Star rearguard spoke volumes about the enormous depth of their farm system. When Harry Lumley went down with an injury, the Wings promoted goaltender Terry Sawchuk from their Indianapolis farm team. Sawchuk had an outstanding

Jumping Junior

Having never played Junior A hockey, goaltender Jack Gelineau became the first player to jump directly to the NHL from the collegiate ranks. The former McGill University netminder was so impressive in his debut with the 1949-50 Boston Bruins, he was awarded the Calder Trophy as the NHL's top rookie.

debut, winning four games and recording his first NHL shutout. With solid netminding and the most productive offense in the league, the Wings cruised to the top of the league standings, capturing the regular-season crown by 11 points over the second-place Montreal Canadiens. All-Star rearguard Red Kelly took over for the departed Quackenbush, leading all defensemen in the NHL with 15 goals and 25 assists. The Production Line of Lindsay, Abel, and Howe finished 1–2–3 in the scoring race, combining for 92 goals and 215 points.

"Terrible Ted" Lindsay captured the scoring title and cemented his image as one of the league's toughest competitors, leading his team with 141 penalty minutes to miss by three minutes earning the "bad-boy" title for the season to Toronto's "Wild Bill" Ezinicki.

After a slow start, the Montreal Canadiens rebounded to finish the season strongly and earn second place in the standings. Hampered by injuries in the first half of the schedule, the Habs were forced to play a game against the Rangers on December 21 with only fourteen players in the lineup. As the season progressed, and their injured stars returned, the Canadiens recovered to go undefeated in their last six matches. Rocket Richard, who had slumped to only 28 goals in 1948-49, bounced back to lead the league with 43 goals. Bill Durnan won his sixth Vezina Trophy in seven years, ensuring his place in hockey history as one of the game's greatest netminders.

The "Battle of the Bulge" overshadowed much of the hockey action in Toronto, where Turk Broda was benched for a short spell by general manager Conn Smythe for being overweight. Certainly, the Leafs' 6–10–3 start was a cause for concern, but canny Conn was really using the bulky Broda as a pawn in his plan to put the Leafs back on track and get football out of the newspapers. The ploy worked, as Broda dropped the required pounds and recorded a shutout in his first game back, and the Leafs broke off a losing skid to climb from fifth to third place. Sid Smith, Ted Kennedy, and Max Bentley each reached the 20-goal plateau, while Broda led the NHL with nine shutouts.

Perhaps the biggest disappointment was the play of the Boston Bruins, who, despite acquiring Quackenbush and finishing third in goals scored, dropped from second to fifth place, winning only three of their final thirteen games down the stretch. The Chicago Black Hawks continued to encounter problems on the ice and at the box-office, dropping to last place, even though their roster featured five 20-goal scorers.

There was a revival on Broadway during the 1949-50 season, written by coach Lynn Patrick and orchestrated by general manager Frank Boucher. After a season of turmoil left them in sixth place in 1948-49, the Rangers rebounded to fourth in the NHL standings. The secret to the Rangers' success was a well-rounded attack, with nine different players reaching double figures in goals. Their overall record of 28–31–11 was

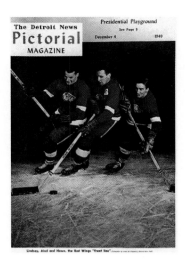

The NHL's most explosive forward unit during the 1949-50 campaign was Detroit's Production Line of Ted Lindsay, Sid Abel, and Gordie Howe. The trio combined for 92 goals and 215 points during the season to finish 1–2–3 in league scoring.

Santa Wore a Blue Suit

On December 25, 1950, the Red Wings beat the Rangers, 4–1, ending a streak that began in 1929, in which the Rangers were undefeated on Christmas Day. During that period, the Blueshirts posted a record of 15 wins and one tie. Their only other previous Christmas defeat was a 1–0 loss to the New York Americans in 1928.

Bert Olmstead led all rookie scorers in 1949-50 with 20 goals and 49 points for the sixth-place Chicago Black Hawks. The following season, Olmstead was traded to the Red Wings, who immediately dispatched the promising youngster to Montreal, where he went on to post the finest numbers of his career.

BABANDO SCORES CUP WINNER IN GAME SEVEN, DOUBLE OVERTIME

Pete Babando's winner, the final playoff goal of his career, capped a remarkable comeback by the Wings, who came from behind in games six and seven to win the Stanley Cup.

April 23, 1950
at Detroit Olympia
Detroit 4, New York 3

FIRST PERIOD
1) NY Stanley 2 (Leswick) PPG 11:14
2) NY Leswick 2 (O'Connor, Laprade) PPG 12:18
PENALTIES – Pavelich DET (holding) 6:12; Laprade NY (roughing), Lindsay DET (roughing, slashing) 8:18; Pavelich DET (slashing) 11:27; O'Connor NY (tripping) 12:42; Slowinski NY (tripping) 19:14.

SECOND PERIOD
3) DET Babando 1 (Kelly, Couture) PPG 5:09
4) DET Abel 6 (Dewsbury) PPG 5:30
5) NY O'Connor 4 (Mickoski) 11:42
6) DET McFadden 2 (Peters) 15:57
PENALTIES – Stanley NY (interference) 3:56.

THIRD PERIOD
No Scoring
PENALTIES – Kyle NY (hooking) :24; Dewsbury DET (holding) 1:33.

FIRST OVERTIME PERIOD
No Scoring
PENALTIES – None

SECOND OVERTIME PERIOD
7) Babando 2 (Gee) 8:31
PENALTIES – None

GOALTENDERS		TIME	GA	ENG	DEC
NY	Rayner	88:31	4	0	L
DET	Lumley	88:31	3	0	W

PP CONVERSIONS NY 2/4 DET 2/4

misleading, for the team underwent its only slump of the season in the final days of the schedule.

In the playoffs, the Rangers rallied to defeat the Montreal Canadiens in five games, their only loss coming in overtime in game four. In the finals, the New Yorkers met the heavily favored Detroit Red Wings, who had ended the Toronto Maple Leafs' hopes of a fourth straight Stanley Cup title with a 1–0 overtime win in game seven of the semi-finals. The dramatic victory by the Red Wings was overshadowed

by an incident in game one of the series. Midway through that match, Gordie Howe collided with Leafs captain Ted Kennedy and fell heavily into the boards. The exact circumstances of the incident remain unclear to this day; some claim Kennedy caught Howe with his stick, others say Howe slammed into the boards after missing Kennedy with a bodycheck. Regardless, Howe sustained a serious head injury and needed a series of operations to relieve pressure on his brain. The Wings used the incident as a rallying point and went on to upset the defending champions.

Forced to play all their games on the road because the circus was occupying Madison Square Garden, New York battled Detroit through seven evenly matched games. The Rangers, who held a 3–2 margin in games after Don "Bones" Raleigh became the first player to score two overtime goals in the same final series, also had a lead in both games six and seven before finally running out of miracles and losing in double overtime in the decisive seventh game. Pete Babando was the hero for the Red Wings when his wrist shot from the right circle escaped the grasp of a screened Chuck Rayner.

Rayner, the Rangers' roving goaltender, captured the Hart Trophy as league MVP, while teammate Edgar Laprade was the Lady Byng recipient.

Maurice Richard rocketed back to the top of the NHL's goal-scoring leader board in 1949-50, firing 43 pucks past opposing goaltenders. Goaltender Al Rollins (right), played for minor-league clubs in Edmonton, Kansas City, Cleveland, and Pittsburgh before making his NHL debut with the Leafs on Christmas Eve, 1949.

101 PTS.　　95 PTS.　　65 PTS.　　62 PTS.　　61 PTS.　　36 PTS.

1950-51
All-Overtime Final Ends on Barilko's Winner

After three seasons in which he was plagued by injury, Milt Schmidt finally returned to Hall-of-Fame form in 1950-51, compiling 22 goals and 61 points, the second-highest totals of his career.

THERE WERE A NUMBER OF DEVELOPMENTS THAT CHANGED THE FACE OF HOCKEY IN the 1950-51 season. In addition to four coaching changes and a history-making trade, there was a brief appearance by a pair of players who would become two of the game's greatest performers. Both Bernie "Boom-Boom" Geoffrion and Jean Béliveau suited up for the Montreal Canadiens on January 27, giving the Habs' fans a glimpse of their team's future. Both players scored in a 4–2 win over Chicago.

Lynn Patrick, who played a key role in the resurgence of the New York Rangers, resigned to take a coaching position with Victoria in the Western Hockey League. However, before he could begin that job, he accepted the head coaching portfolio with the Boston Bruins, who had released George Boucher after failing to make the playoffs in 1949-50. The Bruins' offer to Patrick included a promise that he would replace Art Ross as general manager of the team within three years.

The Toronto Maple Leafs also made a coaching change, elevating Joe Primeau to replace Hap Day. Primeau, who had already led the Toronto Marlboro juniors to the Memorial Cup and the Marlboro seniors to the Allan Cup, was only the fifth coach in team history.

In New York, Neil Colville was given the task of continuing Patrick's rebuilding program. Colville, a long-time Rangers star who had retired after the 1948-49 campaign, had only one year of coaching experience, having piloted the New Haven entry in the AHL during the 1949-50 season. Chicago also switched coaches, with Charlie Conacher surrendering the reins after two disappointing seasons with the Black Hawks. His replacement, Ebbie Goodfellow, would have even less luck in turning the fortunes of the team around.

The Detroit Red Wings were clear favorites to repeat as Stanley Cup champions, but that didn't prevent them from retooling their roster. In the largest trade in NHL history, the Wings sent Harry Lumley, Jack Stewart, Al Dewsbury, Don Morrison, and Pete Babando to Chicago for "Sugar Jim" Henry, Bob Goldham, Gaye Stewart, and Metro Prystai. Lumley, who had led the league in victories in his last two seasons in Detroit, was deemed expendable because of the outstanding play of Terry Sawchuk, who had proved in his brief stint during the 1949-50 season that he was

Gordie Howe, who briefly wore a helmet during the 1950-51 schedule after suffering a serious head injury during the 1950 playoffs, became the first player to lead the NHL in goals, assists, and points since Howie Morenz topped the scoring tables in 1927-28. Howe finished with 43 goals, 43 assists, and 86 points.

ready to assume the Red Wings' goaltending chores. Henry, acquired as insurance for Sawchuk, was pegged for the Wings' Indianapolis farm team, but Goldham, Prystai, and Stewart all played key roles in a record-setting year by the Red Wings.

During the summer meetings, the NHL decided to continue the 70-game schedule they had introduced the season before. The Red Wings took advantage of these ten extra games to set a number of new NHL records, including milestones for wins (44) and points (101). Terry Sawchuk was in net for each of those victories, establishing an NHL mark for goaltenders. Gordie Howe, despite his serious injury in the 1950 playoffs, set a new NHL record with 86 points to win his first scoring title. Red Kelly established a record for defensemen, with 17 goals and 37 assists.

It was clearly a two-horse race in the NHL during the 1950-51 campaign. As dominant as the Wings were, the Toronto Maple Leafs battled them most of the way, finishing only six points back after setting team

Allan Stanley, who went on to become a Hall-of-Fame defenseman with the Toronto Maple Leafs, was jeered by fans in Madison Square Garden for seven seasons before being traded to Chicago in 1954-55. He wasn't the first, and certainly wasn't the last, player to be booed off Broadway.

Getting Their Numbers

Beginning February 1, 1951, NHL on-ice officials began wearing numbers on the backs of their colored sweaters. Referees were assigned numbers 1 through 5, while linesmen wore numbers 11 through 22. No number 13 was assigned.

marks for wins (41) and points (96). After losing their season opener to Chicago 2–1, the Leafs embarked on a team-record eleven-game unbeaten streak, winning eight games and tying three over the month-long undefeated string. Although the four remaining clubs finished with records of below .500, the competition was fierce, with only four points separating the third-, fourth- and fifth-place teams.

Once again, a poor late-season showing by the Rangers cost the club a playoff spot, as they won only one of their final seven games to miss the post-season by a single point. The Rangers, Stanley Cup finalists the previous spring, missed the post-season for the seventh time in the previous nine seasons. Montreal clinched a spot in the playoffs after a 2–2 tie on March 18, while the Bruins squeezed past the Rangers with a 6–5 victory over the last-place Black Hawks on March 21.

One of the early-season surprises was the play of the Chicago Black Hawks. The Hawks, who had missed the playoffs for four straight seasons, started the campaign by going 11–10–6 in the first 27 games. However, Chicago won only two of their remaining 43 contests, including a club-record 21-game winless streak during a stretch in which they played 24 times in 50 days.

Goaltending was to provide the league with both great moments and bitter controversy over the course of the 1950-51 campaign. Four of the six teams started the season with new goaltenders in the starting lineup, including Montreal, where Bill Durnan surprised team officials by announcing his retirement after only seven years of NHL service. Gerry McNeil, who had seen action in both the 1947-48 and 1949-50 seasons, was given the task of replacing Durnan. Chicago, which had earlier traded for Harry Lumley, lost Frank Brimsek to retirement after only one season with the Black Hawks. Although Toronto still had Turk Broda, he was sharing duties with Al Rollins in a unique tandem situation, creating the league's first two-goaltender system.

One of the highlights of the season was the play of rookie goaltender Terry Sawchuk, who appeared in all 70 games for the Red Wings, recording a league-leading 11 shutouts and an outstanding goals-against average of 1.99. Sawchuk was selected as the league's rookie of the year, adding to the freshman honors he received in the USHL and the AHL. However, Sawchuk missed out on the Vezina Trophy when the league awarded the trophy to Toronto's Al Rollins, who completed the schedule with a goals-against average of 1.77. Detroit management argued bitterly that Sawchuk, who appeared in all 70 games as opposed to Rollins's 40 appearances, should be given the award, but the league held fast on its decision, since the Toronto team had allowed one less goal than the Detroit club.

In the playoffs, the Montreal Canadiens outlasted the Detroit Red Wings in a hard-fought six-game semi-final. The opening game required three full periods of overtime before Maurice Richard scored at the 1:09 mark of the fourth overtime. Richard settled matters in overtime again in the second game, firing the puck past a dazed Terry Sawchuk after 42 minutes of extra time to give the Canadiens a 1–0 victory. The Red Wings stormed back to tie the series with a pair of victories at the Olympia, but Montreal took the next two games to reach the finals.

Montreal's opponent in the championship round was the Toronto Maple Leafs, who had downed the Boston Bruins in five games. Because of Sunday curfew laws in Toronto, game two of the semi-final was declared a tie after one period of overtime. It was the first time since March 23, 1935, that a Stanley Cup playoff game was played without a winner being declared.

For the only time in Stanley Cup history, every game of the 1951 finals went into overtime. In game one, Sid Smith scored six minutes into extra time to give the Leafs a 3–2 win and an early series lead. Maurice Richard scored his third overtime goal of the playoffs in game two, picking up a pass from Doug Harvey and drilling it past Turk Broda for a 3–2 win. Teeder Kennedy and Harry Watson took turns in the spotlight in games three and four, each scoring early in the extra session to put the Leafs one win away from their fourth Stanley Cup in five years.

It appeared that the Canadiens were poised to pull within a game of the Leafs in the fifth contest, as the Habs nursed a 2–1 lead into the final minute of the game. However, with goalie Al Rollins on the bench for the extra attacker, Toronto's Tod Sloan scored to tie the game, setting up the fifth overtime of the series. Early in the additional period, Leaf defenseman Bill Barilko spotted a loose puck near the Habs crease, dove in from the blueline, and lifted a backhander over Gerry McNeil's outstretched arm to seal the victory and give the Leafs their seventh Stanley Cup title. The famous Turofsky Brothers photo of Barilko diving through the air as the puck settles into the netting behind McNeil is one of the most enduring images in the history of the sport.

Only three months after scoring his most famous goal, Barilko was reported missing on a fishing trip near Rupert House on James Bay in northern Ontario. The pilot of the plane was Dr. Henry Hudson, whose brother Lou was a member of the 1928 University of Toronto Grads hockey club that won the gold medal at the 1928 Winter Olympics in St. Moritz, Switzerland. Conn Smythe ordered a massive air search for the missing hero, but no sign of the plane was found. It would not be until the summer of 1962 that the wreckage containing Barilko's body would be discovered.

(continued on p. 55)

BARILKO'S GOAL CLINCHES LEAFS' CUP IN ALL-OVERTIME FINAL

Toronto's Tod Sloan scored with only 32 seconds remaining in the third period to tie the game and set the stage for Barilko's heroics.

April 21, 1951
at Maple Leaf Gardens
Toronto 3, Montreal 2

FIRST PERIOD

No Scoring

PENALTIES – Dawes MTL (slashing) :27; Barilko TOR (charging) 16:04.

SECOND PERIOD

1) MTL Richard 9 (MacPherson) 8:56
2) TOR Sloan 3 (Kennedy) 12:00

PENALTIES – None

THIRD PERIOD

3) MTL Meger 1 (Harvey) 4:47
4) TOR Sloan 4 (Bentley, Smith) 19:28

PENALTIES – Barilko TOR (roughing), Johnson MTL (roughing), Reay MTL (misconduct) 10:36.

FIRST OVERTIME PERIOD

5) TOR Barilko 3 (Meeker, Watson) 2:53

PENALTIES – None

GOALTENDERS		TIME	GA	ENG	DEC
MTL	McNeil	62:53	3	0	L
TOR	Rollins	62:23*	2	0	W

*unofficial estimate, left net for extra skater late in third period.

PP CONVERSIONS   MTL 0/1   TOR 0/1

Close Call

Traveling home following a 6–1 pasting by Toronto on December 21, 1950, the slumping Montreal Canadiens were thrown from their sleeping berths when their train derailed on a bridge that spanned the Ottawa River. Had the train tipped right instead of left, the cars would have plunged thirty feet into the freezing water. Coach Dick Irvin remarked, "I was planning a shake-up, but not quite as drastic as that."

Day's Decade: The 1940s Leafs

by Milt Dunnell

Hap Day, seen here sharing the Stanley Cup spotlight with Nick Metz (left) and Wally Stanowski, compiled a .714 winning percentage in the finals, winning 20 games while losing only eight.

It commenced with a miracle and ended with a tragedy that never will be explained. Call it the Decade of Hap Day, during which the Toronto Maple Leafs – yes, the Toronto Maple Leafs – held the Stanley Cup for six of ten seasons, the final one with a freshman coach.

Or it could be recalled as Conn Smythe's "Cycle of Supercenters," in which he gave up an entire starting lineup, minus the goalie, for one playmaker whom he felt he must have to keep the club's series of successes alive. It worked.

Smythe had been able to showcase the Governor General's fifty-dollar rose bowl at the brand new Maple Leaf Gardens in the spring of 1932, when the famous Kid Line of Joe Primeau, Charlie Conacher, and Harvey "Busher" Jackson was manning the guns, King Clancy, Hap Day, and Red Horner were back of the blueline, Lorne Chabot in the cage, and wily Dick Irvin behind the bench.

If the townsfolk expected that glimpse of the Cup to be an annual ritual – and they did – they were due for a long spell of disappointment. The Leafs reached the finals and lost six times from 1933 to 1940, which accounted for considerable pessimism in the spring of 1942, when the Leafs found themselves in what would prove to be the last Cup final before the NHL took on the cozy, six-team configuration it would wear for the next twenty-five seasons. The Red Wings beat the Leafs in the first two games of the series. The public experienced a strong sense of *déjà vu*, which was usually voiced in terms that family gazettes declined to print.

Then, the Red Wings made it three–zip for the series. They were back on their home pond at the old Olympia, and Jack Adams, who turned Detroit into one of the hottest towns in hockey, ordered the champagne put on ice. As far as the Leafs knew, the bubbly never got uncorked. It may have been saved for the next year, when Detroit did get the job done, but that was against the Bruins.

Down three games to none, with the fourth game in Detroit, the Leafs were abandoned by even their closest friends. No other team in the history of the NHL ever got itself over such a barrel and emerged with the Stanley Cup. The Leafs did.

Different reasons were given for the amazing turn-around. One was a change of horses for younger legs, which involved benching Gordie Drillon, their leading goal-getter during this season and in four of the past five years.

Coach Hap Day, in later years, was to claim it was done by hoisting the Red Wings on their own petard, as the Bard might have said. Day claimed that the Red Wings were beating his team by dumping the puck into Toronto's defensive zone and beating them to it, and Day wanted to play the same game, but Smythe objected. It was a style of hockey he didn't like, but after three defeats, he gave the okay. The Leafs won the fourth game, 4–3, and then really sent the Red Wings grasping for the panic button by walloping them, 9–3, on Toronto ice in game five and 3–0 in Detroit in game six.

The seventh game took place in Maple Leaf Gardens, and the fact that no team had ever come all the way back from a three-game deficit to win the Stanley Cup was the only thing the Leafs had going against them. They overcame that, too. On the night of April 18, they beat the Red Wings, 3–1, and it was firecracker night all over town.

Neither Smythe nor Day was fooled by the greatest bounce-back the game had seen. They had a team that had accomplished the impossible, but by the dawn of the six-team era in 1942-43, it was getting old. Some of the club's elder statesmen, who had not been deemed eligible for military service, hung on to win again in 1944-45, but nobody was misled.

Two vital cogs in the Leaf machine – goalie Turk Broda and center Syl Apps, both in the army – were missing from that victory celebration, but both would be back for the three-year reign that Day was to launch in 1946. Once again, he would be making history. Since the inception of the NHL in 1917, no club had been able to win the Stanley Cup in three consecutive seasons.

Practically unnoticed, an important element of what would prove to be Day's dynasty was put in place on March 3, 1943, when "Teeder" Kennedy, a seventeen-year-old boy from Port Colborne, Ontario, signed a Leaf contract. Teeder paid almost immediate dividends, playing an important role in the Leafs' surprise Cup victory two seasons later.

Four nights after joining the Leafs, he made his NHL debut against the Rangers at Madison Square Garden, playing right wing on the club's third line with Bud Poile and Gaye Stewart. Day told him: "All I want you to do is stay with your check and keep him from scoring. Don't wander." Kennedy wandered enough to help his line

An astute judge of athletic talent both on and off the ice, Conn Smythe built the Toronto Maple Leafs into the NHL's first powerhouse, winning six Stanley Cup championships between 1942 and 1951.

score three goals in a 5–5 tie and made a strong case for a shift to center. His agility and creativity made him a natural center-ice man, a position at which Smythe's teams inevitably were well served.

In the early 1940s, the club's first-string center, of course, was Syl Apps, who was well on his way to the Hockey Hall of Fame. Behind him were Nick Metz and Bud Poile. Both Smythe and Day believed that strength down the middle was as essential in hockey as it was in baseball. In baseball, this strength meant that a team's catcher, second baseman, shortstop, and center-fielder had to be solid. In hockey, Smythe and Day felt that a team's backbone was a product of its corps of centers and its goaltender. Apps, Kennedy, Metz, and Poile gave the Leafs a superb group of centers and, with Turk Broda between the pipes, the Leafs had one of hockey's best big-game goaltenders.

It was when Apps neared the end of the line that Smythe made one of the astounding deals in sports history. On November 4, 1948, sports editors gave feature coverage to the story of five Leafs: Gus Bodnar, Gaye Stewart, and Bud Poile, along with blueliners Ernie Dickens and Bob Goldham, who were going to the Black Hawks for Max Bentley and Cy Thomas. Bentley, who

Max Bentley, the "Dipsy-Doodling Dandy from Delisle,"
collected 14 points in three Stanley Cup final-series
appearances as a member of the Maple Leafs.

was coming off three consecutive seasons with more than 25 goals, was the key to the whole transaction. Thomas was slated for trivia immortality.

Before the 1948-49 season began, Smythe had dealt with the Rangers for Bill Juzda, a railroader out of Winnipeg who hit with the force of the locomotives that he jockeyed in the off-seasons. In one of his more memorable games with the Rangers, Juzda had bodychecked Toe Blake of the Montreal Canadiens so heavily that Blake's skate became lodged in the boards. When he fell, Blake's leg was badly broken, and his playing career was over.

Blake went on to win an NHL-record eight Stanley Cup championships as a coach. Juzda became the defense-mate of Bill Barilko, and, in one of the most memorable moments of Stanley Cup play, he was on the ice when Barilko scored the winning overtime goal that became almost as famous as Bill Mazeroski's 1960 World Series home run.

This, of course, was on the night of April 21, 1951, at Maple Leaf Gardens. The Barilko goal, at 2:53 of overtime, became much bigger than just a sports event when Barilko disappeared in August on a fishing trip to James Bay, along with a Timmins, Ontario, dentist friend named Henry Hudson. Their disappearance touched off

one of the biggest and most-prolonged aerial rescue operations in the history of the North, but the remains of Hudson's single-engine, pontoon-equipped Fairchild aircraft wouldn't be discovered until eleven years later.

Barilko, big, green, and rough, had signed with the Leafs in the fall of 1945, but wasn't considered to be ready for a spot with the Leafs' Pittsburgh farm club in the American Hockey League. Instead, he was shipped to the Hollywood Wolves of the Pacific Coast League, where his good looks earned him the nickname "Hollywood Bill." By 1947, he had caught the eye of Johnny Mitchell, a Toronto scout, who recommended that the Leafs give him a shot.

Barilko arrived just in time to become a part of hockey lore. Hap Day, with only seven members of his 1942 miracle-makers still in uniform, was launching what would turn out to be a three-year clutch on the Stanley Cup in 1946-47. Those were rugged times in the NHL, and Barilko fitted right into the action.

The third game of the 1948 semi-final with the Boston Bruins was indicative of the temper of the times. Fans attacked Day and Garth Boesch as they went to the dressing room between periods. The officials, referee George Gravel and linesman George Hayes, were harassed by other irate Bruin partisans.

King Clancy, the stand-by referee, became involved. He eventually was charged with assault by one Bostonian who claimed that King, who was famous for never having won a fight in his life, pushed him into the referee's room, where he was roughed up.

When the case finally came to trial, Clancy, as everyone expected, was exonerated. Lester Patrick, who had been the NHL governor in charge of that particular series, told Clancy: "I think those police officers who testified were Irish." Clancy laughed and said: "How about the judge, Lester? Did you think he was Chinese?"

In the old six-team league, players battled each other so frequently that feuds were inevitable and were carried from game to game. One of the more-publicized set-tos during the Leafs' Stanley Cup three-peat involved Cal Gardner of the Leafs and Ken Reardon, the rugged Montreal Canadiens rearguard. They engaged in a stick duel at Maple Leaf Gardens that earned match

penalties. League president Clarence Campbell later reviewed the incident. He fined Gardner $250 and Reardon $200, sums that at that time represented big bites from each player's paycheque.

The chances of the Leafs capturing a third consecutive Cup championship seemed remote as the 1948-49 season wore on. They just couldn't score goals, finishing in fourth place after scoring just 147 goals in 60 games, the club's lowest single-season total since 1940-41, when the Leafs had scored 145 times over a 48-game schedule.

Apps and Nick Metz had retired. Roy Conacher and Doug Bentley, both Black Hawks, finished one–two in scoring. The top Leaf was Harry Watson, with 26 goals. Max Bentley had 19 goals; Kennedy had 18. The Leafs were still a solid club, but few believed that Hap Day would soon enjoy his third straight chance to dip a finger into the champagne and lick off the bubbly. (As a strict teetotaler, that's as close as Day ever came to alcohol.)

Bill Barilko's Stanley Cup-winning goal in game five of the 1951 finals signaled the end of an era in Maple Leaf hockey history. The franchise would struggle through an eleven-year drought before tasting victory again in 1962.

The playoffs, however, proved to be a soft touch for the Leafs. The Bruins, whom they met in the first round, couldn't win at home. In the finals, the Red Wings came up empty after winning a bitter seven-game semi-final set with the Canadiens, and didn't win a heat against the Leafs. In the end, Toronto toasted its three-time Stanley Cup champions.

It had been so easy that a previously-unheard-of four-year Stanley Cup stranglehold appeared to be in the works. This prediction ignored all the odds, as well as the fact that Detroit's famed Production Line of Gordie Howe, Ted Lindsay, and Sid Abel seemed to be getting ready to take the league apart.

The 1950 Cup semi-final, which was to end the

Captain Ted Kennedy accepts the Stanley Cup from NHL president Clarence Campbell after the Leafs downed the Detroit Red Wings 3–1 on April 16, 1949, to complete a four-game sweep of the championship series.

Leafs' three-year domination, turned into one of the most hostile series of all time between the Leafs and the Red Wings. Trouble came in the very first game, when Howe was badly injured in a collision along the boards with Ted Kennedy. Although there was no penalty on the play, the Detroit media created the impression that it had been a dirty check.

The Red Wings finally triumphed in the seventh game of the series on an overtime goal by Leo Reise. After the game, Smythe congratulated his troops on their long campaign and revealed that Day would become the Leafs' assistant general manager. Joe Primeau was to become the new coach.

This was the same Primeau who had stood at center ice with his wife, Helen, in 1936 and received a silver tea service in recognition of his career with the Leafs. At age thirty he had announced his retirement. Little did he know then that, fifteen years later, he would be accepting the Stanley Cup in exactly the same spot. In sport, fact frequently makes a sucker out of fiction.

Only nine years had elapsed since Day's miracle team. Yet only Broda of that club suited up for Primeau's 1950-51 team. Turk actually was on the way out, since Al Rollins had taken over as the Leafs' number-one netminder. Primeau's club was still strong at center, with Bentley and Kennedy, and he conceded nothing to anybody on defense, where he had Jim Thomson, Gus Mortson, Barilko, Juzda, and Fern Flaman.

"There is no doubt about how the Leafs dominated in that decade," Juzda agrees. "Strength down the middle: we had that with Rollins in goal."

When Barilko blasted the winning goal past the Montreal Canadiens' Gerry McNeil in the fifth overtime game of the 1951 finals, Juzda recalls how he grabbed Barilko and started to lug him around the Gardens' ice in triumph.

Then, the players remembered who got them there. They hoisted Primeau aloft, while the capacity crowd roared. As center of the Leafs' Kid Line in the 1930s, Primeau usually was in the shadow of his mates, Charlie Conacher and Busher Jackson. Now he had the limelight all to himself. And he didn't like it. He wanted out. Coaching at the big-league level was not his idea of living.

Smythe put heavy pressure on Primeau to stay. Only

Left to right: Coach Joe Primeau with Ted Kennedy, Jim Thompson, Harry Watson, Sid Smith, Tod Sloan, and Gus Mortson shortly after taking over the reins of the Maple Leafs from Hap Day. Primeau, who had already guided teams to the Allan Cup and Memorial Cup as a head coach, added the Stanley Cup to his trophy case after piloting the Leafs to the championship in 1950-51.

half jokingly, he said: "It wouldn't be fair for Joe to quit. He hasn't suffered enough." Against his will, Primeau would put in two more seasons.

Unbelievably, the news that Barilko and Hudson were missing on their fishing trip in August was received with some skepticism. The cynics saw it as one of Smythe's publicity ploys. He was famous for them. Smythe, himself, was undisturbed for a day or so. Barilko,

he said, was the kind of guy who would overcome whatever difficulty was encountered. Later, he offered a $10,000 reward to anyone who could find the missing pair.

The last persons known to have seen the star of the 1951 Stanley Cup alive were at Rupert House, on the south shore of James Bay. There were 120 pounds of fish in the pontoons, Hudson and Barilko had said. A storm was threatening, but they insisted they had to get home or the fish would spoil.

"All for a bunch of fish," Smythe lamented when it became obvious he had lost one of his favorite hockey players.

Juzda adds an epitaph: "The fans never got to see how good Barilko might have been. He still hadn't reached his potential. This guy was destined to be great."

And Howe:
The Wings Take Flight
1951-52 to 1954-55

100 PTS.   78 PTS.   74 PTS.   66 PTS.   59 PTS.   43 PTS.

1951-52
Sensational Sawchuk Spins Four Playoff Shutouts

IT WAS AN EVENTFUL OFF-SEASON FOR MANY NHL CLUBS. DESPITE A FIRST-PLACE finish in 1950-51, the Detroit Red Wings continued to revamp their lineup, sending six players – Jim McFadden, George Gee, Jim Peters, Clare Martin, Clarence "Rags" Raglan, and Max McNab – to the Chicago Black Hawks. Detroit received a cash payment and Hugh Coflin, who never played a game for the team. McFadden, Peters, and Gee had combined to score 48 goals for the Wings in 1950-51, but Jack Adams was confident that rookie Alex Delvecchio and newcomer Tony Leswick would compensate for their missing firepower. It was a testament to the depth of the Detroit farm system that the Wings remained the league's best team in 1951-52.

Boston also made numerous personnel changes, purchasing the contract of Sugar Jim Henry from Detroit, while adding Hal Laycoe, Adam Brown, and Gus Kyle. George "Red" Sullivan and Dave Creighton, both of whom had disappointed in 1950-51, were given another opportunity to make the team, and both responded with excellent efforts. Montreal added Dollard St. Laurent and gave Bernie Geoffrion a full-time job after an eighteen-game stint in 1950-51. The defending-champion Maple Leafs, without Turk Broda and Bill Barilko, were on the lookout for blueline help. The New York Rangers lost five players to retirement, and their search for suitable replacements went unrewarded.

The annual All-Star Game was played October 9 in Toronto and featured a new format for the pre-season classic. Instead of a team of All-Stars playing the defending Stanley Cup champions, two teams of All-Stars faced off against each other. The First All-Star Team was bolstered with players from the league's four American clubs. The Second

Opposite: Sid Abel (right) and Terry Sawchuk savor the sweet taste of success after the Red Wings won the 1952 Stanley Cup, their second championship title in three years. Sawchuk's playoff performance, which included eight consecutive wins and four straight shutouts on home ice, was one of the most remarkable in Stanley Cup history.

Bill Mosienko puts the finishing touches on the fastest hat-trick in NHL history by sliding this shot past New York Rangers goaltender Lorne Anderson. Mosienko's three goals in 21 seconds were recorded on the final night of the 1951-52 season and signaled the end of Anderson's brief NHL career.

All-Star Team was supplemented with players from the two Canadian teams. Toronto fans, incensed that Montreal coach Dick Irvin didn't add Al Rollins, the Vezina Trophy winner, to the All-Star squad, gained a small measure of satisfaction when Tod Sloan scored one goal and set up another in the 2–2 All-Star draw.

Early in the season, it appeared that the Montreal Canadiens had the finest young talent. Geoffrion, who earned the nickname "Boom-Boom" because of his overwhelming slapshot, scored 30 goals in his freshman campaign. Dick Gamble, from Moncton, New Brunswick, also made a bold impression, firing 23 goals past opposition goaltenders. Another rookie, Dickie Moore, joined the team on December 15 and went on to collect 33 points in 33 games. Gamble never regained his rookie form,

Terry Sawchuk, who in 1950-51 became the first goaltender in NHL history to win 40 games in a single season, continued to be the NHL's dominant backstop in 1951-52. The Winnipeg native won 44 games, recorded 12 shutouts and posted a miserly 1.90 goals-against average in guiding the Red Wings to their fourth straight regular-season crown.

but both Geoffrion and Moore would play crucial roles in the Canadiens' success throughout the 1950s.

Even though the Habs were rich in young talent, Detroit was still the league's top team, motoring to a 21–6–8 mark by the halfway point of the season. Red Kelly was the league's best defenseman, merging tough defense and scoring savvy to collect 47 points for the Wings. Gordie Howe, Ted Lindsay, and Sid Abel were the top offensive unit in the game, combining for 94 of the team's 215 goals. Terry Sawchuk delivered 12 shutouts and a record-tying 44 victories, in addition to a sparkling goals-against average of 1.90, to win the Vezina Trophy for the first time.

The Canadiens, who were without Maurice Richard for a good portion of the season, still managed a second-place finish with a 34–26–10 record. Elmer Lach led the league with 50 assists, and newcomer Paul Meger became the fourth rookie in the club's history to score at least 18 goals, adding 24 markers to the Habs' attack.

Toronto finished four points behind the Canadiens, struggling most of the season to mount an effective offense. The Leafs, who managed just

Action in the Crease

As part of a group of rule changes concerning goaltenders and the goal area for the 1951-52 season, the goal crease was enlarged from three feet by six feet to four feet by seven feet. Further, if a defending player other than the goaltender picked up a puck in the crease with his hands, a penalty shot would now be awarded to the attacking team. It was also proposed (and later rejected) that, if a goaltender were fouled from behind by an attacker while in the crease, a penalty shot would be awarded to the goaltender's team.

Toronto's Jim Thomson was the only NHL defenseman to play all seventy games without scoring a goal during the 1951-52 season. Thomson's job, however, was preventing goals rather than scoring them. He was rewarded for his excellent defensive play with a berth on the NHL's Second All-Star Team.

New Icing Rule

Beginning in the 1951-52 season, icing would no longer be called if the goaltender was the first member of the defending team to touch the puck. This rule change forced defensemen to hustle back to reach the puck before an opponent. The icing rule was again amended in 1957-58, stipulating that icing would be automatically waved off if a cleared puck passed through the goal crease.

168 goals in the 70-game schedule, were led by Sid Smith, Tod Sloan, Harry Watson, and Max Bentley, each of whom reached the 20-goal plateau. In the final game of the season, a 4–2 loss to Boston, Turk Broda came out of retirement for "Turk Broda Night" and started in the Leafs' net. Broda showed the cobwebs of inactivity, allowing three goals in thirty minutes before being replaced by Rollins. Broda pulled on the pads again in the playoffs, earning a standing ovation from the Detroit fans at the Olympia in a 1–0 loss to the Wings in the second game of the Leafs–Red Wings semi-final. "Ol' Turkey Eyes" started game three as well, but he was ineffective in a 6–2 drubbing. That appearance, his 101st in Stanley Cup play, was the last game of his marvelous career.

Boston sewed up the final playoff spot thanks, in part, to 20-goal efforts from Milt Schmidt, Johnny Peirson, and Dave Creighton. Both Schmidt and Peirson tied for tenth place in the scoring race, while Jim Henry was one of three NHL goaltenders to play every minute of every game in 1951-52. There was an ownership change in Boston during the season. President Weston Adams resigned and sold 60 per cent of the team to Walter Brown, operating director of Boston Garden. The transfer of power had no visible effect on the on-ice operation of the Bruins, as both general manager Art Ross and coach Lynn Patrick were retained. One of the special moments of the Boston season came on March 18, when Bobby Bauer came out of a four-year retirement to play one game with his Kraut Line teammates. Bauer looked in peak form, scoring one goal and setting up Milt Schmidt's 200th career goal as the Beantowners blanked the Black Hawks, 4–0.

The bottom rungs of the NHL ladder were held by the Rangers and Black Hawks, both of whom struggled once again. The Rangers lost five of their last seven games to finish seven points shy of earning a playoff berth. Don "Bones" Raleigh led the Broadway Blues in scoring, collecting 61 points, the fourth-best total in the NHL. Another outstanding rookie in a banner year for freshmen was the Rangers' right-winger, Wally Hergesheimer, who fired 26 goals for his fifth-place team. Another promising newcomer was Herb Dickinson, who compiled 27 points in just 37 games after joining the Rangers early in the season.

It was another disappointing season in the Windy City, as the Black Hawks, under coach Ebbie Goodfellow, finished in the NHL basement with a record of 17 wins, 44 losses, and 9 ties. The only bright light for the Hawks was center Billy Mosienko, who scored 31 goals and added 22 assists for 53 points. Mosienko also put his name in the record books during the final game of the 1951-52 season, scoring three goals in just 21 seconds, all on set-ups from Gus Bodnar. Mosienko's rapid-fire heroics erased a three-goal New York lead and earned a 7–6 win for the Hawks. Victimized was Rangers goaltender Lorne Anderson, who never played in the NHL again. Chicago also entered the record books on

November 25, 1951, when their trainer, Moe Roberts, a former goalie, was called on to replace an injured Harry Lumley in the Chicago net. Roberts closed the door on the first-place Detroit Red Wings and, at age forty-six, became the oldest goalie ever to appear in an NHL game. It was Roberts's first appearance in the NHL since 1934, when he dressed for six games with the New York Americans.

Montreal reached the finals after a tough seven-game series with the Bruins. The key moment of the series came in game six, with the Habs down 3–2 in games and on the verge of elimination. In the third period, with the Bruins nursing a 2–1 lead, Rocket Richard tied the match to send the game into overtime. In the second extra period, Paul Masnick took a pass from Doug Harvey and sent the puck past sprawling goaltender Sugar Jim Henry to tie the series. In game seven, Rocket Richard was crushed by a Leo Labine body check and spent most of the third period on the bench with blood flowing down his brow from a deep cut above his eye. In the closing minutes of the frame, with the score tied 1–1, Richard ignored the pain and took to the ice. Butch Bouchard dug a loose puck out the corner and passed it to the Rocket, who blasted through the entire Bruins team to score the winning goal that sent the Canadiens to the championship round. Following the game, Richard paused to congratulate Sugar Jim Henry, who had played superbly, despite two blackened eyes and a broken nose. For many, this moment epitomized the rugged brand of hockey played in the six-team NHL.

However, the real heroes of the Stanley Cup playoffs were Terry Sawchuk and the rest of the Detroit Red Wings. Detroit won eight straight games in the post-season, sweeping both Toronto and Montreal to win its fourth Stanley Cup title. Sawchuk held opposing shooters scoreless on home ice in the entire playoffs, racking up four shutouts and a minuscule goals-against average of 0.62.

In a year that featured a number of outstanding rookie performances, Bernie Geoffrion was saluted as the league's best newcomer. Gordie Howe won the Art Ross Trophy and the Hart Trophy, while Sid Smith of the Leafs brought home the Lady Byng Trophy as the league's most gentlemanly player.

In the off-season, the NHL received an application from a group in Cleveland, requesting an NHL franchise. The group, headed by Jim Hendy and William Lavery, were given six conditions to meet before a franchise could be granted to the Lake Erie city. Although NHL president Clarence Campbell was sympathetic to the Cleveland bid, they failed to satisfy the league's requirements, and their application was denied. Spokesman Jim Hendy, who was also the general manager of the Barons, Cleveland's successful AHL franchise, announced that his consortium would continue to attempt to convince the NHL's Board of Governors that Cleveland was a viable hockey town.

THREE GOALS IN 21 SECONDS: NEW RECORD FOR MOSIENKO

Gus Bodnar set up all three of Mosienko's goals to establish an NHL record for the fastest three assists. Rangers' goaltender Lorne Anderson never played in the NHL again.

March 23, 1952
at Madison Square Garden
Chicago 7, New York 6

FIRST PERIOD
1) CHI Bodnar 14 (Gadsby, Mosienko) :44
2) NY Eddolls 3 4:50
3) NY Raleigh 19 (Stewart, Stanley) 17:12
4) NY Slowinski 20 (Raleigh, Stewart) 18:35
5) CHI Horeck 9 (Hucul, Finney) 18:47
PENALTIES — None

SECOND PERIOD
6) NY Stewart 15 (Slowinski) 13:19
7) NY Dickenson 14 (Hergesheimer, Ronty) 15:55
PENALTIES — None

THIRD PERIOD
8) NY Slowinski 21 (Raleigh) 3:37
9) CHI Mosienko 29 (Bodnar) 6:09
10) CHI Mosienko 30 (Bodnar) 6:20
11) CHI Mosienko 31 (Bodnar, Gee) 6:30
12) CHI Finney 5 (Hucul, Fogolin) 13:50
13) CHI Finney 6 (Gadsby) 19:22
PENALTIES — None

GOALTENDERS	TIME	GA	ENG	DEC
CHI Lumley	60:00	6	0	W
NY Anderson	60:00	7	0	L

PP CONVERSIONS   CHI 0/0   NY 0/0

90 PTS.   75 PTS.   69 PTS.   69 PTS.   67 PTS.   50 PTS.

1952-53
Goals Galore and an NHL Points Record

AMONG THE TOP STORIES BREAKING IN THE NHL DURING THE OFF-SEASON WAS AN ownership change in Chicago. On September 11, 1952, the owners of Chicago Stadium – James Norris, Sr., James D. Norris, Jr., and Arthur Wirtz – acquired control of the Black Hawks. The new-look Hawks named Sid Abel, the Red Wings' former captain and the Hart Trophy winner in 1949, as the club's playing coach, ending his thirteen-year career in Motown. Abel would have his work cut out for him. The Hawks were the NHL's least-successful team, finishing last in five of the previous six years. To give Abel some needed support, the Hawks' brass played their only trump card before the season commenced, trading Harry Lumley to Toronto for Al Rollins, Ray Hannigan, Gus Mortson, and Cal Gardner. The moves paid instant dividends for the Hawks, who finally made it back to the playoffs under Abel's confident coaching.

The Montreal roster remained virtually unchanged for the 1952-53 season, although both Gamble and Geoffrion suffered the sophomore jinx. Gamble dropped to 11 goals, while Geoffrion slipped from 30 goals to 22. Jean Béliveau and Jacques Plante were called up for three-game trials during the campaign. Béliveau delivered five goals in his brief visit to the NHL, while Plante went undefeated in his trio of appearances, allowing only four goals-against.

Although Detroit lost Sid Abel to the Hawks, his place on the Production Line was ably filled by sophomore Alex Delvecchio. Each of Detroit's front-line wingers hit double figures in goals scored, providing the team with the league's most potent attack. Newcomers Reg Sinclair and goaltender Glenn Hall each made contributions to the Red Wings' first-place finish. The Boston Bruins concentrated on solidifying their defense, adding Warren Godfrey and Bob Armstrong to their blueline crew. Joe Klukay was acquired from the Leafs, and he pitched in with 13 goals and 16 assists in his first season in Boston.

No team made more personnel changes than the New York Rangers, who over the course of the season had fourteen new faces in the lineup. Edgar Laprade, who had retired following the 1951-52 season, was asked by coach Bill Cook to return to action after Don Raleigh broke his wrist. Laprade's return was delayed because he had been claimed on waivers

Traded to Chicago by Toronto in September of 1952, Al Rollins helped lead the Black Hawks into the playoffs for the first time since 1945-46. Rollins won 27 games, posted six shutouts, and compiled a goals-against average of 2.50 in 1952-53.

by both Toronto and Chicago, although both teams eventually withdrew their claims. Laprade would spend two more seasons with the Rangers, before retiring for a second and final time following the 1954-55 campaign. Although the New Yorkers fell into the NHL cellar, there was room for optimism on Broadway. Harry Howell, Dean Prentice, Lorne "Gump" Worsley, Andy Bathgate, and Ron Murphy all made appearances with the Rangers in 1952-53. This core of players would greatly enhance the team's fortunes later in the decade.

There was concern among Toronto Maple Leafs fans in 1952-53 that the team was growing old, with few top prospects being polished in the farm system. Ron Stewart, George Armstrong, Leo Boivin, and Tim Horton showed the most promise, but, once again, consistent offense

Montreal goaltender Gerry McNeil (left) and defenseman Butch Bouchard combine to thwart this scoring bid by Toronto's Sid Smith. Smith would record six consecutive 20-goal seasons with the Leafs.

was Toronto's major shortcoming. It was a season of turmoil for the Leafs, who had as many as six top-line players in sick bay. Although the Leafs remained competitive during the first half of 1952-53, they faltered late in the season, due in large part to injuries and player defections. In late February, a depressed Max Bentley suddenly quit the team and returned home to Delisle, Saskatchewan. Although he would later return to Toronto, his withdrawal from the team was another obstacle the Leafs couldn't overcome. For the first time since 1946, the Leafs missed the playoffs, despite going undefeated in their final five games. Sid Smith was the Leafs' leading scorer, but his 39 points was the lowest team-leading total since the 1935-36 season. There was a bright light amid the gloom, however. Harry Lumley was one of the NHL's top goaltenders, appearing in every game of the 70-game schedule. "Apple Cheeks" owned the league's third-best goals-against average (2.39) and tied for the league lead in shutouts with ten zeros.

Much of the attention during the 1952-53 season was focused on Detroit, where Gordie Howe was making a bid to join Maurice Richard as the NHL's only 50-goal scorer. Howe scored his 49th in a 6–1 victory over Boston on March 19, leaving him with two games to tie Richard's record. After being blanked in a 4–3 loss to Chicago, Howe went into the last game of the season against the Montreal Canadiens, who used a variety of checkers in an attempt to prevent him from matching the Rocket's mark. The ploy worked, as Howe was held off the scoresheet in a 2–1

Montreal victory. Still, Howe finished the season with an NHL record 95 points, earning him his third straight Art Ross Trophy. He was joined by teammates Ted Lindsay (71 points) and Alex Delvecchio (59 points) among the NHL's elite scorers.

Detroit finished first overall for the fifth consecutive season, leading the league in goals-for (222) and goals-against (133), numbers almost identical to their 1951-52 marks of excellence. Terry Sawchuk led the league in wins (32) for the third consecutive season, despite missing seven games due to a broken bone in his foot. In his place, the Wings recalled a young Glenn Hall, who won four times in his six-game stint with Detroit, including a 4–0 blanking of the Bruins on January 9. The season was not without adversity, however. The Wings had to overcome the death of team owner James Norris, Sr., who passed away on December 4 after suffering a heart attack. His daughter, Marguerite, replaced him as team president, becoming the first female executive in NHL history.

The most pleasant surprise of the season was the play of the Chicago Black Hawks, who earned their first post-season berth in seven seasons after posting a 27–28–15 record. In addition to Sid Abel contributing both behind the bench and on the ice, the Hawks received career-best efforts from Jim McFadden, Jim Peters, and Gerry "Doc" Couture. Bill Gadsby and Al Dewsbury excelled on the blueline and Al Rollins was solid in goal for the much-improved Hawks.

In Montreal, all eyes were on Maurice Richard as he approached Nels Stewart's NHL record of 324 goals scored. On November 8, in front of an overflow crowd at the Montreal Forum, Richard whipped a wrist shot past Chicago's Al Rollins for the 325th goal of his career. That goal made the intense right-winger the all-time leading marksman in the history of the NHL. Richard, who had missed 22 games in 1951-52 because of stress and exhaustion, joined defenseman Tom Johnson as the only Montreal players to appear in all 70 games during the 1952-53 schedule. The Canadiens finished second in the league with a 28–23–19 record.

Montreal defenseman Doug Harvey earned the second of what would prove to be seven consecutive selections to the NHL's First All-Star Team. Another feature of note during the 1952-53 campaign was the debut of hockey on national television in Canada. On October 11, the first French-language broadcast took place during a match between the Canadiens and the Red Wings. Three weeks later, on November 1, the Toronto Maple Leafs were featured coast to coast on CBC television, as the Leafs downed the Boston Bruins, 3–2.

The struggle for the final playoff berths behind Detroit was a year-long race, with only eight points separating second from fifth place. Montreal and Boston each compiled 28 victories, while Chicago and

Wally Hergesheimer, the AHL's rookie of the year in 1951, scored 30 goals in 1952-53, his sophomore season with the Rangers.

A Real Bruin

In February 1953, Maine Governor Burton M. Cross presented the Boston Bruins with a seven-foot stuffed black bear named "Buster," which would serve as the team's mascot. It was the Bruins' first mascot since a live cub on a leash wandered the Garden halls in 1928.

Toronto stood with 27 wins apiece when the final game of the schedule had been played. The Leafs lost two more games than the rebuilding Hawks and were eliminated from the post-season parade. Boston tied the Black Hawks with 69 points, but earned a third-place finish, because they had one more victory than Chicago. Some Boston supporters wondered if the Bruins might concede their third spot to the Hawks, because all it earned them was a semi-final date with the defending-champion Detroit Red Wings in the playoffs. The Bruins had lost 10 of the 14 games between the teams during the campaign, and most critics were predicting a four-game sweep for the Red Wings. Those feelings appeared validated after the first game of the semi-finals, in which the Bruins were buried 7–0 by Detroit. However, the Bruins bounced back to win the next three games, including a 2–1 victory in game three on Jack McIntyre's goal at 12:29 of the first overtime period. After Detroit staved off elimination with a 6–4 win on home ice, the Bruins pulled the upset of the decade by downing the Red Wings, 4–2, in game six. The victory propelled the Bruins into the finals for the first time since 1946.

In the other semi-final matchup, the Chicago Black Hawks surprised even their most ardent fans by rebounding from a two-game deficit to take a three-games-to-two lead in the best-of-seven set against the Montreal Canadiens. The turning point in the series came when Montreal coach Dick Irvin decided to recall rookie Jacques Plante to replace incumbent Gerry McNeil. In the first post-season appearance of his NHL career, Plante blanked the Hawks, 3–0, to tie the series before thwarting the Black Hawks, 4–1, in game seven.

Plante was in goal to start the Stanley Cup finals as well, and he was steady in the Habs' 4–2 win in the opening game. After the Canadiens dropped a 4–1 decision in the second game, Irvin went back to Gerry McNeil, who played strongly for the remainder of the series. The series was decided in game five, as the Canadiens eked out a 1–0 victory. The winning goal was scored by veteran Elmer Lach after only 1:22 of overtime. Lach took a pass from Rocket Richard behind the net, wheeled out in front of the Bruins' cage, and, using Richard as a decoy, flipped a waist-high backhander past a startled Sugar Jim Henry. After watching him fire the winning marker, Maurice Richard hugged Lach with such force that he broke his linemate's nose. The win capped a brilliant coaching effort by Irvin, who managed his lineup with precision. It was the first Stanley Cup title for the city of Montreal since 1946.

Prior to the start of the playoffs, it was announced that the Cleveland Barons of the AHL had issued a challenge for the Stanley Cup. Jim Hendy, who had attempted to secure an expansion franchise for the city of Cleveland the previous summer, presented the proposal to the NHL in March. League officials turned down the challenge on two fronts: first,

After a persistent Boston defense held Maurice Richard to a single goal through the first three games of the 1953 Stanley Cup finals, the Rocket exploded for three goals in the Canadiens' 7–3 victory over the Bruins in game four. It was the fifth post-season hat-trick of Richard's career.

BÉLIVEAU NETS HAT-TRICK TO BEGIN THREE-GAME NHL TRIAL

Jean Béliveau had five goals in his three-game trial with the Canadiens before returning to the Quebec Aces of the Quebec Senior Hockey League.

December 18, 1952
at Montreal Forum
Montreal 6, New York 2

FIRST PERIOD
1) MTL Béliveau 1 (Richard, Harvey) 10:05
2) MTL Geoffrion 11 (Meger, Reay) 15:37
PENALTIES – None

SECOND PERIOD
3) NY Mickoski 8 (Stoddard) 3:30
4) NY Ronty 9 (Strain, Hergesheimer) 9:35
5) MTL Béliveau 2 (Harvey, Richard) PPG 12:53
6) MTL Béliveau 3 (Richard) 14:43
PENALTIES – Strain NY (hooking) 6:32; MacIntosh NY (tripping), Stanley NY (fighting – major), MacPherson MTL (fighting – major) 12:36.

THIRD PERIOD
7) MTL Geoffrion 12 (Reay, Meger) 9:42
8) MTL Geoffrion 13 (Reay, Meger) 16:04
PENALTIES – Kullman NY (interference) 3:32; Buller NY (holding) 19:47.

SHOTS ON GOAL	1	2	3	T
NEW YORK	8	8	6	22
MONTREAL	11	13	8	32

GOALTENDERS	TIME	SA	GA	ENG	W/L
NY Rayner	60:00	26	6	0	L
MTL McNeil	60:00	20	2	0	W

PP CONVERSIONS NY 0/0 MTL 1/4

the challenge was premature, because the Barons had not yet won the AHL championship, and second, the Stanley Cup was for competition between teams of major-league caliber, and the Cleveland squad, as good as it might have been, was operating in a minor professional league.

Post-season awards went to New York Rangers' goaltender Gump Worsley, as rookie of the year, and Red Kelly, who earned the Lady Byng Trophy after spending only eight minutes in the penalty box.

(continued on p. 74)

Gordie Howe: The Power and the Glory

by Charles Wilkins

October 16, 1946
Detroit Olympia
Toronto 3, Detroit 3

STARTING LINEUP

#	TORONTO		#	DETROIT
1	Broda	G	1	Lumley
2	Goldham	D	3	Quackenbush
18	Boesch	D	21	Simon
10	Apps	C	12	Abel
12	Ezinicki	W	**17**	**Howe**
4	Watson	W	11	Brown

FIRST PERIOD

No scoring.
PENALTIES — Ezinicki TOR 1:44; Ezinicki TOR 9:59; Lundy DET 12:54; Jackson DET 18:29.

SECOND PERIOD

1) DET Brown 1 (Abel) PPG 7:02
2) TOR Goldham 1 (Ezinicki, Watson) 12:59
3) DET Howe 1 (Abel, Brown) 13:39
4) TOR Watson 1 (Apps) 19:01
PENALTIES — Meeker TOR 5:31; Ezinicki TOR, **Howe DET 8:53**; Meeker TOR 14:47.

THIRD PERIOD

5) TOR Boesch 1 (Kennedy) 16:17
6) DET Abel 1 (Simpson) 19:49
PENALTIES — Thomson TOR, Mortson TOR, Brown DET (major) 7:31; Lynn TOR 10:39.

GOALTENDERS		TIME	GA	ENG	DEC
TOR	Broda	60:00	3	0	T
DET	Lumley	59:30*	3	0	T

*unofficial, left net for extra skater late in third period.

PP CONVERSIONS   TOR 0/3   DET 1/6

In his first taste of NHL action on October 16, 1946, Gordie Howe started on right wing with Sid Abel and Adam Brown, beat Turk Broda for his first NHL goal, and tangled with Leaf tough-guy "Wild Bill" Ezinicki.

The war was over, and the city of Detroit was on the threshold of giddy prosperity. The first wave of baby-boomers had been born, and the local automakers were tooling up to produce the millions of vehicles that would carry the post-war generation from Michigan Avenue to the furthest reaches of the continent.

On the hockey front, there was reason to believe that the Red Wings were on the rise. The players who had served overseas – Sid Abel among them – had rekindled their careers, and a sophomore left-winger named Ted Lindsay had given notice that he might well have the stuff to propel the team to the top.

Understandably, the pre-game atmosphere at the Olympia on the evening of October 16, 1946, bristled with optimism for the new season. The air might have been doubly charged had the crowd realized that it was about to witness the beginning of the most extraordinary career in the history of big-league hockey – some would say of big-league sport.

In the hour before faceoff, eighteen-year-old Gordie Howe – a prairie boy with a demeanor that combined equal parts of Li'l Abner and Captain Hook – had taken his warm-ups under the relaxed assumption that he would be spending most or all of his first NHL game on the bench. But as the minutes ticked down, the muscular teenager was summoned by his coach Jack Adams and told that he would be starting the game at right wing.

"To keep from fainting from nervousness during the national anthem," recalls Howe, "I stood there thinking about various combinations of numbers in pinochle, a game the guys had been teaching me during training camp."

Within seconds of the opening faceoff, Howe was welcomed to the big time by a rattling high stick that knocked out four of his teeth.

During the second period he bulldozed in from the blueline – around, over, and through the Toronto Maple Leaf checkers – and smacked in the first of the 1,071 goals he would score in the NHL and the WHA (three nights later, he would log the first of 1,518 assists).

Fifteen hundred miles away, in Saskatoon, Saskatchewan, his parents sat listening to their son's exploits on a live radio broadcast. Decades later, his father, Ab, would remember that, on that first night, he and his wife, Kathleen, had been "terribly" worried that their son would get into a fight and put someone in the cemetery. "He's got a blow that can kill a man," said Ab, who had often seen Gordie lift two or more ninety-pound cement bags in each hand.

And, sure enough, during that first game, Gordie did fight, as he had fought time and again throughout the pre-season and during the previous year as a member of the Omaha Knights. "My rough play in Omaha had been so successful," says Howe, "that when I got to the Red Wings camp, I fought everybody in sight, even my own players. I could care less, I didn't know 'em anyway. If I had to take a beating to get the job, I'd take one."

Howe fought so prolifically during the early season that Jack Adams eventually took him aside and said, "We know you can fight, son, but can you play hockey?"

He could.

By the time he was twenty-two, he had shown that he could play as well as anyone.

By twenty-four, he could play better than anyone. He was strong; he was fast, both on his skates and with his hands and stick. He was endlessly inventive in his play-making, and from having spent his boyhood shooting a million pucks a year against the house in Saskatoon, he could fire bull's-eyes into any part of the net.

"And of course you have to remember that I was crazy," he said in 1989. "I was never afraid of getting hurt."

Howe exulted in the virulent mess of elbows and high sticks that all but defined play in the corners and crease; he willingly blocked shots from the likes of Bobby Hull. "One night I dropped in front of Bob, and his shot crushed my shin pad, split my shin to the bone. It took eight stitches to close the cut. I missed a couple of shifts and was back out there."

The curious thing about Howe was that, in spite of his vast talent, he didn't always appear to be doing that much on the ice. "My skating style was so smooth," he once said, "that a lot of people thought I was lazy." His subtlety was such that he could often accomplish in one motion what other players took two or three moves to

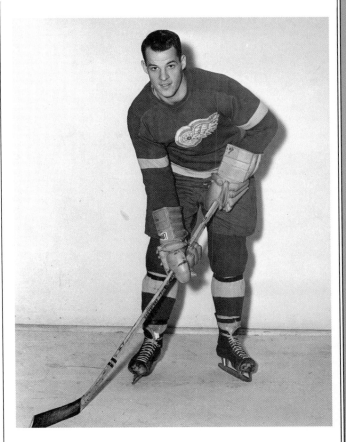

In addition to Howe's exceptional strength and speed, the "slope-shouldered giant" was able to fire the puck with astounding accuracy both right-handed and left-handed.

achieve. If, for instance, he was being checked from the right side (his shooting side), instead of shifting frantically, or whirling, or powering to a stop, he would often simply switch his stick to the other side of his body, change the position of his hands on it, and drill the puck ambidextrously from the left.

Not surprisingly, the 1950s and 1960s were a raving binge of success for Howe. For twenty straight seasons, beginning in 1949-50, he finished among the NHL's top six scorers. During the same period, he played in twenty-one NHL All-Star games and won the Hart Trophy as the league's most valuable player six times. He also won six scoring titles.

Through the late 1940s and early 1950s, he and his linemates, Sid Abel and Ted Lindsay, were considered the finest trio of forwards ever assembled. They were dubbed the Production Line during the 1949-50 season, when they claimed the top three rungs on the

Boston's Eddie Johnston sprawls to stop a patented Howe wrist shot as (left to right) Alex Delvecchio, Murray Oliver, Pat Stapleton, Parker MacDonald, and Ted Green fight for position near the Bruins' crease.

league scoring ladder, a feat that has not been accomplished since.

But during the first game of the playoffs that year, the reckless physicality of Gordie's play, and some disastrously bad luck, combined to mar his season, and nearly claimed his life. "We were playing the Maple Leafs in Detroit," he says of the events of March 28, 1950. "I was chasing Teeder Kennedy. He was coming down the left side of the rink, to my right, and I was going to run him into the boards. But my first thought was to intercept the pass I figured he'd make to Sid Smith, who was coming down the center of the ice. I glanced back at Smith and put my stick down where I thought the pass might be going. What I didn't know as I turned back toward Kennedy was that, in the instant I'd turned away, he'd let the pass go, and now he was bringing up his stick to protect himself from my hitting him. I was still low, and the blade of the stick caught me in the face — tore my right eyeball, broke my nose and cheekbone. As if this wasn't bad enough, I then smashed into the boards head first, giving myself a whale of a concussion.

"They took me to the hospital in an ambulance, and within minutes I was on the operating table and

they were drilling a hole in the side of my skull to relieve the pressure. I was awake through all this; I could hear the drill against the bone. But what was really on my mind was that they'd shaved part of my head. I was at an age when I needed my hair, and I was thinking, 'Oh, gosh, no, what am I going to look like?'"

Worried that he wouldn't live, Red Wing officials sent for Howe's mother and sister, who flew to his bedside from Saskatoon. "For a couple of days, nobody let me sleep," he recalls. "They were afraid I'd go into a coma and never come out. They'd come along and scrape the bottoms of my feet every few minutes and say, 'Don't go to sleep on us.'"

After several weeks in the hospital, Howe was well enough to visit the Olympia to watch the Red Wings win the Stanley Cup with a 4–3 victory over the New

Less than a month after suffering a nearly fatal head injury in game one of the 1950 semi-finals, Gordie Howe was back on the ice celebrating the Red Wings' Stanley Cup victory with linemate Sid Abel, coach Tommy Ivan, and NHL president Clarence Campbell.

York Rangers. "My injury had been a big story in the papers," he says, "and, as the Cup was being presented, the crowd started calling for me; I'd been watching from a seat near the bench. But as I went out on the ice, my worst fear came to pass. Someone grabbed my hat, and there I was in front of 16,000 fans with a big bald patch on my head. Oh, it was awful!"

Howe's assessment of the Production Line's brilliance is as level as the prairie horizon: "We could all carry the puck, we could all skate and check, and we could all make plays. Abel and Lindsay knew how to get into position for a pass."

Unlike some forwards, Lindsay and Howe also made a science of using the end and corner boards, firing the puck in at just the right angle to send it caroming out to the opposite wing.

According to Abel, Gordie's best year came in 1952-53, when he scored 49 goals. "He did score his 50th," says Abel, "but he didn't get credit for it. He tipped in a goal in Boston on a shot Red Kelly took from the blue-line, and they gave it to Kelly. Gordie didn't argue. He had a couple of games left to get his 50th. He could be very patient."

And at times very impatient. "One night in Montreal," Gordie laughs, "the Rocket had a breakaway against us. At the time, I was closing in on his goal-scoring record, and there was no way I wanted him to score. So I jumped off the bench and checked him. The fans went nuts. All we got was a two-minute penalty for having too many men on the ice."

Howe and Richard. Richard and Howe. Throughout the 1950s, newsmen and fans fueled an ongoing debate over which of these mid-century titans was the greater player. And ultimately there is no conclusive answer. Although the competition between them was fierce during their prime, each has now mellowed in his view of the other. "I was never a natural like Gordie," explained the Rocket in 1990. "He was stronger, more fluid, better with the puck. I used to say to him, 'Gordie, you're much better than I am, but you don't have the drive to score the big goals, win the big games, like I do.'"

Gordie willingly acknowledges the Rocket's superiority around the net. "There was nobody like him for putting the puck in; he was so accurate with his shot – and determined! You could see it in those crazy eyes. They'd open right up like sockets or camera lenses as he was going in on goal. . . . One big difference between us was that Rocket kept getting heavier as he got older. I weighed 204 when I came in; he was 165 or so. When he retired he was 220 or 230; I was 206. As he got bigger, of course, he slowed down, and, oh, I loved nailing him. He'd come across the ice at the blueline, and I'd leave my wing and just paste him. When we fought, it was pretty even, although one night I got the better of him. We were all tangled up, and his head suddenly came up between my knees like an unprotected duck on a pond, and I gave him a good shot. The funny thing was that when we were back on our feet, Abel came over and said, 'You dirty so-and-so; you finally got what you deserve.' And before Abel knew it, Rocket had flattened him, hit him right on the nose."

From day one of his career, Gordie played by a credo that he has often described as "religious hockey" – it is better to give than to receive. And give he did – with the rudest of generosity. Hockey lore shivers with stories of the gruesome punishments he inflicted on opponents who ran afoul of him. "If somebody hit me in the back with a cross-check," he admitted recently, "I'd immediately bring my stick back over my right or left shoulder, wherever I thought he was. And after a few stitches on the top of the head, they'd lay off my back . . . . When anybody hooked me, I'd grab his stick, pull it until he was alongside me, and give him an elbow in the head."

Gordie's vengeance could also be less immediate in its deployment. "In the old six-team league, we'd play a team fourteen times a year, so if somebody did something dirty to me, I could afford to wait five, six, seven games to get even. I'd play with the guy, tease him about what I was going to do to him, but he always knew that sooner or later he'd pay."

Black Hawk Hall-of-Famer Stan Mikita recalls that in the early days of his career, a period of particular insolence for the young centerman, he decided to take a run at the legendary number nine. "Unfortunately, my stick came up a little higher than it should have, and I cut him under the eye for a few stitches. He went into the dressing room to get fixed up, and the next time he skated by me, he said, 'It's a long season, kid.' I didn't think much about it; I probably laughed at him and went about my business.

"Nothing happened for the longest time; then one night a couple of months later, we were playing in Detroit, and Gordie and I were both turning in the Red Wings' end of the rink. The last thing I remember was him going by me. I woke up a few minutes later, flat on

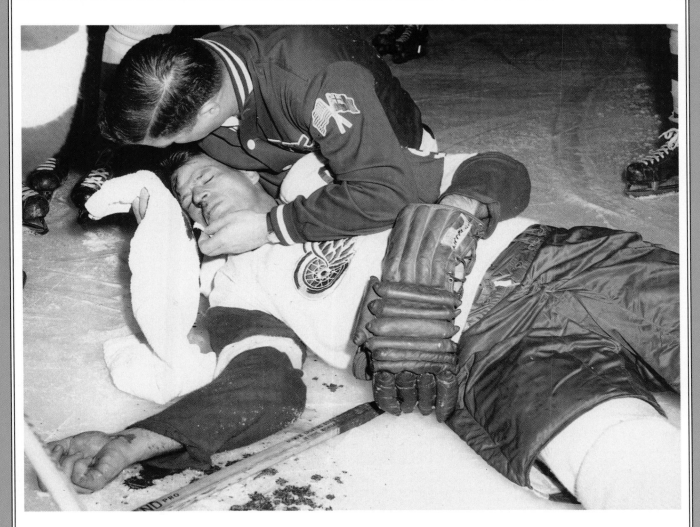

my back. They carried me to the bench, and Denis DeJordy, our backup goalie, told me that, as Gordie had skated past me, he'd slipped his right hand up under his armpit, pulled his fist out of his glove and given me a quick pop flush on the chin. A minute later Gordie himself skated by the bench and said, "Did you get the number of that truck, Stan?" And from that point on we left one another alone."

Lest anyone get the wrong impression, Gordie makes it clear that under normal circumstances – that is, circumstances in which he was not in the process of a retributive strike – he played, in his words, "like an angel." Live and let live. On at least two occasions he actually codified this attitude by making private agreements of mutual non-hostility with opposition players. "In one of my early Detroit training camps, before I turned pro," he says, "we had an exhibition game with

In a moment eerily similar to one that occurred during the 1950 playoffs, Gordie Howe was decked by Toronto's Eddie Shack in this Detroit–Toronto match-up on January 4, 1961. Although Howe suffered a severe cut and a concussion, he missed only four games.

Toronto. As I skated into the corner early in the game, Harry Watson skated in beside me, ready to cream me. But just before he lowered his shoulder, he yelled, 'Look out, kid!', and I just had time to relax and take the hit without getting hurt. Later in the game, when I was about to hit him, I returned the favor by calling, 'Look out, Mr. Watson!' He took the hit in stride, and, as he skated away, he said to me, 'I can see we're gonna get along fine, young fella.' He was a big, strong man, and for fifteen years after that he always covered me when we played the Leafs. And he never once took advantage, and neither did I."

After Toronto defeated the Red Wings 3–1 in game five of the 1963 finals, Howe went to the Leafs' dressing room and raised a celebratory toast to Punch Imlach, coach of the Stanley Cup-champion Maple Leafs.

Howe's arrangement with Eddie Shack, while less reverential, was equally binding: "Eddie often used to go at me verbally," says Howe. "Then one summer we played golf together, and as we had a drink afterwards, he said, 'You're not as bad a guy as I thought you were.' And I said, 'And you're not as dumb as I thought you were.' We clicked glasses, and I said, 'Let's have a little agreement here. We won't hit one another.' And from then on we never did. Funny thing is, Eddie'd come up to me in the heat of a game, when other guys were fighting or some-

thing, and he'd grab me by the sweater and he'd be jawing away as if he were gonna tear me apart, but what he'd be saying was, 'Listen to the crowd, Gordie, they think I'm givin' it to ya. Listen to 'em. They love it. Ya getting any golf in?' And I'd have to tell him, 'Get outa here, Eddie. If I start laughing, Adams'll send me so far away you won't be able to reach me with a postcard.' I mean, we'd run into one another if it was in the course of play. We had to. But there were never any elbows or sticks or crawling over top of one another, that sort of thing."

It is curious that, in the endless myth-making that appends Gordie's career – and to which almost everyone who writes about him seems compelled to contribute – there is generally less attention paid to his trophies and scoring and Stanley Cups than to the more primitive aspects of his game, the fists and elbows and retribution. Gordie himself admits to having less memory of the goals and glories than for the more combative episodes of his life in hockey.

"What's most important to remember," says Jean Béliveau, "is that Gordie was first and foremost a brilliant hockey player, a play-maker, a goal scorer." Indeed, given the tough defensive standards under which he played in his prime, his 801 regular-season goals are an all-but-unaccountable achievement – the equivalent of twenty 40-goal seasons at a time when a 20-goal season was the benchmark of offensive excellence. His thirty-two-year pro career – a career nearly twice as long as the Rocket's and nearly three times as long as Bobby Orr's – is an unprecedented accomplishment in any major-league sport. It is an oft-repeated truth that, by the time Howe retired at the age of fifty-two, he had played NHL hockey in five decades.

Off ice, his unassuming grace has elevated him above the precincts of mere sports idolatry and earned him an enduring portion of public appreciation and respect. He is a man of the profoundly common touch and is seldom happier, for instance, than when he is signing an autograph for a child. Or teenager. Or adult. No matter how long the line of autograph-seekers, he has a kind word, a joke, a reassuring smile for everyone.

As if by uncanny prescience, Howe realized at the age of eight that he would one day be dispensing his signature in volume. He says, "My older brother Vern's wife says she can remember me writing my name several different ways, then tugging at my mother's skirt, asking which one she liked best. The one she chose, the one I still use, I practiced like anything. When Mom said, 'What are you doing?' I said, 'That's for when I become famous.'"

The renowned signature, like any person's signature, has become a symbol of the man who dispenses it. But in the case of Gordie's signature, there's a difference, in that he has written and given away millions of

Howe practiced for hours as a youngster perfecting one of the most famous signatures in hockey history. From his first stardom in the NHL in the 1940s to his appearances as a popular guest at sports-trading-card shows in the 1990s, Howe continues to be one of the game's most popular heroes.

them – more perhaps than anyone in history. By his own estimation, he can sign a thousand times in an hour.

By a curious distortion of values, however, Gordie's signature is deemed to be of little worth in the mercenary world of sports memorabilia . . . though for the most honorable of reasons: there is too great a supply of them out there. "People who are selling them told me recently that mine is worth about a tenth of what a particular young football player's is worth," says Howe without rancor. "Yet if I had it to do over, I'd sign every one of them again. I worked hard for the privilege. In fact, there isn't a thing about my hockey career that I wouldn't do over again."

Gordie once attended a gathering of sportsmen with American track legend Jesse Owens. "Afterwards," says Howe, "I was standing beside Owens, and someone came up and asked me how I explained my success. Jesse piped up, 'I'll answer that. If you listen to the man, it's obvious that he's totally in love with what he does.'"

And millions of hockey fans – five decades worth of them – have been the beneficiaries.

88 PTS. 81 PTS. 78 PTS. 74 PTS. 68 PTS. 31 PTS.

1953-54
Wings Clinch Cup on
Leswick's Fluke Goal in Overtime

A NEW PIECE OF SILVERWARE WAS ADDED TO THE POST-SEASON PRIZE TABLE FOR the 1953-54 season. For years, NHL blueliners had been lobbying for a trophy to recognize the league's best defenseman. In August 1953, the Norris family, owners of the Detroit Red Wings, presented the NHL with the James Norris Memorial Trophy, to be awarded to the "defense player who demonstrates throughout the season the greatest all-round ability at that position."

Following three years of negotiations and almost a decade of publicity, the Montreal Canadiens finally signed Jean Béliveau to an NHL contract on October 4, 1953. Béliveau, the star of the Quebec Senior Hockey League's Quebec Aces, stated that he had delayed moving up to the NHL because he wanted to thank the Quebec fans, who had treated him so well, by playing another season with the Aces. Of course, he also admitted that he was making the equivalent of a major-league salary with the team, an income that some estimated as being similar to Maurice Richard's contract with the Habs. The defending Cup champions made no other major revisions to their lineup, feeling that Eddie Mazur, who had two goals and two assists in seven playoff games in 1953, could fill the skates of Billy Reay, who retired after the Cup victory.

More changes were being made in New York, where Calder Trophy-winner Gump Worsley lost his job to another rookie, Johnny Bower. Bill Cook, who was dismissed as coach following the Rangers' last-place finish, was replaced by general manager Frank Boucher, who had guided the team to its last Stanley Cup in 1940. Eight players were released or elected to retire, leaving the Rangers with a lineup of unproven youngsters. One of the most exciting new prospects was Camille "The Eel" Henry, a speedster with good hands and a canny hockey sense. The Rangers also signed former Toronto and Chicago star, Max Bentley, who had decided to play one last NHL season.

After the Maple Leafs missed the playoffs, coach Joe Primeau retired, handing the reins of the young team to King Clancy, who had directed the Leafs' farm club in Pittsburgh to the AHL title in 1952. The power on the

Toronto club was stationed on the blueline, where Jim Morrison, Tim Horton, Fernie Flaman, and Leo Boivin blended size and skill to form one of the league's best defensive units. Eric Nesterenko and George Armstrong appeared ready to take some of the offensive load off the shoulders of Tod Sloan and Sid Smith.

Optimism was the key word in the Black Hawks' camp as they attempted to build on the previous season's success. Still, there was a large turnover in the roster, with five players being released to make room for Larry Zeidel and Larry Wilson, who were purchased from the Red Wings. One newcomer who would play a major role in the rebirth of the Hawks franchise, Ken Wharram, appeared in 29 games for the Hawks.

Despite Detroit's early exit from the 1953 playoffs, general manager Jack Adams was content with his lineup, adding only Bill Dineen and Earl "Dutch" Reibel to his everyday core of stars. Terry Sawchuk, shaky at best during the previous post-season, looked strong in camp and was assured of starting the campaign as the team's number-one goaltender, although a reliable Glenn Hall was waiting in the wings should his services be required. The surprising play of Reibel earned him a spot centering the club's big line between Howe and Lindsay, and the rookie responded with 48 points.

Once again, the 1953-54 season featured a tight playoff race. The Detroit Red Wings were still the NHL's best club, winning their sixth consecutive regular-season crown with 37 wins and 88 points. Gordie Howe,

The Toronto Maple Leafs traded four players to Chicago to acquire Harry Lumley in 1952. Lumley rewarded his new employers with 32 victories, a league-leading 1.86 goals-against average, and a team-record 13 shutouts during the 1953-54 campaign.

Left to right: Johnny Peirson (21 goals), Fleming Mackell (47 points), "Sugar Jim" Henry (2.59 GAA), and Leo Labine (16 goals) were four ingredients in the recipe that allowed the Boston Bruins to win 32 games during the 1953-54 season. It marked the most victories by the Bruins since the club's Stanley Cup-winning squad of 1939.

who once again led all skaters with 81 points, also led the league in assists, setting up 48 goals over the course of the campaign. Terry Sawchuk, who led the league with 35 victories, registered 12 shutouts and a superb 1.92 goals-against average. Another key contributor to Detroit's championship club was rearguard Red Kelly, who amassed 16 goals and 49 points from his station on the blueline. Another "rookie" who made his NHL debut during the season was Ross "Lefty" Wilson, Detroit's legendary trainer and practice goaltender. Wilson was forced to don the pads and replace Terry Sawchuk on October 20, holding the Habs off the scoresheet in his twenty minutes of play, although the Wings ended up on the short end of a 4–1 score. Rookie Dutch Reibel took advantage of his assignment between Howe and Lindsay, setting an NHL record for assists by a rookie when he set up four goals in his first NHL game.

The Canadiens earned a second-place finish, even though they were burdened by injuries, suspensions, and controversy. Jean Béliveau broke his ankle early in the season and was limited to only 44 games, while Dickie Moore broke his jaw and missed all but 13 contests. Another budding superstar, Bernie Geoffrion, earned a pair of suspensions for shoving referee Frank Udvari and for a vicious stick-swinging duel with Ron Murphy of the Rangers. Geoffrion was suspended from playing against

New York for the rest of the season, which was equivalent to a seven-game hiatus. This created another cloud of controversy, much of it centered over the head of Maurice Richard. Richard, writing in a weekly Montreal newspaper, *Samedi Dimanche*, called NHL president Clarence Campbell a dictator for his handling of the Geoffrion suspension. Further trouble was avoided when Richard retracted his statement and offered an apology to Mr. Campbell.

Richard seemed bolstered by the altercation, and, as a result, he returned to his old form. The Rocket led the league with 37 goals, his highest total in three seasons, and added 30 assists to finish second to Howe in the scoring parade. Geoffrion chipped in with 29 goals in only 54 games, and Kenny Mosdell surpassed the 20-goal mark for the first time in his career, slipping 22 pucks behind enemy goalies in 67 games. Bert Olmstead had an evening to remember on January 9 in a 12–1 win over Chicago. The flashy Montreal left-winger collected four goals and four assists to tie Maurice Richard's mark, established in 1944.

King Clancy's first season behind the Leafs' bench was a success, as Toronto rose from fifth to third, only three points behind the Canadiens. Clancy realized the Leafs were weak offensively, so he stressed team defense. His charges took the message to heart, allowing a league-low 131 goals-against. Harry Lumley led the NHL, with a miserly goals-against average of 1.86, and he also established a modern-day mark for shutouts, blanking the opposition 13 times in 69 games. Lumley's shutout total was the NHL's highest since the 1928-29 season. Much of the inspiration for the Leafs' improvement came from captain Teeder Kennedy, who was expected to retire at the end of the season. Kennedy collected 38 points for the defensively motivated Leaf team, while Sid Smith and Harry Watson each contributed 20-goal campaigns.

In Boston, the Bruins were most impressed with the play of rookie rearguard Doug Mohns. The Capreol, Ontario, native collected 13 goals and 14 assists to lead all Boston blueliners in scoring. Joe Klukay, a cast-off from the Maple Leafs who was sold to Boston in 1952, registered his first 20-goal campaign and was joined by Dave Creighton and Johnny Peirson as Bruins who scored 20 or more goals. Once again, Sugar Jim Henry was solid in goal, appearing in all 70 games for the third consecutive year. A nine-game unbeaten streak strung together in March put the Bruins into the post-season.

The results were not quite so favorable in New York, where the Rangers compiled a 29–31–10 mark to miss the post-season by six points. In every other way, however, it was a positive season for the Broadway Blues, who rebounded nicely from a poor start to barely miss the fourth playoff spot. Ironically, the 68 points the Rangers collected was the highest point total in the history of the franchise. Frank Boucher, who added

"Iron Man" Johnny Wilson, who went eight straight seasons without missing a game from 1952-53 to 1959-60, was one of many contributors to the Red Wings' sixth straight first-place finish in 1953-54. Wilson collected 34 points for Detroit, the fourth-highest total on the team.

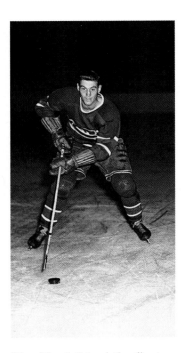

Ken Mosdell had the first 20-goal season of his career with the Canadiens during the 1953-54 season. The Montreal native scored 22 goals and added 24 assists for the Habs and was named to the league's Second All-Star Team. Mosdell, who made his NHL debut with the Brooklyn Americans in 1941-42, became the last player who had worn the star-spangled jersey of the Amerks to retire from the NHL when he ended his playing career after the 1957-58 season.

the coaching title to his managerial duties prior to the season, lasted only 38 games behind the bench. On January 13, 1954, he relinquished the coaching portfolio to Muzz Patrick, who brought the team home with an encouraging 17–11–4 record.

One of the highlights of the 1953-54 season occurred on January 20, when Doug Bentley came out of retirement to join his brother Max on the Rangers' roster. Placed on a line with Max and Edgar Laprade, Doug scored one goal and added three assists as the New Yorkers downed Boston, 8–3. It was a family reunion for another set of brothers as well. The Bruins were coached by Lynn Patrick, brother of newly hired Rangers pilot, Muzz Patrick. It marked only the second time in NHL history that two brothers had faced each other as coaches.

In Chicago, the Black Hawks fell back into the basement with a resounding thud, winning only 12 games. The Hawks opened the season by going winless in their first eight games, and the team was unable to overcome this early-season deficit. In November, Al Rollins was ill, and the Hawks signed former Calder Trophy-winner Jack Gelineau as a replacement. Gelineau's career with Chicago lasted only two games, as he was bombed for 18 goals in 9–0 and 9–4 back-to-back losses to Detroit. Bill Mosienko, Gus Bodnar, Doc Couture, and Jim McFadden also missed time due to injuries, as the Hawks allowed a league-high 242 goals while scoring only 133 times. Halfway through the dismal campaign, there were rumors that the team was about to fold, but owner Arthur Wirtz denied that the team was in jeopardy, despite the fact that attendance averaged only 6,574 fans a game.

In the playoffs, both the Montreal Canadiens and the Detroit Red Wings had little trouble moving into the finals. The Red Wings motored past the Maple Leafs in five games, although it took a goal in the final three minutes to clinch game four by a 2–1 score, as well as an overtime goal by Ted Lindsay in game five to sew up the series. Montreal had an easier time with the Bruins, outscoring Boston, 16–4, in a four-game series.

In the finals, the Canadiens and the Red Wings played one of the most exciting Stanley Cup series in league history. Detroit used a two-goal third period to take the series lead with a 3–1 decision in game one, but the Habs bounced back with a three-goal first period in game two, then hung on for the series-tying 3–1 victory. Detroit rolled into the Montreal Forum and put the Canadiens one loss away from elimination with back-to-back road victories. Back at the Olympia for game five, the teams battled through sixty minutes of regulation time without a goal being scored. Almost six minutes into the first overtime session, Kenny Mosdell snared a loose puck at the Wings' blueline and ripped a shot past Terry Sawchuk to give the Habs a 1–0 victory and keep them alive in the series. The revitalized Habs scored three unanswered goals in less than three minutes during the second period of game six on their way to a 4–1 victory, setting up a classic seventh-game struggle.

In the deciding game, the Canadiens brought a 1–0 lead into the second period, but Detroit's Red Kelly sparked the Wings with a power-play goal at 1:17 of the middle frame. The score remained deadlocked through sixty minutes of play, setting up the second seventh-game overtime of the decade and the second in Stanley Cup final-series history. Early in the overtime session, Montreal's steadiest defenseman, Doug Harvey, corralled the puck behind the net and fired it around the boards. The clearing attempt deflected off Glen Skov directly to Tony Leswick, a defensive specialist that the Red Wings used to shadow the opposition's top scorers. Leswick lifted a shot towards the Canadiens' net, but, as Harvey reached up to glove the puck, it glanced off his glove and over the shoulder of a stunned Gerry McNeil. With that fortuitous bounce, the Red Wings were crowned Stanley Cup champions for 1954.

The Habs, visibly upset, left the ice without bothering to shake hands with the victorious Red Wings, ignoring the token gesture of good will that was a Stanley Cup tradition. Only Gaye Stewart, himself a former Red Wing, stayed behind to offer his hand to the new champions. Montreal's action was met with outrage by reporters and broadcasters. Coach Dick Irvin shrugged off the critical reaction, explaining that he would have been a hypocrite to stay on the ice and congratulate the team that had just defeated him. At an NHL Board of Governors meeting on April 20, Montreal managing director Frank Selke offered his "sincere congratulations" to the Detroit team on their Stanley Cup victory, dispelling rumors that the Canadiens had left the ice on instructions from the Montreal front office.

At the annual NHL meetings in March, Conn Smythe introduced his idea for a "waiver-draft" system, whereby excess talent would be made available to other teams for a set price. It was suggested that each NHL team protect eighteen skaters and two goaltenders, and that restrictions, or "options," be placed on the number of times a player could be called up from, and returned to, the minors. When a player's options had been exhausted, he must either be placed on his club's twenty-man protected list or made available to any other team willing to pay the $15,000 waiver price.

Post-season awards went to Red Kelly, who in addition to winning his third Lady Byng Trophy was also named as the first winner of the Norris Trophy. Gordie Howe repeated as the Art Ross Trophy winner, while Chicago's Al Rollins, who lost an NHL-record 47 games but still compiled a decent 3.23 goals-against average, was named the Hart Trophy winner. Harry Lumley won the Vezina Trophy, while the Rangers' exciting speedster, Camille Henry, was judged to be the best rookie.

Black Hawk blueliner Bill Gadsby finished second in team scoring in 1953-54, collecting 12 goals and 29 assists. A consistent contributor on both offense and defense, Gadsby and Detroit's Red Kelly were the only defensemen to finish among the NHL's top ten scorers during the 1950s.

STRANGE GOAL BY LESWICK WINS CUP FOR WINGS

"Tough Tony" Leswick's shot from the point deflected off Doug Harvey's glove past Montreal goalie Gerry McNeil to give the Red Wings the Stanley Cup victory.

**April 16, 1954
at Detroit Olympia
Detroit 2, Montreal 1**

FIRST PERIOD
1) MTL Curry 4 (Masnick) 9:17
PENALTIES — Harvey MTL (holding) 14:20; Skov DET (hooking) 17:11.

SECOND PERIOD
2) DET Kelly 5 (Lindsay, Delvecchio) PPG 1:17
PENALTIES — Masnick MTL (hooking) :20.

THIRD PERIOD
No Scoring
PENALTIES — None

FIRST OVERTIME PERIOD
3) DET Leswick 3 (Skov) 4:29
PENALTIES — None

SHOTS ON GOAL	1	2	3	1OT	T
MONTREAL	5	5	12	1	23
DETROIT	12	13	6	2	33

GOALTENDERS	TIME	SA	GA	ENG	W/L
MTL McNeil	64:29	31	2	0	L
DET Sawchuk	64:29	22	1	0	W

PP CONVERSIONS MTL 0/1 DET 1/2

95 PTS.   93 PTS.   70 PTS.   67 PTS.   52 PTS.   43 PTS.

1954-55
Rocket Suspended: Richard Riot Rocks Montreal

THERE WERE A NUMBER OF SURPRISING DEVELOPMENTS DURING THE OFF-SEA-SON, most notably the decision of Red Wings' head coach Tommy Ivan to leave Detroit to tackle the general manager's duties of the Chicago Black Hawks. Ivan, who had guided the Red Wings to six straight first-place finishes and three Stanley Cup titles, was entrusted with the task of rebuilding a franchise that had finished out of the playoffs in eight of the previous ten seasons.

Another blockbuster move came in Boston, where an era ended when Art Ross announced his resignation on September 15. Ross, a star defenseman from the first days of organized hockey, had helped both the Kenora Thistles and the Montreal Wanderers win the Stanley Cup. He joined the Boston organization as general manager when the team was formed in 1924, and guided the team for thirty years. Now, after winning three Stanley Cup titles with the Bruins, Ross handed over the manager's job to his successor, Lynn Patrick, who had been promised the position when he took over the coaching job in 1950.

Two other long-time Bruins also retired. Woody Dumart, a valued member of the Kraut Line since 1936, decided to retire after collecting only seven points in 69 games in 1953-54. Johnny Peirson, who scored 21 goals for Boston the previous year, also decided to leave after eight seasons with the club. Other changes in the Bruins' lineup included the acquisition of Fernie Flaman, plus the addition of Lorne Ferguson and Don McKenney, both of whom would make worthy contributions. However, it was another roster maneuver that caught many Bruins fans by surprise. Boston decided that "Long John" Henderson, a twenty-one-year-old rookie, would share netminding duties with Sugar Jim Henry.

In Montreal, Elmer Lach decided to retire after 14 seasons, 215 goals, and 623 points. He was joined by goaltender Gerry McNeil, who suc-cumbed to the pressures of playing the most difficult position in the game. Jacques Plante was awarded the number-one goaltending job after two seasons of NHL tutorials. Two new recruits who were expected to fill the gap left behind by Lach were Don Marshall and Jack Leclair.

Getting the Point

In October 1954, former Black Hawk star Johnny Gottselig proposed a solution to the contentious issue of how assists were awarded. Gottselig, then the club's public-relations direc-tor, suggested that, when a goal was scored, the scorer should be awarded two points and all of his team-mates on the ice should be awarded one point. Though Gottselig's suggestion was never adopted, in 1956, NHL official scorers began keeping track of defending players on the ice when a goal was scored. The next season, they began charting members of the scoring team. These changes antici-pated the development of the plus/minus system, developed by Rangers general manager Emile Francis in the early 1960s. Plus/minus became a pub-lished NHL statistic in 1982.

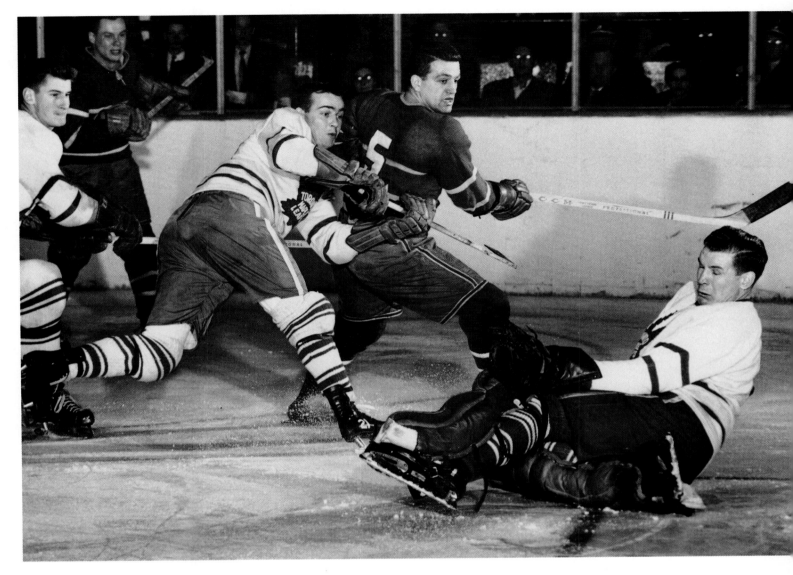

Toronto was also the scene of a surprising front-office shuffle. Conn Smythe retired as general manager of the Maple Leafs and was replaced by former coach Clarence "Hap" Day. Smythe would still hold a controlling interest in the fortunes of the club, but the everyday maintenance of the roster was in the hands of Day. After their third-place finish in 1954, the Leafs were cautiously optimistic as the 1954-55 season began, though the team was reluctant to make any major moves, especially after Ted Kennedy agreed to return for at least one more season. Howie Meeker had retired due to political commitments (he had been elected Member of Parliament for Kitchener–Waterloo), and his roster space was filled by rookies Parker MacDonald and Brian Cullen.

The greatest roster-shuffling took place in Chicago, where the Hawks were attempting to regain some measure of respectability. Sid

Bernie "Boom-Boom" Geoffrion, shown here eluding the grasp of Toronto's Jim Thomson for a scoring chance against Harry Lumley, became the first player in eight years to score five goals in an NHL game when he slipped a handful of pucks past Gump Worsley in Montreal's 10–2 win over the New York Rangers on February 19, 1955.

Boston freshman Don McKenney blasts a shot past Harry Lumley during his rookie campaign of 1954-55. McKenney, who had managed only 13 goals with the AHL's Hershey Bears the previous season, collected 22 goals for the Bruins, the second-highest total on the club.

Abel resigned after the club's disastrous 1953-54 season and was replaced by Frank Eddolls, who had never coached in the NHL before and, after one long year with the Black Hawks, would never coach in the league again. There was concern among NHL executives that, unless the Chicago situation improved, the team would have to fold. The NHL's waiver-draft program, whereby the "have" teams with excess talent on the roster would help the "have-nots," gave the Chicago squad a number of prospects, including Dave Creighton, Bob Hassard, and Harry Watson from Toronto; Metro Prystai from Detroit; and Ed Litzenberger, Dick Gamble, and Paul Masnick from Montreal. Despite the incoming relief from other organizations, the Hawks were expected to have a very rough year.

The New York Rangers, who set a franchise record for points, despite missing the playoffs in 1954, made only minor adjustments to their roster. The revolving door in goal continued to spin, with Gump Worsley, back in nets after a year in the minors, replacing Johnny Bower, who returned to the Western Hockey League's Vancouver Canucks. Other newcomers included a rambunctious defenseman known as "Leapin' Lou" Fontinato and former Leafs Bill Ezinicki and Danny Lewicki.

Terry Sawchuk won 40 games for the third time in his career during 1954-55 to lead all big-league netminders. He also topped the NHL with 12 shutouts and compiled a goals-against average of 1.96, the fifth consecutive season he allowed fewer than two goals a game.

The defending Stanley Cup-champion Red Wings were content to enter the 1954-55 season with the same basic on-ice cast, although Larry Hillman was added to the defense corps. The greatest change came in the coaching ranks, where Jack Adams surprised the hockey world by selecting Jimmy Skinner as bench boss of the Wings over Bud Poile, who had coached Detroit's top farm club, the Edmonton Flyers. Skinner, who served as captain of the USHL's Omaha Knights and coach of the Hamilton Cubs junior team, had spent his entire career in the Detroit system. Adams's move was to pay instant dividends, as Skinner quickly proved he could gain and maintain the confidence of his players.

The eighth NHL All-Star Game, held on October 2, 1954, at the Detroit Olympia, was also subject to controversy. The game's format had reverted to the All-Stars playing the defending Cup champions the previous year, and, since Tommy Ivan had resigned as coach of the Red Wings, his place behind the bench of the defending champs was taken by his successor Jimmy Skinner. The coach of the All-Stars was supposed to be

Heed the Heels

Beginning in the fall of 1954, the NHL decreed that players' uniform numbers be painted on the heels of their skates. This was done so that the players could be more easily identified on television and in photographs.

Montreal's Dick Irvin, but Irvin stated he couldn't afford the time to coach the squad, so Toronto's King Clancy was given the opportunity. Irvin's refusal only added more fuel to the feud between the Canadiens and the Red Wings. The Stars and the defending Cup champions battled to a 2–2 draw.

In the first half of the season, Montreal and Detroit battled neck-and-neck for first place, despite injuries to key personnel. Gordie Howe suffered a shoulder injury and was forced out of the lineup for six games. Although the loss of Howe reduced the Wings' offensive output, Detroit rode into first place on the coattails of Terry Sawchuk, who recorded three consecutive shutouts in late November. By the mid-point of the campaign, the Wings were atop the standings by a slim four-point margin over the Canadiens.

Montreal also suffered through early-season adversity, yet continued to stick close to the surging Wings. Jacques Plante suffered a fractured cheekbone on November 11 and was replaced by a trio of goaltenders: Charlie Hodge, André Binette, and Claude Evans. The threesome combined for a 10–5 record over the course of the season to keep the Habs in the race. The depth of the Montreal roster was proven on December 10, when they sent promising rookie Ed Litzenberger to the Black Hawks as part of the "haves and have-nots" campaign to help the suffering franchise. One week later, on December 18, Rocket Richard became the first NHL player to score 400 goals when his shot trickled through Al Rollins's pads in a 4–2 victory over Chicago.

The Toronto Maple Leafs continued to emphasize team defense. As a result, the Leafs scored 147 goals, fewer than any other team in the league, but allowed only 135 goals-against. Detroit manager Jack Adams was outspoken in his criticism of the Leafs' defensive style, calling it "meaningless and boring." Sid Smith was the only Leaf to rise above the 20-goal plateau, scoring 33 goals over the course of the campaign. In early November, the Leafs dealt from their strength, sending defenseman Leo Boivin to Boston for Joe Klukay. Klukay had potted 20 goals for the Bruins in 1953-54 but he was only able to find the net eight times for the Maple Leafs.

Although the Leafs struggled to score, they had great success preventing goals. On March 10, they held the Montreal Canadiens to a 0–0 tie, a match that was uninteresting except for a new ice-cleaning machine that made its first appearance in an NHL arena. The device, called a Zamboni, was a marvel in ice maintenance and would soon be found in every rink in North America. Toronto finished in third place with a 24–24–22 record. The 22 ties established a new NHL record for draws in a single season.

The Boston Bruins earned the final playoff berth, with much of their success coming after Lynn Patrick surrendered the coaching duties to

In his four seasons with the Toronto Maple Leafs, Danny Lewicki had managed to score only 21 goals. However, after he connected a career-high 36 times with the AHL's Pittsburgh Hornets in 1953-54, the New York Rangers purchased Lewicki's contract. The smooth-skating left-winger turned in his finest NHL campaign for New York, scoring 29 goals in 1954-55.

Milt Schmidt, who had retired as a player 30 games into the schedule. Schmidt brought the Bruins home with a 13–12–15 record in his 40 games behind the bench. The Long John Henderson experiment proved successful, as the rookie recorded a 2.49 goals-against average in 44 games. Réal Chevrefils, Don McKenney, and Leo Labine were the offensive leaders, while newcomer Leo Boivin was a crowd favorite with his body-crunching checks and timely contributions on the scoresheet.

The New York Rangers and the Chicago Black Hawks both missed the post-season, and the only battle they staged was for fifth spot. The Broadway Blues stayed out of the basement, due in part to the efforts of newcomer Danny Lewicki, who amassed 53 points to lead the team. Lewicki collected 29 goals in 70 games, eight more than he had scored in 123 games with the Toronto Maple Leafs. Andy Bathgate was an emerging new star, but Camille Henry was a great disappointment and was sent back to the minors to get his game in gear.

In an effort to revive the Chicago Black Hawks' shrinking bank account, the team decided to play eight "home" games on the road in non-NHL cities. Six matches were held in St. Louis, and single games were played in St. Paul and Omaha. Five of the games ended in ties, a fitting result for these "neutral site" encounters. Frank Eddolls's troops fought

Detroit general manager Jack Adams puts the lid on a crowning performance by Gordie Howe after the superstar fired a hat-trick in the Red Wings' 5–1 victory over Montreal in game five of the Stanley Cup finals. Alex Delvecchio (left) contributed 15 post-season points to the Red Wings' Stanley Cup romp in 1955.

Floyd Curry, shown here wearing the traditional reward for a three-goal game, did his best to pick up the scoring slack for the Montreal Canadiens after Rocket Richard was suspended for the 1955 play-offs. He scored a career-high eight goals during the post-season.

bravely, but with thin talent and thinner finances, the Hawks won only 13 games. One bright spot was the play of rookie Ed Litzenberger, sold to the Hawks by Montreal in December. The Neudorf, Sask-atchewan, native collected 23 goals and 28 assists to win the rookie-of-the-year award, becoming only the second freshman to play with two teams in the same year he won the Calder Trophy.

The battle for first place between Montreal and Detroit coincided with an intense struggle for the NHL scoring lead. Rocket Richard, who had never captured the Art Ross Trophy in his career, was in a neck-and-neck clash with teammate Bernie Geoffrion for the points crown. On March 13, the Canadiens met the Boston Bruins in the Garden on the back end of a home-and-home weekend series. The Habs were two points up on the Detroit Red Wings, and the Rocket was two points ahead of the Boomer. With only six minutes left in the game, Richard and former teammate Hal Laycoe became involved in a stick-swinging duel that linesman Cliff Thompson repeatedly tried to break up. During the fracas, Richard clashed with the linesman, earning himself a match penalty and a meeting with NHL president Clarence Campbell.

The Canadiens weren't scheduled to play again until March 17, so a meeting between Richard, the on-ice officials, and Campbell was held on the sixteenth. As a result of Richard's on-ice actions, the Rocket was suspended not only for the rest of the season, but for the playoffs as well. The reaction in Montreal was one of outrage and disbelief. Death threats were made against President Campbell and he was warned not to attend the March 17 Canadiens home game against the Red Wings. However, with both teams now tied for first place, Campbell was equally adamant that he would attend the game.

The Red Wings quickly assumed control of the contest, building a quick 4–0 first-period lead before the Rocket-less Habs got on the score-board. Throughout the opening twenty minutes, Campbell was verbally harassed, but when a fan threw a punch at the NHL president, the situation got out of hand. During the first intermission, a smoke bomb was released in the Forum, forcing the fire marshal to order that the building be cleared. Once outside, the crowd swelled in size and a riot ensued, the crowd growing in number as it moved along Ste. Catherine Street. The riot lasted most of the night, as gangs looted stores and overturned cars. The Canadiens forfeited the game to the Wings, and it went into the books as a 4–1 Detroit win.

The following day, Richard spoke on radio in both French and English, pleading with his fans to cease their violent behavior. It was only after Richard's speech that peace was finally restored to Montreal's streets. The Canadiens defeated the Rangers in their next game, but fell 6–0 to Detroit in the final match of the season to finish two points back of the Red Wings in the standings. Bernie Geoffrion collected a point on three of the final four goals the team scored after Richard's suspension and took the scoring title by a single point. When Boom-Boom skated onto the Forum ice for the start of the playoffs against Boston, he was booed by his own fans for depriving the Rocket of the Art Ross Trophy.

In the playoffs, both Detroit and Montreal eased through the semi-finals, setting up a Stanley Cup final-series rematch. Each team won on home ice through the first six games of the set, with the smallest margin of victory being two goals. Montreal won 4–2, 5–3, and 6–3 at the Forum, while the Red Wings slammed the Habs 4–2, 7–1, and 5–1 in the Olympia. Bernie Geoffrion and Floyd Curry were both outstanding for Montreal in the Rocket's absence, combining for 16 goals. However, Gordie Howe scored what proved to be the winning marker for Detroit in game seven. After Alex Delvecchio opened the scoring, Howe took a pass from Marcel Pronovost and snapped the puck behind Jacques Plante to give Detroit a 2–0 lead with only 21 seconds remaining in the second period. With the score 3–0, Curry broke Sawchuk's shutout, but the damage was done, and the Red Wings were repeat Stanley Cup champions.

Howe, who set a playoff record with 20 post-season points, joined Ted Lindsay and Marguerite Norris to receive the Stanley Cup from Clarence Campbell. It was the last time in the decade that a player wearing a jersey other than that of the Montreal Canadiens would be awarded the celebrated trophy. At the post-season awards banquet, Doug Harvey won the Norris Trophy, Geoffrion took the Art Ross, Sawchuk won the Vezina, and Ed Litzenberger received the Calder. The only surprise came when Ted Kennedy, one of the NHL's most respected gentlemen, was awarded the Hart Trophy as the league's MVP. Although Kennedy finished with just 52 points in 1954-55, he was an acknowledged team leader and was a worthy winner of the league's most prestigious individual award.

(continued on p. 99)

DON CHERRY PLAYS FIRST AND ONLY NHL GAME

Though he played professionally in four different minor leagues until 1971-72, this proved to be Cherry's sole game in the NHL. After retiring as a player, he turned to coaching and, later, broadcasting, acquiring a wide following as a hockey commentator.

March 31, 1955
at Montreal Forum
Montreal 5, Boston 1

STARTING LINEUP

#	BOSTON		#	MONTREAL
1	Henderson	G	1	Plante
11	Quackenbush	D	2	Harvey
24	**Cherry**	D	19	St. Laurent
17	McKenney	C	18	Mosdell
16	Labine	RW	6	Curry
12	Chevrefils	LW	11	MacKay

FIRST PERIOD
1) MTL Leclair 2 (Harvey, Moore) 3:43
2) MTL Moore 1 (Béliveau, Olmstead) PPG 14:43
PENALTIES — Sandford BOS (roughing), Johnson MTL (roughing) 8:45; Corcoran BOS (holding) 10:17; Labine BOS (elbowing) 13:37; Johnson MTL (holding) 16:20.

SECOND PERIOD
3) MTL Curry 3 (Mosdell, Harvey) 7:55
4) MTL Leclair 3 (Marshall, St. Laurent) 11:18
5) BOS Ferguson 1 (Quackenbush) PPG 15:52
PENALTIES — Geoffrion MTL (holding) 14:57; Corcoran BOS (hooking) 18:18.

THIRD PERIOD
6) MTL Béliveau 3 (St. Laurent) 8:14
PENALTIES — Labine BOS (highsticking), Bouchard MTL (highsticking) 19:59.

SHOTS ON GOAL	1	2	3	T
BOSTON	6	5	3	14
MONTREAL	8	12	13	33

GOALTENDERS		TIME	SA	GA	ENG	W/L
BOS	Henderson	60:00	28	5	0	L
MTL	Plante	60:00	13	1	0	W

PP CONVERSIONS BOS 1/2 MTL 1/3

Waivers, Drafts, and the Sponsorship List

by Donald R. Ellis

The NHL's six-team era was a time that saw many of the game's greatest stars begin their hockey careers, but with the passing of years, much of the detail that describes the intricate paths players followed to reach the NHL has been lost.

Player recruitment is one of the few aspects of modern hockey that actually is simpler today than it was in the six-team years. Today, all players are subject to the NHL's annual Entry Draft when they turn eighteen. Those who aren't drafted by the time they are twenty can be signed as free agents. In the six-team years, however, many young players played for junior and, occasionally, for juvenile or midget teams that were sponsored by NHL clubs or their minor pro affiliates. A maximum of eighteen players from each sponsored club could be placed on an NHL organization's sponsorship list.

This list was maintained in the NHL's Montreal office. The department that kept track of this information and everything else regarding player movement was known as the Central Registry Bureau of Player Information, or CR for short, and I had the pleasure of serving as the director of CR for thirty years, beginning in 1953. Our office maintained the records of players, both professional and amateur, recording signed contracts, transfers, loans, draft and waiver claims, and all pertinent data relating to the rights of players held by pro clubs. There were no computers during the six-team years, so everything was written by hand.

Each player would be assigned a file number when his name was first submitted to CR. This number would stay with the player until he retired. Each transaction or change in a player's status was recorded on a white 3 x 5 index card, which was maintained for each player. This was backed up by lists that I kept in hardbacked ledger books. In these books I would maintain the various lists of players under the control of both NHL and minor pro clubs. These included players on each team's reserve, protected, negotiation, sponsored, retired, inactive, and goalkeeper lists.

As each change to a player's status was received, his listing in the current year's ledger book was also updated. A player's name could be recorded in only one spot. If his status changed – if, for example, he was traded from one team to another – his name would be stroked out on one list in red pencil and written in on his new team's list in ink. These procedures were based on NHL president Clarence Campbell's army experience, in which record-keeping was based on the premise that a soldier could be in only one place at a time.

One of the most persistent myths about recruiting amateur players into the old NHL is that the clubs had carved up the map of Canada into six protected territories. This was not true. There were no amateur territorial rights. Clubs in the NHL did, however, have rights to players on their sponsorship lists, and retained these rights until the players turned twenty and their junior eligibility ended.

To register the sponsorship of a junior team with Central Registry, an NHL club had to file proof of affiliation or a working agreement with each sponsored club. Payments made by NHL clubs to their sponsored junior clubs were used by the junior teams to defray expenses. Proof of a player's eligibility to play with a junior or other amateur club was confirmed by his Canadian Amateur Hockey Association (CAHA) player's card. This was filed each season with CR. There was no minimum age requirement for inclusion on a sponsored list. Bobby Orr was a junior all-star with Oshawa as a fourteen-year-old, and

The Peterborough Petes celebrate their 1959 OHA championship. The junior club was sponsored by the Montreal Canadiens and featured future NHLers Wayne Connelly, Jacques Caron, Denis DeJordy, and Jim Roberts. Scott Bowman (second row, far right) was behind the bench for the Petes. He later went on to a successful coaching career with St. Louis, Montreal, Buffalo, Pittsburgh, and Detroit, setting an NHL record for most wins by a coach.

was, of course, on the Boston Bruins' sponsored list.

Each NHL club was permitted two sponsored clubs under its own name and was also permitted two more sponsored clubs under each of its minor pro affiliates.

The maximum number of players on each sponsored list was eighteen. Thus an NHL club with four minor pro affiliates could have a total of ten sponsored junior clubs or 180 players on its sponsored list. These clubs could be located anywhere.

In addition, the sponsorship list for each sponsored junior club could also include players from a maximum of three affiliated teams in lower classifications such as Junior B, Juvenile, or Midget hockey. This enabled NHL clubs to evaluate players not yet ready for Junior A hockey.

When the NHL expansion came in 1967, the old sponsorship system was replaced with a Universal

Glenn Hall was born in Saskatchewan, but played his junior hockey with the Windsor Spitfires, an Ontario-based junior club sponsored by the Detroit Red Wings.

Amateur Draft. Sponsored lists were frozen on August 15, 1966. No new players were added, and, as players reached their twentieth birthdays, they were removed from the list. The last players recruited under the old sponsorship system came off the sponsored list in 1970.

In addition to the sponsored list, each club in the six-team NHL was entitled to protect the rights of thirty players and three goaltenders on its *reserve list*. Minor pro clubs in leagues like the American, Western, Quebec, United States, and, later, Eastern Pro and Central Pro leagues – almost all of which had affiliations with NHL teams – had their own reserve lists of twenty-five skaters and three goaltenders. The NHL clubs would usually place their top amateur prospects on the reserve lists of their minor pro affiliates if they were unable to accommodate them on the reserve list of the NHL club itself.

Whether pro or amateur, each player on a reserve list had to have signed either a player's contract or one of three standard documents – the "A," "B," or "C" forms – that governed either an agreement to try out or an option on the player's professional services.

The Tryout A Form was signed by an amateur player of at least eighteen years of age who agreed to try out at an NHL training camp to demonstrate his qualifications. This age restriction was increased to nineteen in 1965.

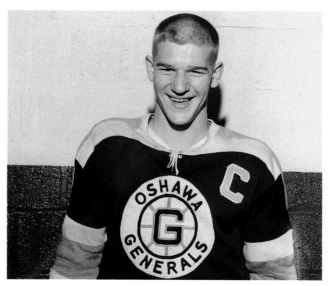

Bobby Orr was the best-known junior player in Canada during his tenure with the Oshawa Generals of the Ontario Hockey Association. The Generals were sponsored by the Boston Bruins.

If the club decided to offer him a contract, the player agreed to accept terms that were mutually agreed upon. The club also agreed to pay any expenses that the player incurred by reporting to training camp.

Pro clubs were required to add the names of A Form players to their reserve lists, but during September training camps, these players were removed from the reserve list so that clubs couldn't use amateur tryouts to hide talented players from other NHL organizations. If a club was convinced that a player who had signed an A Form was ready for a professional career, they could retain his rights either by signing him or by putting him on a negotiation list to protect him. If the player wasn't signed, he was removed from the reserve list, enabling other clubs to sign him to a contract or an option agreement. If no other club picked him up, the original club could restore him to its reserve list, either by signing another A Form or by placing him on its negotiation list.

The *negotiation list* was made up of a maximum of four players per club. Players eligible for this list were unclaimed free agents. In order to add a name to its negotiation list, clubs would file claims for a player's services between midnight and noon on the day of his

ARBOUR, AL

Defense. Shoots left. 6', 180 lbs. Born, Sudbury, Ontario, November 1, 1932.

Season	Club	League	Regular Season GP	G	A	PTS	PIM	Playoffs GP	G	A	PTS	PIM
1950-51	Windsor	OHA	31	5	4	9	....	....	....	....	....	....
1951-52	Windsor	OHA	52	7	12	19	....	....	....	....	....	....
1952-53	Windsor	OHA	56	5	7	12	....	....	....	....	....	....
	Edmonton	WHL	8	0	1	1	2	15	0	5	5	10
1953-54	**Detroit**	**NHL**	36	0	1	1	18	....	....	....	....	....
	Sherbrooke	QHL	19	1	3	4	24	2	0	0	0	2
1954-55	Edmonton	WHL	41	3	9	12	39	....	....	....	....	....
a	Quebec	QHL	20	4	5	9	55	4	0	0	0	2
1955-56 b	Edmonton	WHL	70	5	14	19	109	3	0	0	0	4
	Detroit	**NHL**	....	....	....	....	....	4	0	1	1	0
1956-57	Detroit	NHL	44	1	6	7	38	5	0	0	0	6
	Edmonton	WHL	24	2	3	5	24	....	....	....	....	....
1957-58	Detroit	NHL	69	1	6	7	104	4	0	1	1	4
1958-59	Chicago	NHL	70	2	10	12	86	6	1	2	3	26
1959-60	Chicago	NHL	57	1	5	6	66	4	0	0	0	4
1960-61	Chicago	NHL	53	3	2	5	40	7	0	0	0	2
1961-62	Toronto	NHL	52	1	6	7	68	8	0	0	0	6
1962-63	Toronto	NHL	4	1	0	1	4	....	....	....	....	....
c	Rochester	AHL	63	6	21	27	97	2	0	2	2	2
1963-64	Toronto	NHL	6	0	1	1	0	1	0	0	0	0
c	Rochester	AHL	60	3	19	22	62	2	1	0	1	0
1964-65 cd	Rochester	AHL	71	1	16	17	88	10	0	1	1	16
	Toronto	NHL	....	....	....	....	....	1	0	0	0	2
1965-66	Toronto	NHL	4	0	1	1	2	....	....	....	....	....
c	Rochester	AHL	59	2	11	13	86	12	0	2	2	8
1966-67	Rochester	AHL	71	3	19	22	48	13	0	1	1	16
	NHL TOTALS		**395**	**10**	**37**	**47**	**426**	**40**	**1**	**4**	**5**	**50**

a   QHL Second All-Star Team (1955)
b   WHL Second All-Star Team (1956)
c   AHL First All-Star Team (1963, 1964, 1965, 1966)
d   Won Eddie Shore Plaque (AHL's Top Defenseman) (1965)

Signed as a free agent by **Detroit**. Drafted by **Chicago** from **Detroit** in Intra-League Draft, June 1958. Drafted by **Toronto** from **Chicago** in Intra-League Draft, June 1961. Claimed by **St. Louis** from **Toronto** in Expansion Draft, June 6, 1967.

Player data panel for Al Arbour from the 1967-68 NHL Guide. Note that Arbour was claimed in the Intra-League Draft on two occasions: he moved from the Red Wings to the Black Hawks in 1958 and from the Black Hawks to the Maple Leafs in 1961. After the NHL's 1967 expansion, Arbour would finish his playing career with the St. Louis Blues. He went on to coach the Blues and, later, won four Stanley Cup championships as coach of the New York Islanders.

eighteenth birthday. If more than one club filed to negotiate with a player, the rights to negotiate with him were awarded to the club that was lowest in the standings on the day of his birthday. Rights to this player were retained for one year from the date of listing. At the end of this year, the club could apply to the league president, demonstrating that they had made a fair effort to sign him. Mr. Campbell could, at his discretion, extend a player's negotiation status for an additional year. Players in college, of course, couldn't be signed to

TRY-OUT AGREEMENT "A"
(Form "A")

MEMORANDUM
OF AGREEMENT
BETWEEN:

DATE..............

....
hereinafter called the "Player"

— and —

....
hereinafter called the "Club"

In consideration of the agreement by the Club to pay the expenses (including hotel room, meals and railroad fare) from:..............................
(Place of residence or other base of Player)

and return, the Player agrees to present himself, when called upon to do so, at the Club's training camp for the purpose of demonstrating, to the best of his ability, his qualifications as a hockey player; and further agrees that if such qualifications, in the opinion of the Club, justify the Club in offering him a contract as a professional hockey player, he will sign such contract on terms to be mutually agreed upon.

And the Player further agrees that in case of refusal or failure on his part to attend the training camp and try-out as agreed, the Club shall have the right to request the suspension of the Player by all professional and amateur organizations until the Player has carried out this Try-out Agreement.

The Player also agrees that the Club shall have the right to transfer this agreement and the rights created by it to any other professional hockey club, and the Player agrees that he will report and try out with such transferee club on the basis set out in this Agreement.

WITNESS: .... PLAYER

.... ADDRESS

....
CITY   PROVINCE OR STATE

WITNESS: .... CLUB

PER............................

FOR PLAYER ONLY

NAME IN FULL............................

PLACE OF BIRTH............................

DAY............MONTH............YEAR............

HEIGHT............WEIGHT............

POSITION............SHOOTS............   FORM "A"
                (R or L)

(Read instructions for completion and registration on reverse side.)

Players signed to an "A" form could be brought up to the NHL in mid-season for a three-game trial. Frank Mahovlich's first taste of NHL action came during a three-game trial with the Maple Leafs at the end of the 1956-57 season.

pro contracts, so they frequently spent more than one year on an NHL club's negotiation list.

Players who had signed A Forms could also be brought up to the NHL in mid-season to play games as part of an amateur tryout. These tryouts were restricted to a maximum of three games, though this was increased to five games in the early 1960s.

Permission for players to participate in these tryouts was obtained from the CAHA or the Amateur Hockey Association of the United States (AHAUS), and they did not jeopardize a player's amateur status. Provision also existed for an additional three-game call-up under bona fide emergency conditions, such as

OPTION AGREEMENT "B"

(Form "B")

MEMORANDUM
OF AGREEMENT
DATE..............................

BETWEEN:

....
hereinafter called the "Player"

— and —

....
hereinafter called the "Club"

In consideration of the sum of...Dollars ($) which the Player acknowledges he has received from the Club, the Player hereby grants to the Club an exclusive option on his services as a professional hockey player. The Player further agrees that he will present himself at the Club's training camp, at the Club's expense (including hotel room, meals and railroad fare), when requested to do so, for the purpose of demonstrating his skill and ability as a hockey player, and that he will, on request of the Club, sign a Standard Player's Contract (professional) on terms to be mutually agreed upon.

And it is further agreed that the option hereby granted is a continuing option exercisable by the Club so long as the Club is prepared to tender and does tender to the Player, upon demand in writing being made by him at any time when he is eligible and available to play, a Standard Player's Contract at a rate of salary equal to the fair average salary of the League in which the Club is a member.

And it is further agreed that if the Club defaults in the performance of any of its obligations under this Agreement the Player may notify the Club in writing the particulars of such default. Should the Club not make good such default within fifteen days from the receipt of such notice all rights hereby created shall thereafter cease and determine.

The Player agrees that the Club shall have the right to transfer this agreement and the rights created by it to any other professional hockey club, and the Player agrees that he will carry out the terms of this Agreement on the same basis as if it had been made with the transferee club.

WITNESS:..   .... PLAYER

.... ADDRESS

CITY   PROVINCE OR STATE

WITNESS:..   .... CLUB

FOR PLAYER ONLY   PER..

NAME IN FULL..

PLACE OF BIRTH..

DAY............MONTH............................YEAR............

HEIGHT............................WEIGHT............

POSITION....................SHOOTS............
(R or L)   FORM "B"

(Read instructions for completion and registration on reverse side.)

The option "B" form was a unique contract because the player could decide when he wanted to sign an NHL contract. Jean Béliveau signed a "B" form while he was with the Quebec Aces of the Quebec Senior Hockey League.

injury to players on the NHL roster. So by the early 1960s, it was possible for an amateur player to play up to eight games in the NHL while remaining an amateur, though minor pro players were most often called up for these emergency fill-ins.

If signed before September 1, an A Form remained in effect to the end of October. If signed after September 1, it remained in effect to the end of October of the following calendar year, in effect guaranteeing the player an invitation to the team's next full training camp, though, like all A Form players, he would still be dropped from the club's reserve list for the suspension period.

There was also a temporary training-camp list of players invited to pro training camps. The protection offered by this list was short-term, expiring with the first regular-season game each season.

The Option B Form was very rarely used and was unique because it gave the player the right to demand a contract. Signing required a minimum fifty-dollar payment to the player. Like the A Form, the B Form player agreed to attend training camp and, if offered a contract, to sign on terms mutually acceptable to the club and the player. As long as the form was in force, the player also had the option to indicate to the club when he wished to sign, and the club had to comply with an offer equal to the fair average salary in the NHL. This form was not renewable, but remained in effect until the player signed with an NHL organization or retired from hockey. Jean Béliveau, whose courtship by the Canadiens took several seasons, signed a B Form with Montreal while he was playing with the senior Quebec Aces. Very few B Forms were signed, largely because they gave control to the player.

The Option C Form was considered the most important of the NHL's three standard documents, as it generally led to a Standard Player's Contract. It was the form that promising young players signed. People have somehow misunderstood the C Form, thinking that it was a document signed by very young players, tying them to NHL clubs. This wasn't the case. Parental consent was not re-quired to sign, and, as with the A and B forms, a player had to be eighteen years old to sign a C Form. It re-quired a minimum payment to the player of fifty dollars, as well as a future guaranteed minimum salary in the NHL and in each of the minor leagues in the event of a future assignment by the NHL club. If the player had not signed a pro contract within one year of the signing date, the C Form could be renewed for an additional year by the completion of a Renewal of Option C Form, which retained the same clauses as the original Option C.

No new signings under these forms were permitted after May 1, 1968. Combined with the freezing of sponsored lists in 1966, the termination of all the A, B, and C forms turned the Universal Amateur Draft first staged in 1969 into the number-one source of new players. Almost all traces of sponsorship had been eliminated by the time of this draft, which saw 84 players taken.

OPTION AGREEMENT "C"

(Form "C")

MEMORANDUM OF AGREEMENT

DATE.................................

BETWEEN :

....

— and —

hereinafter called the "Player"

....

hereinafter called the "Club"

In consideration of the sum of .... Dollars ($) which the Player acknowledges he has received from the Club, the Player covenants and agrees with the Club that he will, upon request of the Club made within one year from the date hereof, sign a contract with the Club to serve the Club as a hockey player for a period of .... year(s), subject to the terms and conditions set out in the Standard Player's Contract (a copy of which has been shown to and examined by the Player), and for the following remuneration payable to the Player by the Club :

....Dollars ($)
payable forthwith upon the signing of a Standard Player's Contract,

— and —

....Dollars ($)
per hockey season if the player is assigned by the Club to play for a club in the Quebec Hockey League Inc.

— or —

....Dollars ($)
per hockey season if the player is assigned by the Club to play for a club in the Western Hockey League,

— or —

....Dollars ($)
per hockey season if the player is assigned by the Club to play for a club in the American Hockey League,

— or —

....Dollars ($)
per hockey season if the player is assigned by the Club to play for a club in the National Hockey League.

ALL such payments, excepting the .... payable for signing the contract, shall be pro rated according to the proportion of the hockey season for which the Player is employed in each of such Leagues.

The Player further agrees that he will present himself at the Club's training camp at the Club's expense (hotel, meals and railway fare) whenever requested to do so by the Club during the currency of this Agreement, or extension thereof, for the purpose of demonstrating his skill and ability as a hockey player.

During the currency of this Agreement or extension thereof, the Player covenants and agrees that he will play hockey only for such hockey team as may be designated by the Club.

(TURN OVER)

OPTION AGREEMENT "C" (continued)

It is mutually agreed that the Club shall have the right to sell, exchange, assign or otherwise transfer this contract and the rights to the Player's services to any professional hockey Club, and the Player agrees to accept and be bound by such sale, exchange, assignment or transfer, and to faithfully perform and carry out the terms of the Agreement with the same force and effect as if it had been entered into by the Player and the assignee club.

This Agreement may be extended for further periods of one year each upon payment to the Player by the Club before the expiration of this Agreement or any extension thereof the sum of ....Dollars ($) for each such extension.

DATED AT .... this .... day of .... 19......

WITNESS : ....   PLAYER

....   ADDRESS

CITY   PROVINCE OR STATE

WITNESS : ....   CLUB

FOR PLAYER ONLY   PER ....

NAME IN FULL ....

PLACE OF BIRTH ....

DAY .... MONTH .... YEAR ....

HEIGHT .... WEIGHT ....

POSITION .... SHOOTS ....
(R or L)   FORM "C"

The option "C" form was the standard agreement signed by most young prospects. A player had to be eighteen years of age to sign the sheet, which could be renewed for a year if the player had yet to sign a pro contract.

Sponsorship was completely gone by 1970, when 115 players were selected.

The NHL's modern draft era began in 1969, after almost all sponsored and C Form players had passed through the system. Previous to the implementation of this Universal Amateur Draft, the NHL had held an annual *Amateur Draft* beginning in June 1963. Its purpose was to provide a mechanism for NHL clubs to acquire the rights to amateur players not already on sponsored lists or negotiation lists. It also served as an incentive to amateur clubs to develop players, because the claiming price paid for each player ($2,000, increased to $3,000 in 1964) was shared by the clubs the draftee had played with in each of the previous two seasons. Those players were eligible who had turned seventeen between August 1 and July 31 following the draft. When this draft was first held, the majority of talented young players were already on sponsored and negotiation lists, so few players were eligible and few were taken. Garry Monahan was the first, and he was selected by the Canadiens. Pete Mahovlich was taken second overall by Detroit.

Each NHL club could take up to four players. The name of each player taken was placed on a special amateur-draft list and was retained there until the player's eighteenth birthday, at which time the player had to be either released outright or signed to an agreement and placed on a club's reserve or negotiation lists.

In the first year, drafted players who went on to play in the NHL included Mahovlich, Monahan, Gerry Meehan, Jim McKenny, and Walt McKechnie, though only McKenny and Mahovlich played during the six-team era.

In 1965, the claiming age was advanced to eighteen, with removal from the draft list at nineteen.

An NHL by-law passed in 1962 had given the Montreal Canadiens an option to use the first and

NHL AMATEUR DRAFT
PLAYERS SELECTED 1963-1966

PLAYER	DRAFTED BY	PLAYER	DRAFTED BY
1963		**1965**	
1 **Garry Monahan**	Montreal	1 Andre Veilleux	New York
2 **Peter Mahovlich**	Detroit	2 Andrew Culligan	Chicago
3 Orest Romashyma	Boston	3 George Forgie	Detroit
4 Al Osborne	New York	4 Joe Bailey	Boston
5 Art Hampson	Chicago	5 **Pierre Bouchard**	Montreal
6 **Walt McKechnie**	Toronto	6 George Surmay	New York
7 Rodney Presswood	Montreal	7 Brian McKenney	Chicago
8 **Randy Osborne**	Detroit	8 Bob Birdsell	Detroit
9 Terrance Lane	Boston	9 Bill Ramsay	Boston
10 Terry Jones	New York	10 **Michel Parizeau**	New York
11 Wayne Davidson	Chicago		
12 Neil Clairmont	Toronto	**1966**	
13 Roy Pugh	Montreal	1 **Barry Gibbs**	Boston
14 Roger Bamburak	Boston	2 **Brad Park**	New York
15 Mike Cummings	New York	3 **Terry Caffery**	Chicago
16 Bill Carson	Chicago	4 **John Wright**	Toronto
17 **Jim McKenny**	Toronto	5 **Phil Myre**	Montreal
18 Glen Shirton	Montreal	6 **Steve Atkinson**	Detroit
19 Jim Blair	Boston	7 **Rick Smith**	Boston
20 Campbell Alleson	New York	8 **Joey Johnston**	New York
21 **Gerry Meehan**	Toronto	9 Ron Dussiaume	Chicago
		10 Cam Crosby	Toronto
1964		11 Maurice St. Jacques	Montreal
1 Claude Gauthier	Detroit	12 Jim Whitaker	Detroit
2 Alec Campbell	Boston	13 **Garnet Bailey**	Boston
3 Robert Graham	New York	14 **Don Luce**	New York
4 Richard Bayes	Chicago	15 Larry Gibbons	Chicago
5 **Tom Martin**	Toronto	16 **Rick Ley**	Toronto
6 Claude Chagnon	Montreal	17 **Jude Drouin**	Montreal
7 **Brian Watts**	Detroit	18 Lee Carpenter	Detroit
8 Jim Booth	Boston	19 **Tom Webster**	Boston
9 **Tim Ecclestone**	New York	20 **Jack Egers**	New York
10 Jan Popiel	Chicago	21 Brian Morenz	Chicago
11 Dave Cotey	Toronto	22 Dale MacLeish	Toronto
12 Guy Allen	Montreal	23 Bob Pate	Montreal
13 Ralph Buchanan	Detroit	24 Grant Cole	Detroit
14 **Ken Dryden**	Boston		
15 Gordon Lowe	New York		
16 Carl Hadfield	Chicago		
17 **Mike Pelyk**	Toronto		
18 Paul Reid	Montreal		
19 **Renald LeClerc**	Detroit		
20 Allister Blair	Boston	*Players who later played*	
21 Syl Apps, Jr.	New York	*one or more games in*	
22 **Maurice L'Abbé**	Chicago	*the* NHL *are listed in*	
23 **Jim Dorey**	Toronto	*bold.*	
24 Michel Jacques	Montreal		

The results of the NHL's Amateur Draft from 1963 to 1966. Future Hall-of-Fame members Ken Dryden and Brad Park were both selected in these early years of the draft.

second picks in the amateur draft to select eligible players who were the sons of French-Canadian fathers living in the province of Quebec at the time of the draft. The purpose of this concession was to enable Montreal to maintain its image as a French-Canadian club. This

option remained in place up to and including the 1969 Amateur Draft in which the Canadiens used the first two picks to select Réjean Houle and Marc Tardif.

The roots of this special concession to the Canadiens went back to the mid-1930s, when the Canadiens were doing poorly in the standings and at the gate. With the Maroons, Montreal's other NHL club, also drawing small crowds – 1937-38 would be their last season – it was felt that the NHL needed to bolster the Canadiens with French-Canadian talent so that Montreal's huge francophone community would embrace the team.

For much of the six-team era, players were swapped between NHL organizations and minor pro clubs through three drafts – the Inter-League, the Intra-League, and the Reverse drafts – that were held consecutively at the NHL's June meetings each year.

The *Inter-League Draft*, established in 1948, was the first of the three drafts staged each year. Eligible were players on the reserve lists of minor pro clubs, whether they were owned by NHL teams or by the minor pro clubs themselves. Players on NHL reserve lists weren't eligible. The claiming price of $20,000 – later raised to $30,000 – was paid to the club that owned the player. Players who were under twenty years of age or under option or tryout agreements were not eligible. Clubs were required to freeze their protected lists between the end of the playoffs to June 15, so that players couldn't be hidden by last-minute shuffling onto NHL reserve lists.

Players selected in this draft had to be accommodated on the selecting NHL club's reserve list. These players could not be drafted by an NHL club and then lent to a minor pro club without first being offered back to the player's original minor pro club for half of the draft price. If not reclaimed by his minor pro club, the player would then be offered on waivers to the other clubs in the NHL. Only then, if the minor pro club had declined him and the remaining NHL clubs had passed, could he be lent to another minor pro club. This ensured that players claimed in the Inter-League Draft were selected because they were considered to be of NHL caliber.

NHL Intra-League Draft
Players Selected 1954-1966

Player	Drafted By	Drafted From	Price	Player	Drafted By	Drafted From	Price	Player	Drafted By	Drafted From	Price
Sept. '54				**June '60**				**June '64**			
John McCormack	Chicago	Montreal	$15,000	Ted Green	Boston	Montreal	$20,000	Bob Woytowich	Boston	New York	$20,000
				Jim Bartlett	Boston	New York	$20,000	Gary Bergman	Detroit	Montreal	$20,000
Sept. '56				Tom Thurlby	Boston	Montreal	$20,000	George Gardner	Detroit	Boston	$20,000
Tom McCarthy	Detroit	New York	$15,000	Parker MacDonald	Detroit	New York	$20,000	Murray Hall	Detroit	Chicago	$20,000
Larry Cahan	New York	Toronto	$15,000	Billy McNeill	New York	Detroit	$20,000	James Mikol	New York	Boston	$20,000
				Ted Hampson	New York	Toronto	$20,000	Dickie Moore	Toronto	Montreal	$20,000
June '57				Jim Morrison	New York	Chicago	$20,000	Terry Sawchuk	Toronto	Detroit	$20,000
Norm Johnson	Boston	New York	$15,000	Larry Hillman	Toronto	Boston	$20,000				
Bronco Horvath	Boston	Montreal	$15,000	Guy Rousseau	Toronto	Montreal	$20,000	**June '65**			
Larry Hillman	Chicago	Detroit	$15,000					Gerry Cheevers	Boston	Toronto	$30,000
Bob Bailey	Chicago	Detroit	$15,000	**June '61**				Poul Popiel	Boston	Chicago	$30,000
John Hanna	New York	Montreal	$15,000	Pat Stapleton	Boston	Chicago	$20,000	Norm Schmitz	Boston	Montreal	$30,000
				Earl Balfour	Boston	Chicago	$20,000	Keith Wright	Boston	New York	$30,000
June '58				Orland Kurtenbach	Boston	New York	$20,000	Pat Stapleton	Chicago	Toronto	$30,000
Jean-Guy Gendron	Boston	New York	$15,000	Bronco Horvath	Chicago	Boston	$20,000	Bryan Watson	Detroit	Chicago	$30,000
Gord Redahl	Boston	New York	$15,000	Autry Erickson	Chicago	Boston	$20,000	Earl Ingarfield	New York	Montreal	$30,000
Earl Reibel	Boston	Chicago	$15,000	Jean-Guy Gendron	New York	Montreal	$20,000				
Jack Evans	Chicago	New York	$15,000	Vic Hadfield	New York	Chicago	$20,000	**June '66**			
Earl Balfour	Chicago	Toronto	$15,000	Al Arbour	Toronto	Chicago	$20,000	Ted Taylor	Detroit	Montreal	$30,000
Al Arbour	Chicago	Detroit	$15,000					Al Lebrun	Detroit	New York	$30,000
Danny Lewicki	Montreal	New York	$15,000	**June '62**				Ray Cullen	Detroit	New York	$30,000
Dave Creighton	Montreal	New York	$15,000	Jean-Guy Gendron	Boston	New York	$20,000	Pat Quinn	Montreal	Detroit	$30,000
Bert Olmstead	Toronto	Montreal	$15,000	Warren Godfrey	Boston	Detroit	$20,000	Wally Boyer	Montreal	Toronto	$30,000
Gerry Wilson	Toronto	Montreal	$15,000	Irv Spencer	Boston	New York	$20,000	Wally Boyer	Chicago	Montreal	$30,000
				Alex Faulkner	Detroit	Toronto	$20,000	Al MacNeil	Montreal	Chicago	$30,000
June '59				Barclay Plager	Detroit	Montreal	$20,000	Al MacNeil	New York	Montreal	$30,000
Bruce Gamble	Boston	New York	$20,000	Floyd Smith	Detroit	New York	$20,000	Mike McMahon	Montreal	New York	$30,000
Autry Erickson	Boston	Chicago	$20,000	Bert Olmstead	New York	Toronto	$20,000	Orland Kurtenbach	New York	Toronto	$30,000
Charlie Burns	Boston	Detroit	$20,000	Bronco Horvath	New York	Chicago	$20,000	Max Mestinsek	New York	Detroit	$30,000
Gary Aldcorn	Detroit	Toronto	$20,000	Ed Van Impe	Toronto	Chicago	$20,000	Brian Campbell	New York	Detroit	$30,000
John McKenzie	Detroit	Chicago	$20,000					Don Blackburn	Toronto	Montreal	$30,000
Irv Spencer	New York	Montreal	$20,000	**June '63**				John Brenneman	Toronto	New York	$30,000
Ian Cushenan	New York	Chicago	$20,000	Andy Hebenton	Boston	New York	$20,000				
Brian Cullen	New York	Toronto	$20,000	Wayne Rivers	Boston	Detroit	$20,000				
				Irv Spencer	Detroit	Boston	$20,000				
				Ted Hampson	Detroit	New York	$20,000				
				Art Stratton	Detroit	Chicago	$20,000				
				Val Fonteyne	New York	Detroit	$20,000				

Results of the NHL Intra-League Draft, from 1954 to 1966. The Boston Bruins grabbed All-Star goalie Gerry Cheevers from the Maple Leafs in the 1965 draft.

Each minor pro club could lose a maximum of one player that it owned outright. There was no restriction on the number of minor pro players owned by an NHL club that could be taken.

The *Intra-League Draft* was established in 1952. In the Intra-League Draft, NHL clubs drafted players from other NHL organizations. Each NHL club filed a protected list of players and goaltenders who could not be drafted. Until 1965, all clubs protected eighteen skaters and two goalies. Starting that year, the league's sixth-place club was allowed to protect two additional skaters; the fifth-place, one additional.

Any other player not on the protected list – with the exception of first-year pros – could be drafted for a claiming price that began at $15,000 and was later raised to $20,000 and then $30,000. Players owned outright by minor pro clubs were ineligible. The order of draft was in inverse order of the final standings in the NHL season just completed.

A player acquired in the Intra-League Draft had to be accommodated on the protected list of the club that had drafted him. The team acquiring a player was required to drop someone from its protected list to make room for its

Two of the most successful junior operations of the 1950s, the St. Michael Majors and the St. Catharines TeePees, battle each other at Maple Leaf Gardens during the 1959-60 OHA playoffs.

new acquisition. This newly unprotected player was then eligible to be selected by another club, but the club that had lost the original player in this transaction was entitled to make first claim. No club could lose more than three players in an Intra-League Draft.

At the end of the Intra-League Draft, players who were not on protected lists and who had not been claimed by another NHL club were deemed to have cleared waivers and could then be assigned to a minor pro club.

After the Intra-League Draft was concluded, the *Reverse Draft* took place. This was a procedure by which the top minor pro clubs could draft unprotected players from NHL organizations. Clarence Campbell would give the presidents of the AHL and WHL a list of sixty players, made up of ten from each of the six NHL organizations. These players had to have a minimum of one year of professional hockey experience and have played a minimum of sixty pro games. They also were required to have participated in a minimum of thirty-five games in the previous season. These players were available for outright sale to the minor pro clubs for $10,000 per player.

When a team lost interest in a player on its reserve list or wanted to place him in the minors, he could not be released or assigned outright. Instead, he had to be offered to the other NHL organizations, each of which would have seventy-two hours to make a claim on the player. This process was known as being placed on waivers. If another club claimed a player who was on waivers, they had to pay the club losing the player a standard waiver price. This sum was $7,500 up until 1954, $15,000 from 1954 to 1965, and $30,000 thereafter.

Once a year, players could be placed on waivers with a right of recall. In these instances, a player who was claimed on waivers could be withdrawn by the club that had originally offered him. If the same player was placed on waivers a second time, the waivers were irrevocable. If claimed, the player was lost to the organization that placed him on waivers.

Between sponsorship agreements, A, B, and C forms, reserve, protected, and negotiation lists, waivers, and four different drafts, a player's path through pro hockey could be a complicated one. It was Central Registry's job to track each and every movement. Clarence Campbell was responsible for the origin of the department, and throughout his career he remained the most impartial man I've ever met in sports. Someone once described him as a stern Canadian who was very much in charge, which was accurate. He was dependable, very fair, and possessed exceptional organizational skills and a keen legal mind. He refined the entire system of sponsorship agreements and drafts, having thought out all the angles to establish a system that gave the least-successful NHL franchises a chance to improve their hockey clubs.

NHL FARM SYSTEMS: Sponsored Junior and Affiliated Minor Pro Clubs, 1965-66

BOSTON BRUINS
Niagara Falls Flyers OHA Jr. A
Stamford Jr. B
Stamford Midget
Estevan Bruins
North Battleford Jr. B
Estevan Midgets

HERSHEY BEARS (AHL)
Oshawa Generals OHA Jr. A
Oshawa Jr. B
Oshawa Midgets
Winnipeg Monarchs Jr. A

SAN FRANCISCO SEALS (WHL)
Shawinigan Bruins Jr. A
Shawinigan Juveniles
Shawinigan Midgets
Waterloo Siskins Jr. B
Waterloo Siskins Juveniles
Waterloo Siskins Midgets

OKLAHOMA CITY BLAZERS (CPHL)
Winnipeg Warriors Jr. A
Winnipeg Braves Jr. A

CHICAGO BLACK HAWKS
St. Catharines TeePees OHA Jr. A
St. Catharines Jr. B
St. Catharines Lions
"Tiger" Midgets
Dixie Beehives Jr. B
Dixie Major Midgets

BUFFALO BISONS (AHL)
Brockville Braves Jr. A
Brockville Braves Juveniles
Brockville Braves Midgets
Sarnia Jr. B Legionnaires
Sarnia Juvenile Legionnaires
Sarnia Midget Legionnaires

LOS ANGELES BLADES (WHL)
Sorel Hawks Jr. A
St. Gabriel Jr. B
Saskatoon Blades Jr. A
Saskatoon Jr. B

ST. LOUIS BRAVES (CPHL)
Sudbury Wolves Jr. A
Sudbury Cubs Jr. B
St. Jean Painters Midgets
Moose Jaw Canucks Jr. A

DETROIT RED WINGS
Weyburn Red Wings Jr. A
Lashburn Jr. B
Weyburn Midgets
Hamilton Red Wings OHA Jr. A

PITTSBURGH HORNETS (AHL)
Stratford Jr. A
Stratford Juveniles
Stratford Midgets
St. Jerome Alouettes Jr. A
Lachute Jr. B
St. Jerome Alouettes Midgets

PORTLAND BUCKEROOS (WHL)
Flin Flon Bombers Jr. A
Flin Flon Juveniles
Flin Flon Midgets
Fredericton Jr. A
Fredericton Minor Hockey

MEMPHIS WINGS (CPHL)
Edmonton Oil Kings Jr. A
South Side Jr. B Red Wings
Edmonton Canadians A.C.
Universal Concrete Juveniles
Cockshutt Arrows Midgets

MONTREAL CANADIENS
Montreal Junior Canadiens OHA Jr. A
Rosemount Jr. B
Peterborough TPT OHA Jr. A

CLEVELAND BARONS (AHL)
Kirkland Lake Legion Jr. A
Verdun Maple Leafs Jr. A
Verdun Police Jr. B

PROVIDENCE REDS (AHL)
Nationale Jr. A
St. Laurent Jets Jr. B
Maisonneuve Braves Jr. A

QUEBEC ACES (AHL)
Regina Pats Jr. A
Regina Pats Jr. B
Regina Pats Midgets

SEATTLE TOTEMS (WHL)
Columbus Canadiens Jr.
Eperviers de Hull Jr. A.
Loisirs Juveniles
Loisirs Midgets

HOUSTON APOLLOS (CPHL)
Lachine Maroons Jr. B
Lasalle Tides Juveniles
Chatham Jr. B
Chatham Juveniles
Chatham Midgets

NEW YORK RANGERS
Kitchener Rangers OHA Jr. A
Burlington Mohawks Jr. A

BALTIMORE CLIPPERS (AHL)
Kitchener Greenshirts Jr. B

ROCHESTER AMERICANS (AHL)
Three Rivers Reds Jr. A (fi interest)
St. Marguerite Juveniles
Cornwall Royals Jr. A

VANCOUVER CANUCKS (WHL)
Winnipeg Rangers Jr. A
Kingston Frontenacs Jr. A

MINNESOTA RANGERS (CPHL)
Brandon Wheat Kings Jr. A
Brandon Hockey Association
North Bay Trappers Jr. A

TORONTO MAPLE LEAFS
Toronto Marlboros OHA Jr. A
York Steel Jr. B
Toronto Marlboro Midgets
Ottawa Capitals Jr. A

ROCHESTER AMERICANS
Three Rivers Reds Jr. A (fi interest)
St. Marguerite Juveniles
Winnipeg Monarchs Jr. A

VICTORIA MAPLE LEAFS (WHL)
Calgary Buffalos Jr. A
Calgary Stampeders Juveniles
Calgary Rangers Juveniles
Melville Millionaires Jr. A

TULSA OILERS (CPHL)
London Nationals OHA Jr. A
Markham Waxers Jr. B

A total of 133 midget, juvenile, junior, and minor pro clubs were either sponsored by or affiliated with the NHL's six franchises in 1965-66.

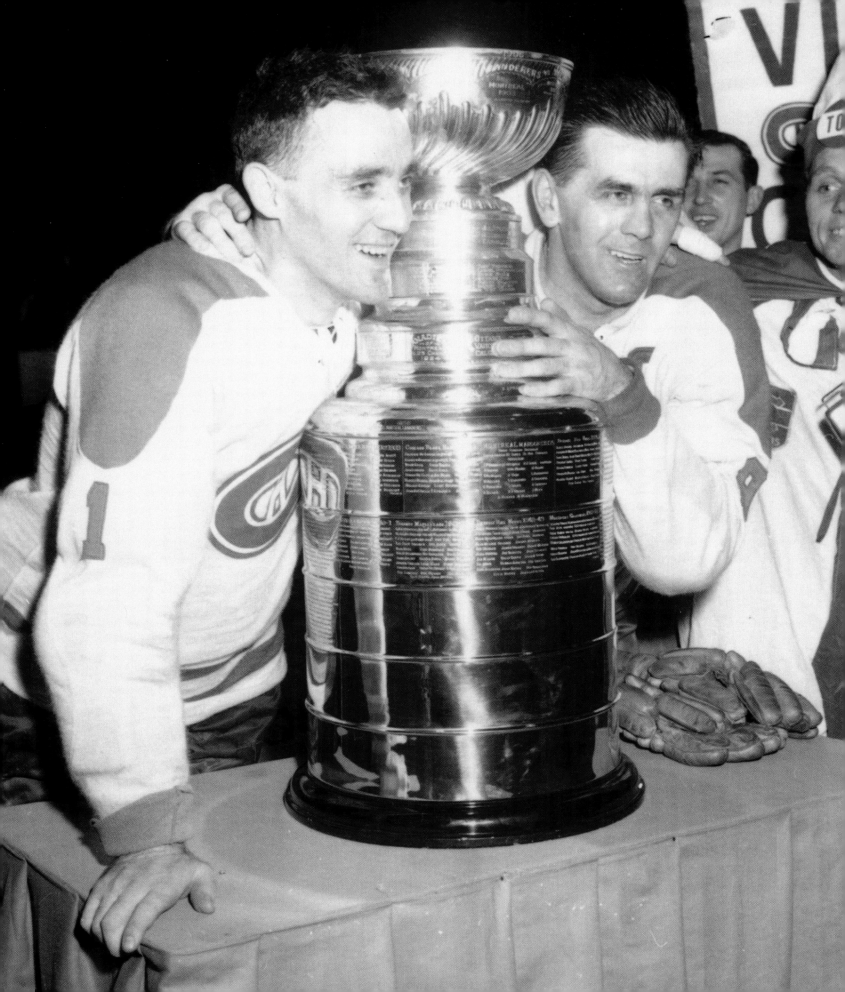

Les Canadiens sont là:
The Birth of a Dynasty
1955-56 to 1959-60

| 100 PTS. | 76 PTS. | 74 PTS. | 61 PTS. | 59 PTS. | 50 PTS. |

1955-56
Béliveau Captures Scoring Title as
Coach Blake Launches Cup Dynasty

TWO STRAIGHT LOSSES TO DETROIT IN THE STANLEY CUP FINALS, COMBINED WITH the simmering feud between the Canadiens and the Red Wings, forced the Montreal Canadiens to make a coaching change over the off-season. Dick Irvin was replaced with former Habs star Hector "Toe" Blake, who had become a successful coach with Houston of the USHL and Valleyfield of the QSHL. Irvin agreed to return to Chicago, where he had started his NHL coaching career in 1930. Montreal managing director Frank Selke confided that it was Irvin's inability to harness Rocket Richard that eventually led to his dismissal. It was felt that Blake would be able to control Richard's volatile temper, while still getting passionate performances out of the feisty right-winger.

The transition behind the bench was only one of a number of roster adjustments that the Canadiens would make in preparing for the 1955-56 season. Butch Bouchard, a stalwart on the Canadiens' defense for thirteen years, played only thirty-six games during the season, opening up a spot for newcomer Bob Turner, who assumed Bouchard's regular spot along the blueline. Henri Richard, the Rocket's younger brother, made his NHL debut, as did Claude Provost. Both players would play key roles in building the Canadiens' dynasty over the next fifteen years.

The coaching change in Montreal was a surprise, but it paled in comparison to the bombshell that fell in Detroit. Terry Sawchuk, the NHL's best goaltender, was traded to Boston, along with teammates Vic Stasiuk, Marcel Bonin, and Lorne Davis, for Norm Corcoran, Gilles Boisvert, Warren Godfrey, Ed Sandford, and Réal Chevrefils. Of the five players Detroit received, only Godfrey was still with the team when the 1955-56

Opposite: In a scene that was to be repeated every April from 1956 to 1960, Maurice Richard and Jacques Plante pose with the Stanley Cup after another Canadiens victory. Eleven players, including Richard and Plante, were members of all five Cup-winning teams.

Glenn Hall steers a rebound out of the reach of attacking Maple Leaf forwards George Armstrong (left) and Tod Sloan during a Detroit–Toronto match during the 1955-56 campaign. Hall, who had been most impressive in a six-game trial in 1952-53 and in a two-game stint in 1954-55, played all seventy games for the Red Wings in 1955-56, and finished with 12 shutouts and a 2.11 goals-against average.

season was completed. While Detroit general manager Jack Adams obviously felt that Glenn Hall was ready to take over as the club's top goaltender, most Detroit fans felt that Sawchuk should have been traded for at least one front-line player. When the Wings broke camp to begin the defense of their Stanley Cup crown, only nine players remained from the team that had captured the championship in 1955.

In an effort to resurrect the Black Hawk franchise, an airlift of talent continued to flow into Chicago. John Wilson, Glen Skov, Tony Leswick, and Benny Woit were among the new recruits who were pegged to help the Hawks climb out of the basement. Dick Irvin returned to Chicago to handle the coaching duties, while Hank Bassen was on board to back up overworked goaltender Al Rollins. Despite the influx of new players, it was generally agreed that the key to the Hawks' future was the development of the talent in their farm system.

There were high expectations in both Boston and New York. The addition of Terry Sawchuk was expected to boost the Bruins into the

NHL's top tier. Johnny Peirson came out of retirement to rejoin the Bruins, while both Vic Stasiuk and Marcel Bonin, obtained in the Sawchuk deal, were assured regular spots in the lineup. The Rangers, with Phil Watson stepping in as head coach, were vastly improved. For the first time in many seasons, the club's roster was stable. Gump Worsley was given a vote of confidence and returned as the team's number-one goaltender. Bill Gadsby, acquired from Chicago in November 1954 for Allan Stanley, was the team leader along the blueline, ably supported by Harry Howell. Andy Bathgate was coming off his first 20-goal season, while rookie Andy Hebenton impressed everyone in training camp and was penciled in on right wing.

Once again, a lack of goal-scoring appeared to be the Toronto Maple Leafs' greatest shortcoming, and it was hoped that rookies Dick Duff, Billy Harris, and Ron Hurst could add some much-needed punch to the Leafs' weak attack.

In the early going, the Montreal Canadiens jumped into a commanding lead in the standings. Jacques Plante was outstanding in goal, and he was the center of media attention for his wandering ways outside of the

Alex Delvecchio (far left) leads the attack as the Red Wings and the Black Hawks clash in the crease during the 1955-56 season. Chicago netminder Hank Bassen holds the fort as Black Hawk defenders Allan Stanley (4) and Glen Skov (14) attempt to clear Detroit's Marty Pavelich (11) from the slot.

Although he had seen only limited action with the AHL's Pittsburgh Hornets and Buffalo Bisons in his first three seasons as a professional, Ed Chadwick was outstanding in his brief trial with the Maple Leafs in 1955-56. In his first five NHL games, Chadwick recorded two shutouts and a remarkable 0.60 goals-against average, a performance that earned him the Leafs' number-one goaltending job the following year.

Red's Reversal

On October 16, 1955, three-time Lady Byng Trophy-winner Red Kelly of Detroit received twenty-two penalty minutes in one period. Kelly was assessed a two-minute minor, then fought with Toronto's Eric Nesterenko and got a double major and a ten-minute misconduct. Until that time, Kelly had a career average of less than sixteen penalty minutes a season.

Canadiens' goal crease. Plante would roam behind the goal to stop the puck for his defenseman or pass it up to his backchecking forwards. He would also leave the crease and dive on loose pucks, freezing the disc to create a stoppage in play. This habit caught the attention of the league's rule committee, and they soon passed a new edict, forbidding goalies from leaving the crease to smother loose pucks unless an opposing player was on the verge of getting a scoring chance.

The most powerful aspect of the Canadiens' attack was their devastating power play, which accounted for 25 goals in the team's first 22 games. (At this time, a penalized player served his full two minutes, even if the team with the manpower advantage scored a goal.) In a game against Boston on November 5, Jean Béliveau scored three goals in forty-four seconds on the same power play, while Hal Laycoe of the Bruins sat in the penalty box.

Béliveau's hat-trick was the second-fastest three-goal effort in NHL history. Even an injury to Jacques Plante failed to stem the Habs' tide. With Plante out with a broken nose, substitute goaltender Robert "Miche" Perreault won three of the six games he appeared in, compiling a goals-against average of 2.00. At the mid-point of the season, the Canadiens held a commanding lead over the surprising Rangers and the faltering Red Wings.

The 1955-56 season marked the coming of age of Jean Béliveau, who put all aspects of his game together to collect 47 goals and lead the NHL in scoring with 88 points. Maurice Richard was also back on track, playing alongside his younger brother, Henri. The Rocket's 38 goals were the most he had scored since he notched 42 in 1950-51. Dickie Moore, Bert Olmstead, and Bernie Geoffrion also had stellar seasons for the Canadiens, who joined the Red Wings as the only teams to finish with 100 points in the standings. Jacques Plante recorded 42 victories, seven shutouts, and a miserly 1.86 goals-against average.

With the roster-shuffling in Detroit, it took the team some time to finally click. While many experts felt the trading of Sawchuk would hamper the team defensively, Glenn Hall was spectacular in the Wings' net. Offensively, however, the Wings struggled. Coach Jimmy Skinner moved Red Kelly up to the forward line in an attempt to bolster the team's sagging goal totals, but the strategy was shortlived. At the halfway mark of the season, the Wings stood mired in third place, the first time since 1948 that Detroit wasn't in top spot at the mid-season break. In the second half of the season, Gordie Howe went on a tear, scoring 12 goals in eight games as the Wings climbed above the slumping Rangers into second place. Although they were much improved, the Wings were unable to overcome their poor start and finished second to the Canadiens, twenty-four points behind Montreal. Freshman Norm Ullman, who starred for the Wings' farm team in Edmonton, made his NHL debut, amassing 18 points in 66 games.

Phil Watson was given much of the credit for the improved play of the Rangers. The Broadway Blueshirts had the finest season in their history, setting team records for points with 74 and for wins with 32 to finish in third place, only two points behind the Red Wings. Individual stars for the Rangers included Andy Hebenton, who fired 24 goals in his rookie season, Andy Bathgate, who collected 66 points, and Bill Gadsby, who led all NHL rearguards in scoring with 51 points. Over the course of the season, the Rangers sacrificed defense for a

Terry Sawchuk, who notched nine shutouts for the Bruins in his first season in the Boston net, watches teammate Fernie Flaman and Detroit's Lorne Ferguson (14) battle for a high-flying loose puck. Doug Mohns (left), Metro Prystai (12), and Bill Dineen (17) are the other interested observers.

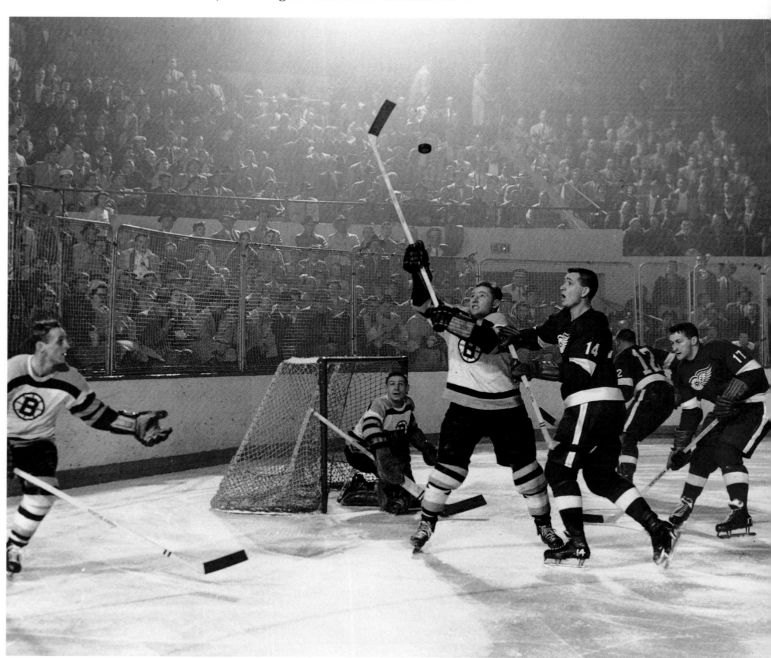

Jean Béliveau's break-through season with the Canadiens occurred in 1955-56 when "le Gros Bill" led the league in goals (47) and points (88).

The Detroit Red Wings' attempt to match the Toronto Maple Leafs' mark of three successive Stanley Cup titles was derailed by the Montreal Canadiens in the 1955-56 finals. The Habs, bolstered by Jean Béliveau's seven goals, defeated the Red Wings in five games.

potent, consistent attack. They scored a team-record 204 goals, with nine of the squad's forwards reaching double figures in goals.

The decline of the Toronto Maple Leafs continued in 1955-56, as the team fell into fourth place with a 24–33–13 record. Coach King Clancy was at a loss to find an offensive scheme that would help the Leafs, who managed only 153 goals in the 70-game schedule. Tod Sloan was Toronto's lone bright light, scoring 37 goals and adding 29 assists to lead the club in scoring. Eric Nesterenko, once touted as the team's future superstar, was dispatched to the Winnipeg Warriors of the minor pro WHL. The Leafs' fortunes took a further dive when Harry Lumley was injured and was forced to miss 11 games. Replacement Gilles Mayer lost five of the six games he appeared in, but Ed Chadwick showed great promise, going undefeated in five games with a commendable 0.60 goals-against average. One of the highlights of the season was the play of winger Gerry James. James, a halfback and place kicker for football's Winnipeg Blue Bombers, was named a Western Inter-provincial Football Union all-star. He joined the Leafs after the football season and picked up six points in 46 games.

One season after leading the NHL in victories, Terry Sawchuk led the league in defeats during the 1955-56 season. Boston, touted as a possible league champion in the early-season polls, dropped to fifth place, going 4–5–1 in their last ten games to finish two points behind the fourth-place Maple Leafs. The Bruins' top scorer was Vic Stasiuk, who managed 37 points over the season, despite missing a month of play after the removal of a blood clot in his leg. Injuries and dissension were key factors in the Bruins' decline, as only Cal Gardner and veteran Bill Quackenbush, in his final NHL season, managed to play all 70 games.

The Chicago Black Hawks improved slightly in 1955-56, but it wasn't enough to keep them out of the NHL cellar. Red Sullivan, Nick Mickoski, Ed Litzenberger, and Johnny Wilson were the leading scorers on the last-place club. As was the case in the previous season, the team played some games in non-NHL rinks, with four contests set for St. Louis and one for Omaha.

At the NHL Board of Governors meeting in December, it was decided to change the uniform worn by referees and linesmen from the orange sweater with black piping that was currently in use to a black-and-white striped jersey that could easily be distinguished from players' uniforms by television viewers.

The Rangers' reward for making the playoffs was a first-round encounter with the Montreal Canadiens. In the opening game, the Habs blitzed the Rangers, scoring six goals in the final two periods to win, 7–1. Gump Worsley was burdened by a gimpy knee and didn't look sharp for New York, prompting a goaltending change. In game two, Gordie Bell was promoted from Trois Rivières to take Worsley's place. Bell, who hadn't played in the NHL since the 1945-46 season, was spectacular in leading the Rangers to a 4–2 victory over the Canadiens. The Habs heeded this wake-up call, sweeping the remaining three games, including a 7–0 shutout in game five. Maurice Richard tied an NHL record with five assists in the game, as the Canadiens earned a berth in the Stanley Cup finals for a sixth consecutive year. The Canadiens' opponent in the championship round was the Red Wings, setting up the possibility of a third consecutive Cup championship for Detroit. While it was true that the Wings looked sharp in downing the Leafs in a five-game semi-final series win, they would have their hands full slowing down Montreal's high-powered attack.

Game one of the finals proved to be a case in point. The Red Wings controlled the flow of play over the opening forty minutes, and entered the final frame with a commanding 4–2 advantage. Early in the third period, Jack Leclair, Bernie Geoffrion, and Jean Béliveau scored in a two-minute span to erase the Canadiens' deficit en route to a 6–4 win by the Habs.

Montreal continued its relentless assault in game two, using a short-handed goal by Don Marshall to take a quick 1–0 lead in the first period. The Richard brothers, Bernie Geoffrion, and Jean Béliveau also scored for Montreal as the Habs took a two-game lead in the championship final. Detroit won the third game, 3–1, with a pair of late third-period goals to get back into the series, but the Canadiens responded with a 3–0 win in game four to move within a single victory of their seventh Stanley Cup title.

Game five was played cautiously, with no scoring until the mid-point of the match. Then, with Marcel Pronovost of the Red Wings in the penalty box for tripping, the vaunted Montreal power play went to work, connecting for a pair of goals in a fifty-two-second span. The eventual Stanley Cup-winning goal was scored by Maurice Richard, who had been suspended from the previous season's playoffs. Bernie Geoffrion added a third goal just thirteen seconds into the final period to put the victory and the Stanley Cup banner in the Canadiens' hands. Alex Delvecchio attempted to mount a Detroit comeback with a goal only twenty-two seconds after Geoffrion's marker, but the Canadiens held on for a 3–1 win. Jean Béliveau led the way for the Habs with 12 goals in 10 games and joined Richard and Butch Bouchard in receiving the Stanley Cup. Bouchard, who dressed for most of the games but saw on-ice action in only one contest, announced his retirement shortly after the victorious Canadiens returned to Montreal.

In the post-season award presentations, Glenn Hall won the Calder Trophy, Doug Harvey narrowly defeated Bill Gadsby for the Norris Trophy, Jean Béliveau took home both the Art Ross and the Hart trophies, while Dutch Reibel of Detroit won the Lady Byng.

HABS DEFEAT DETROIT TO WIN '56 CUP

Jean Béliveau and Rocket Richard each scored during a second-period penalty to Marcel Pronovost. This would prove to be the last time in NHL history that two goals would be scored on the same minor penalty. Beginning in 1956-57, players serving a minor penalty were allowed to return to the ice if their team was scored upon.

April 10, 1956
at Montreal Forum
Montreal 3, Detroit 1

FIRST PERIOD
No Scoring
PENALTIES — Hillman DET (elbowing) 2:48; Provost MTL (slashing) 6:42; H. Richard MTL (hooking) 9:35; Howe DET (charging), Harvey MTL (slashing) 10:47.

SECOND PERIOD
1) MTL Béliveau 12 (Curry, Harvey) PPG 14:16
2) MTL M. Richard 5 (Geoffrion, Béliveau) PPG 15:08
PENALTIES — Harvey MTL (holding) :42; Lindsay DET (highsticking), Béliveau MTL (highsticking) 6:30; St. Laurent MTL (highsticking) 9:56; Pronovost DET (tripping) 13:50.

THIRD PERIOD
3) MTL Geoffrion 5 (Béliveau, Olmstead) :13
4) DET Delvecchio 7 (Lindsay) :35
PENALTIES — Kelly DET (tripping) 7:07; M. Richard MTL (hooking) 12:11.

SHOTS ON GOAL	1	2	3	T
DETROIT	7	10	9	26
MONTREAL	11	8	11	30

GOALTENDERS	TIME	SA	GA	ENG	W/L
DET Hall	60:00	27	3	0	L
MTL Plante	60:00	25	1	0	W

PP CONVERSIONS   DET 0/5   MTL 2/3

88 PTS.   82 PTS.   80 PTS.   66 PTS.   57 PTS.   47 PTS.

1956-57

Howe Tops Scoring,
but Montreal Defeats Boston for Second Cup

THE NHL MADE ONE MAJOR RULE CHANGE FOR THE 1956-57 SEASON. AFTER watching the Montreal Canadiens' devastating power play throughout the 1955-56 campaign, Clarence Campbell, now in his second decade as the NHL's president, devised a new rule that allowed a player serving a two-minute minor penalty to return to the ice if his team was scored upon while he was in the penalty box. This rule limited the "price" paid by the team committing an infraction to a maximum of one goal-against.

There were only minor roster changes when the six franchises opened their pre-season training camps in the fall of 1956. Most clubs preferred to stand pat on the trade front, promoting talent from within their organizations.

In Montreal, the defending Stanley Cup champions approached the new season with the same cast of superstars, especially behind the blueline. The Habs' back-line crew of Plante, Harvey, Jean-Guy Talbot, Johnson, Turner, and St. Laurent was so strong that even the retirement of future Hall-of-Famer Butch Bouchard didn't weaken the team defensively. André Pronovost, a young left-winger from Shawinigan, Quebec, was given a full-time spot on the Habs' roster, replacing Kenny Mosdell, who was loaned to Chicago for the season.

After losing both their regular-season and playoff crowns to Montreal, it was expected that the Wings would undergo a makeover, but Jack Adams resisted tampering with his team. Al Arbour was added to replace retiring veteran Bob Goldham, while Billy Dea, obtained from the Rangers in 1955, was finally promoted to the big club.

Milt Schmidt and his Boston Bruins appeared to be capable of a much better effort than that of the previous year. Boston's defense, which allowed 185 goals in 1955-56, was their major concern. Two veteran defenders, Hal Laycoe and Bill Quackenbush, retired, leaving two roster spots open. Allan Stanley, a steady, no-nonsense rearguard, was acquired from Chicago. Although Stanley was "booed off Broadway" when he was a member of the New York Rangers, he was expected to stabilize a shaky Boston blueline. Jack Bionda, picked up as a Toronto Maple Leaf castoff, was the Bruins' fifth rearguard.

There was a change behind the Maple Leafs' bench for the 1956-57 season. King Clancy stepped aside and Howie Meeker, who had retired as a player in 1954, was named as his replacement. The Leafs had struggled for most of the decade, but continued to build from within their farm system. Bob Pulford, Bob Baun, and Al MacNeil all saw NHL duty during the season. Perhaps the biggest roster surprise was the promotion of Ed Chadwick as the Leafs' number-one goaltender. Harry Lumley and Eric Nesterenko were sold to Chicago on May 21, 1956.

Another coaching change occurred in Chicago, where Dick Irvin resigned as coach because of health problems, and Black Hawk general manager Tommy Ivan added the club's coaching duties to his portfolio. Teams around the NHL continued to offer their excess talent to the Black Hawks, but it was the young players who were the key to the Black Hawks' fortunes. Elmer "Moose" Vasko joined Pierre Pilote on the Hawks' defense to add size and strength to Pilote's natural offensive abilities. Stocky center Forbes Kennedy was the Hawks' lone rookie forward.

After their most successful regular season in history, the New York Rangers were confident that the likes of Bathgate, Hebenton, Prentice, Gadsby, and Howell would lead the Blueshirts back into the post-season.

Two keys to the Montreal Canadiens' success in 1956-57 was an explosive offensive attack and a stubborn defense led by All-Star rearguard Doug Harvey and Vezina Trophy-winning goaltender Jacques Plante. Harvey, who led all NHL blueliners with 50 points, captured his third consecutive Norris Trophy as the league's top defenseman.

Coach Phil Watson was hesitant to disrupt his solid mix of youth and age, adding only Parker MacDonald and Gerry Foley, both purchased from the Leafs, to the roster.

An assortment of injuries to the front-running Montreal Canadiens made the playoff sprint a four-team race in 1956-57. Three Canadiens stars, Geoffrion, Maurice Richard, and Henri Richard, all suffered elbow injuries. Both Richard brothers missed seven games, while Geoffrion was out of action for twenty-nine matches. Jacques Plante, suffering from chronic asthma, was out of the Canadiens' lineup for nine games, during which the Habs won four and lost five. Gerry McNeil, who came out of retirement in 1954 to coach in the Quebec junior league and, later, to play in the Quebec Professional Hockey League, played the final nine games of his NHL career in Plante's absence.

The change in the power-play rules didn't seem to affect the Habs' dynamic offense, as they scored a league-high 210 goals over the course of the season. Jean Béliveau, who led the Canadiens in assists (51) and points (84), also tied Rocket Richard for the team lead in goals with 33. The Canadiens, led by Jacques Plante's league-leading 2.02 goals-against average, had the NHL's lowest goals-against total, allowing just 155 goals in 70 games.

Detroit took full advantage of Montreal's misfortunes to return to first place, although only eight points separated first from third. The tandem of Gordie Howe and Ted Lindsay finished one–two in the NHL points race, with Howe edging out his teammate for the scoring crown by four points. Howe led the NHL in goals with 44, while Lindsay led all set-up artists with 55 assists. Both of the Red Wings' big-gunners reached career milestones during the season. On November 18, Lindsay became the fourth player in NHL history to score 300 career goals, when he connected twice in the Wings' 8–3 victory over Montreal. On December 15, Howe scored his 325th career goal, surpassing Nels Stewart to become the second-highest scorer in league history. Al Rollins, who surrendered Howe's 200th and 300th career goals, was victimized again for his 325th. Glenn Hall continued his impressive play in goal for Detroit, compiling a 2.24 goals-against average with four shutouts.

One of the surprises of the season was the play of the Boston Bruins. Expected to be a Stanley Cup contender in the previous campaign, the Bruins reached those expectations in 1956-57, despite being forced to play without All-Star goaltender Terry Sawchuk, who was unable to participate due to stress-related illness. The Bruins, who didn't have a single 20-goal scorer in 1955-56, had four players reach the 20-goal plateau in 1956-57, led by Réal Chevrefils, who connected for 31 goals. Forwards Don McKenney, Fleming Mackell, and Vic Stasiuk all had excellent offensive campaigns for the improving Bruins, as did rearguards Fernie Flaman and Allan Stanley. Rookie right-winger Larry Regan also

Réal Chevrefils, who played briefly in Detroit in 1955-56 before being traded back to Boston, had the finest season of his career in 1956-57, collecting 31 goals and 48 points in 70 games for the third-place Bruins.

Real Chevrefils

impressed the Boston fans, collecting 33 points in his first skate around NHL rinks.

In December, Terry Sawchuk became ill with a blood disorder and was hospitalized for two weeks. After returning to the lineup for a couple of games, Sawchuk left the team on January 16, citing exhaustion and emotional strain. He later retired and would not return to the team for the remainder of the campaign. Sawchuk's departure forced the Bruins to acquire rookie goaltender Don Simmons from Springfield of the AHL. Simmons was a major factor in Boston's third-place finish, registering 13 victories, 4 shutouts, and a 2.42 goals-against average.

The Rangers earned the fourth playoff spot, but the team struggled most of the season, finishing the campaign with a record of 26–30–14. Andy Bathgate led all Rangers in scoring with 27 goals and 50 assists. The Rangers had an effective offensive attack with Bathgate, Hebenton,

The woes in Chicago continued through 1956-57, as the Black Hawks finished in the league basement for the fourth consecutive season. Despite the club's poor overall performance, one bright spot was goaltender Al Rollins, seen here battling his former Maple Leaf teammates. Rollins registered three shutouts and a goals-against average of 3.21.

Montreal sharpshooter Bernie "Boom-Boom" Geoffrion fires the puck past Gump Worsley in the Canadiens' 7–3 win over the New York Rangers in game three of the 1957 semi-finals. Geoffrion would go on to lead all post-season scorers in 1957 with 11 goals and 18 points as Montreal downed the Rangers and Bruins to win their second straight Stanley Cup title.

Prentice, and Creighton, but coach Phil Watson's biggest problems were on defense and in goal. Struggling behind a porous defense, Gump Worsley slumped to a 3.24 goals-against average, while the team allowed a league-high 227 goals.

Howie Meeker's Toronto Maple Leafs continued their downward spiral, and, for the fourth consecutive season, the offense was among the league's worst. Only the Black Hawks scored fewer goals than the Leafs in 1956-57. In an effort to raise team morale and punch up the attack, Ted Kennedy came out of retirement and joined the team for the second half of the schedule. Kennedy collected 22 points in 30 games, but it wasn't enough to boost the Leafs into a playoff spot. They managed only 174 goals in the 70-game schedule, fourteen of those coming in a 14–1 shelling of the Rangers on March 16. Dick Duff led the team with 26 goals, the only Leaf to reach the 20-goal plateau. Ed Chadwick appeared in all 70 games for Toronto, and although he registered a respectable 2.74 goals-against average, he couldn't lift the team by himself. Yet there was promise on the horizon. Pulford, Horton, Armstrong, and Duff formed the basis of a strong nucleus, while rookie Frank Mahovlich, who made his debut at the conclusion of the regular season, was expected to be the offensive sparkplug the team so desperately needed.

There was not much improvement in Chicago, where Tommy Ivan's troops finished in the basement for the fourth consecutive season. Featuring a roster stocked with veterans, the team clearly needed a healthy infusion of young talent if it were going to overcome its dismal showing. Ed Litzenberger continued to be the club's best forward, finishing in fifth place in the NHL scoring race with 32 goals and an equal number of assists.

In the semi-finals, the much-improved Boston Bruins threw a tight-checking blanket around Detroit's top unit of Howe, Lindsay, and Delvecchio and escaped with a five-game victory in the best-of-seven series. Detroit managed only seven goals in their four losses to the confident Bruins, while Boston received stellar efforts from Simmons, Chevrefils, and Mackell in winning 3–1, 4–3, 2–0, and 4–3. In the other semi-final series, the Montreal Canadiens defeated the New York Rangers in five games, but needed an overtime goal by Rocket Richard to win game five.

The 1957 Stanley Cup finals began on April 6 at the Montreal Forum, and the game proved to be one of Rocket Richard's greatest playoff performances. He connected for a quartet of goals in Montreal's 5–1 win, the third time in his career that he had scored at least four goals in a Stanley Cup playoff game. The Bruins were able to collar Richard in game two, but, in playing their tight defensive game, were unable to maintain any attack of their own. Jean Béliveau scored the only goal the Canadiens would need at 2:27 of the second period, and Jacques Plante closed the door from there, as Montreal took a commanding two-game advantage.

In game three, the Canadiens pounced on the Boston defense for three first-period goals, including a pair from the stick of Bernie Geoffrion. The Habs hung on to win 4–2, putting them one victory away from their first back-to-back titles since 1929-30 and 1930-31. Reverting to the style that worked against the Red Wings, the Bruins were able to combine opportunistic scoring and airtight defense to stay alive in the series with a 2–0 victory in game four. Fleming Mackell connected for both Boston goals, and Don Simmons registered his first Stanley Cup-final shutout. Dickie Moore was the star of the fifth game for Montreal, assisting on a pair of goals while scoring what eventually turned out to be the Stanley Cup-winning goal at the fourteen-second mark of the second period. André Pronovost, Bernie Geoffrion, Donnie Marshall, and Floyd Curry added goals, as the Habs defended their Stanley Cup title with a 5–1 victory.

In addition to winning his fifth Art Ross Trophy, Gordie Howe captured his third Hart Trophy and earned a berth on the First All-Star Team. Jacques Plante took home the Vezina, Doug Harvey captured the Norris for the third time, and Boston's Larry Regan won Calder as the league's best rookie.

Dick Irvin, the pioneer player who went on to win 690 games as a coach in the NHL, passed away on May 16, 1957, shortly after being hospitalized for anemia. He was sixty-four. Teams coached by Irvin had reached the Stanley Cup finals in 16 of 26 seasons.

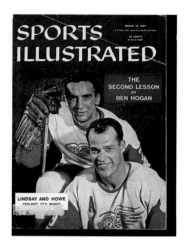

Sports Illustrated *saluted Detroit Red Wing stars Ted Lindsay and Gordie Howe during the 1956-57 season. Lindsay topped all NHL playmakers with 55 assists, while Howe returned to top of the league's scoring ladder with 44 goals and 89 points.*

BOSTON UPSETS DETROIT IN FINALE OF '57 SEMI-FINALS

Boston's semi-final victory over Detroit ended the Red Wings' hopes of meeting Montreal in the final for the fourth consecutive year.

April 4, 1957
at Detroit Olympia
Boston 4, Detroit 3

FIRST PERIOD
1) DET Delvecchio 3 (Howe, Lindsay) 9:52
PENALTIES – Caffery BOS (charging) 7:52; Pronovost DET (spearing) 14:32; Gardner BOS (highsticking), Howe DET (crosschecking) 15:38; Caffery BOS (tripping) 16:55.

SECOND PERIOD
2) BOS Boone 1 (Mackell, Mohns) 12:10
PENALTIES – Pavelich DET (highsticking) 2:44; Pavelich DET (highsticking) 10:02; Boivin BOS (boarding) 13:12.

THIRD PERIOD
3) DET Lindsay 2 (Howe) :36
4) BOS Labine 1 (McKenney, Mohns) 6:18
5) BOS Mohns 2 (McKenney) 10:21
6) BOS Gardner 2 (Bionda, Peirson) 15:16
7) DET Prystai 2 (Delvecchio, Bailey) 17:59
PENALTIES – None

SHOTS ON GOAL	1	2	3	T
BOSTON	3	6	6	15
DETROIT	11	6	9	26

GOALTENDERS	TIME	SA	GA	ENG	W/L
BOS Simmons	60:00	23	3	0	W
DET Hall	59:10*	11	4	0	L

*unofficial estimate, left net for extra skater late in third period.

PP CONVERSIONS BOS 0/3 DET 0/3

| 96 PTS. | 77 PTS. | 70 PTS. | 69 PTS. | 55 PTS. | 53 PTS. |

1957-58
Dickie Moore Earns Scoring Crown
Despite Broken Wrist

IN FEBRUARY 1957, A GROUP OF PLAYERS, SPEARHEADED BY DETROIT'S TED Lindsay, Toronto's Jim Thomson, and Montreal's Doug Harvey, gathered to discuss plans for the formation of an association of NHL players. Conn Smythe was one of the more vocal opponents to the new union and, in his annual year-end address to the media after the conclusion of the 1956-57 season, voiced his disappointment in Thomson for serving as the association's secretary. Later that summer, Smythe sold Thomson to the Black Hawks, last-place finishers in nine of the last eleven seasons. Thomson was soon joined in exile by NHLPA president Ted Lindsay, who was dispatched to Chicago by Jack Adams.

While the owners may have disapproved of the fledgling union, the players continued to gather strength and confidence over the course of the 1957-58 season. One of the association's first actions was to launch a $3,000,000 lawsuit against the NHL, its member clubs, and seven individuals including NHL president Clarence Campbell. The lawsuit sought increased pension benefits and a larger share of television revenues for the players. In Toronto, members of the Maple Leafs applied to the Ontario Labour Relations Board, seeking official certification as a bargaining unit. However, as time went on, there was growing dissension amongst the players. Detroit captain Red Kelly informed Lindsay and the rest of the NHLPA members that Red Wing players were withdrawing from the union, feeling that the lawsuit brought against the NHL represented bad-faith bargaining on the part of the players.

On February 5, 1958, the players' association and the owners met for the first time. Although the owners refused to recognize the existence of the union, they did submit to a few of its demands. In return for the withdrawal of the lawsuit, the NHL agreed to increase player pensions, enhance hospitalization benefits, increase minimum NHL salaries to $7,000, pay the players a larger share of the playoff pool, and reduce the number of pre-season exhibition games.

While peace was restored, it was a cautious truce. Many owners and team executives were concerned about the effects of the failed union and stifled any future attempts to re-form the organization. It would be eight years before the players gathered enough support to try again.

Fashion Statement

Beginning in 1957-58, the New York Rangers had their gloves painted red, white, and blue. This was the first time that an NHL club coordinated the color of its gloves with that of its uniforms. The Toronto Maple Leafs switched to colored gloves the following season. The Detroit Red Wings were the last club to retain natural-colored gloves, wearing them to the end of the six-team era.

There were a number of transactions during the off-season, with the Detroit Red Wings leading the trade parade. In a surprise move, Jack Adams swapped John Bucyk to the Bruins to re-acquire Terry Sawchuk, who promised he would come out of retirement to join the Wings. He then traded Ted Lindsay and goaltender Glenn Hall to Chicago for Johnny Wilson, Hank Bassen, William Preston, and Forbes Kennedy. Neither move brought the desired result for Detroit, as Sawchuk struggled to regain his previous form while Hall and Bucyk would go on to star in the NHL until the 1970s.

The main beneficiaries of this player movement were the Chicago Black Hawks, who received a star goaltender in Hall, a steady defender in Jim Thomson, and a veteran presence in the dressing room in Lindsay. With promising newcomer Bobby Hull joining the team, and steady winger Ron Murphy coming over from the Rangers, the Black Hawks were poised to end years of frustration.

In Boston, the Stanley Cup-finalist Bruins added two important players to their roster. Johnny Bucyk was acquired from Detroit, and Joseph "Bronco" Horvath was claimed from Montreal in the Intra-League Draft. Both players would play key roles in the success of the franchise in the rest of the 1950s. Other additions included Harry Lumley, signed to back up Don Simmons, and rearguard Larry Hillman, who arrived from Detroit.

Confusion ruled the day in Toronto, where Howie Meeker became the first man to be fired as general manager before his team played a game under his control. Meeker had coached the Leafs in 1956-57, but after Conn Smythe pressured Hap Day into retiring, he gave Meeker the general manager's job while simultaneously replacing him with Billy Reay as coach. It didn't sound as if Meeker had the confidence of the crusty Smythe, who said, "All theory and no practice was Meeker's problem. If he had a team made up of Rocket Richard and four more like him, he still couldn't win."

During the off-season, Smythe had turned control of the Leafs over to his son, Stafford, whose first order of business was to fire Meeker, saying he didn't have the experience to be a general manager. Stafford Smythe told the media that he and his six partners, known collectively as the "Silver Seven," would run the club for the 1957-58 season. The other members of the glittering septet – Harold Ballard, John Bassett, George Mara, Jack Amell, George Gardiner, and Bill Hatch – were all members of the Leafs' new board of governors.

Things were not much smoother for the Leafs on the ice. With the front office undergoing a major overhaul, it was decided to stay with basically the same squad that had missed the playoffs in 1956-57. Frank Mahovlich, a talented left-winger who scored one goal in his three-game trial at the conclusion of the 1956-57 season, was the lone newcomer.

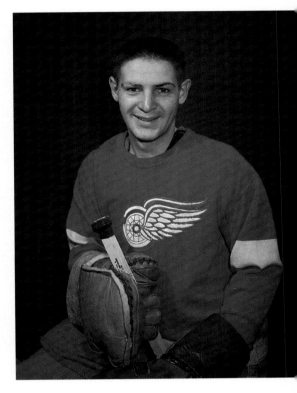

After Detroit failed to reach the Stanley Cup finals for the first time in three seasons, Jack Adams sent John Bucyk to Boston to re-acquire Terry Sawchuk. Sawchuk played all 70 games for the Red Wings in 1957-58, winning 29 and posting a trio of shutouts.

Montreal's dynamic Richard brothers, Maurice (left) and Henri, both contributed to the Habs' success in 1957-58. Henri, dubbed the "Pocket Rocket," led all NHL playmakers with 52 regular-season assists. The Rocket enjoyed one of his greatest postseasons, scoring 11 playoff goals, including his NHL-record sixth overtime marker in game five of the Boston–Montreal final.

A Checkered Past

At the suggestion of retired Bruins ex-manager Art Ross, the NHL altered the center red line from a solid red band to a checkered pattern during the late 1950s. The checkered line could be easily distinguished from the bluelines on black-and-white television.

Coach Phil Watson was hesitant to tamper with the lineup of his New York Ranger team, adding only Marcel Paille and Henry Ciesla to the everyday lineup. With Camille Henry back from a tutorial in the minors, and Andy Bathgate ready to assume superstar status, Watson was confident the Rangers could make a concerted run at the Stanley Cup.

In Montreal, coach Toe Blake could sit back and admire the most powerful lineup ever assembled in the history of the NHL. He had potent scoring in Moore, Olmstead, Béliveau, and Richard, hard-checking forwards in Marshall and Provost, two of the league's top defensemen in Harvey and Johnson, and one of hockey's finest goaltenders in Jacques Plante. It's not surprising that the Habs ran away with the NHL title in 1957-58, becoming the first team to score 250 goals in a 70-game schedule. Dickie Moore led the league in goals (36) and points (84), while the "Pocket Rocket," Henri Richard, assumed the league lead in assists, setting up 52 goals over the course of the season. On October 19, Rocket Richard became the first player to reach the 500-goal bracket when he slid a pass from Jean Béliveau past Chicago's Glenn Hall for the milestone goal. It was to be the only bright spot in an otherwise gloomy period for the NHL's all-time scorer. On November 13, in a game against Toronto, the Rocket severed his Achilles' tendon and missed 42 games.

The depth of the Montreal organization would be severely tested during this season. Besides the Rocket's injury, Geoffrion, Béliveau, Olmstead, and Plante would also miss considerable time. Béliveau was out for 15 games, Olmstead missed 13, while Geoffrion suffered a ruptured bowel and was in critical condition for a few days. He missed a total of 28 games. Plante, who again suffered from asthma, was absent from the lineup for 12 games, but was replaced by Charlie Hodge, Len Broderick, and Don Aiken. Interestingly, both Broderick and Aiken were amateur goalies, called in at the last moment to replace Plante. Rightwinger Dickie Moore fractured his wrist, but continued to play and lead the league in scoring while wearing a cast. Despite this injury toll, the Habs rolled to the league title with 43 wins and 96 points.

It was a season to remember in New York, where the Rangers climbed to second place, their highest finish since 1941-42. Both Andy Bathgate and Camille Henry reached the 30-goal mark, while Dave Creighton, Dean Prentice, and Andy Hebenton continued to supply steady production. The defense, anchored by Bill Gadsby, who had 46 points, and by Harry Howell, drastically reduced the team's goals-against, allowing Gump Worsley to return to form with an excellent 2.32 goals-against average.

There was great concern in Detroit, where the Red Wings struggled in the early stages of the season. When the season started, coach Jimmy Skinner had Howe and Delvecchio paired with rookie Guyle Fielder.

Fielder, a prodigious scorer in the minor leagues, lasted only six games before being returned to the farm. He would go on to be the first player in hockey history to collect 2,000 career points, but he never registered a single point in the NHL. The team was still floundering in fifth place in mid-December when Jack Adams engineered an eight-player trade with Chicago, sending Dutch Reibel, Bill Dineen, Billy Dea, and Lorne Ferguson to the Black Hawks for Bob Bailey, Jack McIntyre, Nick Mickoski, and Hec Lalande. Shortly after making the trade, Adams fired Skinner as coach, replacing him with former Red Wing captain Sid Abel. These moves lit a fire under the underachieving Wings, who were resting comfortably in third place by the end of the season.

When Boston bench boss Milt Schmidt decided to place three players of Ukrainian descent on the same line, the fortunes of the Bruins took a decided upswing. John Bucyk, Vic Stasiuk, and Bronco Horvath, known collectively as the "Uke Line," combined to score 72 goals and 174 points. Six members of the Boston team hit the 20-goal plateau: the three Ukes, plus the club's second line of Don McKenney, Fleming Mackell, and Jerry Toppazzini.

The Bruins needed a diversified offense, as they were required to dress five different goaltenders during the season. Don Simmons was injured for much of the campaign, forcing Schmidt to use Harry Lumley, Al

The New York Rangers climbed into second place during the 1957-58 season, thanks in part to outstanding performances by Andy Bathgate (first row, far right) and Bill Gadsby (second row, far right). Bathgate finished third in league scoring with 78 points, while Gadsby topped all blueliners with 46 points.

The "Topper," Jerry Toppazzini, was tops for the Bruins during the 1957-58 playoffs, turning in the performance of his career. Toppazzini, who had failed to score a goal in his previous twenty-one playoff games, connected nine times for the Bruins, who were defeated by the Canadiens in a six-game final series.

The Other Crease

To halt the practice of players chasing officials all over the ice to argue a decision, in 1957-58 a semi-circle with a ten-foot diameter was painted on the ice in front of the scorer's bench. Players were prohibited from entering this referee's crease to argue with officials during stoppages in play.

Millar, and Claude Evans in his place. In a December 29 tilt against Detroit, Boston was forced to use Red Wings trainer Lefty Wilson in goal after Simmons dislocated his shoulder. It was the third time Wilson was called upon to play goal in an NHL game, and he kept his undefeated record intact as the Bruins and Wings battled to a 2–2 tie. Boston scored 199 goals during the season, the second-highest total to that point in team history, but the team also allowed 194 goals, which kept it in fourth place with a 27–28–15 record.

A piece of history was recorded on February 1, when the Bruins became the first NHL team to dress a black player. Willie O'Ree, a talented winger who scored 22 goals with Quebec in 1956-57, was promoted to the Bruins and appeared in two games.

Despite compiling the third-highest point total in franchise history, the Chicago Black Hawks missed the playoffs for the twelfth time in fourteen seasons, though there were signs that the Hawks were finally on the road to respectability. Manager Tommy Ivan hired Rudy Pilous of the Memorial Cup-winning St. Catharines juniors to serve as head coach. With Ted Lindsay and Jim Thomson providing veteran leadership, the Hawks climbed to fifth place, two points ahead of the last-place Toronto Maple Leafs. Ed Litzenberger continued to be the main offensive weapon for Chicago, finishing tied for third in the league with 32 goals.

However, the story of the season was the battle for the Calder Trophy between Chicago's Bobby Hull and Toronto's Frank Mahovlich. Hull, a strapping left-winger with impressive speed and strength, collected 47 points in his rookie season. Mahovlich, a natural centerman who blossomed into a potent scorer when he was shifted to left wing, scored 20 goals for the last-place Leafs and narrowly beat out Hull for the rookie prize.

Mahovlich's performance aside, it was a dismal season for the Leafs, who finished in last place for the first time since Conn Smythe purchased the team in 1927. Ironically, after struggling offensively for six straight seasons, the Leafs managed to score 192 goals over the course of the 70-game schedule, with Dick Duff and Brian Cullen joining Mahovlich in the 20-goal club. The Leafs' problems came on defense, where the main blue-line corps of Horton, Marc Réaume, Baun, Morrison, and goaltender Ed Chadwick allowed a league-high 226 goals.

The 1958 playoffs opened in Montreal and New York, where the Canadiens hosted the Red Wings and the Rangers entertained the Bruins. In Montreal, the Canadiens had little trouble with the Red Wings, swamping Detroit 8–1 and 5–1 in the opening two games. Phil Goyette led the attack in game one with three goals, while the Rocket, fully recovered from his Achilles'-tendon injury, paced the Habs in game two with a pair of goals. Although the Wings played considerably better at the Olympia, the powerhouse Canadiens were unstoppable. After André Pronovost gave the Habs a 2–1 overtime win in the third match, Rocket Richard caught fire in game four, collecting his seventh post-season hat-trick in Montreal's 4–3 victory. The Canadiens' win set up a Stanley Cup rematch with the Boston Bruins, who outlasted the Rangers in six high-scoring games.

While many pundits expected the Canadiens to defeat Boston easily, the Bruins proved to be stubborn opponents and entered the fifth game of the series tied with the Habs at two wins apiece. Boston opened the scoring late in the first period on a goal by Fleming Mackell, who was playing inspired hockey for the Bruins, but Montreal moved into the lead with a pair of second-period goals, with Geoffrion and Béliveau connecting only 42 seconds apart. As they had been doing through most of the series, the Bruins fought back, and Bronco Horvath tied the game at 2–2 midway through the final frame.

As the teams prepared for overtime, all eyes were on Maurice Richard, who was having one of the best post-seasons of his illustrious career. Early into the extra session, Henri Richard gathered in the puck and fed a pass to Dickie Moore, who spotted the Rocket just inside the Bruins zone. Moore put the puck on the Rocket's stick, and Richard let go a quick wrist shot that escaped the grasp of a screened Don Simmons to put the Habs one win away from a record-tying third-straight Stanley Cup.

The Canadiens seized control early in the sixth game with Geoffrion and Maurice Richard both scoring in the game's opening moments. The brave Bruins battled back to within a goal late in the third period, but Doug Harvey's empty-net insurance marker sealed Montreal's 5–3 Cup-clinching win. The city of Montreal was already celebrating when the Rocket, whose 11 goals in the playoffs were the second-highest total of his career, accepted a remodeled Stanley Cup trophy from President Campbell at center ice in the Boston Garden.

For 1958, the base of the Cup trophy had been rebuilt as a wide barrel, made up of five equal-size silver bands. The entire Cup from bowl to base was now a one-piece trophy, weighing 32 pounds (14fi kilograms). With the exception of the engraving of additional names on the trophy each year, the Stanley Cup would remain unchanged from this point until 1992, when the top band of the barrel was removed and a new blank band was added at the bottom to accommodate the rosters of additional winning teams.

Gordie Howe retained the Hart Trophy, Dickie Moore won the Art Ross, and teammate Doug Harvey engraved his name on the Norris Trophy for the fourth straight time. Camille Henry completed his comeback from the sophomore jinx, winning the Lady Byng Trophy after a season in which he spent only two minutes in the penalty box.

Dickie Moore, who had managed only 11 goals just two seasons earlier, led all NHL marksmen in goals (36) and points (84) in 1957-58. Moore played in pain after breaking his wrist early in the new year.

RICHARD'S OVERTIME MARKER WINS FIFTH GAME OF '58 FINAL

Richard's extra-session marker in game five was the sixth and final overtime goal of his career.

**April 17, 1958
at Montreal Forum
Montreal 3, Boston 2**

FIRST PERIOD

1) BOS Mackell 5 (Stanley, Toppazzini) PPG 18:43
PENALTIES – Bucyk BOS (tripping) 3:27; Mohns BOS (roughing), Moore MTL (roughing) 4:54; M. Richard MTL (highsticking) 13:33; Béliveau MTL (highsticking) 17:03.

SECOND PERIOD

2) MTL Geoffrion 4 (Béliveau) 2:20
3) MTL Béliveau 3 (Geoffrion) 3:02
PENALTIES – Pronovost MTL (kneeing) 4:37; Mohns BOS (holding) 5:30.

THIRD PERIOD

4) BOS Horvath 5 (Stasiuk, Boivin) 10:35
PENALTIES – None

FIRST OVERTIME PERIOD

5) MTL M. Richard 10 (Moore, H. Richard) 5:45
PENALTIES – None

SHOTS ON GOAL	1	2	3	1OT	T
BOSTON	14	10	11	5	40
MONTREAL	18	13	12	4	47

GOALTENDERS	TIME	SA	GA	ENG	W/L
BOS Simmons	65:45	44	3	0	L
MTL Plante	65:45	38	2	0	W

PP CONVERSIONS BOS 1/3   MTL 0/2

(continued on p. 126)

The Boston Bruins: Schmidt, the Uke Line, and the End of DNQ

by Fran Rosa

After being rejected by Toronto's Conn Smythe as being "too small" at a Maple Leafs tryout camp in the mid-1930s, Milt Schmidt went on to spend thirty-six years with the Boston Bruins as a Hall-of-Fame center, successful coach, and respected general manager.

The last fifteen years of the NHL's six-team era brought the Boston Bruins modest success, a precipitous decline, and the seeds of a renaissance. No matter what, when the history of Boston's hockey team is examined, there is Milt Schmidt, a player – and what a great player he was – a coach, a manager, and a Hall-of-Famer. On this day, he sits in the manager's office of the Boston Garden Club and turns the crystal ball into reverse to recall the past, a past that carried him through a lifetime in Boston, from youth to middle age to "My, don't you look good." He stops when the counter says 1954.

"Let's see," he begins. "It's the 1954-55 season. We're in Chicago. Both my knees are tightly taped and there's no guarantee the skin won't come with it when you peel it off. The next morning, I met coach Lynn Patrick in the lobby of the hotel. We're walking to the railroad station. My knees are raw and bleeding, and I tell him I'm going to retire. He said, 'I knew this was coming and now you're the coach of the Bruins if Walter Brown [the team president] and Weston Adams [the owner] okay it.' So now I was a coach."

Schmidt had broken in with the Bruins in 1936.

Among his teammates were Boston legends Eddie Shore, Dit Clapper, and Cecil "Tiny" Thompson, and, later, Frankie Brimsek, all Hall-of-Famers. His linemates were Woody Dumart and Bobby Bauer and they would become legends too, as the Kitchener Kids or the Kraut Line. It's a little scary to think how close he came to quitting hockey.

"At nineteen I almost called it a career," he said. "The Bruins were going on a road trip, and Art Ross sent me down to Providence. When I got there, Providence was going on a road trip and I was sent back to Boston. I spent a week in a hotel room, and I was so depressed. I felt unwanted and I asked myself, 'Where am I going?'

I was ready to go home. Then I decided to wait until the Bruins came home and see what was going on. I don't know why I stayed; I guess I had something to prove." Whatever it was that kept Schmidt in hockey, Boston and hockey should feel blessed he didn't end his career almost before it started.

Milt had won Stanley Cup championships in 1939 and 1941. In 1953, Detroit had finished first, a whopping 21 points ahead of Boston, but the Bruins erased the Red Wings in a gigantic upset, one of the biggest in NHL history. Schmidt was a key man in the series.

Johnny Peirson, who was a member of the 1953 Bruins, remembers that series. "I'll never forget that series and the coaching job Lynn Patrick did," he said. "Detroit had a great team and they clobbered us all season, winning ten of the fourteen games against us and usually by big scores. The Red Wings had set a record for points, and we supposedly didn't have a chance. Before the first game, Lynn called a team meeting to discuss strategy, and it was agreed we'd play Milt Schmidt, Porky Dumart, and Joe Klukay against Detroit's top line of Gordie Howe, Ted Lindsay, and Marty Pavelich, I think. Detroit pounded us 7–0 in that game, and we had another team meeting before game two. Lynn said we were going to stay with the same

Lynn Patrick (right), who spent his entire ten-year on-ice career with the New York Rangers, moved up the coast and behind the bench with the Bruins, guiding Boston into the Stanley Cup finals in 1952-53.

strategy, and we all agreed. Dumart did a great job on Gordie, and we went on to win the series, 4–2, and go on to the finals against Montreal. They beat us for the Cup."

Eddie Sandford, another Bruin of the era, agreed that "Detroit had a great team. They had Howe and Lindsay and Red Kelly, and Terry Sawchuk in goal. Lynn put down the plan and told us if we worked at it, we'd have a shot at winning." The execution of the Patrick plan left Howe with just two goals in six games in the face of Dumart's checking. Patrick coached the Bruins for five seasons, beginning in 1950-51. He added the general manager's portfolio in 1953-54, before making Schmidt his coach the following season.

"I learned coaching from him," said Schmidt. "He was far and away the best coach I ever had." Schmidt would coach the Bruins into two Stanley Cup final-series appearances in his first three seasons, as life behind the bench became fun for this fierce competitor. Each time, they lost to Montreal in the final – which, of course, wasn't much fun. The famous Montreal jinx over

Boston was blossoming, but no one had recognized it yet. It would last until the 1980s.

Schmidt had played for the strong-minded and penny-pinching Art Ross, coach and general manager of the Bruins. "Every year I was a hold-out," said Schmidt. "I even asked to be traded, but Ross said to me, 'You've got a job here when your career is finished.' After we reached the finals in two of my first three years as coach, *rigor mortis* set in. The talent level of our team declined. There were all those sleepless nights with a weak team, and I really didn't enjoy coaching very much. In the beginning, the toughest part was coaching guys I had played with and had a beer with. The players made the transition easier for me, but coaching is the toughest job in hockey. Playing was easy, managing was easy, coaching was definitely the toughest."

So was playing against Detroit's "Black Jack" Stewart. Stewart versus Schmidt became one of the great feuds in hockey. "We didn't have stick fights," Schmidt recalled, "and we didn't fight too much. We just ran at each other as hard as we could. We became bitter enemies. I never knew how it started until Joe Carveth came over to Boston from Detroit, and I asked if he knew what it was all about. He said, 'Stewart claims you hit him with your stick in the testicles so

Milt Schmidt displayed the same enthusiasm and winning spirit as a coach as he had as a player, despite suffering through six consecutive "Did Not Qualify" seasons with his eager, but talent-thin, Bruins.

hard that they swelled up.' I can honestly say I couldn't remember that, but if I did, it wasn't intentional."

The feud progressed, and one night when the Bruins were playing Detroit, Ross told Schmidt, "You're not dressing tonight." Schmidt answered, "Don't you dare do that to me. That will be an insult, and I'll be the laughing stock of the league." On one occasion that Schmidt remembers, he had a little run-in on the ice with Gordie Howe, and "Stewart skated over to Gordie and said, 'Leave him alone, he's mine.' Years later I was coaching, and Stewart was in Boston on a business trip. He came into our dressing room after practice. I looked up and saw him and my fists clenched automatically. But he held out his hand, we shook hands and embraced, and he said to me, 'Weren't we a couple of crazy fools.' That was one of the highlights of my career. We were bitter enemies and then we became friends. The battles that we had created a deep respect for each other."

Patrick went to the expansion St. Louis Blues in 1965 when that club was first being organized. Hap Emms became the general manager of the Bruins, and

Schmidt became his assistant after serving two terms as coach: 1955-56 to 1960-61 and 1962-63 to 1965-66. It was a trade Schmidt made over the objections of Emms that launched the Bruins' powerhouses of the early 1970s. The Bruins' stat sheet from 1959-60 to 1966-67 carried the notation "Did Not Qualify" for the playoffs for eight consecutive years, which became known as the DNQ seasons. Seven times they finished last in the six-team league, and once they managed to climb to fifth. But the Bobby Orr–Phil Esposito era was dawning, and it was Schmidt who engineered the trade with Chicago that brought Esposito to Boston and, eventually, brought two Stanley Cup championships as well. But that's another story, and it's getting ahead of this one.

Hockey in the NHL of the 1950s was another kind of game from the one played today. It was a more controlled, grinding style that was physically tougher than 1990s hockey. The Bruins were in step with the six-team style and its emphasis on defense. "We carried the puck in, made plays, and, if we lost the puck, the wingers picked up their men and came back," said Schmidt.

"Art Ross would say, 'Don't give up the puck to the other team.' If you did, he'd have your head," Peirson remembered.

"We skated our lanes," said Sandford. "We weren't as innovative as today's players. There was no crossing over. You just skated your wing. We used just one forechecker, and when you lost the puck, you picked up your man and backchecked. We didn't shoot the puck in. We tried to make plays. Our philosophy was that, if you controlled the puck, you had a chance of scoring. We were taught that way as juniors, and we were coached that way. It made it easier to play defense, but it was pretty dreary hockey. A 2–0 lead was murder. No one lost with a 2–0 lead."

"The difference in players then and now is huge," Schmidt maintains. "We were all so hungry. If you failed, you went down to the minors and, with only six teams, you might never get back to the NHL. It made you work harder and it made you play hurt. There was so much more hitting. The hardest hitters I remember were Bill Barilko, Leo Boivin, and Johnny Bucyk, maybe the three best hip-checkers of all time. No one was better with the hip check."

Peirson described the Bruins of the 1950s this way: "We were sort of a Lunch Pail Gang – before Don Cherry popularized that expression in the 1970s. We used just thirteen players most of the time, three lines and two pairs of defensemen. We played a positional game. Lynn Patrick would say, 'You worked too hard to get the puck, don't give it away.' I remember he brought up Leo Labine from Barrie and told him, 'Stir up some trouble and don't worry about the fines, I'll pay them.' Labine picked up seventeen penalty minutes in a minute and a half on his first shift. Of course, you played each of the other five teams fourteen times, and personal rivalries were inevitable. I'll tell you, I saw enough of Ted Lindsay to last me a lifetime."

Another outstanding Bruin of the era was Don McKenney, a graceful, skilled player who had "a great backhand shot," said Peirson. And there were many others, including Fernie Flaman, Bill Quackenbush, and Leo Boivin – all of whom are now Hall-of-Famers – and Doug Mohns, Eddie Sandford, and Fleming Mackell.

Sandford, now an investment broker in Boston, is the crew chief of the off-ice officials and the official scorer at the Bruins' home games. Hardly anyone in Boston remembers that he led all scorers in the 1953 playoffs with 11 points – 8 goals and 3 assists – in 11 games. "Oh sure, I was the leader," he chuckled. "But not many goals were scored in the playoffs. Guys like Richard and Howe had two men on their backs all the time."

Games against the same opponent were so frequent, there was no time to forget challenges. Instead they were met head-on, usually the next day. "In many ways, it's a tougher game today," said Sandford. "But we had great rivalries in our era. Some grudges developed because we played each other so often and we all knew each other with all those weekend series against the same opponent. Some of those grudges didn't last long, but some lasted a lifetime." So, there was no fraternizing.

"Sometimes we'd travel on the same train," pointed out Tom Johnson, a Hall-of-Fame defenseman with Montreal, who finished his career as a Bruin and now is

Hal Laycoe, who retired as an active player only one year after the infamous Richard incident in 1955, spent fourteen seasons behind the bench in the Western Hockey League before becoming the first coach of the NHL's Vancouver Canucks.

Harry Sinden's assistant. "We wouldn't even walk through the other team's car to get to the diner. We hardly ever spoke to each other. The Bruins of the 1950s were always the toughest games for us. I remember a game in 1956. Each team had only one goalie, and

if anything happened to him, the home team had to supply a substitute who was usually its practice goalie. In Montreal, our practice goalie was Claude Pronovost, Marcel's brother. We'd put 15 or 20 goals past him every time we practiced. This night Long John Henderson, the Boston goalie, couldn't play, because his equipment was lost. We loaned them Pronovost for the game, and what do you think he did? He shut us out, 2–0."

Fan interest was as high in those days as it is today. "When we upset Detroit in 1953, we took a train to Montreal for the finals," said Schmidt. "The train stopped in London, Ontario, and there were about two hundred people at the station. Word had gotten around that we were on the train, and people had come to the station to get a look at the team that beat Detroit. Rivalries between clubs also sparked fan interest. Every team had a big line, and those lines often played against each other."

The Bruins lost to the Canadiens in the 1953 finals and in the semi-finals of 1952, 1954, and 1955. Montreal also defeated Boston in the finals in 1957 and 1958, making six playoff defeats by the Habs during the decade. "Some people may think it was easier to win the Cup in those days," says Schmidt, "because you had to win only two series, eight games. But those eight games took a lot of winning. With the rivalries of the six-team league, winning two series was a pretty tough task."

There was a wild scene between Montreal and Boston late in the 1954-55 regular season that produced hockey's darkest hour. It triggered rioting in Montreal and probably cost Maurice Richard the scoring title, making league president Clarence Campbell and Boston defenseman Hal Laycoe public enemies number one and two in Montreal. It all sprang out of an incident in Boston Garden on March 13, 1955. Richard exploded after being cut on the head in a clash with Laycoe, who had apparently highsticked the Rocket. Referee Frank Udvari put his arm up for a delayed penalty. When play stopped, Richard claimed Laycoe had cut him, pointing to his head and skating at the Boston player. According to reports, he swung his stick at Laycoe, hitting him on the shoulder and side of his face. Richard lost his stick, then picked up another, and started swinging at Laycoe again. This time he broke his stick on Laycoe's back.

"Then," Sandford recalls, "Doug Harvey picked up a stick on the ice and handed it to Richard. The officials kept trying to restrain Richard, and he kept breaking free." Richard went after Laycoe a third time. Linesman Cliff Thompson, from Stoneham, Massachusetts (a suburb of Boston), tried to wrestle Richard to the ice. Again he broke loose and punched Thompson in the face twice. After a hearing, Campbell suspended Richard for the remainder of the season and the playoffs.

The reaction in Montreal to Campbell's ruling produced a frightening night and one of hockey's most shameful incidents. One night after the ruling, Detroit was in Montreal for a game, and Campbell decided to attend. The Red Wings took a 4–1 lead in the first period, and unruly fans began to heckle the league president. A smoke bomb was thrown on the ice, fans rushed for the exits, and the game was forfeited to Detroit. The fans then poured out onto Ste. Catherine Street and the "Richard Riot" ensued.

"A few days later we had to go there for a game," said Sandford, "and I drew Laycoe as my taxi teammate. When we got to the Forum, the police were waiting for us, and they escorted us into the building and to the dressing room past a bunch of angry fans. Then every time Laycoe came on the ice, the crowd booed him."

As the decade wore on, Lynn Patrick made some moves to strengthen the team. The major maneuver was to get goalie Terry Sawchuk from Detroit for the 1955-56 campaign. Although he would play just two seasons in a Boston uniform, Sawchuk was eventually traded for Johnny Bucyk, a man who would become a Bruins legend and play twenty-one seasons for the club.

Sawchuk was unhappy in Boston and, in the middle of the 1956-57 season, he walked out on the Bruins, who traded him back to Detroit after the season was completed. Bucyk, who came to the Bruins in return, stayed in Boston for the remainder of his career and has lived there ever since. He's still with the club as the game analyst on the Bruins' radio network and as the organizer of

The oldest player to score 50 goals in a season in NHL history, John Bucyk was the heart, soul, and backbone of the Boston Bruins franchise for twenty-one seasons.

the Bruins' alumni, a group of former players that has raised more than a million dollars for various charities over the last five years.

In Boston, Bucyk became one of the game's greatest left-wingers. He was a key man on three of Boston's best lines, first with Vic Stasiuk and Bronco Horvath on the Uke Line, then with Murray Oliver and Tommy Williams

on the B-O-W Line, and, later, with Fred Stanfield and Johnny McKenzie on Boston's Stanley Cup championship clubs of 1970 and 1972.

Harry Sinden, general manager of the Bruins since 1972-73, rates Bucyk as "one of the best passing forwards of all time." Attesting to that are the 813 assists and 1,369 points he accumulated – both league records for left-wingers.

For the 1957-58 season, the Bruins had picked up Horvath from Montreal and Bucyk from Detroit. Stasiuk was already on the roster, and Schmidt put them together to form the Uke Line. The line produced 72 goals that season and helped the Bruins get into the playoffs. The club upset the Rangers in the first round, but again lost to Montreal. It was becoming a bad habit. Fleming Mackell and Don McKenney led the playoff scorers with 19 and 17 points, respectively.

The Uke Line, with 70 goals, led the Bruins into second place the following season, but now it was the Bruins' turn to be on the short end of a playoff upset,

All three members of Boston's famed "Uke Line," which included Vic Stasiuk (left) and Bronco Horvath, seen here mounting an attack against the Maple Leafs, played in the Detroit Red Wings' system before joining the Bruins.

as fourth-place Toronto won a seven-game series.

Now a black curtain would fall over the Bruins. Beginning in 1959-60, the dreaded DNQ appeared alongside the Bruins' record as the club began its long string of fifth- and sixth-place finishes. This was the *rigor mortis* stage that Schmidt had mentioned.

Sinden arrived to coach the team in 1966-67, the same season that saw the long-anticipated arrival of Bobby Orr. Orr wasn't merely the light at the end of the tunnel, he was the guiding star that would light Boston's hockey sky. All through the down years, the Bruins had still played to 87 per cent of capacity, frequently selling all 13,909 tickets to games in Boston Garden. With Orr's arrival, tickets became scarce. He would revolutionize the role of the defenseman, lead the Bruins to two Stanley Cup championships, and

become Boston's most popular athlete since Ted Williams played for the Red Sox.

With Orr in the lineup, all the Bruins had to do was fill in the players around him, which Schmidt did with one big move, engineering a blockbuster trade with Chicago. "We needed some help on the forward line," said Schmidt, "and I kept talking with Tommy Ivan of Chicago on the phone. Hap Emms was still the general manager, and I was his assistant. Chicago had Phil Esposito, who wasn't very happy there. They had Ken Hodge, who was sitting at the end of the bench, and Freddy Stanfield, who was sitting in the stands. We'd give them Pit Martin, goalie Jack Norris, and another player. The player Ivan wanted was defenseman Gilles Marotte. That was the key. But Marotte had played for Emms in junior, and Hap didn't want to give him up. I was ready to let him go because we needed forwards.

Phil Esposito helped transform the Bruins franchise into a consistent winner, leading the NHL in either goals or assists in each of his eight full seasons in Boston.

"I finally got the okay to make the trade over his objections, and Emms was furious with me." After that, the Bruins vaulted out of the NHL's first expansion season to become the best team in the league, a swashbuckling gang that played hard, lived high, and thoroughly enjoyed life on and off the ice.

Since then, the Bruins have won the Stanley Cup twice, have reached the finals on five other occasions, and have made the playoffs in each of twenty-six consecutive seasons from 1967-68 to 1993-94, an achievement unmatched by any team in any sport.

They, indeed, have come a long way from the DNQ seasons.

91 PTS.　　73 PTS.　　69 PTS.　　65 PTS.　　64 PTS.　　58 PTS.

1958-59
Imlach Rallies Leafs to Cup Finals

WHEN ASKED ABOUT THE SUCCESS OF THE MONTREAL CANADIENS FOLLOWING THE 1957-58 season, Detroit general manager Jack Adams noted that "every good hockey club disintegrates about every five years." While he couldn't have known it at the time, he was predicting the fate of his own club in 1958-59. Adams continued to shuffle the Red Wings' lineup. Gus Mortson arrived from Chicago, but his best days were behind him and he lasted only 36 games in Detroit. Other newcomers were Charlie Burns, Len Lunde, and Gerry Ehman, who was quickly grabbed by the Leafs when Adams tried to sneak him through waivers.

There was continued confusion in Toronto, where the Leafs were still without a full-time general manager. Stafford Smythe partially addressed the problem by hiring George "Punch" Imlach as an assistant general manager. Imlach was the former player, coach, manager, and co-owner of the Quebec Aces who had played a central role in the development of Jean Béliveau. One of his first moves was to grab former Rangers goaltender Johnny Bower off the waiver wire. Bower was thirty-three years old, but Imlach had seen him stop the best shooters in minor pro hockey for a decade and felt he was the veteran who could solidify the Leafs' defense. Carl Brewer, a rambunctious rookie who was impressive in a two-game trial during the 1957-58 season, was given a full-time blueline spot along with Allan Stanley, who was obtained from Boston in exchange for Jim Morrison. Under Imlach's tutoring, Stanley was about to become an NHL All-Star. Another veteran, four-time Stanley Cup-winner Bert Olmstead, was claimed in the Intra-League Draft, after the Canadiens left him off their protected list.

A promising season was expected in Chicago, where the Hawks were building a noteworthy roster. Already blessed with two excellent defensemen in Vasko and Pilote, the Hawks supplemented their blueline corps with three more experienced rearguards: Dollard St. Laurent from Montreal, Al Arbour from Detroit, and Jack Evans from New York. Tod Sloan, made expendable by the Leafs after the acquisition of Bert Olmstead, was purchased from Toronto, while Kenny Wharram, who had been in the Hawks' system since making his NHL debut in 1951-52, was finally given the opportunity to play a full season in the NHL.

A New Start

For the 1958-59 season, the Red Wings introduced 2 p.m. matinees and moved the start times of their evening games to 7 p.m. on Sundays and 8 p.m. on weeknights. When the team first moved to Detroit from Victoria in 1926, all games had begun at 8:30 p.m.

As expected, the Montreal Canadiens were hesitant to vary their winning combination, but they did make three roster revisions. Albert "Junior" Langlois, who filled in admirably during the 1957-58 season, was rewarded with Dollard St. Laurent's spot on the blueline. Ab McDonald, a productive farm hand in Rochester, replaced Bert Olmstead, and rookie Ralph Backstrom was penciled in as the twelfth forward.

With Andy Bathgate established as one of the league's most talented players, it seemed certain that the Rangers would challenge in the Stanley Cup race. Coach Phil Watson added forwards Earl Ingarfield and Eddie Shack, while signing John Hanna for the blueline. If the Rangers had a weakness, it was in goal, where Gump Worsley had a tendency to falter as the season progressed.

Once again, the Montreal Canadiens were the class act of the NHL, gliding into first place early in the season. Dickie Moore, his wrist completely healed, established a single-season NHL record with 96 points, breaking the mark set by Gordie Howe in 1952-53. Jean Béliveau returned to the top of the goal-scoring ladder, connecting for 45 goals in 64 games. Once again, however, injuries tested the depth of the Montreal roster, as only Moore, Tom Johnson, Donnie Marshall, and André Pronovost, were able to skate in all 70 games. Bonin, Harvey, and Geoffrion all suffered an assortment of injuries, but the worst damage was suffered by Rocket Richard. Richard, who missed 42 games in 1957-58, played only 42 in 1958-59 after breaking his ankle on January 18. Jacques Plante continued to be the NHL's best goalie, leading the league in wins (38) and goals-against average (2.16).

The Boston Bruins climbed into second place on the strength of the Uke Line of Bucyk, Stasiuk, and Horvath. Left-winger Don McKenney led the Bruins, with 32 goals and 62 points. Horvath was slowed by a broken jaw through most of the season, but still managed to connect for 19 goals and 39 points in 45 games. A strong second half was the key to Boston's success, as the team recovered from a 14–18–5 mid-season mark to finish with a 32–29–9 record. Harry Lumley compiled an 8–2–1 record, while Don Simmons recovered from a thumb injury, to keep the Bruins in the race.

As expected, the Chicago Black Hawks were much improved, finishing in third spot with a 28–29–13 record. The Hawks were strong in net, with two-time All-Star Glenn Hall patroling the crease, solid on defense, with a sound combination of youth and experience, and well balanced up front. Ed Litzenberger had his third straight 30-goal season, while Ted Lindsay and Tod Sloan each chipped in with 20-goal campaigns. Bobby Hull, who was becoming a fan favorite with his movie-star good looks and explosive slap shot, added 18 goals and 50 points to the Hawks' attack.

In Detroit, coach Sid Abel had his hands full with the Red Wings, who slumped badly in the second half of the season and fell to last place for the first time since 1937-38. Terry Sawchuk, who had led the league in

Andy Hebenton's consecutive-games streak eventually reached 630 in the NHL, but it actually began in the Western Hockey League, where he played 210 consecutive games with Victoria before joining the NHL. Hebenton's 33 goals in 1958-59 ranked him fourth in the league and marked a career high.

There was a noticeable resurgence of hockey interest in Chicago in 1958-59 as the Black Hawks rose from fifth spot to third. Two reasons for this renewed enthusiasm were the play of defenseman Elmer "Moose" Vasko and goaltender Glenn Hall. Vasko punished any forward who entered the Hawks' zone with solid bodychecks and, if the attackers were able to evade the Moose, Hall was often there to close the door.

Segregated Sin Bins

Prior to the start of the 1959 playoffs, the Black Hawks became the first NHL team to separate penalized players from fans by completely enclosing the penalty bench with a wire screen. Until then, penalty boxes were situated among the spectators' seats near the boards.

victories for three straight years in the early 1950s, led the league in losses as the Red Wings went 12–24–1 in the second half of the season. In an attempt to shake up the team, Abel levied fines for inferior play on every player on his roster, with the exception of Gordie Howe and three others. The ploy failed, however, and the Wings were forced to watch the playoffs from the sidelines.

One of the great stories of the 1958-59 season was the rebirth of the Toronto Maple Leafs. After a dismal 5–10–3 start, the Leafs' front office held an emergency meeting and gave Punch Imlach complete power to make whatever changes he deemed necessary to save the season. Imlach's first order of business was to fire coach Billy Reay and install himself temporarily behind the bench. Imlach wanted Alf Pike of the Western Hockey League's Vancouver Canucks to take the Leaf post, but Pike was hesitant to leave the security of the WHL. Punch decided to stay on, appointed Bert Olmstead as his assistant coach, and, slowly, the Leafs began to turn things around. Imlach's positive attitude, combined with Olmstead's determination, energized the club. Imlach told anyone who would listen that the Leafs would catch the Rangers for the last playoff spot and, once in the post-season, would down both Boston and Montreal to win the Stanley Cup. Rangers coach Phil Watson countered by saying, "Always he's predicting what the Leafs are going to do. The only crystal ball he's got is on his shoulders. What a beautiful head of skin."

Whatever his system, the bald prognosticator and his young group of Maple Leafs entered the stretch drive seven points behind the Rangers with five games left to play. The Leafs won all five of their remaining games, including crucial home-and-home victories against New York and a 6–3 win over Montreal at the Forum. The Canadiens' choice of goaltenders for this game was controversial. Instead of having to face Jacques Plante, who was sidelined by a case of boils, the Leafs were opposed by a pair of minor-league netminders, Claude Pronovost and

Left to right: Fernie Flaman, Don Simmons, and Jim Morrison were three principals in the Boston Bruins' second-place finish in 1958-59. Defense partners Flaman and Morrison had both been tutored in the Toronto Maple Leafs' system. Morrison contributed eight goals and 25 points in his first season in Boston.

Claude Cyr. Yet, when Montreal faced New York on the last night of the season, veteran Charlie Hodge was in goal. He set down the Rangers, 4–2, while the Leafs overcame a 2–0 deficit in Detroit to clinch the last playoff spot. While the Leafs were red hot down the stretch, the Rangers were ice cold, losing six of their last seven games to finish a single point behind Toronto.

The 1959 playoffs began on March 24, with the Canadiens hosting the Black Hawks and the Bruins entertaining the Maple Leafs. As expected, both home teams easily defeated their visiting rivals. Montreal jumped out to a two-game lead with 4–2 and 5–1 victories, while Boston, ignoring Imlach's predictions, downed the Leafs 5–1 and 4–2 behind the goaltending of former Leaf Harry Lumley. However, back in Chicago and Toronto, the underdogs overachieved. Goalie Glenn Hall and second-string forward Lorne Ferguson were outstanding, as the Black Hawks pulled even with the Habs with 4–2 and 3–1 victories. Jean Béliveau was injured in the third game and was forced to sit out the remainder of the series. Ken Mosdell, who played with Chicago in 1957-58 before being returned to Montreal, was called up to replace Béliveau.

In Toronto, the Leafs won only their third playoff game since 1951 with a 3–2 overtime victory in game three. Gerry Ehman tied the game late in the third with a wrist shot just inside the post, and later won the game with a pretty goal five minutes into sudden death. Ehman, who had played for Imlach in Springfield and Quebec, was acquired from Detroit just days after Imlach took over as the Leafs' general manager. Buoyed by this victory, the Leafs used a similar script in game four to once again edge past the Bruins, 3–2, in overtime. Frank Mahovlich, on a set-up from Olmstead and Brewer, scored the first playoff goal of his career eleven minutes into the extra period, while the Bruins were attempting to kill a five-minute major penalty to Jean-Guy Gendron. Toronto went on to capture the series in seven games, with Ehman once again being crowned as

The Friendly Skies

The Bruins, Maple Leafs, and Black Hawks all chartered airplanes for their 1959 playoff series, leaving the Canadiens the only NHL club that refused to fly.

Rookie sensation Ralph Backstrom (6) challenges Toronto goaltender Johnny Bower during the Montreal forward's first full NHL season. Backstrom won the Calder Trophy as the league's best freshman in 1958-59, collecting 18 goals and 40 points for the Stanley Cup-champion Canadiens.

the hero. In game seven, he scored the series-winning goal, with two minutes remaining in the third period. The Leafs returned to the Stanley Cup finals for the first time since 1951, and their opponents would once again be the Montreal Canadiens.

After watching Chicago tie their best-of-seven semi-final, the Habs bounced back to take the next two games, 4–2 and 5–4. The decisive game was a hard-fought, rowdy contest, in which referee Red Storey had his hands full handling both the players and the fans. Late in the match, with the score tied at 4–4, Marcel Bonin tripped up Bobby Hull, but no call was made. The Black Hawk players, expecting a penalty, actually stopped skating, allowing Montreal's Claude Provost to pick up the puck and coolly stuff what would prove to be the winning goal past Glenn Hall. The game was delayed for over thirty minutes, as fans littered the ice and attempted to attack the referee. After the game, NHL president Clarence Campbell told Bill Westwick, an old friend and a Canadian Press reporter, that Storey "froze" on a couple of plays and that penalties should have been called. Although Campbell was speaking off the record, the story was printed. The following day, Storey resigned as an NHL referee, explaining, "When you don't have the support of your superiors, it is time to quit."

The 1959 Stanley Cup finals began amid controversy, with Eddie Powers taking over for the departed Storey, who had been slated to referee the finals. The Canadiens, despite the loss of Béliveau, had scored

Left: Marcel Bonin, who had never scored a post-season goal in his career, topped all Stanley Cup marksmen with 10 goals in the 1959 playoffs.

Right: In his first taste of post-season action, Gerry Ehman collected a team-leading 13 points for the Maple Leafs in the 1959 playoffs.

nine power-play goals against the Black Hawks. Against the upstart Leafs, they were simply too strong. They wore the young team down with their relentless speed, aggressive forechecking, and potent power play. Five of their 18 goals in the series were scored with the man advantage.

The teams were tied entering the third period in three of the first four games, but the Canadiens emerged victorious in all three matches, winning 5–3, 3–1, and 3–2. Toronto did manage to win game three on Dick Duff's overtime goal, but Montreal wrapped up the package in five games. Marcel Bonin, who would register only 11 playoff markers in his entire career, led all post-season scorers with 10 goals. Maurice Richard, who returned from his injury to appear in four games during the finals, failed to register a single point. As team captain, however, he accepted the Cup from President Campbell for an NHL-record fourth consecutive time.

Following the series, Red Storey refused to accept an apology from Campbell, ending his officiating career. Despite winning his second straight Art Ross Trophy, Dickie Moore was overlooked for Hart Trophy consideration, as Rangers forward Andy Bathgate was selected as the league's MVP. Alex Delvecchio took home the Lady Byng Trophy, Plante retained the Vezina Trophy, and Ralph Backstrom of the Canadiens won the Calder Trophy as rookie of the year. Tom Johnson, Doug Harvey's defense partner, captured the Norris Trophy.

At a post-season banquet in Boston, Bruins' president Weston Adams praised Toronto's Conn Smythe for his work in gaining support for the NHL's waiver-draft system earlier in the 1950s. Adams felt the system gave each team an equal chance to improve and was responsible for the league's renewed success at the box office.

(continued on p. 140)

TORONTO GAINS PLAYOFF BERTH ON FINAL NIGHT OF SEASON

STANDINGS ON MARCH 9, 1959

TEAM	GP	W	L	T	PTS
Montreal	63	36	15	12	84
Chicago	64	26	25	13	65
Boston	64	27	28	9	63
New York	63	25	26	12	62
Toronto	64	22	31	11	55
Detroit	64	23	34	7	53

March 22, 1959
at Detroit Olympia
Toronto 6, Detroit 4

FIRST PERIOD
1) DET Ullman 21 (Howe, Wilson) PPG 7:12
2) DET Pronovost 10 (Kennedy) 12:38
PENALTIES – Pulford TOR (highsticking) 5:46; Baun TOR (charging) 15:27.

SECOND PERIOD
3) TOR Regan 8 (Armstrong, Duff) 2:41
4) TOR Baun 1 (Stewart) 4:15
5) DET Ullman 22 (Wilson, S. McNeill) 15:16
6) TOR Brewer 3 (Mahovlich, Regan) PPG 17:08
7) TOR Regan 9 (Duff, Armstrong) 17:29
8) DET Pronovost 11 (Ullman, Delvecchio) 18:58
PENALTIES – S. McNeill DET (tripping) 15:44.

THIRD PERIOD
9) TOR Duff 29 (Regan) 2:51
10) TOR Harris 22 (Baun) 14:40
PENALTIES – None

SHOTS ON GOAL	1	2	3	T	
TORONTO	12	10	12	34	
DETROIT	12	8	10	30	

GOALTENDERS		TIME	SA	GA	ENG	W/L
TOR	Bower	60:00	26	4	0	W
DET	Sawchuk	60:00	28	6	0	L

PP CONVERSIONS TOR 1/1 DET 1/2

The Toronto Maple Leafs won their remaining five games to capture the NHL's final playoff spot. The Leafs' strong finish eliminated the Rangers, who lost six of their final seven games.

FINAL REGULAR-SEASON STANDINGS

TEAM	GP	W	L	T	PTS
Montreal	70	39	18	13	91
Boston	70	32	29	9	73
Chicago	70	28	29	13	69
Toronto	70	27	32	11	65
New York	70	26	32	12	64
Detroit	70	25	37	8	58

Biltmores on Broadway: The Rangers of the 1950s

by Ira Gitler

Between their inception in 1926-27 and their winning of the NHL's regular-season championship in 1941-42, the New York Rangers finished under .500 only once (and that by one game) and won the Stanley Cup in 1928, 1933, and 1940. Military service in the Second World War took many of the best players, not only from the Rangers but from their previously productive farm system as well. The club next reached the playoffs in 1947-48, but during training camp in the fall of 1948, an auto accident injured four players and started the team on a downward spiral that ended in a last-place finish.

Prior to the 1949-50 campaign, the consensus of experts consigned the Rangers to the very same cellar, but they played surprisingly well under new coach Lynn Patrick to finish fourth. They then proceeded to upset the Canadiens, 4–1, in the semi-finals and took the first-place Detroit Red Wings to double overtime of the Cup's seventh and deciding game before losing – this despite the fact that the presence of the circus in Madison Square Garden forced the club to play all seven games on the road. If a goalpost hadn't gotten in the way during the first overtime, Rangers detractors of the early 1990s might well have chanted "1950, 1950!" instead of "1940, 1940!"

However, the fact that they came within inches of winning the Stanley Cup with a particularly valiant effort to open the 1950s did not herald an imminent Rangers renaissance. That wasn't to come until midway through the decade, when three seasons of prosperity were followed by an abrupt fall from second place that would close the decade on a sour note.

General manager Frank Boucher tried everything in 1950-51. Hypnotist Dr. David Tracy, who had once attempted to inspire baseball's St. Louis Browns, was called in after the Rangers had won only once in their first seventeen games, but this experiment was short-lived. Later in the season, a magic elixir that was mixed and delivered to the dressing room in a mysterious black bottle by restaurateur Gene Leone, fueled a surge by the team that fell short when center Edgar Laprade broke his leg. The Rangers missed the last playoff spot by a point.

Laprade's injury was but one in a long list that would be part of an overall hex hanging over the franchise, which persisted until the Rangers won the Stanley Cup in 1994. In 1951-52 they seemed headed for a playoff position, when, in late February, big Jack Stoddard – one of the few players to wear number 13 – broke his wrist in the midst of a hot streak. In 1952-53, Herb Dickinson, a very promising left-winger, was hit in the eye with a puck during a pre-game warmup in Toronto, ending his career. Without going into an entire litany of injuries, it must be noted that these were among the preliminaries that presaged the crucial ankle breaks to Jean Ratelle in 1972 and Ulf Nilsson in 1979, the only seasons between 1950 and 1994 that saw the Rangers advance to the Stanley Cup finals.

Four members of the Guelph Biltmores, who had captured Canada's junior hockey championship, the Memorial Cup, made their debuts with the Rangers in 1952-53: Andy Bathgate, Harry Howell, Dean Prentice, and Ron Murphy all played their first games in Madison Square Garden, as did goaltender Gump Worsley, who had played junior hockey in the Montreal suburb of Verdun. Although the Broadway Blueshirts finished in

Andy Bathgate, captain of the Guelph Biltmores, proudly poses with the Memorial Cup after his team downed the Regina Pats in four straight games to capture the junior hockey championship of Canada in 1952.

sixth-and-last place that season, these players were to become part of the nucleus of those three mid-1950s playoff teams. Pressed into major-league service prematurely, some logged time in the minors before finally sticking with the parent club; others never left the NHL, learning on the job the hard way.

Bathgate, the eventual superstar, took a while to establish himself as a bona fide major-leaguer. A talented

center in junior, he arrived in New York with a slipping left kneecap that was corrected by the insertion of a small metal plate. Later, he played with a brace on his right knee as well. Given his achievements, it makes one wonder what heights he could have attained with two healthy knee joints.

The Rangers first asked Bathgate to play the role of a checking left-winger for the team's top offensive combination of Paul Ronty and Wally Hergesheimer, but he was sent to Vancouver of the Western Hockey League for additional seasoning. In 1953-54, he divided his time between Vancouver and Cleveland of the American

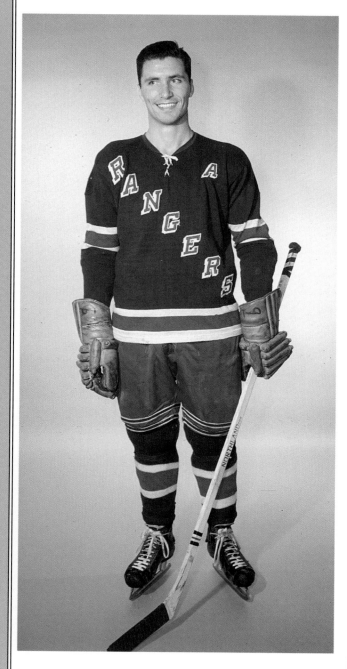

After two seasons of tutorial time with Cleveland of the AHL and Vancouver of the WHL, Andy Bathgate made it to Broadway to stay in 1954-55, collecting an impressive 20 goals and 20 assists as a rookie for the Rangers.

Hockey League and the Rangers. A year later, he was in New York for the whole campaign, registering twenty goals and twenty assists while playing right wing and manning the right point on the power play.

Whether stationary at the point or on the fly,

Bathgate had one of the hardest slap shots in the game, but he also possessed an effective, accurate wrist shot and passed the puck with precision. As a stickhandler, his skill level brought to mind the dextrous stars of earlier eras. In a game against Chicago in Madison Square Garden, he astounded foe and fan alike with a series of dazzling moves. The puck had come out of the Black Hawks' defensive end to the neutral zone when "Handy Andy" (as he was sometimes called) took command. A right-hand shot, he was facing away from defenseman Moose Vasko when he passed diagonally behind his back from right to left, spun around, and left the Moose flat-hooved before picking up the puck to skate in alone on the net, feint goalie Glenn Hall out of position, and score.

Bathgate didn't go looking for trouble, but as the Rangers' top gunner he was often the target of enemy bullies. He provided his own protection. The same lightning reflexes that served him as a goal-scorer and playmaker made him equally quick with his fists. When Detroit's bad boy, Howie Young, wouldn't stop tormenting him with his stick, Andy ripped the lumber out of Howie's hands, dropped his gloves, and cleaned Young's clock. Hulking Vic Stasiuk of the Bruins challenged Bathgate with his fists in the first and third periods of a game and came off second best on both occasions.

Before he left the Rangers in February of 1964, Bathgate had become team captain and owned a host of club scoring records. His mark of ten consecutive games in which he scored at least one goal still stands. In 719 games he scored 272 goals and added 457 assists for 729 points, third-highest total on the team's all-time list. His 40 goals and 88 points in 1958-59 helped to win him the Hart Trophy as the most valuable player in the league. The Stanley Cup that eluded him as a Ranger came in the spring of 1964, after he was traded to the Toronto Maple Leafs. Two years later he made another run at it, this time as a member of the Red Wings, but the Canadiens defeated Detroit, 4–2.

Bathgate's teammates on the 1965-66 Red Wings included his old Guelph and Rangers buddy Dean Prentice. This hard-working left-winger had been a fixture in New York until February 1963, when he was traded to Boston for Don McKenney. Ten years earlier, he had been absorbing his NHL lumps while Bathgate was still down on the farm in Vancouver. One night Prentice lined up for a faceoff against Gordie Howe, who called him a "busher" and offered to remove a few of his front teeth. Dean grinned a gap-mouthed smile and added, "Someone beat you to it."

Prentice did learn to keep his head up that first season. On one occasion he neglected to do so and was run over by a tank named Lee Fogolin, Sr., who patroled the blueline for the Chicago Black Hawks. Prentice steadily improved his scoring totals, and when Bathgate arrived for keeps, Dean notched 16 goals as the two were placed on a line with center Larry Popein. Prentice scored a total of 186 goals and 422 points with the Rangers, and was a valuable two-way player who went on to play a total of 22 NHL seasons. A skate cut tore his calf muscles during the 1957-58 season and, as a result, he wasn't at his best when the Bruins eliminated the Rangers in a six-game semi-final series. His name was never engraved on the Stanley Cup.

Another who never played on a Cup championship, despite an illustrious career, was Harry Howell, the Rangers' all-time games-played leader, with 1,160. The way fans booed him at times, it's a wonder he lasted in the Big Apple at all. Howell was a steady defender and an efficient bodychecker, who played with little apparent flair. Fans in Madison Square Garden, who were a notoriously tough crowd, had hooted Allan Stanley, a defenseman of similar characteristics, all the way to Chicago in 1954-55. Howell, however, persevered, and, from the fall of 1955 through the spring of 1957, he was one of the youngest captains in the NHL.

He played well under pressure, bending but never breaking while being razzed from the balcony. In 1966-67, he won the Norris Trophy as the league's best defenseman, one year before a kid named Orr literally took over the award. Howell's 12 goals and 40 points in 1966-67 were career highs. He remained a Ranger for two more seasons and, in the end, departed as one of the most popular players in team history. Howell finally did see his name on the Stanley Cup as a scout with the Edmonton Oilers in 1990.

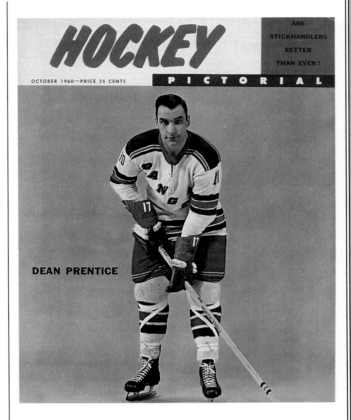

HOCKEY PICTORIAL

ARE STICKHANDLERS BETTER THAN EVER?

OCTOBER 1960—PRICE 35 CENTS

DEAN PRENTICE

A versatile performer who was noted both for his scoring skills and for his defensive abilities, Dean Prentice reached double figures in goals in nine of the eleven seasons he spent with the Rangers.

Ron Murphy joined Bathgate, Howell, and Prentice as the fourth member of the Guelph contingent. He played fifteen games as a Ranger rookie in 1952-53, and had earned a regular spot on the team the following season when, on December 20, 1953, he and Boom-Boom Geoffrion of the Canadiens became involved in a stick-swinging incident that grew out of a scuffle between the Boomer and another Ranger, Bob Chrystal. A crowd of 13,615 spectators looked on at Madison Square Garden as Geoffrion pole-axed Murphy, fracturing his jaw high on the side of his face. Dr. Kazuo Yanagisawa, the Rangers' doctor, said, "If he had been hit a little bit higher, he would have been dead right away."

After recovering, Murphy finished the season at Saskatoon in the Western League. In 1954-55, he finally put in a full season in New York, registering 14 goals and 16 assists. The next season, he upped his totals to 16 goals and 28 assists and helped the Rangers make the

One of the most popular players to patrol the blueline at Madison Square Garden, Harry Howell spent seventeen seasons with the Rangers without appearing in a Stanley Cup final-series game.

goaltender Lorne "Gump" Worsley, who would go on to a long, checkered, and colorful career in the NHL. Although he played for a non-playoff team and posted a 3.06 goals-against average, he was awarded the Calder Trophy as the NHL's rookie of the year. Nevertheless, the next season found him back in the minors. Johnny Bower, a long-time star in the American Hockey League, was in the Rangers' goal. Bower didn't lead the Rangers to the playoffs either, but did post a solid 2.60 goals-against average. The club switched back in 1954-55, as Bower played in Vancouver and Worsley returned to the Rangers. He remained the club's primary netminder until he was traded to Montreal before the start of the 1963-64 season. Worsley was always quotable in a Yogi Berra-ish sort of way, and it was during some of the bleak seasons of the early 1960s that, when asked to name the NHL team that gave him the most trouble, he replied, "The Rangers."

Sometimes the statisticians at Madison Square Garden were accused of padding the shots-against totals for Worsley, but that wouldn't really have been necessary. The diminutive, brush-cut Gumper saw a lot of rubber. There were more than a few nights of 50-plus shots, and often the opposition would score on the second or third rebound. When he joined the Canadiens he benefited from defensemen who could clear the puck and from forwards who often held the rubber in the other team's end. He wound up as part of four Cup champions in Montreal.

But by the mid-1950s, the Rangers' defense was coming together in front of a maturing Worsley. To Howell had been added future Hall-of-Famer Bill Gadsby from Chicago, as well as Western Leaguers Jack Evans and Lou Fontinato. Gadsby teamed with Bathgate on the points of a fine power-play unit. Lantern-jawed Evans was a strong, silent type, whose poker face earned him the nickname "Tex." Fontinato, the last of the Guelph championship team to make it to the majors, was a heavy bodychecker and brawler, whom reporters quickly christened "Leapin' Lou."

Up front, the Rangers had acquired some solid players in Andy Hebenton, a twenty-six-year-old rookie from the Western League; center Dave Creighton, a veteran

playoffs for the first time since 1949-50. That campaign was to be his best as a Blueshirt, however, and he was dealt to Chicago two seasons later. There he flourished for several years and was a member of the Hawks' Cup-winning squad in 1961.

The last of the significant arrivals of 1952-53 was

who had spent most of his career in Boston; and left-winger Camille Henry. Dubbed "The Eel" because of his ability to slip in, out, around, and behind opposing defensemen, Henry was a short, slight man with a goal-scorer's touch. He had a magical "deke," with which he pulled goaltenders out of position, and an uncanny sense of timing in deflecting shots into the net from around the crease. Henry, operating primarily as a power-play special-ist, scored 24 goals and won the Calder Trophy in 1953-54. He played parts of the next two seasons in the minors, but

It's been said that Gump Worsley always marched to a different drummer, but he certainly kept the beat for the defensively weak Rangers of the 1950s, winning the Calder Trophy in 1952-53 and consistently posting a goals-against average near three goals per game.

was promoted to full-time status with the Rangers midway through the 1956-57 season. He contributed five playoff points in each of the 1957 and 1958 semi-finals.

The man whose appearance behind the bench coin-cided with the Rangers' return to the playoffs was Phil

Watson, a fiery French-Canadian, who had been an out-standing center on the Rangers' 1940 championship team before working his way up the coaching ladder through the club's farm system. Watson was a martinet, who emphasized curfews and conditioning. He had coached Worsley with the New York Rovers, a Rangers farm team in the Eastern Amateur League, and he immediately resumed his old harangue about the Gump's pot belly and his fondness for beer. "Beer is the poor man's champagne," countered Worsley. "I'm strictly a V.O. [rye] man."

The Rangers finished third and fourth in the first two seasons of Watson's regime, but each time they ran into the Canadiens in the semi-finals. *Les Habitants* just happened to be starting a run of five straight Cup cham-pionships with a team that was so overpowering that the league was forced to change its rules for minor penal-ties, so that, once a team scored with the man advan-tage, the penalized player came out of the box. Before this rule change, it was "all you can score in two min-utes," and Montreal often took advantage of this oppor-tunity. In each of their two playoff meetings with the Rangers, the Canadiens prevailed, 4–1.

Phil Watson, who spent five seasons behind the bench in New York before joining the Boston Bruins, later became the first former NHL coach to accept a coaching position in the WHA, leading the Philadelphia Blazers to a third-place finish in 1972-73.

In 1957-58, by finishing second, the Rangers avoided the Canadiens and drew Boston, the fourth-place team that had trailed them by eight points. The Rangers won the opener at home, 5–3, but it was a costly victory. Vic Stasiuk had skated the width of the rink and crashed into Red Sullivan, fracturing Sullivan's jaw and splinter-ing the Rangers' playoff hopes. Two nights later, also at Madison Square Garden, the Bruins came from behind, and, when Jerry Toppazzini's shot from just inside the blueline beat Worsley at 4:36 of overtime, the series was not only tied, it was over. The circus shooed the Rangers out of the Garden until the next fall; all the remaining games would be played in Boston. The Rangers managed a win to tie the series in game four, but were blown out in the last two games.

Prior to the 1958-59 season, the Rangers lost four players in the Intra-League Draft: Evans, Creighton, Jean-Guy Gendron, and Danny Lewicki. Evans was probably the most missed, as he had developed into a strong back-liner. General manager Muzz Patrick, who had taken over from Frank Boucher in 1955-56, explained that he had chosen to protect his rookie crop. "I could be wrong," he said. "Maybe the inexperience will show. But I'm convinced that the longer the season goes, the better equipped we'll be for Stanley Cup competition."

Patrick was never able to test his theory, because the Rangers failed to qualify for post-season festivities. The club started well and was sailing along through January. On the first day of February, they defeated Detroit at the Garden, 5–4, but Howe bested Fontinato in what has become a storied fight. Some say that that's when the decline began, but the Rangers went to Detroit four nights later and shut the Wings out, 5–0.

Then their troubles began. After four consecutive losses, they lost 5–1 to the Canadiens at home on February 15. With ten minutes to play, Worsley was nursing a 1–0 shutout. The Habs broke through with five unanswered goals, three of which were scored in four minutes, and the Rangers moped back to the dressing room. "Don't take off your uniforms," screamed Watson. Worsley was the only one spared, as Phil put the rest of the squad through grueling skating drills.

The players responded with four wins and two ties in their next eight games, but on March 11 began another string of five straight losses, including back-to-back defeats at the hands of the Toronto Maple Leafs, the team that eventually bested them for fourth place. The second loss, a 6–5 setback at home on March 15, was especially bitter. The game turned when Worsley misplayed a shot from beyond the blueline by Bob Pulford.

Watson's needle, which seemed to energize his players during the first part of his reign, had been injected too many times. His bullying tactics had worn thin, and his players no longer heeded his call. When Muzz Patrick was asked if the collapse was the fault of the club's rookies, he answered: "No. Why blame the kids? They did all right. I could easily point my finger at some of the veterans. But why cry over spilt milk? In the long run, [by playing the rookies] we'll be much better off."

What Patrick didn't know was that the "long run"

would not happen until the arrival of Emile Francis, who had come to the Rangers as a substitute goaltender in 1948-49 and later coached in Guelph. Francis replaced Patrick as the club's general manager in 1964-65. He added the coaching portfolio midway through 1965-66, and, as the six-team era drew to a close in 1966-67, led the Rangers to a 25-point improvement in the standings and the first of nine consecutive berths in the playoffs.

By 1967-68, the maturing Rangers, schooled in the six-team era, were one of the NHL's better teams, finishing with 90 points. They would go on to improve on this total in each of the next six seasons.

Muzz Patrick, who spent nine seasons as the general manager of the New York Rangers, also took three turns behind the bench in 1953-54, 1954-55, and 1962-63. Despite a solid nucleus of promising talent, the Rangers lacked the defensive discipline to become a consistent playoff contender.

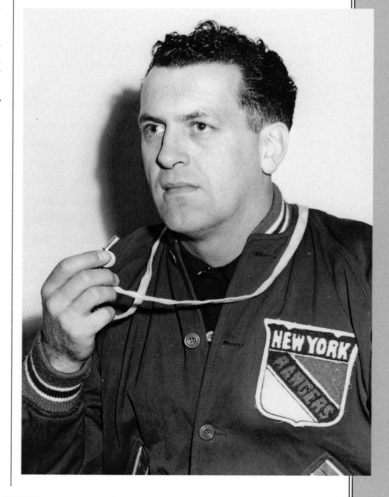

92 PTS.   79 PTS.   69 PTS.   67 PTS.   64 PTS.   49 PTS.

1959-60
Rocket's Last Glare:
Habs Clinch Fifth Consecutive Cup Crown

THE 1959-60 SEASON ACCENTUATED THE EXCEPTIONAL TALENTS OF CHICAGO'S Bobby Hull, who was involved in one of the tightest point-scoring races in recent memory. Hull, nicknamed the "Golden Jet" because of his blond hair and his spectacular speed, captured the imagination of fans throughout the league. His season-long battle for the Art Ross Trophy with Boston's Bronco Horvath was a highlight in a new decade of NHL action.

Roster revisions were limited when the six NHL teams regrouped for training camp in 1959. As expected, the Red Wings were rebuilding, centering around their main core of Howe, Ullman, Kelly, Pronovost, Delvecchio, and Sawchuk. Jack Adams continued to pursue veteran players, although most sports columnists felt he should be rebuilding with youth. Jim Morrison, Gary Aldcorn, Barry Cullen, and John McKenzie were acquired from other NHL squads, and all four made respectable contributions to the Red Wings' reconstruction program. Newcomers included Murray Oliver and Val Fonteyne, both of whom were keys to Detroit's climb from sixth to fourth place.

Coach Toe Blake, while concerned about the age of his defending-champion Canadiens, agreed with Frank Selke that the team needed only cosmetic repairs. The only newcomer to make a contribution was Billy Hicke, the AHL's leading scorer and rookie of the year with the Rochester Americans in the previous season. He would suit up for 43 games with the Canadiens in 1959-60. Jean-Claude Tremblay, Reg Fleming, and Cecil Hoekstra also made appearances with the Canadiens during the campaign.

In spite of a third-place finish in 1958-59, the Chicago Black Hawks continued to make player adjustments. Bill Hay and Murray Balfour, two players deemed expendable by the talent-rich Canadiens, both made the team in training camp. Coach Rudy Pilous placed the two speedsters on a line with Hull, and the prototype "Scooter Line" was born. Stan Mikita, who was born in Czechoslovakia but raised in Canada, also made the club. He centered Ted Lindsay and Kenny Wharram. There were no questions about the Hawks' goaltending, since Glenn Hall hadn't missed a single minute of NHL action since he joined the league to stay in 1955.

Bronco Horvath finished second in scoring in 1959-60 and also set an NHL record by recording at least one point in twenty-two consecutive regular-season games. Scoring streaks weren't officially tabulated by the NHL's statisticians in the late 1950s, so Horvath's achievement went unnoticed until 1971-72.

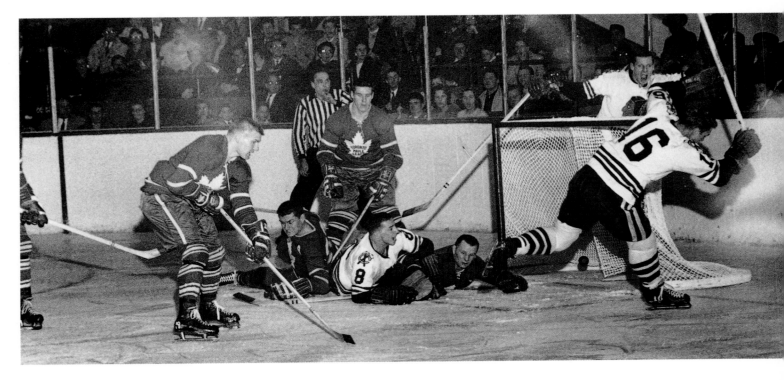

Punch Imlach, who had rebuilt the Leafs into a finely tuned machine, made very few changes, not wanting to disrupt the chemistry he had established in the playoffs. Imlach sent Barry Cullen to Detroit for Johnny Wilson and waived Brian Cullen, who was claimed in the Intra-League Draft by the Rangers. Johnny Bower, the venerable "China Wall," was back in nets, while forwards Ted Hampson and Gerry Edmundson both saw significant action during the season.

It was a year of setbacks in Boston and New York, both of whom made only minor changes and fell out of the playoff picture. Boston, Stanley Cup finalists in two of the past three seasons, obtained Aut Erickson from Chicago and promoted Dallas Smith to provide extra help along the blueline. The Bruins also acquired center Charlie Burns from Detroit.

In New York, Phil Watson was still unsure about Gump Worsley in goal, although he had given him a vote of confidence after the 1958-59 season. Clearly, Worsley had to share part of the blame for the Rangers' poor showing down the stretch, but his defensemen were not making his job any easier. Yet, the club started the 1959-60 campaign with the same cast of rearguards: Gadsby, Howell, Fontinato, John Hanna, and Jack Bownass. Rookie Kenny Schinkel was a good-looking prospect, joining Brian Cullen, Bob Kabel, and Earl Ingarfield up front.

The Rangers' slide during the final month of the 1958-59 season continued, as the New Yorkers won only three of their first fifteen games in 1959-60. On November 10, coach Phil Watson was hospitalized with ulcers, forcing Muzz Patrick to stand in for a few games. Rumors circulated that Watson was through, and when Alf Pike appeared on the scene as

Maple Leafs goaltender Johnny Bower, seen here entangled with Black Hawk forward Murray Balfour and Toronto blue-liner Allan Stanley, watches helplessly as Bobby Hull slides a rebound into the Toronto net. Hull, who turned twenty-one midway through the 1959-60 season, became the youngest player in NHL history to win the Art Ross Trophy when he captured the scoring crown with 81 points.

Jacques Plante, who had worn a mask for years during practices before finally wearing one full-time in game action, was outstanding in the 1959-60 playoffs, posting three shutouts and a 1.38 goals-against average.

The Reel Thing

In October 1960, Red Wings manager Jack Adams became the first club executive to hire film crews to cover all of his team's home games. Adams and coach Sid Abel ran the films at team meetings, pointing out right and wrong moves to the players.

an assistant coach, this gossip seemed to be true. By November 18, Pike was alone behind the Rangers' bench, and he guided the team for the rest of the season. One of Pike's first moves was to demote Worsley in favor of Marcel Paille. In all, five goaltenders would play for New York during the season, including Al Rollins, who saw his first NHL action in three seasons, practice goalie Joe Schaefer, who was called in to replace Worsley in a 5–1 loss to Chicago on February 17, and Olympic hero Jack McCartan. Despite 32 goals by Dean Prentice and 74 points by Andy Bathgate, the Rangers finished in last place, 15 points behind fifth-place Boston.

McCartan's play was one of the only shining moments in a dreary Rangers season. After leading the U.S. Olympic Team to the gold medal at the Winter Olympics in Squaw Valley, California, McCartan made his NHL debut on March 6, backstopping the Rangers to a 3–1 victory over Detroit. He finished with a 2–1–1 mark and a 1.75 goals-against average, raising hopes for the next season.

In an odd way, the Toronto Maple Leafs were able to take advantage of New York's misfortune. On February 4, the Rangers traded Eddie Shack and Bill Gadsby to Detroit for All-Star defenseman Red Kelly and Billy McNeill. However, Kelly refused to report to New York, effectively canceling the deal. Punch Imlach jumped on the opportunity and offered journeyman rearguard Marc Réaume to the Wings in exchange for Kelly. Jack Adams accepted, and so did Kelly, who would go on to lead the Leafs to four Stanley Cup titles in the 1960s. When Kelly arrived in Toronto, Imlach informed the eight-time All-Star that he was not going to play defense. Instead, he was being moved to center to take advantage of his puck-handling skills. It was a master stroke by the Leafs' coach, for Kelly proved to be a perfect fit for left-winger Frank Mahovlich, who was in the midst of a season-long slump and was rumored to be on the trading block himself.

The Leafs continued their upward climb in 1959-60, finishing in second place with a 35–26–9 record. Bob Pulford and George Armstrong were the top-scoring forwards, and Allan Stanley led all NHL defenders with ten goals. Stanley was Imlach's personal reclamation project, and he constantly put the big defenseman in pressure situations, from penalty-killing to taking key faceoffs in the defensive zone. Johnny Bower, whose signature move was a diving poke-check that confused opposing players, won 34 games and compiled a 2.73 goals-against average with five shutouts.

After four years behind the bench, Toe Blake was convinced that his 1959-60 club was the finest group he had ever directed. The Canadiens had an eighteen-game unbeaten streak in the opening months of the season, and were in first place by nine points at the halfway mark of the campaign. Midway through that streak, on November 1 in New York, Jacques Plante was severely cut when an Andy Bathgate backhander ripped his nose and upper lip. Plante went to the clinic to get stitched up, but refused to return to the ice unless he could wear the fiberglass face-mask that he often wore in practice. Toe Blake reluctantly agreed to Plante's demands, and the goalie returned to the net wearing the crude face protection. With the mask on, Plante and the Habs went another 11 games without a loss before the Leafs eked out a 1–0 victory on December 1. Although Blake had to admit that Plante was playing better than ever with the mask on, he still tried to convince his goaltender to play without it. Finally, on March 8, Plante played barefaced, but seemed shaky in a 3–0 loss to Detroit. He would never play another game in the league without a mask.

On January 10, Boston's Don Simmons became the second goalie in the modern era to employ a mask, wearing a model designed by Plante. Simmons became a convert after blanking the Leafs, 4–0, and the Rangers, 6–0, in his first two games with facial protection. The introduction of the "banana blade" curved stick, combined with the velocity of the now-popular slap shot, would soon compel many other goalies to don masks.

Gordie Howe, who assumed the captaincy of the Detroit Red Wings prior to the 1958-59 season, registered his eleventh consecutive season with 20 or more goals in 1959-60, notching 28 goals and 45 assists for the Red Wings.

The Bruins ended the 1959-60 season with a series of lost opportunities. Boston went 4–9–3 down the stretch to miss the playoffs by three points, and Bronco Horvath ended up losing the scoring title to Bobby Hull by one point. Horvath had established career highs in goals (39), assists (41), and points (80) when he entered the final game of the season, ironically against Chicago, one point ahead of Hull. Early in the second period, Horvath was struck in the face by a shot and had to go to the hospital for repairs. While Horvath was gone, Hull scored his thirty-ninth goal of the season to tie for the lead. Horvath returned for the third period, but the Hawks threw a defensive cloak around him, and he couldn't manage a point. With less than five minutes remaining, Hull made one of his patented end-to-end rushes. As Boston defenseman Dallas Smith was ramming him into the end boards, Hull threw a centering pass through the crease that deflected off teammate Eric Nesterenko's skate and skittered past Boston goalie Don Simmons. The assist marked Hull's eighty-first point, earning him his first Art Ross Trophy.

Many Boston fans pointed to another incident that summed up their season. In a November 8 game, the Black Hawks' Al Arbour threw his stick in an attempt to impede Bronco Horvath's breakaway on Glenn Hall. Referee Dalton McArthur called for a penalty shot, but was obviously confused as to the proper application of this rarely employed rule, since it was only the tenth penalty shot that had been called in the last ten years. Instead of allowing the Bruins to name their shooter, as the guidelines stated, he allowed the Chicago bench to choose the marksman. Naturally, the Boston team was incensed. The Bruins' general manager Lynn Patrick came down to the bench waving a rule book, and even offered to pay coach Milt Schmidt's fine if he went on the ice to point out

Maurice Richard (left) drills the final goal of his NHL career past Maple Leaf defender Tim Horton (7) and goaltender Johnny Bower at 11:07 of the third period on April 12, 1960. Allan Stanley (26), Henri Richard (16), Dickie Moore (12), and Gerry Ehman (17) are the other on-ice witnesses to Richard's final moment in the spotlight.

The Sixth Attacker

On October 20, 1960, Boston's Milt Schmidt became the first coach to remove a goalie for an extra attacker during a delayed penalty. When referee John Ashley signaled a delayed penalty against Detroit's Gerry Odrowski, Bronco Horvath jumped on for Don Simmons and stayed on for ten seconds before the penalty was whistled. Schmidt attempted the tactic in Detroit because the players' benches at the Olympia were closer to the goals than in other arenas. On other occasions, Schmidt had replaced his goalie with an extra attacker with under five seconds to go in a period and a faceoff in the offensive zone.

the miscarriage of justice. Little-used forward Larry Leach was chosen to take the shot, and Glenn Hall easily stopped the attempt. Bronco Horvath, in the midst of a NHL-record 22-game points streak, would have been the Bruins' obvious choice to take the penalty shot.

There was great concern in Chicago, where the Black Hawks won only two of their first twenty games. Bobby Hull was electrifying fans around the league, but the rest of the team was not responding to coach Pilous. Nonetheless, by the halfway point of the season, the Hawks had climbed to within three points of fourth place, and were finally playing as a cohesive unit. On January 19, Ed Litzenberger was involved in a serious car accident that took the life of his wife and left him out of action for eighteen games, but the Hawks overcame the adversity to finish in third place with a 28–29–13 record. Only Tod Sloan was able to join Bobby Hull as a 20-goal scorer, but the defense compensated for the lack of scoring production. Although Glenn Hall led the NHL in losses, he led the Vezina Trophy race until the last night of the season, when he surrendered five goals to Boston. Hall missed winning his second Vezina by just two goals.

The Montreal Canadiens began the defense of their Stanley Cup title against the Hawks on March 24. Chicago, already suffering from a lack of offensive punch, was missing both Hull and Mikita in the first game of the semi-finals and dropped a 4–3 decision to the Habs. Montreal was holding a 3–2 lead in the second game, when, with less than a minute remaining, Bill Hay stole the puck from Doug Harvey and slipped it past a startled Jacques Plante. Harvey quickly redeemed himself by scoring the winning goal in overtime. Jacques Plante and a smothering Montreal defense took over from there, blanking the Hawks 4–0 and 2–0 to move the Habs into their tenth consecutive Stanley Cup final. Claude Provost, assigned to check Bobby Hull, limited the NHL's scoring leader to one goal in the series.

The other semi-final featured the Leafs and the Red Wings, and although the Leafs emerged victorious, the Wings played well in the six-game series. Len Haley, a little-used winger, scored the winner for Detroit in the opening game, but Toronto rebounded for a 4–2 victory in game two. Game three was a back-and-forth marathon that took three overtime periods to decide. With the scored tied 4–4, Frank Mahovlich, well rested after spending five minutes in the penalty box following a tussle with Pete Goegan, scored three minutes into the third extra period to give the Leafs the series lead. Detroit tied the set with an overtime victory of their own in game four, but the Leafs nailed down the series with 5–4 and 4–2 wins in the next two games to reach the finals for the second straight year.

The Canadiens, heavy favorites to defeat the Leafs, had little trouble with Toronto in the finals, sweeping the Leafs in straight games to equal the Detroit Red Wings' 1952 record of eight straight victories in a single playoff season. In the third period of game three, Maurice Richard scored his only goal of the post-season, slipping a rebound past Johnny Bower in Montreal's 5–2 win. After scoring the goal, his thirty-fourth in Stanley Cup final-series play, Richard reached into the net and retrieved the puck, leading to speculation that he was planning to retire after the season. Jean Béliveau and Doug Harvey scored 28 seconds apart in the first period of game four, and Jacques Plante made 30 saves in the Cup-clinching 4–0 win. The victory represented the end of an era in NHL play and the end of the greatest dynasty in hockey history. By the time the Canadiens won their next Stanley Cup title in 1965, eight members of the team who were part of all five Cup-winning teams during the 1950s would be gone. Rocket Richard, Jacques Plante, Doug Harvey, Tom Johnson, Dickie Moore, Don Marshall, Bernie Geoffrion, and general manager Frank Selke would no longer be with the franchise.

Chicago's Bill Hay, the first U.S.-college-trained player to star in the NHL, won the Calder Trophy after collecting 18 goals and 37 assists. Gordie Howe won his fifth Hart Trophy, Doug Harvey took home his fifth Norris Trophy in six years, and Jacques Plante, who won 40 games and appeared in a career-high 69, captured the Vezina Trophy. Don McKenney, who led the league with 49 assists, won the Lady Byng Trophy.

In June, two pioneer players who went on to become great architects of the modern game of hockey, brothers Lester and Frank Patrick, passed away within weeks of each other in Victoria, British Columbia.

Bill "Red" Hay, a collegiate star with the Colorado College Tigers before turning pro with the WHL's Calgary Stampeders, captured NHL rookie-of-the-year honors after his 18-goal, 37-assist effort in 1959-60.

U.S. OLYMPIC HERO JACK McCARTAN GOLDEN IN NHL DEBUT

McCartan, who backstopped the U.S. Olympic Team to a gold medal at the 1960 Winter Games in Squaw Valley, California, played four games with the New York Rangers during the 1959-60 season, compiling a goals-against average of 1.75.

March 6, 1960
at Madison Square Garden
New York 3, Detroit 1

FIRST PERIOD
1) NY Cullen 7 (Bathgate, Hebenton) 18:29
PENALTIES – Ullman DET (hooking), Prentice NY (slashing) 11:47.

SECOND PERIOD
2) DET Delvecchio 17 (Oliver, Howe) 16:18
3) NY Hebenton 16 (Prentice, Cullen) PPG 17:50
PENALTIES – Aldcorn DET (hooking) 17:07; Fontinato NY (holding) 18:36.

THIRD PERIOD
4) NY Prentice 27 (Cullen) 11:30
PENALTIES – Cullen NY (holding) 3:44; Spencer NY (hooking) 6:38; Spencer NY (crosschecking) 15:47.

SHOTS ON GOAL	1	2	3	T
DETROIT	11	9	14	34
NEW YORK	17	8	6	31

GOALTENDERS	TIME	SA	GA	ENG	W/L
DET Sawchuk	60:00	28	3	0	L
NY McCartan	**60:00**	**33**	**1**	**0**	**W**

PP CONVERSIONS DET 0/4 NY 1/1

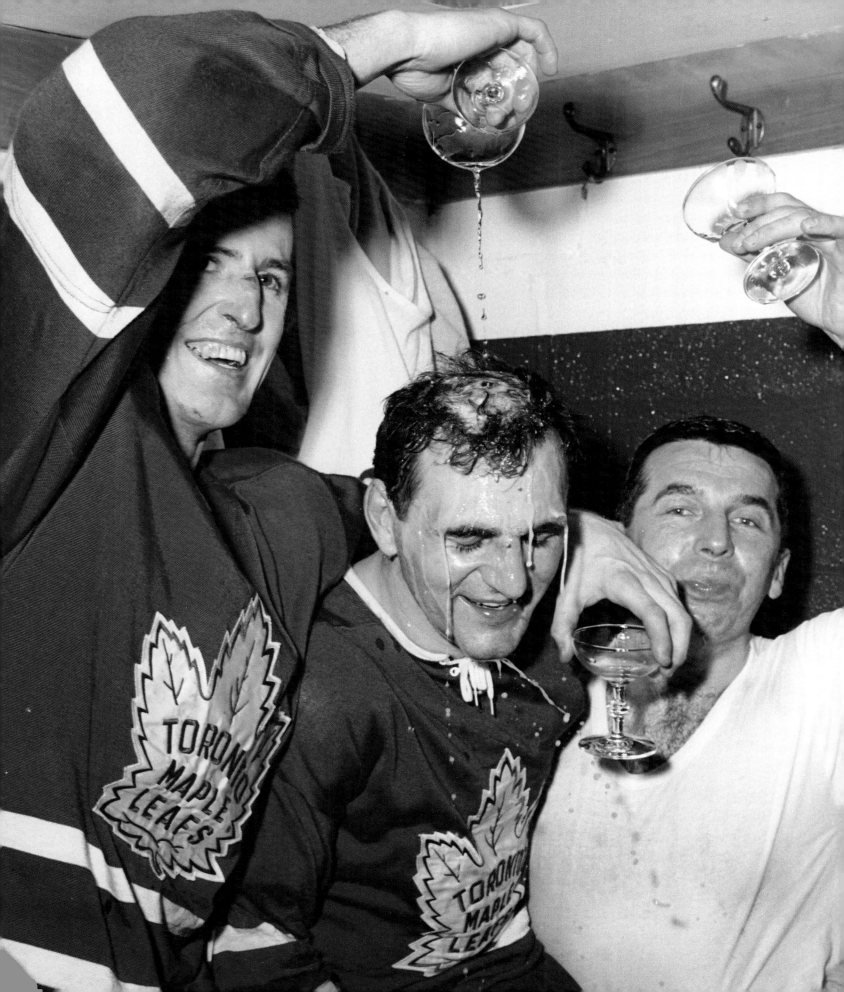

Punch Time: Lord Stanley Returns to Toronto

1960-61 to 1963-64

| 92 PTS. | 90 PTS. | 75 PTS. | 66 PTS. | 54 PTS. | 43 PTS. |

1960-61
Hawks' Rebuild Completed by Cup; Geoffrion Scores 50

THE 1960-61 SEASON WAS HIGHLIGHTED BY A YEAR-LONG ON-ICE RIVALRY between the two offensive superstars of the Montreal Canadiens and the Toronto Maple Leafs, Bernie Geoffrion and Frank Mahovlich. The Leafs and Habs staged a 70-game clash for first place, while Geoffrion and Mahovlich both went to the wire in their competition to match Rocket Richard's record of 50 goals in a season.

Throughout the summer, the Montreal newspapers were full of rumors about the Rocket's imminent retirement. Although, when training camp opened, he was in attendance, only hours after scoring four goals in a inter-squad scrimmage on September 15, Richard announced that his marvelous career was over. The Rocket departed having scored 544 regular-season and 82 playoff goals, but, more importantly, his departure took with it a significant part of the heart and passion that drove the Montreal machine. The team would continue to vault up the NHL standings, but when playoff time came around, the absence of the game's greatest playoff performer would prove telling.

Despite the loss of Richard, the Canadiens made few roster revisions in preparation for their defense of the Stanley Cup. Ab McDonald was traded to Chicago for Glen Skov, but Skov was unable to crack the talented Habs lineup. Bill Hicke was assigned Richard's right-wing spot, and rookies Gilles Tremblay and Bobby Rousseau were both promoted during the season and saw limited action.

Punch Imlach's Maple Leafs had a pair of outstanding rookies make their NHL debuts during the 1960-61 season. Bob Nevin, who had seen periodic action in both 1958 and 1959, was employed for a full

Opposite: Stanley Cup hero Bobby Baun (center) receives a champagne shower from teammates Billy Harris (left) and Ron Stewart after the Toronto Maple Leafs' third straight Stanley Cup victory in 1963-64. After eight years of either missing the playoffs or being eliminated in the first round, the Leafs made it to the championship finals in five of six years from 1958-59 to 1963-64.

Former teammates and defense partners Red Kelly (left) and Marcel Pronovost battle for a loose puck behind the Red Wings' net shortly after Kelly was dealt to Toronto. In part, it was the emergence of Pronovost as an All-Star defenseman that had made Kelly expendable. Pronovost earned the first of four consecutive All-Star berths in 1957-58.

season in 1960-61, scoring 21 goals. Dave Keon came straight out of St. Michael's College in Toronto to the Leafs and impressed fans with his maturity and skating skills. Imlach also nabbed Larry Hillman in the Intra-League Draft from the Bruins. The six-year veteran played a significant role in establishing the Leafs as the league's finest defensive team. Red Kelly returned to the forward line, centering Mahovlich and Nevin.

Chicago lost Ted Lindsay to retirement, but replaced him by obtaining Ab McDonald from the Canadiens. The Habs were reluctant to give up on the Winnipeg native, but he was jeered so loudly at the Forum after he replaced fan favorite Marcel Bonin on the second line that his performance had suffered. The addition of McDonald was the only major roster move the Hawks would make, as they were able to

go through the entire season without major injuries. Only one player, Wayne Hicks, was needed to complement the lineup during the campaign.

Jack Adams continued to roll the dice in Detroit, drafting Parker MacDonald from New York and Al Johnson from Montreal and acquiring Howie Glover from Chicago in exchange for Jim Morrison. Adams also elevated farm hands Gerry Odrowski and Bruce MacGregor and demoted Lou Marcon, Forbes Kennedy, Billy McNeill, Barry Cullen, and Jack McIntyre. Hank Bassen was penciled in to spell Terry Sawchuk, and he ended up playing only two fewer games than the veteran.

Alf Pike, back behind the bench for the Rangers, revamped his lineup by including newcomers Floyd Smith, Ted Hampson, Don Johns, and Orland Kurtenbach. Once again, the Rangers' most pressing problem appeared to be in goal, where there was no clear incumbent. Gump Worsley won the job in training camp, but Jack McCartan, Marcel Paille, and Joe Schaefer all made appearances in the New York nets during the season.

An era came to an close in Boston when Fleming Mackell retired to become the playing coach of the American Hockey League's Quebec Aces. A thirteen-year veteran, Mackell had delivered performances in the 1953 and 1958 finals that were the highlights of his career. Jim Bartlett was acquired from New York to take Mackell's place, one of eight different players the Bruins auditioned over the 70-game schedule.

The "Big M," Frank Mahovlich, unleashes a backhander that Boston's Bruce Gamble just manages to kick away in this Toronto–Boston tilt during the 1960-61 season. Mahovlich's 48 goals in 1960-61 established a Maple Leaf record for goals by a left-winger that stood until 1993-94.

Jean Ratelle made his NHL debut during the 1960-61 season, collecting three points in three games with the New York Rangers. The previous season, Ratelle began his professional career with the EPHL's Trois-Rivières Lions, notching an impressive eight points in only three games.

Milestones Against Maniago

When Bernie "Boom-Boom" Geoffrion became the first player to equal Rocket Richard's mark of 50 goals in a season in 1960-61, the goaltender he victimized was Cesare Maniago. When Bobby Hull became the first player to break the 50-goal mark in 1965-66, Maniago was also in goal.

None of Gary Aldcorn, Orval Tessier, or Dick Meissner could help the club climb out of the NHL cellar.

It was the play of Toronto's Frank Mahovlich that delighted Leaf fans during the 1960-61 season. With Kelly delivering perfect passes and Nevin digging the puck out of corners, Toronto's lanky left-winger was well on his way to equaling Richard's mark of 50 goals established in 1945. Mahovlich, by now known as the "Big M," set a new Leaf mark for goals on January 25, when he scored his 38th and 39th of the season in a 5–3 win over the Canadiens. After 50 games, the Big M had 40 goals and had pulled into second spot in the point-scoring race behind Bernie Geoffrion, although Boom-Boom still trailed Mahovlich by 13 goals.

Montreal was still the league's strongest club, with Béliveau, Moore, and Geoffrion taking turns moving up and down the scoring ladder. However, Moore broke his foot in a 7–4 victory over the Rangers at the Forum, leaving Geoffrion and Béliveau to battle for top spot. It was then that the Boomer caught fire, averaging over a goal per game through to the end of the season, despite a nagging knee injury. The Leafs and Habs jockeyed back and forth in the standings, but the Canadiens finished the schedule, going 7–2–1 to finish in first place, two points ahead of the Leafs.

On March 16, when the Canadiens and Leafs met to decide top spot in the standings, Mahovlich had 48 goals and Geoffrion had potted 49. As they had done with Gordie Howe in 1953, the Canadiens' defenders keyed on Mahovlich, limiting him to one shot on goal. With six minutes remaining in the game, Geoffrion took a relay from Gilles Tremblay and Jean Béliveau and slid the puck past Cesare Maniago for his 50th goal, tying the Rocket's 16-year-old mark. Despite playing only 64 games, Geoffrion won the scoring title with 50 goals and 45 assists, pursued closely by "le Gros Bill," Béliveau, who collected 90 points.

A key move in the Leafs' success was made early in the season, when Imlach acquired Eddie Shack from the Rangers for Pat Hannigan and John Wilson. Shack, a whirling dervish on skates, gave the Leafs some needed scoring touch and extra toughness.

Third place was the property of the Chicago Black Hawks, whose 29–24–17 record earned them 75 points. Under Rudy Pilous, the Hawks had matured into a consistent, evenly paced club, with three good forward lines and a large mobile defense. When they played together as a unit, they were as good as any team in the league. Bobby Hull suffered a let-down after his marvelous 1959-60 season, dropping to 56 points, three behind team leader Bill Hay's 59 points. The Scooter Line of Ab McDonald, Stan Mikita, and Kenny Wharram gave the Hawks an excellent second forward line, and Ron Murphy, Tod Sloan, and Ed Litzenberger provided veteran leadership.

The Detroit Red Wings seized the final playoff berth, largely on the merits of outstanding seasons from Norm Ullman (70 points) and Gordie

Howe (72 points). In the first half of the season, the Wings were a solid third-place club, with a 15–12–8 record. However, after starting the new year by going 3–6–3, Jack Adams swapped youngsters Murray Oliver, Tom McCarthy, and Gary Aldcorn to Boston for Vic Stasiuk and Leo Labine. The move didn't seem to help either team, and the Wings limped to the finish line with a 25–29–16 record.

Alf Pike's New York Rangers performed capably through much of the campaign, but a 5–10–2 finish sealed their fate, and they finished out of the playoffs for the third straight year. The story line was similar to the woes that plagued the Rangers over the past four seasons: efficient

Johnny Bower displays his patented poke-checking style to deflect the puck away from Boston's Leo Labine. Bower led the NHL in victories (33) and goals-against average (2.50) in the 1960-61 season, totals that earned Bower the Vezina Trophy and a spot on the First All-Star Team.

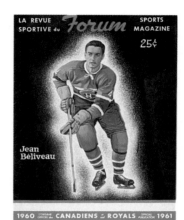

Many of Jean Béliveau's NHL-leading 58 assists in 1960-61 were converted into goals by Bernie Geoffrion, who became the second player to record a 50-goal season.

Murray Balfour's most important goal was the triple-overtime winner in Chicago's 2–1 victory over the defending-champion Montreal Canadiens in game three of the 1961 semi-finals.

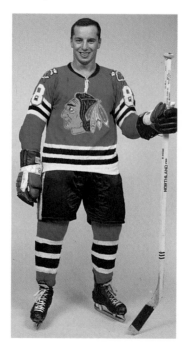

offense coupled with porous defense. Bathgate, Prentice, Hebenton, and Henry all compiled outstanding seasons but, once again, goaltending was a major concern. Jack McCartan shut out the Black Hawks, 2–0, in his season debut, then allowed 36 goals in his next seven games. Gump Worsley, subjected to 40-plus shots every evening, was notable in compiling a 3.33 goals-against average, but his efforts went largely unrewarded. The Rangers were eliminated from the playoff run on March 9 and finished in fifth spot, twelve points in arrears of the Red Wings.

Cellar-dwelling Boston had another disappointing campaign, finishing last with 15 wins, 42 losses, and 13 ties. Age and inconsistency were the Bruins' major obstacles, as Horvath, Stasiuk, and Flaman were approaching the ends of their careers. General manager Lynn Patrick attempted to shake things up, acquiring André Pronovost from Montreal for Jean-Guy Gendron and breaking up the Uke Line by sending Labine and Stasiuk to Detroit. One of the newcomers, Murray Oliver, would go on to have a number of fine seasons in Boston, but Tom McCarthy and Gary Aldcorn would never play in the NHL again after the 1960-61 season. Boston's Willie O'Ree, the first black athlete to play in the league, recorded 4 goals and 14 points in 43 games. It would be O'Ree's last shot at NHL employment, though he would become a perennial All-Star in the minor pro Western Hockey League, playing until 1974.

The defending-champion Montreal Canadiens – healthy for the first time all season – met the Chicago Black Hawks in the 1961 semi-finals. Although the Habs had split their season series with Chicago, each team winning five and tying four, the Hawks were an unpredictable and difficult opponent for the Canadiens. Montreal had an easy time in game one, rolling to a 6–2 win behind four third-period goals. Ed Litzenberger's goal with three minutes left gave Chicago a 4–3 win in game two, and Murray Balfour's pair of markers, including the overtime winner, put Chicago up by a game with a 2–1 triumph.

Balfour's winning goal was scored with Dickie Moore in the penalty box, a call that incensed the Canadiens' bench. At the conclusion of this game's 52-minute marathon overtime, Montreal coach Toe Blake walked out onto the ice and threw a punch at referee Dalton McArthur, earning a $2,000 fine, the largest in NHL history to that point. Remarkably, Blake wasn't suspended, but his actions weighed heavily on the Habs. Montreal was able to tie the series with a 5–2 victory in the fourth game, but Glenn Hall registered a pair of 3–0 shutouts in games five and six to end the Canadiens' reign as NHL champions. The Habs were without Bernie Geoffrion for games four and five, when his sprained knee was placed in a cast, but he managed to play in game six after Doug Harvey cut off the plaster during their train journey back to Chicago.

There was another surprise in the Detroit–Toronto semi-final. The Leafs, who had easily handled the Wings during the regular season, were expected to sweep Detroit, and, after a 3–2 double-overtime win in the opening game, were well on their way to their third straight trip to the finals. However, Terry Sawchuk and the Red Wings' defense toughened up and won the remaining four games to set up the first all-American Stanley Cup final since 1950. The resulting Detroit–Chicago series was also the first final featuring third- and fourth-place clubs since the NHL was formed in 1917.

In game one, Terry Sawchuk suffered a shoulder injury and gave up three first-period goals in a four-minute span. Bobby Hull, who scored twice, and Ken Wharram were the Hawks' marksmen. Sawchuk was replaced by Hank Bassen. The Wings fought to within one, on goals by Len Lunde and Al Johnson, but Glenn Hall held the door shut in a 3–2 Black Hawks win. Bassen was back in goal for the second game, as the Wings tied the series with a 3–1 victory on a pair of goals by Alex Delvecchio and a single tally by Howie Young.

The Black Hawks regained the series lead in game three, bunching second-period goals by Mikita, Balfour, and Murphy for a 3–1 decision. Following Detroit's 2–1 win in game four, the Black Hawks regrouped and outworked the weary Red Wings in the remaining two games. In game five, Stan Mikita scored twice and set up a third goal en route to a 6–3 decision. Using a similar game plan in game six, the Hawks out-hit and outskated the Red Wings, capitalizing on a series of Detroit turnovers to score three unassisted goals in their 5–1 Stanley Cup-clinching victory. The final-series win gave Chicago its third Stanley Cup title, and its first since 1938.

Post-season awards went to Bernie Geoffrion, who took home the Hart and the Art Ross trophies. Johnny Bower's 2.50 goals-against average earned him the Vezina, and Doug Harvey received his sixth Norris. Rookie Dave Keon's excellent two-way play was rewarded with the Calder Trophy, and Red Kelly, who compiled a career-high 70 points in his first full season as a forward, won the Lady Byng.

(*Continued on p. 162*)

BALFOUR'S GOAL IN TRIPLE OVERTIME PUTS HAWKS AHEAD OF HABS IN '61 SEMIS

Chicago went on to defeat the Canadiens in six games, ending Montreal's string of ten straight appearances in the Stanley Cup finals.

March 26, 1961
at Chicago Stadium
Chicago 2, Montreal 1

FIRST PERIOD

No Scoring
PENALTIES – Langlois MTL (highsticking) 1:26; Balfour CHI (charging) 6:44; Richard MTL (roughing), Fleming CHI (roughing) 7:18; Gendron MTL (highsticking), Hay CHI (highsticking) 11:04; Backstrom MTL (highsticking), St. Laurent CHI (highsticking) 18:06.

SECOND PERIOD

1) CHI Balfour 1 (Hay, Hull) 18:33
PENALTIES – Balfour CHI (holding) 7:47; St. Laurent CHI (tripping) 8:12; Johnson MTL (hooking) 12:49; Provost MTL (roughing), Murphy CHI (roughing) 14:07.

THIRD PERIOD

2) MTL Richard 2 (Goyette) PPG 19:24
Penalties – Hicke MTL (spearing, fighting – major, misconduct), Mikita CHI (fighting – major, misconduct) 13:09; Hay CHI (tripping) 18:40.

FIRST OVERTIME PERIOD

No Scoring
Penalties – None

SECOND OVERTIME PERIOD

No Scoring
Penalties – Talbot MTL (tripping) 4:20; St. Laurent CHI (tripping) 10:21; Langlois MTL (hooking) 14:18.

THIRD OVERTIME PERIOD

3) CHI Balfour 2 (Pilote, Mikita) PPG 12:12
PENALTIES – Murphy CHI (tripping) :08; Moore MTL (tripping) 11:44.

SHOTS ON GOAL	1	2	3	1OT	2OT	3OT	T
MONTREAL	13	4	13	8	10	6	54
CHICAGO	7	6	7	8	13	4	45

GOALTENDERS	TIME	SA	GA	ENG	W/L
MTL Plante	112:09*	43	2	0	L
CHI Hall	112:12	53	1	0	W

* unofficial, left net for extra skater late in third period at time of face-off in Chicago's defensive zone.

PP CONVERSIONS MTL 1/6 CHI 1/6

Rebuilding the Black Hawks

by Dan Moulton

By 1954, the fact that the Chicago Black Hawks had been providing new definitions for the words "inept" and "futile" for several seasons was finally starting to show up in Chicago Stadium's box-office figures.

That only four thousand or so were taking the trouble to show up on West Madison Street had to be a bit startling for new owners Arthur Wirtz and Jim Norris because, through most of the team's history, its lack of success on the ice – it had won the Stanley Cup only in 1934 and 1938 – had borne no relationship to success in the counting house. In fact, as recently as 1947-48, the Hawks had set an NHL attendance record while duplicating their sixth-and-last-place finish of the season before.

But the goodwill that had sustained the team almost from its inception had finally run out. The Pony Line of Doug and Max Bentley and Bill Mosienko, which had provided so much entertainment through the 1940s, was no more. And its last vestige, Mosienko, quite obviously would play little part in any resurgence. In fact, he was not offered a contract after scoring 12 goals and 15 assists in 64 games of the 1954-55 season.

There had been a brief flurry in 1952-53 when center Sid Abel had come over from Detroit as a playing coach and pulled a motley collection of youngsters and rejects into fourth place, from which it managed a cou-

ple of victories over the mighty Canadiens in the first round of the playoffs. But that was it. The only bright spot in the 1953-54 season was goalie Al Rollins, who was given the Hart Trophy as most valuable player as a prize for having escaped the season with his life. The team won a grand total of twelve games and was back in the basement.

Clearly, Wirtz and Norris had to make a move. Though they acquired the Black Hawks only in 1954, an earlier deal had given the Wirtz and Norris families control of Chicago Stadium in 1933. The Stadium, which lacked a pro basketball tenant, needed the revenue that a popular NHL team could generate. Without a substantial contribution from these two winter sports, ticket sales from their International Boxing Club fights, ice shows, circuses, and Saturday-night college basketball double-headers weren't going to be enough.

To start, the Black Hawks' front-office organization had to be dragged into the 1950s. For years, manager Bill Tobin had operated virtually without a farm system, picking up other teams' culls and occasionally stealing a kid out of Western Canada. For the most part, he couldn't, or wouldn't, even try to tap into the talent-rich junior teams in Quebec and Ontario. His one bold attempt at a major improvement hadn't worked out. In November 1947, he swung a seven-player deal that sent Max Bentley and Cy Thomas to the Maple Leafs for three forwards and a pair of defensemen, but none of these new Hawks made a lasting impression in Chicago. In fact, only Gus Bodnar lasted long enough to participate in the 1953 playoffs, which was the team's only post-season venture since 1946.

Thomas would play only eight games for Toronto, but Bentley, a clever puckhandler who served as the Leafs' power-play pointman, would help his new club to the Stanley Cup in 1948, 1949, and 1951.

The Hawks needed a complete retooling. To start the job, Wirtz and Norris turned to the Detroit Red Wings. The ownership of the two clubs was closely related. Norris's father, James Norris, Sr., had grown up playing hockey in Montreal, but made his fortune in the Chicago grain market. Norris had hoped to land an NHL franchise for Chicago, but had lost out to coffee brewer

Major Frederic McLaughlin in 1926. Instead, in 1930 he purchased a minor pro hockey club, the Chicago Shamrocks, hoping to acquire an NHL club at a later date. Norris senior's chance to become a big-league hockey owner came less than three years later, when Depression-era economics had forced the owners of the Detroit Falcons and the Olympia arena into receivership. To complete the transactions, Norris senior sent young Chicago real-estate entrepreneur Arthur Wirtz to Detroit. Wirtz joined Norris as an investor in the arena and in the club, which was promptly renamed the Red Wings.

The following year, 1933, the Norrises and Wirtz also acquired control of the Chicago Stadium Corporation, and a later investment brought them control of Madison Square Garden as well. Their enthusiasm for hockey and arena ownership proved to be most fortunate for the league, because Norris's and Wirtz's considerable wealth was a major factor in keeping the NHL afloat during the worst years of the Depression.

By 1954, when the Hawks' need was greatest, the Red Wings were being run by Jim Norris's half-brother, Bruce, and his sister, Marguerite. James Norris, Sr., after whom the NHL's annual award for its top defenseman is named, had passed away in 1952.

Detroit's contribution to the Hawks' renaissance arrived in the form of a new general manager. The day-to-day job of building the Black Hawks was given to Tommy Ivan, who, while serving as coach under manager Jack Adams, had directed the Red Wings to six consecutive league titles and three Stanley Cup championships between 1948-49 and 1953-54.

The diminutive Ivan had no illusions about the job ahead of him. Whereas as coach of the Red Wings he could open the gate and put Gordie Howe, Ted Lindsay, Alex Delvecchio, Marcel Pronovost, and Red Kelly on the ice, as the man in charge of the Hawks he had to make do with earnest young men named Red Sullivan, Bill Gadsby, Pete Conacher, Gord Hollingworth, Lou Jankowski, and Frank Martin.

Sid Abel had left the Hawks at the end of the 1953-54 season, so Ivan's first task was to pick a coach. The job went to Frankie Eddolls, a defenseman who had spent

After coaching the Detroit Red Wings to three Stanley Cup titles in five years, Tommy Ivan (seen here with former Red Wing center Glen Skov) was brought to the Windy City to rebuild the falling Chicago Black Hawks franchise.

two seasons with the Canadiens and five with the Rangers during a thirteen-year professional career. He became the Hawks' nineteenth coach since Pete Muldoon directed the team in its maiden voyage in 1926-27.

The Black Hawks' approach to coaching always had been casual, to say the least. Muldoon, who started the whole thing, lasted only a year, and it took two men, Barney Stanley and Hugh Lehman, to get the team through 1927-28. Herb Gardiner managed it all by himself in 1928-29, but Tom Shaughnessy and Bill Tobin split the job the next year. Dick Irvin, one of the players from the old Portland (Oregon) Rosebuds of the West Coast league, who was sold to Chicago to form the nucleus of the first team, coached the 1930-31 season, but gave way to Tobin again midway through 1931-32.

And so it went. Tommy Gorman was in charge in 1933-34, the year of the team's first Stanley Cup. But he was gone in favor of one Clem Loughlin the next year.

The 1937-38 season was remarkable. The story goes that the singular Major McLaughlin was impressed one afternoon at Wrigley Field when National League umpire Bill Stewart ejected Cubs star Gabby Hartnett, and he decided that a man of such strength of character was just the one to run his team.

However it actually came about, Stewart, a New Englander with some hockey in his background, was, indeed, the coach of the 1937-38 team and became the first U.S.-born coach of a Cup champion. And he didn't even have to quit his "regular" job. That was fortunate since Stewart lasted only part of the next season before being replaced by Paul Thompson.

Ivan may have been new to the team in 1954, but he picked up on the tradition quickly, and Eddolls was fired after his charges managed only thirteen victories, just six of them in the Stadium.

Tommy probably was also aware of the offhand manner in which the team had been run – from an office in McLaughlin's coffee-roasting plant several miles from the Stadium – but he got a graphic demonstration at his first training camp in Pembroke, Ontario. Tobin, who still had a title and an office, had offered to be of use during the camp, and Ivan asked him to take care of the players' travel expenses.

Because player development of any kind had been a foreign concept in Chicago, Ivan would have had no more than twenty or twenty-five players with which to set up some semblance of competition for positions if he hadn't invited several unattached pros and senior amateurs for tryouts.

Ivan knew that there was almost no possibility of a prospect being uncovered among the invitees. They probably knew it, too, and Tobin certainly didn't expect any miracles. But for everyone's sake, it was important that the fiction be maintained that the hopefuls hadn't made the trip in vain.

Not a chance. Shortly after the players assembled, Tobin gathered all the unrostered players, ascertained how much each had spent getting to Pembroke, and issued cheques that covered their costs and also included money for the trip home! So much for confidence-building.

They might not have been visible to the naked eye, but Ivan actually was taking positive steps during Chicago's dismal 1954-55 season. Some eighteen games into the season, he packaged long-time Hawk star Gadsby and Pete Conacher, whose main asset was an illustrious name, and shipped them to New York for defenseman Allan Stanley, who had fallen from favor in the Garden, and journeyman forward Nick Mickoski. Neither had an immediate impact on the team, but a signal had been sent that Ivan would deal.

That particular trade, by coincidence, emphasized how bleak the hockey picture in Chicago had become. Gadsby and Conacher were notified of the deal when they showed up at a train station for a trip to Omaha, where a regular-season game was to be played against the Canadiens. Several Hawk games were farmed out that year, and few in Chicago complained.

One acquisition that year had a long-range impact.

Although he wasn't expected to make the grade, eighteen-year-old Bobby Hull was so impressive at training camp prior to the 1957-58 season that he graduated to the Black Hawks team without ever playing a game in the minor leagues.

The St. Catharines TeePees celebrate their 6–3 victory over the Edmonton Oil Kings in the 1954 Memorial Cup final. Elmer "Moose" Vasko (4), went on to anchor the Black Hawk defense for ten seasons.

Center Eddie Litzenberger arrived from Montreal in what might well have been part of a help-the-Hawks program. He alone from that group would be around for the Stanley Cup in 1961.

Another hopeful sign had been flashed a bit earlier, when scout Bob Wilson, on hand to observe a youngster in a kids'-league game in Ontario, noticed a blond, pudgy fourteen-year-old named Robert Marvin Hull. The young man he'd been sent to scout was quickly forgotten in Wilson's rush to put Master Hull on the Hawks'

sponsorship list in the NHL's Central Registry in Montreal.

That may have been the single most important act in team history, as became apparent soon after eighteen-year-old Robert Marvin arrived in Chicago fresh from Junior A hockey for the 1957-58 season.

A move during the summer of 1955 may be ranked second in its impact on the franchise's future. Eager to start some semblance of a farm system, Ivan convinced Wirtz and Norris to let him purchase the Buffalo franchise in the American Hockey League. Ownership of a minor pro farm team was important, because it provided Ivan with a place in which the Hawks could develop players to their specifications. But of at least equal importance was the fact that Buffalo sponsored a Junior A team in nearby St. Catharines, Ontario, which was the birthplace of the elder Norris.

Having a top junior team was important in itself. But this particular team, the TeePees, owned title to a big, fast, and willing young defenseman named Elmer "Moose" Vasko, who would arrive on the Chicago scene in 1956 and be on hand to join in the Cup celebration in 1961. Already with the Hawks when Vasko arrived was Pierre Pilote, who was playing with Buffalo at the time of the purchase. He also was an important part of the Cup team and went on to capture the Norris Trophy as the league's top defenseman on three occasions.

"I knew Pilote was supposed to be a good prospect," said Ivan years later. "But I had to take other people's word for it. Every time I watched, he played poorly. It's a good job I listened."

The infrastructure repair was fine, but Chicago fans paid little attention to such things and still judged progress by looking at the standings. And there the signs remained negative.

Ivan had replaced Eddolls with the venerable Dick Irvin for the 1955-56 season. Refusing to allow his firing by the Black Hawks in 1932 to spoil his zest for coaching, Irvin had gone on to highly successful careers behind the bench in Toronto and Montreal. By the 1955-56 season, Irvin had been replaced in Montreal by former star Toe Blake, and Ivan, who coached against Irvin for years, saw a chance to get a big-name coach with an impeccable record.

The move paid off, to some degree. Pilote and Litzenberger showed flashes, and Rollins was steady in goal, as he was through most of his Chicago career. But the victory count improved only modestly to 19, and the playoffs again went on without the Hawks. Talent, obviously, was still the problem, and Ivan devoted a good part of the off-season trying to add another body he felt could be of service. The degree of his desperation can be measured by the concessions he made to get his man.

The man was Eric Nesterenko, who had been billed as Toronto's answer to the Canadiens' Jean

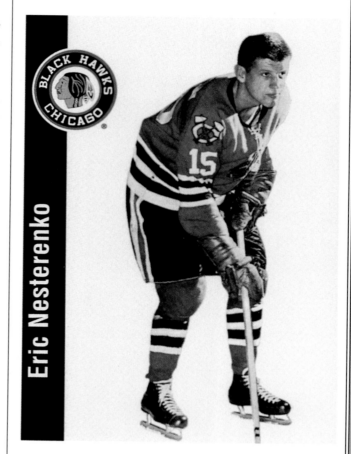

Eric Nesterenko

After five disappointing seasons with the Toronto Maple Leafs, Eric Nesterenko was sold to the Chicago Black Hawks on May 21, 1956, where he became a valued defensive specialist.

Béliveau when he graduated to the Maple Leafs from the St. Michael's Juniors.

Well, he hadn't proven to be the Leafs' answer to much of anything, despite good size, excellent skating ability, and a willing, if somewhat "ethereal," nature.

Ivan got the rights to the native of Flin Flon, Manitoba, but that was just the start of his adventure. Nesterenko promptly decided that he'd had it with hockey and would turn his talents to a different game, as an end on the University of Toronto football team.

"I made a lot of trips to Toronto that summer," Ivan recalled. "But I didn't have much luck. There I'd be, as the university's bus carrying the football team to camp pulled away, waving goodbye to Nesterenko, who would be looking out the back window."

The Hawk manager couldn't afford to drop the

In a move that shocked Motown hockey fans, "Terrible Ted" Lindsay was traded by Detroit to the Black Hawks on July 23, 1957. Lindsay spent three seasons in Chicago, collecting 123 points in 206 games before retiring after the 1959-60 campaign.

matter, though. His team still needed too much, and Nesterenko offered some of what he needed. He could and would check, and Ivan figured him for a solid penalty-killer. Any goals he scored would rate as bonuses. Still, the trick was to get him to Chicago.

A few more miles logged on Trans-Canada Airlines, and an agreement was reached. Nesterenko would study during the week and fly to wherever the Hawks were playing on weekends, making him perhaps the NHL's first weekend warrior.

Before Nesterenko had decided to be part of the Hawks' 1956-57 season, however, tragedy had struck, forcing Ivan to assume the role as coach and manager. Dick Irvin had reported to training camp in St. Catharines on time, but it soon became apparent that he was gravely ill. He returned to his home in the Town of Mount Royal, Quebec, before the team broke camp, and he died before the year was out.

Ivan tried to apply all the coaching skills he'd developed at Detroit. But the talent still wasn't there on the ice. In fact, only Vasko, Pilote, Litzenberger, and Nesterenko lasted long enough to play on the Cup

winner. The result was a dismal sixteen-victory season. The team seemed to be retrogressing.

Ivan's work began paying off during the 1957-58 season, although the team improved by only eight victories to twenty-four and missed the playoffs once again. However, two deals worked out with the talent-rich Red Wings – again – had added the still dangerous Ted Lindsay, center Earl Reibel, wings Bill Dineen, Billy Dea, and Lorne Ferguson, and – fanfare, please – a goalkeeper named Glenn Hall. In addition, Hull had arrived after a Memorial Cup season in St. Catharines.

That St. Catharines connection paid off during the season, too, when TeePees coach Rudy Pilous arrived to relieve Ivan of half of his management portfolio.

The breakthrough came the next season, when Pilous directed the Hawks into third place on the strength of twenty-eight victories. Of decided aid were three defensemen, who joined Vasko and Pilote. Former Ranger Jack Evans came in, along with ex-Canadien Dollard St. Laurent and a bespectacled shot-blocker named Alger Arbour, who had done time in Detroit. Center Tod Sloan also came over from Toronto.

As important as these additions were to the team's eventual success, however, the most portentous part of the season was the three-game tryout of another St. Catharines junior star. On his first trip over

When Rudy Pilous was appointed as the Black Hawks coach prior to the 1957-58 season, he inherited a team blossoming with young talent such as Pierre Pilote, Bobby Hull, Glenn Hall, and Moose Vasko.

the boards, eighteen-year-old Stan Mikita put on a shift that sent the Canadiens' brilliant Doug Harvey spinning, and only a strong effort by the goalie prevented the youngster from scoring on his first NHL shot. This player obviously was a keeper.

Fans had begun returning the previous season, and by 1958-59 the base had been re-established.

The 1959-60 season duplicated the previous year exactly – twenty-eight victories, thirteen ties, third place, first-round elimination by the Canadiens. But Bill Hay and Murray Balfour came aboard. And the stage at last was set.

The next season, another third-place finish was followed by a stunning first-round victory over the Canadiens, ending the Habs' five-year reign as Cup champions. Game three was won by Chicago, 2–1, in triple overtime on a goal by Murray Balfour. The game's conclusion featured Montreal coach Toe Blake taking a poke at the referee after the overtime goal was scored. Blake was fined by the NHL, providing a field day for punning headline writers. "Toe Gets $2,000 Sock" was just one such gem. Long after his retirement, veteran Montreal play-by-play man Danny Gallivan called this the most exciting game he had ever seen.

The Hawks went on to eliminate the Canadiens in six games and then, in their first visit to the finals in seventeen seasons, again needed six games to clinch the Cup. In one of those sweetly symmetrical moments that

Owners Arthur Wirtz (left) and "Big Jim" Norris pose with the Stanley Cup after the Black Hawks won their first title since 1938 by defeating the Detroit Red Wings in the 1961 finals.

sport is uniquely able to provide, the Black Hawks' opponent in their breakthrough Stanley Cup championship series was, of course, the Detroit Red Wings.

The rebuilding of the Black Hawks, begun in earnest in 1954, was at last complete. The club averaged just forty-six points and made the playoffs only three times in the first fifteen years of the six-team era. After winning the Cup in 1961, the franchise has missed the playoffs only once in the ensuing thirty-three seasons. In addition to Wirtz, Norris, Ivan, and Pilous, four players on the Hawks' 1961 Cup-winning roster – Hall, Hull, Mikita, and Pilote – capped their marvelous careers with induction into the Hockey Hall of Fame.

| 98 PTS. | 85 PTS. | 75 PTS. | 64 PTS. | 60 PTS. | 38 PTS. |

1961-62
Golden Jet Grounded as
Leafs End Eleven-Year Cup Drought

A PAIR OF NHL SUPERSTARS WERE THE FEATURED PLAYERS IN THE TALE OF THE 1961-62 season, as Andy Bathgate and Bobby Hull engaged in a season-long duel to decide the scoring championship. An added feature was Hull's attempt to become the first NHL marksman to score more than 50 goals in a single season.

The defending-champion Black Hawks appeared to be even stronger than in the previous year, inserting a number of impressive newcomers into their lineup. The Hawks lost Al Arbour to Toronto, but compensated by trading minor-leaguer Fred Hilts to Montreal for veteran Bob Turner. Larry Hillman's younger brother Wayne was also added to the defensive mix, although he would see action in only 19 games during the season. Bronco Horvath was left unprotected by Boston, and the Hawks jumped at the chance to incorporate the former Uke Line star in their lineup.

Amid calls by the fans and the media to tear apart the Habs' line-up and rebuild, Frank Selke, Toe Blake, and the management of the Montreal Canadiens remained calm as they entered the new season, reasoning that they were still strong at every key position. There was one major change. Doug Harvey, a perennial Norris Trophy-winner and a fourteen-year veteran of the Montreal defense, was allowed to move to New York to become the Rangers' playing coach. "Leapin' Lou" Fontinato was sent to the Habs in return. Junior Langlois was also traded to New York in exchange for John Hanna. Bobby Rousseau, whom Frank Selke described as a $100,000 rookie, was on board for the full campaign, as was Al MacNeil, who had been drafted from the Toronto Maple Leafs.

Despite their disappointing post-season performance, Punch Imlach was convinced the Leafs were the team to beat for the Stanley Cup title in 1961-62. Roster changes were minor, with the only priority being a suitable backup to Johnny Bower. At age thirty-six, Bower had been the best goaltender in the NHL in 1960-61. As insurance, Imlach dealt Ed Chadwick to Boston for Don Simmons, and Larry Regan was dispatched to Rochester to make room for Al Arbour. The Leafs' defense, featuring the "big four" of Horton, Baun, Brewer, and Stanley, was the finest in the league, and Arbour's arrival meant that even the Leafs' fifth defenseman was an experienced NHL competitor.

Gump's Lumps

Hall-of-Fame netminder Gump Worsley had the dubious distinction of surrendering a number of noteworthy goals during the six-team era, including the 600th for Maurice "Rocket" Richard (combined playoffs and regular season); Gordie Howe's 500th, 544th (tying him with Richard for most regular-season goals), and 600th regular-season goals; the 50th for Bobby Hull in the 1961-62 season; and Bobby Orr's 1st goal.

Not surprisingly, Jack Adams decided to stand pat after the Wings' Stanley Cup final-series appearance in the spring of 1961. He did, however, bolster the blueline by finally acquiring Bill Gadsby from New York for minor-leaguer Leslie Hunt. Sid Abel decided to stay with his tandem of Sawchuk and Bassen in goal, even though Sawchuk was vehemently opposed to the system and had requested a trade to a team where he could play every day. Adams was forced to tell the veteran that he had tried to trade him, but no team in the NHL was willing to guarantee that he would play every game.

Numerous changes were made in New York. The defense was re-designed around playing coach Doug Harvey and Junior Langlois from Montreal. Irv Spencer and Larry Cahan, who hadn't played a full season in the NHL since 1956-57, were two other defensemen given the opportunity to stick with the big club in 1961-62. Young forwards Vic Hadfield, who would play 44 games in 1961-62, and Jean Ratelle, who would play 31, bolstered the Rangers' attack.

Another coaching change was made in Boston in an attempt to revive the glory days of the late 1950s. Phil Watson replaced Milt Schmidt behind the bench, and although an assortment of new talent was brought in, the Bruins were destined for another last-place finish. Three rookies – Ted Green, Pat Stapleton, and Ed Westfall – joined veteran Leo Boivin and sophomore Dallas Smith on the Bruins defense. The forward unit was strengthened by rookie Terry Gray and by Wayne Connelly, who had been purchased from the Canadiens. Another freshman, Tommy Williams, made his NHL debut during the season. Williams had been a star with the gold-medal-winning 1960 U.S. Olympic Team and was warmly received by the Boston fans.

The early stories of the 1961-62 season were the success of the Rangers and the slow start of the Black Hawks. The defending-champion Hawks won only once in their first ten games, with their sole victory coming over the lowly Boston Bruins. Lack of offense and lack of grit were the two main reasons cited for the team's decline. The Hawks scored only 19 goals in their first ten games and were without a real leader on the club, despite the presence of veterans like Pilote and Nesterenko. After coach Rudy Pilous criticized his players in the press, the Black Hawks picked up their game, and Bobby Hull began a record run at the 50-goal plateau.

Over the next four months, the Black Hawks were one of the league's best clubs, and Hull was the league's premier forward. After scoring only three goals in his first 12 games and 15 in his first 40, Hull erupted to score 35 goals in the last 30 games of the season, hoisting the team up the standings as the season unfolded. With 20 wins in the last half of the schedule, the Black Hawks finished in third place, with a record of 31 wins, 26 losses and 13 ties.

In his second NHL season, Dave Keon established himself as one of the league's premier defensive forwards. The stylish center, who fired 26 goals for the Maple Leafs while spending only two minutes in the penalty box, won the Lady Byng Trophy and was named to the league's Second All-Star Team.

Doug Harvey motors away from the close pursuit of Boston's John Bucyk in Harvey's first season with the Rangers. After fourteen seasons with the Canadiens, the six-time Norris Trophy winner joined New York in 1961-62 as the Rangers' playing coach.

Hull entered the final game of the season against the Rangers one goal shy of the magical 50 mark. He was also tied for the NHL points-scoring lead with New York's Andy Bathgate. Early in this head-to-head encounter, Hull took a pass from Reg Fleming and rammed his 50th goal of the season past Gump Worsley. Just six minutes later, Bathgate scored to tie both the game score and the individual points-scoring race. Both the Golden Jet and "Dandy Andy" saw over thirty minutes of ice time in the contest, but neither could break their individual deadlock, although the Rangers found the range three more times for a 4–1 victory. For the first time in NHL history, there was a tie atop the scoring column, with both Hull and Bathgate finishing the campaign with 84 points. Hull, however, was awarded the Art Ross Trophy on the basis of having 50 goals to the Ranger superstar's 28.

Bathgate's success was only one chapter in the Broadway revival being performed in New York. Coach Doug Harvey quickly taught his troops that the key to winning was to hate losing, and his charges learned the lesson early. The Rangers began the season by losing only one of their first five games and established themselves as playoff contenders by compiling a 15–13–8 record by the halfway point of the schedule. Dean Prentice, Earl Ingarfield, and Camille Henry joined Bathgate in the 20-goal

club, and Andy Hebenton notched 42 points while playing his sixth consecutive season without missing a game. The club faltered towards the end of the schedule, but earned a spot in the post-season Stanley Cup hunt with 64 points in the standings.

Montreal continued to excel in regular-season competition, finishing atop the standings for the sixth time in the past seven years. Again, the depth of the organization was a key to the team's success. Jean Béliveau injured his knee in a pre-season exhibition contest and was forced to miss the first 27 games of the campaign, but the scoring slack was picked up admirably by Gilles Tremblay and Claude Provost, who tallied 32 and 33 goals respectively. Seven players reached the 20-goal plateau, including Billy Hicke, Bernie Geoffrion, and rookie Bobby Rousseau. Near the end of the season, the Canadiens signed Gordon "Red" Berenson, a graduate of the University of Michigan. Berenson, the first player to move directly from an American university into the NHL, scored his first NHL goal on March 25 in a season-ending 5–2 win over Detroit. Berenson's marker was the 259th goal of the season for the Canadiens, establishing a new NHL record. For the first and only time in his career, Jacques Plante played in every game during the 70-game schedule. Plante won 42 games, registered four shutouts, and led the league with a goals-against average of 2.37.

With the departure of Doug Harvey to the Rangers, Jean-Guy Talbot (right) became a leader on the Canadiens' blueline. Talbot responded with a 47-point season and earned a spot on the NHL's First All-Star Team. Stan Mikita (left) set an NHL record with 21 points in the playoffs as the Black Hawks advanced to the finals for the second consecutive season.

BOBBY HULL

The Golden Jet soared during 1961-62, joining Maurice Richard and Bernie Geoffrion as the third player in league history to score 50 goals in a season. This photo was part of a series of collectibles issued by the St. Lawrence Starch Company.

Slowed by numerous injuries to key personnel, the Toronto Maple Leafs finished 13 points behind Montreal, but still had a solid hold on second place. Red Kelly injured his knee and missed 12 games, and Johnny Bower spent time on the shelf for various ailments. Their places were taken by Ed Litzenberger, grabbed off the waiver wire by Imlach, and by a tandem of Don Simmons and a young Gerry Cheevers in net.

Frank Mahovlich had another outstanding year, leading the Leafs with 33 goals and 71 points to finish fifth in league scoring. Dave Keon, with 26 goals, and George Armstrong, with 21 markers, were also key members of the Leafs, not only for their scoring skills, but for their penalty-killing abilities. Though only in his second season, Keon was already regarded as one of the NHL's top power-play and penalty-killing specialists.

It was another frustrating season in Detroit and Boston, where both teams failed to make the playoffs. After reaching the Stanley Cup finals in 1961, it was felt the Red Wings would be one of the league's top teams, but Sid Abel's team never got untracked, falling to fifth place with just 60 points. Boston, hampered by a young and inexperienced defense, lost 47 games and finished with 38 points for the team's worst showing since their first season in the league. The team endured a 20-game winless streak from January 28 to March 11, collecting only four ties during this span. John Bucyk was proving to be a top-notch NHL performer, collecting 60 points, but the supporting cast, mostly aging veterans and raw youngsters, were unable to keep the Bruins out of the basement. While it went unnoticed by all but the most fervent Boston fans, the Bruins secured their future by signing a fourteen-year-old prospect named Bobby Orr to a "C" form, the standard NHL player-development agreement. Orr was still five seasons away from his NHL debut, but was already recognized as a superstar in the making.

In the semi-finals, the Chicago Black Hawks weren't expected to handle the first-place Canadiens, and these predictions appeared to be true after Montreal won the opening two matches, 2–1 and 4–3. Back at Chicago Stadium, however, the Black Hawks tied the set with 4–1 and 5–3 victories. In the waning minutes of the third match, a Montreal fan named Kenneth Killander pried open a display case housing the Stanley Cup in the front lobby of Chicago Stadium and tried to escape with the trophy. Killander, who was quickly apprehended, explained that he was simply returning the Cup to Montreal where it belonged.

Game four was a rough, aggressive affair, with the Canadiens receiving 12 of the 16 penalties called. As a result, the Hawks were able to score four power-play goals, more than enough to defeat the Canadiens. Coach Toe Blake was furious, and had to be restrained by his players from attacking referee Eddie Powers. That game seemed to take most of the fight out of the Habs, and they went on to lose the next two matches

Left to right: Detroit tough guy Howie Young shares a light moment in the Red Wings' dressing room with Hank Bassen and Alex Delvecchio. Although Bassen recorded a career-best 2.81 goals-against average in 1961-62, the Wings faltered and dropped to fifth place, four points behind the New York Rangers.

by 4–3 and 2–0 counts. The four straight victories assured the Hawks the opportunity to defend their Stanley Cup crown.

The other semi-final, between the Leafs and the Rangers, was also a close affair, which took a parallel path. The Leafs won the opening two games at Maple Leaf Gardens by 4–2 and 2–1 scores, only to have New York fight back to tie the series with a pair of home-ice victories of their own by scores of 5–4 and 4–2. Rookie Rod Gilbert, appearing in only his fourth NHL game, scored two goals in game four.

Game five was a fiercely contested battle that required nearly 25 minutes of overtime to decide. Goals by Stewart and Mahovlich gave Toronto a 2–0 advantage, but the Rangers came back to tie on the strength of goals by Gendron and Ingarfield. In overtime, the Leafs peppered the Rangers net, but were unable to score on an acrobatic Gump Worsley until the second sudden-death period, when Frank Mahovlich fed a pass to Red Kelly, and the converted defenseman slipped the puck in for a 3–2 win. The Rangers had little left for the ensuing game, and the Maple Leafs won easily by a count of 7–1.

The finals began in Toronto, where the Hawks were favorites because of their superior defense and bruising checking style. In the opener,

George Armstrong (left) and Frank Mahovlich flank Tim Horton after the Toronto Maple Leafs returned to the Stanley Cup winner's circle in 1962. Horton's total of 13 post-season assists was a team record for defensemen that stood for thirty-two years.

however, the Leafs proved they could penetrate that defense and take their licks along the boards. Toronto players goaded Eric Nesterenko into taking a trio of foolish penalties and Frank Mahovlich capitalized by scoring the game winner on the power play. The Leafs scored another power-play marker in game two on their way to a 3–2 victory, putting the Leafs up by two games in the championship set.

Back in Chicago Stadium, the Black Hawks were able to confuse and frustrate the Leafs, using a pair of power-play goals to secure 3–0 and 4–1 wins. Stan Mikita and Ab McDonald scored four minutes apart to seal the 3–0 verdict in game three, while Reg Fleming and Bobby Hull had a pair of goals apiece in a series-tying 4–1 triumph in game four. Twenty-one penalties were called in the fourth contest, including game misconducts to Mahovlich and Mikita.

Johnny Bower, who was playing superbly despite a pulled groin, aggravated the injury prior to game five, and Don Simmons was penciled in to take his place. The Leafs turned up the offensive heat and burned the Black Hawks defense for eight goals, including a hat-trick by Bob Pulford and a pair of goals by the Big M. Simmons played effectively in the Leafs net, and his strong performance left Toronto a single victory away from the Stanley Cup.

Simmons was in goal again for the next game, a cautious, close-checking affair that was scoreless through two periods. Midway through the final frame, Bobby Hull broke free from the Leaf checkers to give Chicago a slim 1–0 lead. The Chicago Stadium crowd exploded, littering the ice and causing the game to be delayed for fifteen minutes. This stoppage in play allowed the Leafs to regroup, while taking momentum away from the home-town Hawks. Just 93 seconds after Hull's goal, Bob Nevin scored to tie the game on passes from Mahovlich and Baun. Less than four minutes later, Dave Keon, Reg Fleming, and Glenn Hall became entangled in front of the Hawks' net, giving Dick Duff a vacant cage at which to shoot. Duff made no mistake, flipping the puck in to provide the Leafs with a 2–1 margin with less than six minutes remaining. The Hawks pressed the Leafs, but couldn't get the equalizer past a steady Simmons. When the foghorn at the Stadium blew to signal the end of the game, the Leafs had won their first Stanley Cup since 1951.

Among the Toronto heroes were Bob Pulford, who collected seven goals, and Tim Horton, who set a team record with 13 assists in 12 play-off games. Al Arbour and Ed Litzenberger, who were both members of Chicago's Cup-winning team in 1961, became only the ninth and tenth players to win back-to-back championships with different teams.

On June 6, forty-four days after the Leafs clinched the 1962 Stanley Cup championship, a bush pilot named Gary Fields spotted the wreckage of a light plane in a dense Northern Ontario forest. The downed aircraft contained the remains of Bill Barilko, the Maple Leaf hero who died only months after scoring the Cup-winning goal in overtime in 1951. With the discovery of the crash site, the mystery of Barilko's disappearance and the Leafs' eleven-year Stanley Cup drought were both finally put to rest.

Among the post-season award-winners were Doug Harvey, who won his seventh Norris Trophy in eight seasons, Bob Rousseau, the Calder Trophy recipient, Bobby Hull, the Art Ross Trophy winner, and slick Dave Keon, who was awarded the Lady Byng Trophy. Jacques Plante earned a trio of accolades during the 1961-62 season. He captured his sixth Vezina Trophy, his sixth All-Star selection, and, most importantly, his first Hart Trophy as league MVP.

TORONTO DEFEATS CHICAGO IN GAME SIX OF '62 CUP FINAL

Don Simmons, who replaced an injured Johnny Bower before game five, never played another post-season game.

**April 22, 1962
at Chicago Stadium
Toronto 2, Chicago 1**

FIRST PERIOD

No Scoring
PENALTIES – Evans CHI (holding) 2:57; Hull CHI (boarding) 6:08; Pulford TOR (highsticking) 12:09.

SECOND PERIOD

No Scoring
PENALTIES – Fleming CHI (tripping) 5:19; Nesterenko CHI (highsticking) 7:42; Baun TOR (holding) 11:46; St. Laurent CHI (holding) 18:07.

THIRD PERIOD

1) CHI Hull 8 (Balfour, Hay) 8:56
2) TOR Nevin 2 (Baun, Mahovlich) 10:29
3) TOR Duff 3 (Horton, Armstrong) PPG 14:14
PENALTIES – Horton TOR (tripping) 4:30; Nesterenko CHI (hooking) 13:27; Horton TOR (tripping) 19:02.

SHOTS ON GOAL	1	2	3	T
TORONTO	13	14	10	37
CHICAGO	4	8	9	21

GOALTENDERS	TIME	SA	GA	ENG	W/L
TOR Simmons	60:00	20	1	0	W
CHI Hall	59:02*	35	2	0	L

* unofficial, left net for extra skater late in third period at time of Horton penalty.

PP CONVERSIONS   TOR 1/6   CHI 0/4

82 PTS.   81 PTS.   79 PTS.   77 PTS.   56 PTS.   45 PTS.

1962-63
The Tightest Race in NHL History:
Five Points Separate First Four Teams

THERE WAS A FOUR-TEAM RACE FOR FIRST PLACE IN THE NHL DURING THE 1962-63 season, with only five points separating first from fourth in the tightest season-long competition in league history. For the first time since 1947-48, the Toronto Maple Leafs finished atop the standings, followed closely by Chicago, Montreal, and the rebuilding Detroit Red Wings.

There was a changing of the guard in Detroit, where Jack Adams stepped down as general manager of the Red Wings after thirty-five years on the job. Under Adams's guidance, Detroit had won seven Stanley Cup championships and finished in first place twelve times. Adams wasn't stepping out of hockey altogether, as he was named the first president of the Central Professional Hockey League, an NHL-endorsed development league that was being formed in the United States.

Sid Abel took over the managerial reins of the Red Wings and, after a fifth-place finish in 1962, there were a number of adjustments to be made. One of Abel's first moves was to give the number-one goaltending job back to Terry Sawchuk, who needed that vote of confidence to play his best. Abel decided on a five-man defensive core, led by Marcel Pronovost and Bill Gadsby and supplemented by Howie Young, Pete Goegan, and newcomer Doug Barkley. Barkley, acquired from Chicago for Len Lunde and John McKenzie, had only six games of NHL experience under his belt, but Abel was confident he could secure a shaky Red Wings' blueline.

An offensive nucleus of Delvecchio, Ullman, Howe, and Parker MacDonald ensured that the Wings would have plenty of scoring clout. Floyd Smith, Eddie Joyal, and Alex Faulkner, the first Newfoundland native to play in the NHL, were added as offensive insurance.

With a Stanley Cup title tucked under his ever-present fedora, Punch Imlach was content to enter the new season with virtually the same cast of stars and supporting players. On defense, Imlach decided to replace Al Arbour with rookie Kent Douglas, who the Toronto general manager obtained from Springfield of the AHL for a five-player package that included Wally Boyer and Bill White. Bert Olmstead, whom many of the Leafs credited with supplying the veteran savvy needed to defeat the Black Hawks, was plucked in the Intra-League Draft by the Rangers.

Eddie Shack would replace him on left wing, but no one could replace his leadership in the dressing room. Don Simmons and Johnny Bower returned to handle the goaltending duties.

Few changes were needed in Chicago, where Rudy Pilous had a young, exciting hockey club, brimming with talent. Dollard St. Laurent retired and Al MacNeil, acquired from Montreal for Wayne Hicks, was slated to take his place. Wayne Hillman, who had appeared in 19 games during the 1961-62 campaign, was given a full-time position on the blue-line. On the front lines, the configuration remained the same: Mikita, Hull, Wharram, Balfour, Hay, and McDonald. Chico Maki, a 21-goal scorer with Buffalo in the AHL, had an impressive training camp and was slotted in at right wing.

Despite losing to the Black Hawks in the 1962 semi-finals, the Canadiens made no significant changes to their club. Marcel Bonin retired and was ably relieved by Red Berenson. Three impressive freshmen – Jacques Laperrière, Terry Harper, and Claude Larose – all made appearances over the course of the schedule, but their most significant contributions to the Canadiens were still to come.

In a surprise move, Doug Harvey resigned as coach of the Rangers, setting off two months of speculation about his replacement. Red

Slippery center and power-play specialist Camille "The Eel" Henry notched a career-high 37 goals for the New York Rangers in 1962-63. That total could have been higher had this picture-perfect backhander not rung off the cross bar behind goaltender Don Simmons in a 4–2 Toronto victory on February 16, 1963.

Steady Glenn Hall stymies Norm Ullman during the Detroit–Chicago semi-final in 1963. Ullman led all post-season scorers with 12 assists in the 1963 play-offs. Hall, who had played every minute of 502 consecutive games from the start of the 1955-56 season, saw that streak come to an end on November 7, 1962, when he had to leave a game against the Boston Bruins with a back injury.

Busy Bronco

At various times during the six-team era, Bronco Horvath's playing rights were held by every NHL club. Originally Detroit property, Horvath was traded to the Rangers in 1955, when he broke into the NHL. From there he was sold to Montreal in 1956 before being drafted by Boston in 1957, where he flourished as center of the high-scoring Uke Line. He was drafted by Chicago in 1961, reclaimed by the Rangers in 1962, and then, in January 1963, picked up on waivers by Toronto, completing the circuit.

Sullivan, Emile Francis, and Bert Olmstead were the most prominent names mentioned, but Muzz Patrick was behind the bench when the season opened. When Harvey resigned, it was assumed he wanted out of New York, but he returned for another season on the blueline, where he was joined by incumbents Harry Howell, Junior Langlois, and Larry Cahan, and by newcomer Jim Neilson. Rod Gilbert, who was impressive during the playoffs, was on board for the entire season. Jean Ratelle and Vic Hadfield divided their time between New York and the Rangers' Baltimore farm club in the AHL. Bert Olmstead decided to retire.

There were still considerable problems in Boston, and, with a slim talent pool to choose from, it was doubtful the team would improve. The goaltending trio of Don Head, Bruce Gamble, and Ed Chadwick was released in favor of Ed Johnston and former Montreal Canadien Robert "Miche" Perreault. Doug Mohns was dropped to the blueline to help the sagging defense, and Warren Godfrey was obtained from Detroit just prior to the season opener. The offence, featuring blossoming stars John Bucyk, Murray Oliver, and Tommy Williams, added Forbes Kennedy, Jean-Guy Gendron, and Wayne Hicks. It wouldn't be enough, however. Phil Watson's troops crawled out of the gate, winning only one of their first 14 games, and forcing general manager Milt Schmidt to release Watson and take on the coaching duties himself.

An interesting side note to the season was being written in Toronto, where Frank Mahovlich was embroiled in a contract dispute with Punch Imlach. At a party prior to the annual All-Star Game, Chicago Black Hawks president Jim Norris offered the Maple Leafs $1,000,000 for Mahovlich's services. Harold Ballard, one of the Leafs' co-owners, accepted the deal, but the Maple Leafs' board of directors wouldn't ratify the transaction, and Mahovlich remained in Toronto, where he quickly came to terms with Imlach.

After Mahovlich was signed and sealed, he delivered, leading the Leafs in goals (36) and points (73) as Toronto won the regular-season title. George Armstrong, Dave Keon, and Bob Pulford also had fine

Toronto's "Entertainer," Eddie Shack, attempts to control a loose puck in the Boston crease while being closely observed by defenseman Ted Green (6) and goalie Bob Perreault. Shack would later score the 1963 Stanley Cup-winning goal, connecting at the 13:28 mark of the third period in game five of the finals between the Leafs and Red Wings.

seasons, as did Red Kelly, who became the second active NHL player to juggle hockey with politics. Kelly was elected as a Liberal Member of Parliament for the suburban Toronto constituency of York West. Kent Douglas was a bruising force along the blueline, using his size and reach to thwart numerous scoring opportunities and earn accolades from around the league.

Chicago stayed neck-and-neck with the Leafs throughout the season, thanks to 31-goal efforts from Mikita and Hull. One of the most extraordinary consecutive-game streaks came to an end on November 7, when a sore back forced Glenn Hall to remove himself from the Hawks' goal after playing 502 consecutive complete games. For the first time since Hall joined the team in 1957, Chicago was compelled to use another goalie. Denis DeJordy replaced Hall and appeared in five games over the course of the campaign.

Injuries hampered the Montreal Canadiens during the 1962-63 season, especially along the blueline. Tom Johnson broke his cheekbone when he collided with teammate Bobby Rousseau in practice and was out of action for 27 games. Lou Fontinato experienced the most severe injury when he broke his neck after crashing into the boards attempting to check the Rangers' Vic Hadfield. Fontinato was paralyzed for some time, but

Gordie Howe returned to the scoring-race summit in 1962-63, winning his sixth Art Ross Trophy after leading the league with 38 goals and 86 points. This goal, scored against Johnny Bower, was Howe's 37th of the season, giving Detroit a 1–0 lead on their way to a 2–1 victory over the Maple Leafs on March 23, 1963.

One of the NHL's hardest-hitting defensemen, Toronto's Carl Brewer made his debut on the NHL's First All-Star Team in 1962-63.

eventually recovered full movement in all his limbs. His nine-year hockey career, however, was over. Jacques Laperrière and Terry Harper, a pair of good-looking youngsters, replaced Johnson and Fontinato, and both remained with the club through the playoffs. Gilles Tremblay, Jacques Plante, and Bernie Geoffrion also spent time in the clinic during the season, but Montreal still led the league in goals scored. Team defense was a question mark, however, as the Habs allowed 183 goals, the fourth-highest total in franchise history.

Gordie Howe led the surging Detroit Red Wings back into the playoff hunt by winning his first scoring title in six seasons with 38 goals and 86 points. The Red Wings finished the season with a 32–25–13 record, a full 21 points ahead of the fifth-place Rangers. Terry Sawchuk returned to his former glory, leading the league with a 2.48 goals-against average. Only a serious hand injury, which caused him to miss 18 games, prevented him from a possible Vezina Trophy victory. Parker MacDonald (33 goals), Alex Delvecchio (64 points), and Norm Ullman (26 goals) were the other keys to a Detroit attack that combined to score 200 goals for the first time since 1954-55.

New York and Boston shared the league basement for the second time in three years. Muzz Patrick was released as coach after the Rangers won just 11 of their first 34 games. His replacement, Red Sullivan, a former Ranger player, was unable to fare much better, bringing the team home with a 11–17–8 mark. Andy Bathgate's 81 points and Camille Henry's second 30-goal campaign weren't enough to power the Rangers into the playoffs. Despite having two of the NHL's top offensive defensemen in Doug Harvey and Harry Howell, New York was never in playoff contention.

A similar story was written in Boston, where the Bruins finished out of the playoffs for the fourth consecutive season. John Bucyk, Murray Oliver, Tom Williams, and Jean-Guy Gendron all reached the 20-goal plateau, but the club's young defense allowed a league-high 281 goals-against as Boston won only 14 games in the 70-game schedule. In a dramatic trade, the Bruins and Rangers swapped stars when Boston acquired

Dean Prentice and New York obtained Don McKenney on February 6, 1963. Both players did well in their new cities, but neither team made the playoffs.

Montreal and Toronto met in the first round of the playoffs, and the Leafs ousted the Canadiens in five games. A superior Toronto defense continually frustrated the Canadiens, who managed to score only six goals in the five-game series. Johnny Bower collected a pair of shutout victories, and the Leafs received goals from eight different players to move into the finals for the fourth time in five seasons.

The Chicago Black Hawks, heavy favorites to eliminate the Red Wings, appeared to be well on their way, with 5–4 and 5–2 victories in the opening two games of their semi-final series. Five goals in the first 40 minutes of game one sealed that win, and four power-play markers in game two gave the Hawks a commanding advantage. However, the next four games belonged to the Red Wings, who closed off the neutral zone, stood up on the blueline and, on most occasions, beat the Hawks to the puck. Detroit outshot Chicago 93 to 38 in 4–2 and 4–1 wins in games three and four before wrapping up the series with 4–2 and 7–4 wins. This six-game semi-final-series win qualified the Red Wings for the finals for the second time in three years.

The 1963 final series featured tight defensive play, in which the Leafs prevailed in five evenly matched games. Dick Duff scored a pair of goals in the first minute and eight seconds of game one, and Bob Nevin added two more, as Toronto opened the finals with a 4–2 win. Ron Stewart scored a pair in another 4–2 Toronto victory in the second match. Former Leaf Alex Faulkner's goal at 13:39 of the second period gave Detroit a 3–2 victory in the third contest, but Toronto secured its second straight Stanley Cup win with 4–2 and 3–1 wins in the next two games. The secret to the Leafs' success once again was a punishing defense that continually checked any Red Wing who entered Toronto's defensive zone. Steady, aggressive forechecking led to three shorthanded goals, including a pair from Dave Keon in the final match. Keon's shorthanded double established a new NHL single-game playoff record. Johnny Bower, the grizzled "China Wall" in the Leafs' net, won eight games with a stingy goals-against average of 1.60.

When the NHL distributed its post-season individual awards, Gordie Howe was the big winner, capturing his sixth Art Ross and sixth Hart trophies. Pierre Pilote took home the Norris, Dave Keon won his second straight Lady Byng, and hard-hitting Kent Douglas was named winner of the Calder Trophy as the league's best rookie.

BATHGATE EXTENDS GOAL-SCORING STREAK TO TEN GAMES

Maurice Richard and Bernie Geoffrion shared the modern-day NHL record with goals in nine straight games before Bathgate's performance. His streak ended one night later when Montreal defeated New York, 6–0, at Madison Square Garden. Ten games proved to be the longest goal-scoring streak of the six-team era.

January 5, 1963
at Montreal Forum
New York 2, Montreal 2

FIRST PERIOD
No Scoring
PENALTIES – Ingarfield NY (fighting – major) :45; Fontinato MTL (fighting – major) :45; Béliveau MTL (holding) 6:36; Gauthier MTL (hooking) 14:06; Langlois NY (elbowing), Backstrom MTL (slashing) 17:25.

SECOND PERIOD
1) NY Bathgate 19 (Ingarfield, Harvey) PPG 16:02
PENALTIES – Gilbert NY (spearing), Fontinato MTL (spearing) 14:51; Talbot MTL (tripping) 15:08.

THIRD PERIOD
2) MTL Rousseau 5 (G. Tremblay, Béliveau) 6:40
3) MTL Richard 14 (Moore, Provost) 9:01
4) NY Bathgate 20 (Harvey, Prentice) 14:35
PENALTIES – Gauthier MTL (tripping) 12:18.

SHOTS ON GOAL	1	2	3	T
NEW YORK	10	14	11	35
MONTREAL	7	10	11	28

GOALTENDERS		TIME	SA	GA	ENG	W/L
NY	Worsley	60:00	26	2	0	T
MTL	Plante	60:00	33	2	0	T

PP CONVERSIONS   NY 1/4   MTL 0/0

(Continued on p. 182)

Minor Pro Hockey in the Six-Team Era

by James Duplacey

As much as the quarter-century between 1942 and 1967 is considered a "golden age" for the National Hockey League, it was also an era that witnessed the birth and flourishing of a diverse and dynamic minor-league system. From Don Cherry to Arnie Kullman and Stan Smrke to Enio Sclisizzi, the minors featured some of the most colorful characters to ever play the game.

From 1942 to 1967, almost every skater who saw his name in lights in the NHL first had to endure the life in the "bushes." Of the 448 players listed in the *NHL Guide* for the 1967 season, all but a dozen apprenticed in the minors. For many NHL stars, the minors were merely the first rung on the ladder. However, only a handful were able to combine a respectable minor-league career with a profitable NHL tenure.

Survival for the fledgling minor-league operations was a constant struggle. Four of the seven minor pro organizations that operated during the quarter-century of six-team NHL hockey eventually folded, but not before introducing the game to Texas, California, the Carolinas, and the American Midwest – areas largely unfamiliar with the sport. The men who starred in those leagues and ultimately put fans in the seats played as vital a role in the shaping of the modern twenty-six-team

NHL as did any of the Hall-of-Famers who starred in the six-team league.

At the end of the Second World War, there were two minor professional leagues operating, both centered in the United States. The American Hockey League and the United States Hockey League were made up of independently owned franchises that also served as farm teams for the six NHL clubs. These leagues were quickly joined by the Western Hockey League, which grew out of the Pacific Coast Hockey League, and the Quebec Hockey League, which spawned the Eastern Professional Hockey League and the Central Professional Hockey League in the 1960s.

The oldest and most respected minor-league fraternity, the AHL, was incorporated prior to the 1936-37 season. Operating in large cities like Cleveland, Cincinnati, and Pittsburgh, as well as in smaller towns like Hershey

The St. Louis Flyers were members of the American Hockey League for nine seasons from 1944-45 to 1952-53. The team finished first in 1948-49 with a 41–18–9 record.

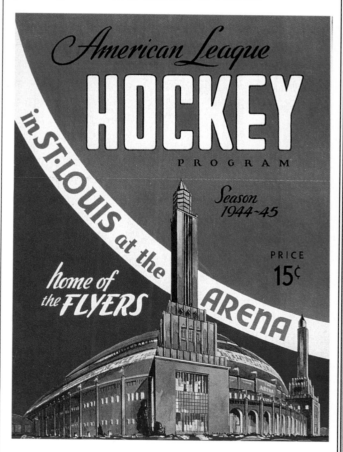

and New Haven, the AHL used dedicated ownership and solid management to stay ahead of its competition. The Cleveland Barons club that attempted to join the NHL in 1952 and issued a challenge for the Stanley Cup in 1953 helped serve notice that the AHL was more than a learning base for unschooled rookies or a viable alternative for veterans whose NHL careers had ended.

The AHL of the six-team era was renowned for producing All-Star quality defensemen and goaltenders. In addition to Johnny Bower, who posted an AHL-record forty-five shutouts before joining Toronto at age thirty-three, Gerry Cheevers, Bernie Parent, Terry Sawchuk, and Gump Worsley all honed their skills in the AHL before earning Hall-of-Fame credentials in the NHL. Rearguards Tim Horton, Allan Stanley, Larry Hillman, and Al Arbour scripted AHL All-Star berths before writing their lengthy NHL résumés. Other star rearguards, like Don Cherry, Frank Mathers, and Pete Backor, could never break an NHL lineup, despite years of success patroling the bluelines in the AHL.

On the other side of the ledger, countless former "big-leaguers" kept their careers alive in the AHL. Carl Liscombe, who became the first AHLer to record a 100-point season and the first pro to score 50 goals in back-to-back campaigns, joined the AHL after a productive nine-year career with the Detroit Red Wings. Gaye Stewart, Jacques Plante, Doug Harvey, Dick Gamble, and Bronco Horvath all continued their pro careers in the AHL after being cut loose by the NHL.

Despite this wide variety of "name" stars, the true charm of the AHL lies in the talents of the league's life-long minor-leaguers. All-time scoring leader Willie Marshall, who had a brief glimpse of the show with Toronto in the early 1950s, collected 535 goals and 1,375 points in his 20-year tenure in the American League. Career AHLers Bruce Cline, Harry Pidhirny, and Bill Sweeney played a combined 36 games in the NHL, but accounted for 2,406 scoring points during their collective 41 seasons in the AHL.

The USHL, which survived only from 1945 to 1951, offered the "world's fastest game" to Houston, Tulsa, Omaha, Denver, and Fort Worth. The USHL's Omaha Knights, an important link in the Detroit Red Wings'

The venerable Johnny Bower won the Les Cunningham Plaque as the AHL's most valuable player in three consecutive seasons, 1955-56, 1956-57, and 1957-58, before joining the Toronto Maple Leafs in 1958-59.

chain of farm teams, saw both Gordie Howe and Terry Sawchuk pass through its ranks on their way to Detroit and the Hockey Hall of Fame. Fred Shero earned his nickname, "The Fog," toiling in the Lone-Star State, while Toe Blake cut his coaching teeth behind the bench in Houston, taking the Huskies to the Loudon Trophy in 1947-48.

In 1949, the Pacific Coast Hockey League, with teams in California and Western Canada, became North America's third minor professional league. The PCHL staked its reputation on well-known veterans like Babe Pratt and young stars such as Guyle Fielder, but the

SEATTLE TOTEMS HOCKEY CLUB

Guyle Fielder led the Western Hockey League in scoring nine times, and holds the league's all-time marks for games played (1,425), assists (1,430), and points (1,846).

product failed to excite fans in the United States, the market the league most wanted to conquer. Fifteen franchises came, and went, in its brief four-year existence. When the league was reorganized as the Western Hockey League in 1952, it concentrated on Western Canada, placing franchises in Regina, Calgary, Saskatoon, Brandon, Edmonton, Winnipeg, Vancouver, New Westminster, and Victoria.

The WHL offered an opportunity for numerous prospects to gain valuable pro experience while enjoying the luxury of remaining close to home. Glenn Hall, Andy Bathgate, John Bucyk, and Norm Ullman were household names on the western circuit long before they were headline news in the NHL. Others, like Bill Mosienko, Doug Bentley, and Don "Bones" Raleigh, returned to the Western League after their NHL careers were completed. During the 1950s, the Detroit Red Wings were the only NHL team to sponsor a WHL club. Although some pundits questioned the viability of the Red Wings' plunge into these uncharted waters, the Detroit commitment was a lifeline for a league unsettled by countless franchise shifts.

It soon became clear that the key to the WHL's survival depended on re-establishing ties with the hockey fans on the West Coast of the United States. By 1962, the league had consolidated itself on the West Coast with six American franchises, including Los Angeles, San Francisco, and Seattle, while maintaining only two Canadian teams. On the ice, the WHL produced a near-NHL-quality product and gradually replaced the AHL as the pre-eminent minor league. In 1965-66, the two rivals faced off against each other in a unique interlocking schedule. The Westerners captured 38 of the 62 games played, and although numerous attempts were made to organize a championship series between the two, they never came to fruition.

Like the AHL, the Western Hockey League had an established stable of star attractions. Gord Fashoway fired 485 goals in only 843 games. Art Jones played his entire career in the WHL, retiring as the league's all-time leading scorer with 578 goals. Andy Hebenton, who played 630 consecutive games in the NHL over nine seasons, played an additional 1,057 games in the PCHL/WHL. Hebenton joined Gordie Howe as the only pro to play in the same league as his son, sharing the stage with goaltender Clay Hebenton in 1973-74. Willie O'Ree, who broke the NHL's color barrier in 1957-58, but couldn't break the Boston Bruins' lineup, was a star attraction in Los Angeles and San Diego until 1974.

The WHL's Guyle Fielder was one of hockey's most productive players. Wayne Gretzky received glowing accolades for surpassing Gordie Howe's numerous scoring records, but it was really Fielder's marks he was shooting for. Fielder, who collected 1,846 points in the WHL, was the first professional player to compile 2,000 career points. However, the only mark he made on an NHL scoresheet was the four minutes in penalties he served. Three different organizations gave Fielder a chance, including Detroit, who placed him on a line with Johnny Wilson and Gordie Howe to start the 1957-58 campaign. Yet, after only six games, Fielder was

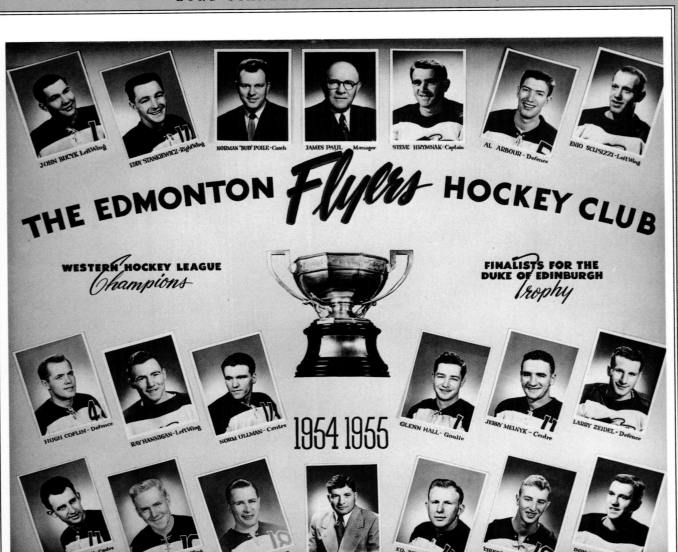

THE EDMONTON *Flyers* HOCKEY CLUB

WESTERN HOCKEY LEAGUE *Champions*

FINALISTS FOR THE DUKE OF EDINBURGH *Trophy*

1954 1955

JOHN BUCYK - Left Wing   EDDY STANKIEWICZ - Right Wing   NORMAN "BUD" POILE - Coach   JAMES PAUL - Manager   STEVE HRYMNAK - Captain   AL ARBOUR - Defence   ENIO SCLISIZZI - Left Wing

HUGH COFLIN - Defence   RAY HANNIGAN - Left Wing   NORM ULLMAN - Centre   GLENN HALL - Goalie   JERRY MELNYK - Centre   LARRY ZEIDEL - Defence

BRONCO HORVATH - Centre   LORNE DAVIS - Right Wing   KEITH ALLEN - Defence   CECIL "TIGER" GOLDSTICK - Trainer   ED. ZENIUK - Defence   "CHUCK" HOLMES - Right Wing   DON POILE - Right Wing

dispatched to the minors again. Disgruntled and disappointed, he vowed never to attempt breaking the tough shell of the majors again.

That resolve held firm the following season when Punch Imlach drafted both Fielder and a veteran goaltender lovingly dubbed the "China Wall" – Johnny Bower – for the struggling Maple Leafs. Bower gambled on the opportunity, but Fielder felt he had rolled the dice once too often. He remained devoted to the WHL, earning nine more All-Star berths before the league folded after the 1973-74 season.

Soon after the West Coast and the central United States made their imprints on the minor-league map, the East Coast of Canada also established its own devel-

The Edmonton Flyers captured the President's Cup as WHL champions three times, including the 1954-55 season, when their team included future NHL stars John Bucyk, Norm Ullman, Al Arbour, Bronco Horvath, and Glenn Hall.

opment leagues. The Quebec Senior Hockey League and its counterpart, the Maritime Major Hockey League, were both semi-pro outfits, considered a tier above Allan Cup senior hockey and a step below the other minor-league systems. Of course, the QSHL had Jean Béliveau in its fold, and "le Gros Bill" kept the turnstiles revolving in every rink.

The MMHL was noted for lengthy schedules, constant financial difficulties, and top-notch names such as Len Haley, Bud Poile, and Willie Marshall. From 1951 to

After being released by the Boston Bruins in 1964, Andy Hebenton continued to play in the Western Hockey League until the league folded following the 1973-74 season.

1953, the champions from the two leagues faced off against each other for the Alexander Cup. However, when the Quebec League became the continent's fourth fully professional minor league prior to the 1953-54 season, it signaled the end of the line for the major senior leagues. The MMHL struggled on for another season, retaining the Alexander Cup as its championship trophy, but folded after the 1953-54 campaign.

The new QHL placed franchises in Ottawa and the Eastern Townships of Quebec, including Shawinigan, Chicoutimi, and Sherbrooke. The alliance gained instant credibility by arranging a post-season series between the QHL champions and their WHL counterparts for the Duke of Edinburgh Trophy, which was emblematic of the minor-league pro championship of Canada.

Though largely remembered as a breeding ground for future Montreal Canadiens stars like Béliveau, Plante, Charlie Hodge, and Marcel Bonin, the senior and professional QHL also had its own regiment of stars. Jacques Locat was the league's all-time scoring leader with 244 goals in 422 games, while Georges Roy holds the QHL mark for games (442) and assists (248). Bob Perreault, who appeared briefly with the Canadiens before making a comeback with the WHA's Los Angeles Sharks in 1973, was the QHL's top goaltender, setting standards for games played (243) and shutouts (19).

After only seven seasons, the Quebec League was disbanded and another pro league, dubbed the Eastern Professional Hockey League, was organized to take its place. In addition to placing franchises in many of the same centers served by the QHL, the EPHL also dipped into the U.S. market with teams in St. Louis and Syracuse. Unlike many of the other minor pro leagues, the majority of players in the EPHL were youngsters. Léon Rochefort, Bobby Rousseau, and Cesare Maniago were distinguished EPHL performers who continued to star in the NHL as players, while others like Harry Sinden and Orval Tessier made the grade in the "bigs" behind the bench.

Despite the excellent quality of the on-ice product, the EPHL folded after the 1962-63 season. One month later, the NHL announced that it would establish its own minor-league system to replace the EPHL, with every NHL club required to sponsor a team. Named the Central Professional Hockey League, the new loop placed its six teams in many of the same towns as the old USHL, including Tulsa and Omaha. Jack Adams, the architect who built the Detroit Red Wings into an NHL power-house, was appointed the league's first commissioner.

The CPHL was designed as a development league, meant to polish the raw talents of the NHL prospects who were tutored there. The league guaranteed that youth would be served: each team was restricted to having only one player over the age of twenty-five and three players over the age of twenty-three. By the time the NHL doubled in size in 1967-68, the CPHL was an established league that was also ready to expand.

There were also two other amateur leagues that the NHL used as minor-league affiliates. The Eastern Hockey League, based mainly in the Carolinas, but also in Philadelphia, Nashville, and New Jersey, was notorious for its turbulent brand of on-ice entertainment. John Brophy, Junie Fontana, and Rocky Rukavina weren't exactly NHL prospects, but their antics kept the seats full. That success caught the eye of the NHL, and by the 1966-67 season, four NHL teams were sponsoring EHL clubs.

Another semi-pro league, the International Hockey League, also gained credibility during the 1960s, when Montreal, Chicago, and Boston all sponsored squads. Today, the IHL is the gem of hockey's minor-pro system, with franchises in most of major American markets not served by the NHL, including Atlanta, Cincinnati, Milwaukee, and San Diego.

The incursion made by these minor leagues played a significant role in establishing the game of hockey in the United States. In 1994, there are five minor pro leagues and eighteen of the NHL's twenty-six franchises operating in the United States. In many ways, the success of the NHL today can be directly traced to the minor-league system that was established during the six-team years.

The semi-pro Quebec Aces were one of the strongest franchises in the Quebec Senior Hockey League, and winners of the Alexander Cup playoff between the champions of the QSHL and the Maritime Major Hockey League in 1953. The Quebec League turned fully professional the following season.

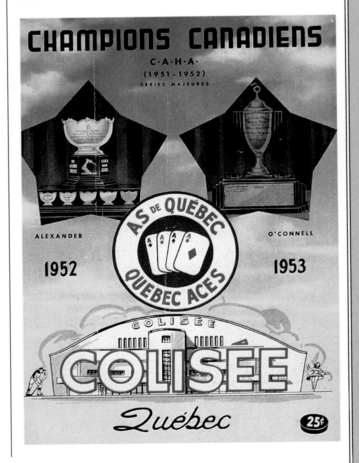

85 PTS.   84 PTS.   78 PTS.   71 PTS.   54 PTS.   48 PTS.

1963-64
Dandy Bathgate Helps Toronto
Repeat in Seven-Game Final

IN DECEMBER 1962, THE NHL'S MANAGERS AND GOVERNORS DETERMINED THAT the league's existing waiver-draft system did not supply enough talent to weaker clubs. In an effort to help the "have-nots," it was decided that a pre-season draft would be held in which any amateur player over the age of seventeen not already on an NHL-sponsored junior team would be eligible to be drafted by interested NHL franchises. In June 1963, the first amateur draft was held, with Montreal, Detroit, Boston, New York, Chicago, and Toronto choosing in that order. Twenty-one juniors were selected, but only a handful made it to the NHL. Garry Monahan, the first player taken, played twelve seasons. Detroit picked Peter Mahovlich, who had a productive sixteen-year career, while three of the four players taken by Toronto – Walt McKechnie, Jim McKenny, and Gerry Meehan – would all go on to become NHL regulars.

A number of major roster moves and blockbuster trades made the 1963-64 season one of the most intriguing campaigns of the six-team era. It was also a year that saw several important milestones equaled and broken, including the NHL's career records for goals and shutouts.

After three early playoff exits, the Montreal Canadiens decided to make a momentous deal with the New York Rangers, who were also suffering post-season woes. The Habs sent Jacques Plante, Phil Goyette, and Don Marshall to the Rangers for Gump Worsley, Dave Balon, Len Ronson, and Léon Rochefort. It was expected that Charlie Hodge would become the Canadiens' number-one goaltender, while Worsley was slated to spend the season with the Quebec Aces of the AHL. Defenseman Tom Johnson and right-winger Dickie Moore, both members of the Canadiens' five Stanley Cup-winning teams from 1956 to 1960, were also missing when training camp opened in September. Johnson had been drafted by Boston. Moore retired. John Ferguson, a tough winger who was noted as a talented lacrosse player in the off-season, was signed to replace Moore.

In Chicago, Rudy Pilous was relieved of his duties and replaced by former Leaf coach Billy Reay. The Black Hawks were content to stay with the same basic cast, adding only Howie Young from Detroit. Young, an aggressive and sometimes-unruly blueliner, was brought in to give

A Separate Peace

A week after Toronto's Bob Pulford and Montreal's Terry Harper continued their on-ice fisticuffs in the penalty box of Maple Leaf Gardens on October 30, 1963, Leaf president Stafford Smythe ordered construction of separate penalty boxes for the home and visiting teams. This was an NHL first. The Canadiens followed shortly thereafter, and had the words *"Visiteurs"* and *"Canadiens"* painted on the penalty-box doors.

added protection to Bobby Hull and Stan Mikita. Mikita had proved he could take care of himself, but his offensive output suffered as his time in the penalty box increased. Phil Esposito, promoted from St. Louis of the Central Pro League, and Aut Erickson, brought up from Buffalo, were added to the squad during the season.

Detroit and Toronto, Stanley Cup finalists in 1963, had differing approaches to the new season. The defending-champion Maple Leafs made only one roster revision, adding Jim Pappin, a graduate of the Toronto Marlboros, who had spent three seasons with Rochester in the AHL. Punch Imlach said he preferred to go with the men he knew, but stressed he wasn't afraid to pull the switch on a deal during the season if any of the old guard failed to produce. Detroit's Sid Abel traded Howie Young to Chicago in exchange for Roger Crozier, who would share goaltending duties with Sawchuk. Other young Red Wings included Eddie Joyal, who scored 29 goals with Pittsburgh in 1962-63, John Miszuk, a good-looking rookie defenseman, and Paul Henderson, a speedy right-winger who had played two games with the Red Wings during the previous season.

The Boston Bruins also made a number of roster revisions. Gary Dornhoefer and Andy Hebenton joined the team for the 1963-64 season while Orland Kurtenbach and Bob Leiter were also back on board. Tom Johnson and Bob McCord were slotted in on the blueline to aid Ted Green, Leo Boivin, and Doug Mohns. Ed Johnston was given the number-one goaltending job.

In addition to the major deal with the Canadiens that brought Plante, Marshall, and Goyette to Broadway, the Rangers also acquired Val Fonteyne through the Intra-League Draft, and Howie Glover and Dick Meissner off the waiver wire. Gilles Villemure was slotted as Plante's backup, and Don Johns was promised a regular shift along the blueline.

Two members of the Detroit Red Wings reached career milestones during the 1963-64 season. Gordie Howe entered the campaign needing only five goals to pass Maurice Richard as the NHL's all-time leading goal-scorer. Howe scored twice in a 5–3 win over Chicago in the season opener, and added another goal in Detroit's 3–0 blanking of Boston. He tied the Rocket with his 544th goal on October 27 against the Canadiens in the Olympia. On November 10, in a game against Montreal, Howe took a pass from Billy McNeill and scored at 15:06 of the second period while killing a five-minute major penalty to Alex Faulkner. That short-handed marker was Howe's 545th goal, establishing a new NHL career-goal-scoring record, while the assist by McNeill would prove to be his last NHL point. The final score of the game was 3–0 for Detroit, and the shutout was the 94th zero of Sawchuk's career, tying him with George Hainsworth for the all-time lead. Sawchuk broke the mark on January 18 with a 2–0 blanking of the Canadiens. Five weeks later, on

George "Red" Sullivan, who spent five seasons with the New York Rangers as a dependable third-line center, replaced Muzz Patrick as the Rangers' head coach midway through the 1962-63 season. Sullivan was back behind the bench to start the 1963-64 campaign and guided the Blueshirts to a 22–38–10 record.

Pierre Pilote solidified his position as the NHL's dominant defenseman during 1963-64 by winning his second consecutive Norris Trophy. Pilote led all NHL rearguards in assists (46) and points (53) as the Black Hawks finished in second place, only one point behind the front-running Montreal Canadiens.

February 22, Sawchuk set a new NHL record for career games played by a goaltender, surpassing Harry Lumley's mark of 804.

The constant media attention that surrounded both Howe and Sawchuk as they pursued these long-held career marks had an adverse effect on the Red Wings, and the team struggled through much of the early part of the season. The club suffered a seven-game winless streak before

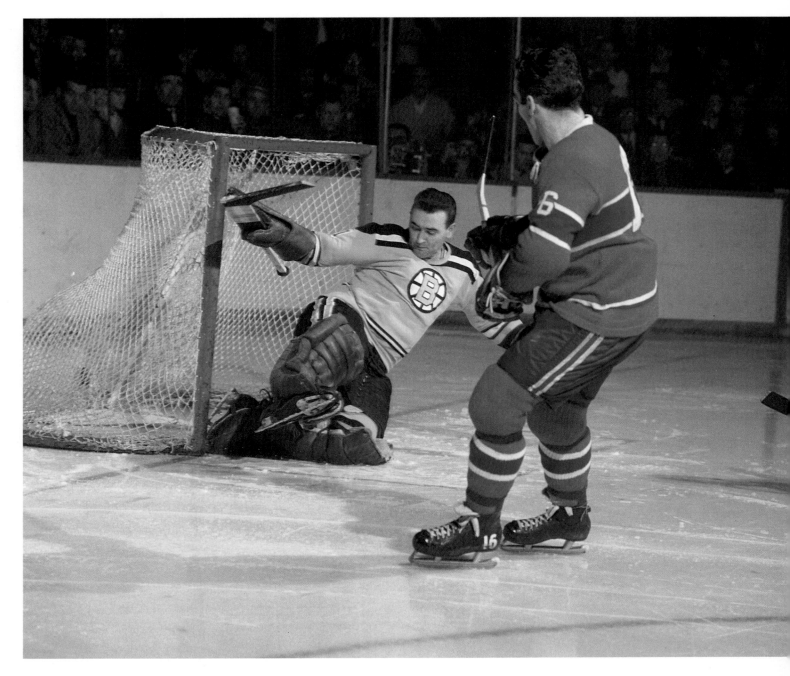

breaking out of its slump in December. After a 12–15–6 first half, in which they scored only 74 goals, the Wings finished the campaign at 30–29–11.

The Chicago Black Hawks and the Montreal Canadiens waged a year-long battle for first place, with Montreal finally ending up on top after beating the Hawks 4–3 in their final meeting before finishing the season with wins over New York and Boston. The first-place finish was a vindication for Frank Selke, who had engineered the deals that dispatched Stanley Cup heroes Plante, Harvey, and Johnson to other clubs. Rookie defenseman Jacques Laperrière had an outstanding season, as did Terry Harper, compensating to a great extent for the loss of Harvey and

Eddie Johnston was the last NHL goalie to play every minute of every game in a season, spending 4,200 minutes between the pipes for the Bruins in 1963-64. Johnston also appeared in all seventy games for the EPHL's Hull–Ottawa Canadiens in 1960-61 and the WHL's Spokane Chiefs in 1961-62.

A backup goalie with the Montreal Canadiens since 1954-55, Charlie Hodge finally became the Habs' number-one netminder in 1963-64. Here, Hodge and defenseman J. C. Tremblay combine to thwart Chicago's Red Hay.

Johnson. Dave Balon, who had never scored more than 11 goals in a single season, fired home 24 for his new team. Bobby Rousseau also had a celebrated season, becoming the first NHL player since Bernie Geoffrion to score five goals in a single game, victimizing Detroit's Roger Crozier in a 9–3 win on February 1. Young Yvan Cournoyer, who was playing in the last match of his five-game trial with the Habs, also scored a pair of goals in this victory. Charlie Hodge, who had made his NHL debut with the Canadiens nine years earlier, appeared in a career-high 62 games for the Habs, with a goals-against average of 2.26, the second-lowest total in the league.

Chicago was the talk of the NHL as Stan Mikita and Bobby Hull dueled for the scoring title. Hull led the league in goals with 43, while Mikita scored 39 goals and added 50 assists for a league-leading 89 points. Another Black Hawk, Kenny Wharram, finished tied for second with Mikita for the goal-scoring title, with a career-high 39. Pierre Pilote was the league's top-scoring defenseman, with 46 assists and 53 points. Glenn Hall, who continued to share some of his goaltending duties with Denis DeJordy, won an NHL-high 34 games with a goals-against average of 2.31. League-leaders for most of the season, the Hawks stumbled down the stretch, and the Canadiens passed them to finish in first place.

It was a season of contrasts for the Toronto Maple Leafs, who received outstanding goaltending from Johnny Bower and brilliant defensive play from the blueline unit, but constantly struggled to put the puck in the net. Frank Mahovlich, in a profound slump most of the year, was shifted from line to line and from position to position by Punch Imlach, who was attempting to lift the left-winger out of his lethargy.

But it wasn't only Mahovlich who had to endure the wrath of Imlach. On January 18, the Boston Bruins shocked the hockey community by blasting the Maple Leafs 11–0 at Maple Leaf Gardens. Don Simmons, replacing an injured Johnny Bower, was in the barrel for all 11 goals and was told by Imlach after the game that he was finished as a Maple Leaf. The Leafs were playing in Chicago the next evening, and Imlach ordered that WHL farm hand Al Millar be flown in from the West Coast for the game. Millar, who had played six NHL games for Boston in 1957-58, also as a replacement for Don Simmons, was unable to reach Chicago in time for the game because of fog and airplane engine trouble. Simmons went back into the Leafs' goal and promptly shut out Chicago 2–0. Millar returned to Victoria of the Western Hockey League and never played in the NHL again.

The Leafs continued to struggle, scoring only two goals in their next four games and falling dangerously close to the fifth-place Rangers. Finally, Imlach swung the deal that the newspapers had been speculating about for weeks. On February 22, the Toronto general manager sent Arnie Brown, Dick Duff, Bill Collins, Bob Nevin, and Rod Seiling to the Rangers for Andy Bathgate and Don McKenney. The impact of the transaction was said to rival the Max Bentley deal of 1947. While it was true that the Leafs had sacrificed part of their future, they received two veteran players who would give their sputtering offense a boost. The Leafs lost only one of their last nine games to climb back into third place with a record of 33 wins, 25 losses, and 12 ties.

Once again, the Rangers and Bruins occupied the bottom rungs of the NHL ladder. In New York, there was outrage at the trading of Bathgate, their only superstar, but the five players the Rangers received would help bring the franchise back to respectability. With young stars such as Jean

LAST-PLACE BOSTON WINS BIG

This 11–0 victory stands as the most decisive shutout win in Boston Bruins history. Despite winning by a lopsided score on this night, the Bruins would finish 30 points behind the Cup-champion Leafs in the 1963-64 regular-season final standings.

January 18, 1964
at Maple Leaf Gardens
Boston 11, Toronto 0

FIRST PERIOD
1) BOS Dornhoefer 3 (Bucyk, Oliver) :53
2) BOS Hebenton 6 (Kurtenbach, Prentice) 6:20
3) BOS Oliver 14 (Bucyk, Boivin) 9:02
4) BOS Prentice 14 (Kurtenbach) 9:28
5) BOS Hebenton 7 (Prentice) 14:51
6) BOS Prentice 15 (Kurtenbach) 19:54
PENALTIES – None

SECOND PERIOD
7) BOS Hebenton 8 (Leiter, Prentice) 12:27
PENALTIES – Shack TOR (highsticking) 1:19; Kurtenbach BOS (elbowing) 3:30; Leiter BOS (fighting – major), Shack TOR (fighting – major) 6:40; TOR (too many men on the ice – served by Stemkowski) 17:03.

THIRD PERIOD
8) BOS Oliver 15 (Bucyk, Green) 2:11
9) BOS Prentice 16 (Hebenton) 6:17
10) BOS Bucyk 8 (Oliver, Dornhoefer) 7:04
11) BOS Gendron 2 (Kennedy, McCord) 15:47
PENALTIES – Kurtenbach BOS (highsticking, roughing), Brown TOR (highsticking, roughing) 16:45; Mohns BOS (slashing) 19:13.

SHOTS ON GOAL	1	2	3	T
BOSTON	15	10	13	38
TORONTO	7	9	10	26

GOALTENDERS	TIME	SA	GA	ENG	W/L
BOS Johnston	60:00	26	0	0	W
TOR Simmons	60:00	27	11	0	L

PP CONVERSIONS BOS 0/2 TOR 0/2

Icy Theaters

Spurred by the successful Maple Leafs closed-circuit TV theater "network," which had grown to seven southern Ontario theaters by 1964, two Detroit movie theaters showed live closed-circuit telecasts of all the Red Wings' 1964 playoff games. The Wings had hoped to get their road playoff games televised over the air, but local stations wanted to broadcast only home games. The Black Hawks also agreed to closed-circuit theater showings of their home playoff games.

Ratelle, Rod Gilbert, and Vic Hadfield, the club appeared to be building a firm foundation.

Boston continued to struggle, winning only 18 games and missing the playoffs by 23 points. Murray Oliver, with 24 goals, and John Bucyk, with 54 points, continued to be the team's top offensive stars, while Ed Johnston became the last NHL goaltender to play every minute of every game in a single season. One of the few bright spots for the Bruins was the play of Andy Hebenton, who set an NHL record for consecutive games played. Hebenton, who made his NHL debut in 1955, never missed a game in his entire NHL career. Nevertheless, at the conclusion of the 1963-64 season, he was released after appearing in 630 consecutive games. He remained in professional hockey, but never played in the NHL again.

For the first time since the best-of-seven playoff format was introduced in 1939, all three series went the distance in 1963-64, creating one of the most exciting post-seasons of the six-team era. The Montreal Canadiens and the Toronto Maple Leafs battled through seven games, with Frank Mahovlich playing inspired hockey. The Big M scored the winner in Toronto's 2–1 win in game two and collected five points in the Leafs' 5–3 victory in game four. Games six and seven belonged to Johnny Bower and Dave Keon, who were playing the best hockey of their respective careers. In game six, with the Leafs on the verge of elimination after a 4–2 Montreal triumph in the fifth match, Bower stopped 25 shots in a 3–0 shutout win. In the decisive seventh game, Bower made 38 saves, and Dave Keon scored all three goals in Toronto's 3–1 series-clinching victory.

Chicago and Detroit also played seven times before the Wings finally emerged victorious. The Black Hawks, who held a 3–2 edge in games, lost the final two matches by a combined score of 11–4. Norm Ullman was the catalyst for the Wings, collecting 13 points in the series. Gordie Howe became the NHL's all-time playoff scoring leader when he registered his 127th post-season point in Chicago's 3–2 win in game five.

The Stanley Cup final was a test of emotions for both teams, as each of the first three games was decided in dramatic fashion. Bob Pulford sealed game one for the Leafs when he cut off a cross-ice pass by Norm Ullman at the Toronto blueline and steamed in all alone on Sawchuk to score a shorthanded goal. Pulford ripped a rising wrist shot from fifteen feet that caught the top corner with two seconds left in the game to give Toronto a 3–2 win. Detroit tied the series with an overtime win in game two. Left-winger Larry Jeffrey tipped in a shot from the edge of the goal crease at the 7:52 mark of sudden death.

The Red Wings needed some late-game magic in the third match as well, losing a 3–0 lead only to have Alex Delvecchio tap in a pass by Gordie Howe with seventeen seconds left to win, 4–3. The teams split victories in the next pair of games, pushing the Wings to within a single victory of the Stanley Cup. One of the NHL's most-chronicled moments

Andy Bathgate sips sweet champagne after scoring the Stanley Cup-winning goal in game seven of finals between Toronto and Detroit on April 25, 1964. The former Hart Trophy-winner appeared in only 22 playoff games during his career with the New York Rangers. He was acquired by the Toronto Maple Leafs on February 22, 1964, in one of the biggest trades of the 1960s.

occurred in game six. With the game tied at 3–3 in the third period, Bob Baun was carted off the ice on a stretcher after taking a slapshot on the ankle. Baun, however, refused to leave the game, insisting that the trainer tape the ankle tightly so he could take a regular shift should the game go into overtime. The match remained deadlocked until the 1:43 mark of the first extra session, when Baun picked up a pass at the blue-line and flipped the puck towards the Detroit net. The puck bounced off Detroit defender Bill Gadsby, skipped by Red Wing rearguard Doug Barkley, and finally found its way past Terry Sawchuk in the Wings' net for a 4–3 Leaf victory.

Fortified by their dramatic success in game six, the Leafs attacked from the opening whistle of game seven. Andy Bathgate scored three minutes into the contest, and Keon, Kelly, and Armstrong scored in the final frame to record a 4–0 Cup-clinching win. Following the game, Red Kelly, who was playing despite severe pain in his legs, collapsed in the shower and had to be taken to hospital by ambulance. Later, Leaf co-owner Harold Ballard brought the Stanley Cup and a bottle of champagne to Kelly's home, and they saluted the victory there.

After the series, Bob Baun disclosed that he had played the over-time period in game six and all of the seventh game on a fractured ankle. He would spend much of the summer wearing a cast. Post-season awards went to Pierre Pilote (Norris), Jean Béliveau (Hart), Jacques Laperrière (Calder), Stan Mikita (Art Ross), Ken Wharram (Lady Byng), and Charlie Hodge (Vezina).

Prime Tickets:
Big Jean and the Golden Jet
1964-65 to 1966-67

| 87 PTS. | 83 PTS. | 76 PTS. | 74 PTS. | 52 PTS. | 48 PTS. |

1964-65
Hawks' Big Shooters Finish 1–2–3 in Goals

NUMEROUS CHANGES WERE IN STORE FOR THE MONTREAL CANADIENS, WHO HAD now gone four straight seasons without reaching the Stanley Cup finals. After eighteen seasons and six championship titles, Frank Selke resigned as managing director of the team and was replaced by Sam Pollock. Montreal also lost Bernie Geoffrion to retirement and Dickie Moore to the Leafs through the Intra-League Draft. Moore, who had retired after the 1962-63 season, returned to action after being claimed by the Leafs.

Charlie Hodge, who had won the Vezina Trophy in 1963-64, was slated to share the Canadiens' goaltending job with Gump Worsley, who played 47 games with Quebec and eight games with the Habs in 1963-64. Ted Harris, a minor-league pro since 1956, looked promising in training camp and earned a berth on the blueline with Laperrière, Harper, J.C. Tremblay, and Talbot. Defensive specialists Jim Roberts and Claude Larose, who led the CPHL in playoff goals in 1963-64, won lineup spots and took turns working with John Ferguson and Ralph Backstrom on the club's main checking line.

One of the NHL's all-time greats decided to make a comeback after four years in retirement. Ted Lindsay, who had last played in 1959-60, decided to return to active duty with the Red Wings and signed a new contract, following an impressive training camp with Detroit's Memphis farm team. Coach Sid Abel was convinced that the Wings were ready to improve upon their fourth-place finish in regular-season play after two successive trips to the finals. Roger Crozier was given the number-one goaltending job when the Wings lost Terry Sawchuk to the Leafs in the Intra-League Draft. Ron Murphy was acquired from Chicago, and Gary

Opposite: Hockey's Dynamic Duo. Stan Mikita (left) and Bobby Hull were the dominant offensive players in the NHL throughout much of the 1960s. Hull broke every existing single-season scoring mark, while Mikita's evolution was slower but equally impressive. Once noted for his aggressive play, Mikita dropped his belligerent behavior to become the NHL's finest playmaking center. Both Black Hawks used banana-bladed sticks.

New York Rangers defenseman Arnie Brown (4) can only watch as this shot escapes the grasp of goaltender Jacques Plante. Plante, a six-time winner of the Vezina Trophy with the Montreal Canadiens and the last goalie to win the Hart Trophy, was dispatched to the AHL's Baltimore Clippers during the 1964-65 season, and retired after the Clippers were eliminated by the Hershey Bears in the first round of the AHL playoffs. He would later make a successful NHL comeback.

A Milestone for Mr. Hockey

Gordie Howe scored goals in each game of a home-and-home series against Gump Worsley of the Montreal Canadiens on February 6 and 7, 1965. These gave him a career total of 100 goals against the Montreal Canadiens and made him the first NHL player to score at least 100 goals against every team in the league.

Bergman, a career minor-leaguer, was given a full-time job as Detroit's fifth defenseman.

The defending-champion Maple Leafs, with Andy Bathgate and Don McKenney aboard for the full season, made no major deals in the off-season. In addition to Sawchuk, Moore was also claimed in the Intra-League Draft, although bad knees were expected to limit his on-ice action. Ron Ellis was the lone rookie to earn an NHL job, while Kent Douglas was back with the Leafs after spending the majority of his sophomore season with Rochester of the AHL. In the 1964 Amateur Draft, the Leafs selected a pair of promising defensemen, Jim Dorey and Mike Pelyk, both of whom would earn berths on the team by the end of the 1960s.

Chicago swung two separate deals with Boston, first acquiring Doug Mohns for Ab McDonald and Reggie Fleming before obtaining Jerry Toppazzini and Matt Ravlich in exchange for fan favorite Murray Balfour. Toppazzini never suited up for the Hawks, but Ravlich became a steady member of the blueline crew. Newcomers included Dennis Hull, the Golden Jet's younger brother, and Phil Esposito, who saw limited duty in 1963-64.

There were few encouraging signs in Boston and New York, although both teams did acquire some fine talent in the league's annual Amateur Draft. Boston selected a young goaltender named Ken Dryden, but when they discovered that Dryden planned to attend university instead of playing junior hockey, they traded his rights to the Montreal Canadiens for Guy Allen and Paul Reid. The Rangers selected Syl Apps, Jr., and Tim Ecclestone, both of whom would become solid NHL players.

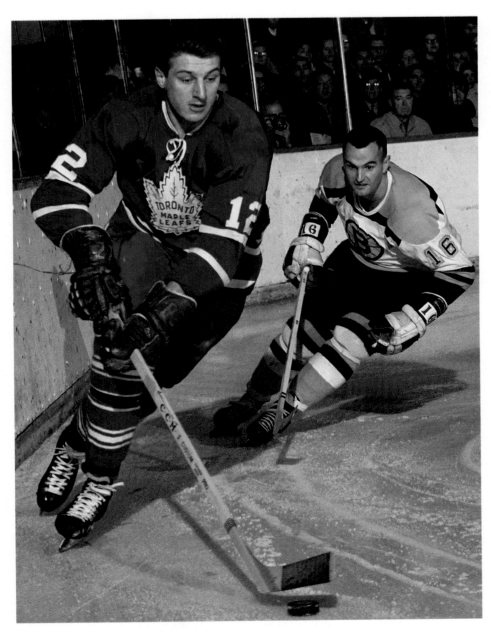

Murray Oliver (16), shown here chasing Toronto forward Pete Stemkowski, was one of the Bruins' most consistent players during his eight years with the club. Boston's number-one center, Oliver recorded three consecutive seasons with 20 or more goals, beginning in 1962-63.

Lou Angotti, a graduate of Michigan Tech University, who had spent the previous two seasons in Rochester, was the lone rookie to make the Rangers' lineup. After six Vezina Trophy wins and seven All-Star selections, Jacques Plante was demoted to Baltimore of the AHL to start the season. Marcel Paille was scheduled to replace him.

Boston introduced a number of new players for 1964-65. Wayne Rivers, Wayne Maxner, and Bill Knibbs were three of the newcomers who stayed with the Bruins through most of the season, in what would prove to be their longest stints in the NHL. Other new faces to see action were Bob Woytowich, Don Awrey, and Joe Watson. Ab McDonald, Reggie Fleming, and Murray Balfour, over from Chicago, joined Bucyk, Prentice, and Oliver as the Bruins' top forwards.

Claude Provost (14), a versatile winger, was a member of nine Stanley Cup-winning teams in his fourteen seasons with the Montreal Canadiens. Equally adept at both ends of the rink, Provost won a berth on the NHL's Second All-Star Team after compiling 27 goals and 37 assists for the Canadiens in 1964-65.

Detroit Ditto, or Red Wing Redux

Recalling his linemate Ted Lindsay's 1949-50 in-season sabbatical, Red Wings' coach and general manager Sid Abel gave rookie goalie Roger Crozier a three-day Miami Beach vacation in January 1965. It worked. Crozier came back, and, over the next nine games, the Wings won seven. He allowed only six goals in the seven wins, and had two shutouts. Crozier would go on to win the Calder Trophy. He was named to the NHL's First All-Star Team and only missed winning the Vezina Trophy on the last night of the season.

The 1964-65 season was highlighted by a three-team race for first place. Detroit's Roger Crozier proved himself to be the league's finest young goaltender, and his acrobatic style won praise throughout the NHL. The Motowners won 25 of their last 39 games, taking advantage of a mid-season slump by the Habs to capture their first regular-season title since 1956-57. Detroit had three of the league's top five scorers in Norm Ullman, Gordie Howe, and Alex Delvecchio.

Norm Ullman, who led all NHL marksmen with 42 goals, was engaged in a lengthy struggle with Bobby Hull for the goal-scoring lead. Ullman played his best hockey down the home stretch, connecting for 15 goals in his final 13 games to finish ahead of Hull. The Golden Jet had opened the campaign by scoring 29 goals in his first 28 games and seemed destined to surpass the 50-goal record he shared with the Rocket and Boom-Boom Geoffrion. Halfway through the schedule, however, he suffered a nagging knee injury that forced him to miss nine games, and he limped through the second half of the season. Still, Hull finished with 39 goals.

Montreal appeared to be in total control through the early part of the 70-game schedule, losing only eight of their first 32 games. However, Jean Béliveau, Gilles Tremblay, and Henri Richard all succumbed to

injuries, and youngsters such as Yvan Cournoyer and Bobby Rousseau were unable to compensate for the loss of firepower. In an attempt to bolster the Habs' depleted lineup, Dick Duff was acquired from New York for Bill Hicke, but Duff could manage only nine goals in his 40 games with the Habs. The Canadiens won only 10 of their last 24 games to finish second behind Detroit with 83 points.

While Chicago proved they had more than enough scoring punch to win the league title, it was becoming evident they had an equally effective defensive system as well. Pierre Pilote, Doug Jarrett, and Elmer "Moose" Vasko combined speed and toughness, while "Mr. Goalie," Glenn Hall, was as steady as any netminder in the NHL. Stan Mikita, one of hockey's finest playmakers, led the NHL with 59 assists and 87 points. He also spent 154 minutes in the penalty box.

It was a season of disappointment in Toronto, where the Leafs were beset by a string of injuries and fell to fourth place with a 30–26–14 record. Andy Bathgate, Allan Stanley, Frank Mahovlich, and George Armstrong all missed considerable amounts of ice time. Mahovlich, according to newspaper reports, was constantly harassed by Imlach. He was hospitalized for a month, suffering from continual fatigue and depression. Red Kelly, still

Left to right: Ed Joyal, Norm Ullman, Paul Henderson, Sid Abel, Alex Delvecchio, and Roger Crozier celebrate the Detroit Red Wings' first-place finish in 1964-65. The Red Wings' surprising rise to the top of the league's standings marked the first time the club had finished higher than fourth since 1957-58.

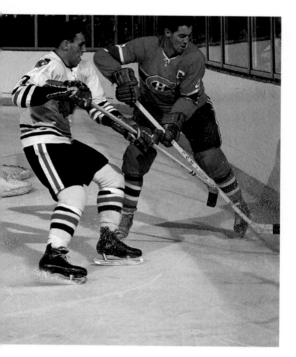

Two future members of the Hockey Hall of Fame, Phil Esposito (left) and Jean Béliveau, battle for a loose puck during the 1964-65 Stanley Cup finals. In his first full season in the league, Espo managed 23 goals and 32 assists in helping the Black Hawks to 34–28–8 record. Béliveau, who scored the winning goal in three of Montreal's four victories in the finals, was the first recipient of the Conn Smythe Trophy as playoff MVP.

juggling politics and hockey, was the only Leaf forward to suit up for all 70 games. Imlach, at a loss to motivate the team, demoted Billy Harris to the minors and moved Tim Horton to right wing. Only three Leafs were able to hit the 20-goal plateau, with rookie Ron Ellis tying Mahovlich for the team lead with 23 goals. But while the team's offense had deteriorated, the blue-line was as solid as ever, winning the Vezina Trophy for the goaltending tandem of Terry Sawchuk and Johnny Bower.

For the third season in succession, the Rangers and Bruins failed to make the playoffs. There was little improvement in either city, prompting the NHL's general managers to meet to discuss ways of aiding the ailing franchises. Muzz Patrick was relieved of his general manager's duties in New York, and Emile "The Cat" Francis was entrusted with the task of rebuilding the Rangers. Francis allowed Red Sullivan to complete the season behind the bench, informing the media that Sullivan was the least of the Rangers' problems. According to Francis, the fact that the Rangers had 67 more goals-against than goals-scored was a more pressing concern. New York made headlines during the season when they signed Swedish Olympic star Ulf Sterner and brought him to North America. Sterner, who collected 44 points in 52 games with the Rangers' AHL farm team in Baltimore, was a skilled player, but he was unable to make an impact in the NHL and he returned to Sweden at the end of the 1964-65 season.

In Boston, the Bruins finished with less than 50 points for the fifth straight season. Ed Westfall was moved from defense to forward, where he made a fine contribution with 12 goals and 27 points, but he was one of only six front-liners to reach double figures in goals. John Bucyk was the club's leading scorer once again with 55 points.

For the first time in NHL history, five of the six NHL clubs used a two-goaltender rotation. The exception was in Detroit, where Roger Crozier became the last NHL goaltender to appear in all 70 games, although he was twice replaced in mid-game by backup Carl Wetzel. In January, the NHL passed legislation that stated that every team was required to have a goaltender on the bench, dressed and ready to play, during the 1965 playoffs. Prior to this rule change, the home team had to provide a spare goalie who was capable of filling in if the starter was injured. These spare goalies were usually amateur netminders, club trainers, or practice goalies. They sat in the stands until needed, delaying the game while they dressed and warmed up. The edict was extended to the regular season for the 1965-66 campaign, ending the days when the names of emergency fill-ins like Lefty Wilson, Len Broderick, Don Aiken, Don Keenan, Julian Klymkiw, and Danny Olesevich would find their way onto NHL scoresheets.

In the 1965 semi-finals, the Toronto Maple Leafs' three-year reign as Stanley Cup champions came to a close, as the Canadiens defeated their rivals in a tight six-game series. The Habs won the first two games on home ice by 3–2 and 3–1 scores, using airtight defense and an opportunistic power play to take a commanding lead in the set. Toronto evened things up back at Maple Leaf Gardens on Dave Keon's overtime goal in game three and a masterful performance by Johnny Bower in Toronto's 4–2 triumph in game four. However, the Canadiens were too strong for the aging Leafs, and they wrapped up the series with a 3–1 win in game five and a 4–3 overtime triumph in game six. Claude Provost scored the series-clinching goal after 16:33 of extra time.

For the second year in a row, the Chicago Black Hawks and the Detroit Red Wings went to seven games before a winner was decided. Chicago reversed the tide in this semi-final playdown, rebounding from a 3–2 deficit in games to move into the finals for the first time since 1962.

The 1965 finals opened in Montreal and marked the third time the Black Hawks and the Canadiens had met in the championship round. Toe Blake decided to start Gump Worsley in goal, giving the twelve-year veteran his first opportunity to play in a Stanley Cup final. The Gumper rewarded Blake's judgment with a convincing display in Montreal's 3–2 game-one win. He notched his first playoff shutout by blanking the Hawks 2–0 in the second encounter. Back in Chicago Stadium, the Hawks' fans roared their approval as Chicago defeated the Habs, 3–1 and 5–1. In these two games the Hawks outscored the Canadiens, 6–0, in third-period play. Charlie Hodge, who saw action in game four, started game five for the Habs in Montreal, backstopping his team to a 6–0 shutout. In the sixth meeting of the series, the Canadiens were fourteen minutes away from their first Stanley Cup in five years, when Elmer Vasko and Doug Mohns connected less than two minutes apart to give Chicago a series-tying 2–1 win.

Game seven was slated for the Montreal Forum, and the Hawks knew it was imperative to get out to a fast start. Bobby Hull stated that, if Chicago could survive the emotions and nerves of the first two minutes, they would win the series. Blake started Worsley in the Canadiens' net and began the game with his top line of Béliveau, Rousseau, and Duff on the ice. That unit combined for three goals in the first sixteen minutes, as the Canadiens captured their twelfth Stanley Cup championship with a 4–0 victory. Jean Béliveau, who scored only 14 seconds into the game to set the tone for the evening, was named the inaugural winner of the Conn Smythe Trophy, awarded to the most valuable performer in the playoffs.

Although it was small consolation, three Black Hawks were honored with post-season awards. Stan Mikita (Art Ross), Bobby Hull (Hart and Lady Byng), and Pierre Pilote (Norris) joined Roger Crozier (Calder) and the tandem of Johnny Bower and Terry Sawchuk (Vezina) as the league's top regular-season performers.

On a sad note, Murray Balfour, a member of the 1961 Stanley Cup-champion Chicago Black Hawks, was diagnosed with cancer in March. Balfour, who started the season with the Boston Bruins, passed away following surgery in July 1965.

DETROIT GAINS FIRST PLACE IN RACE FOR REGULAR-SEASON CHAMPIONSHIP

Standings on March 8, 1965

TEAM	GP	W	L	T	PTS
Chicago	63	33	23	7	73
Detroit	60	33	21	6	72
Montreal	61	30	20	11	71

March 9, 1965
at Detroit Olympia
Detroit 3, Montreal 2

FIRST PERIOD
1) MTL Béliveau 10 (Richard, Talbot) PPG 15:38
PENALTIES — Jeffrey DET (elbowing) 3:08; Harper MTL (holding) 6:35; Balon MTL (crosschecking) 11:51; Laperrière MTL (boarding), Howe DET (roughing) 13:47; Godfrey DET (holding) 14:32; Peters MTL (holding) 17:21.

SECOND PERIOD
2) DET Delvecchio 19 (Howe) 1:32
3) DET Ullman 32 (Howe, MacDonald) PPG 12:20
4) MTL Rousseau 10 (Duff, Béliveau) 16:47
PENALTIES — Laperrière MTL (highsticking) 2:55; Talbot MTL (holding) 9:30; Roberts MTL (holding) 10:22; Gadsby DET (interference) 12:30; Ullman DET (highsticking) 17:54.

THIRD PERIOD
5) DET Delvecchio 20 (Ullman, Howe) 19:55
PENALTIES — Delvecchio DET (hooking) :55; Duff MTL (crosschecking) 5:47; Ferguson MTL (interference), Crozier DET (served by Martin) 11:24.

SHOTS ON GOAL	1	2	3	T
MONTREAL	15	5	7	27
DETROIT	8	8	9	25

GOALTENDERS		TIME	SA	GA	ENG	W/L
MTL	Hodge	60:00	22	3	0	L
DET	Crozier	60:00	25	2	0	W

PP CONVERSIONS   MTL 1/5   DET 1/7

Standings on March 10, 1965

TEAM	GP	W	L	T	PTS
Detroit	61	34	21	6	74
Chicago	63	33	23	7	73
Montreal	62	30	21	11	71

Detroit finished with 6 wins, 2 losses, and 1 tie.
Chicago finished with 1 win, 5 losses, and 1 tie.
Montreal finished with 6 wins and 2 losses.

Detroit clinched the NHL championship on March 25, 1965 with a 7–4 win over New York. It was the club's first regular-season title since 1956-57.

90 PTS.   82 PTS.   79 PTS.   74 PTS.   48 PTS.   47 PTS.

1965-66
Hull Shatters 50-Goal Barrier

FANS OF THE NHL WITNESSED ONE OF THE GREATEST SINGLE-SEASON SCORING feats in hockey history during 1965-66, when Bobby Hull became the first NHL player to score more than 50 goals in a season. The Golden Jet, who had been well on his way to establishing the mark in 1964-65, before a sprained knee hampered his goal production, connected for his record-breaking 51st goal on March 12 in front of 22,000 fans in Chicago Stadium.

The defending-champion Canadiens entered the 1965-66 season with the same cast of stars and role players that had successfully returned the Stanley Cup to Montreal in 1965, though some extra help was added to the defense when the Habs sent Cesare Maniago and Garry Peters to the Rangers for blueliner Noel Price, plus Earl Ingarfield, Gord Labossierre, and Dave McComb. Price, who had played with Detroit, Toronto, and the Rangers, saw only limited duty with the Canadiens, but provided valuable injury insurance. Goaltenders Hodge and Worsley were back, as were all of the club's top forwards. In the June amateur draft, the Canadiens used their only pick to select Pierre Bouchard, the son of former team captain Emile "Butch" Bouchard. The younger Bouchard would play a prominent role in the Canadiens' championship teams of the 1970s.

Chicago combined a formidable offensive lineup, led by Bobby Hull and the Scooter Line of Mikita, Wharram, and Mohns, with a determined, aggressive defense, secured by Vasko, Ravlich, Pilote, MacNeil, and Jarrett. Dave Dryden was engaged to replace Denis DeJordy as a backup to Glenn Hall, while Pat Stapleton was selected in the Intra-League Draft to fill in on defense. Ken Hodge, a six-foot, two-inch, 210-pound winger who was born in England, was awarded a spot on the forward line after an outstanding junior career with the St. Catharines Black Hawks.

Despite winning the regular-season title in 1964-65, the Detroit Red Wings had been unable to win a playoff round, compelling Sid Abel to make several roster adjustments. A pair of veterans, Ab McDonald and Bob McCord, were obtained from Boston for Parker MacDonald and Junior Langlois. Bryan Watson, a rambunctious defenseman, who would quickly earn the nickname "Bugsy," was drafted from Chicago and became a hard-checking force along the blueline.

Pre-Game Show

Prior to the start of the 1965-66 season, the NHL stated that each team's pre-game warm-ups would be conducted separately, and that teams would be allowed to warm up using the entire ice surface. The home team would warm up forty-five minutes prior to game time, while the visitors would skate thirty minutes before the drop of the puck. The system was abandoned after players and coaches objected, feeling that the different warm-up times resulted in uneven pre-game preparation.

Alex Delvecchio, seen here attempting to strip New York Rangers defenseman Bob Plager of the puck, scored 31 goals for the Red Wings in 1965-66, the highest total of his twenty-four-year career. Plager, who saw limited action in three different seasons with the Rangers, went on to anchor the blueline of the expansion St. Louis Blues for eleven seasons.

Abel and Toronto's Punch Imlach completed one of the decade's bigger deals shortly after the conclusion of the 1964-65 season. Detroit sent Marcel Pronovost, Ed Joyal, Aut Erickson, Larry Jeffrey, and Lowell McDonald to the Leafs for Andy Bathgate, Billy Harris, and Gary Jarrett. Bathgate was approaching the end of his career, but he made a considerable contribution to the Red Wings during his brief stay in Motown.

The Toronto Maple Leafs, while noted for having one of the NHL's richest farm systems, were still the league's oldest team. Punch Imlach was hesitant to replace too many of the aging veterans whose careers he had resurrected, so players like Billy Harris and Ron Stewart were made expendable. Stewart was sent to Boston for Orland Kurtenbach, while Harris was part of a deal that sent Bathgate to Detroit. Imlach did introduce three rookies to the lineup for 1965-66, as Brit Selby, Pete Stemkowski, and Wally Boyer all played regular shifts during the campaign. Defenseman Carl Brewer retired after training camp and

Montreal Canadiens' rear-guard Jacques Laperrière (right) won the Norris Trophy and was selected to the NHL's First All-Star Team during the 1965-66 season. Toronto's Eddie Shack (left) collected a career-high 26 goals for the Leafs, despite starting the season with the AHL's Rochester Americans. Shack was also immortalized in a hit song entitled "Clear the Track, Here Comes Shack."

returned to university. He would later apply to have his amateur status restored and go on to play for the Canadian National Team.

The Boston Bruins, last-place finishers for five straight seasons, entered 1965-66 with a prospect-laden roster that would push the club out of the NHL basement. On defense, Ted Green, Don Awrey, Leo Boivin, and Junior Langlois combined veteran savvy with youth. The forwards, led by Bucyk, were enhanced by the addition of Hubert "Pit" Martin, Ron Stewart, Bob Dillabough, and Bill Goldsworthy. In goal, Ed Johnston was joined by promising newcomers Gerry Cheevers and Bernie Parent.

Emile Francis, the new general manager of the Rangers, declined to make a coaching change, preferring to modify his roster in other areas. Jacques Plante, who retired after being demoted to the minors, was

Pat Stapleton joined the Black Hawks in 1965-66. An immediate crowd favorite in Chicago Stadium, he would go on to earn a berth on the NHL's Second All-Star Team.

replaced by minor-league veteran Ed Giacomin, who had spent seven seasons toiling in the Eastern and American leagues. Cesare Maniago, secured from Montreal, was named as Giacomin's backup. Earl Ingarfield was claimed in the Intra-League Draft a day after being dealt to Montreal, and he responded by having one of his finest seasons. Francis decided to rotate six defensemen, including stalwarts Harry Howell, Jim Neilson, and Rod Seiling, but the Rangers still allowed 66 more goals than they scored and finished in sixth place.

Ted Lindsay, who had made an impressive comeback in 1964-65, with 14 goals and 28 points, had retired again after the season to avoid being claimed on waivers. After the new season began, Lindsay applied for reinstatement, but his bid was blocked by league governor Stafford Smythe of the Leafs. No deal could be worked out, and Lindsay remained on the sidelines.

The Red Wings were in a tight three-team race for top spot during the first half of the campaign, despite injuries to Bill Gadsby and Warren Godfrey. Early-season highlights included Gordie Howe scoring his 600th NHL goal, against Gump Worsley and the Canadiens, on November 27. Norm Ullman recorded three goals and three assists in a game against Boston one week later. Detroit continued to play well, and had risen to first place, when Doug Barkley was clipped in the eye by a high stick on January 29. Barkley, a standout on the Wings' blueline, suffered a detached retina, which ended his NHL career. The loss of one of the

The veteran and the freshman. Don Marshall (left), a member of five Stanley Cup-winning teams with the Canadiens in the 1950s, had a career-best 26 goals and 54 points for the New York Rangers during 1965-66. Bernie Parent, who would later become the first player to win the Conn Smythe Trophy in consecutive years in 1974 and 1975, made his NHL debut with the Boston Bruins on November 3, 1965, in a 3–3 tie with the Chicago Black Hawks.

Timely Additions

After NHL president Clarence Campbell recommended an upgrading of timing devices throughout the NHL, Montreal, Detroit, and Toronto all installed new scoreboards for the 1965-66 season. The new four-sided, bilingual model was the first scoreboard to hang over center ice at the Montreal Forum. Previous scoreboards had been mounted on the building's walls. A similar four-sided model was hung over center ice in Toronto. In Detroit, the old center-hung model was replaced by scoreboards mounted at the ends of the arena. All three featured digital timers instead of circular clock faces.

club's best rearguards took the wind out of Detroit's sails, and they slumped to a fourth-place finish with 74 points.

In key late-season moves designed to bolster the Red Wings lineup, the Wings acquired Dean Prentice and Leo Boivin from Boston on February 18. Prentice collected 15 points down the stretch for Detroit, and was a key factor in the club's post-season success. Boivin, a bruising fifteen-year veteran, was a standout on the blueline.

Most of the media's attention during the season was focused on Bobby Hull and the Chicago Black Hawks, as the Golden Jet pursued the 50-goal plateau. The Hawks sat atop the league standings for much of the campaign and were tied for first with Montreal when, on March 2, Hull

became the first player to record two 50-goal seasons. However, the team went into a tailspin and failed to score in three consecutive games, as Hull searched for his 51st tally of the year. Bruce Gamble, standing in for injured goalies Sawchuk and Bower, was outstanding for the Leafs in a 5–0 win by Toronto. Montreal blanked the Hawks 1–0 on March 6, and the lowly Rangers also upset the powerhouse Hawks by a similar 1–0 count three nights later.

Finally, ten days after notching his 50th goal, Hull moved into the record books. At 5:34 of the third period on Saturday, March 12, the Golden Jet moved over the blueline, paused a split second while team-mate Eric Nesterenko moved into position as a screen, and sent a blistering slap shot past the Rangers' Cesare Maniago to establish an NHL record for goals in a single season. Chicago finished with just four wins in their last nine games and fell to second place, eight points behind the Canadiens. Hull, who won the scoring title and set an NHL record with 97 points, finished the season with 54 goals, with a record 22 of them coming on the power play. Teammate Stan Mikita tied for the league lead with 48 assists.

Following a disappointing season in 1964-65, Frank Mahovlich and the Toronto Maple Leafs rebounded to wrap up third spot with a

The career of one of the NHL's all-time great defensemen came to an end following the Red Wings' six-game loss to the Montreal Canadiens in the 1966 Stanley Cup finals. Detroit's Bill Gadsby (4), seen here attempting to block a shot by Montreal's Dick Duff, appeared in 1,248 games with three different teams, but never played on a Stanley Cup winner.

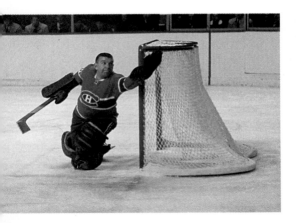

The road the Stanley Cup was long and rocky for Lorne "Gump" Worsley, who played ten seasons with the New York Rangers before joining the Montreal Canadiens in 1963. In his first two trips to the Stanley Cup finals in 1965 and 1966, the Gumper proved himself to be the league's top "money" goalie, twice leading the league in post-season goals-against average and shutouts as the Habs captured back-to-back Stanley Cup titles.

34–25–11 record. The Big M fired 32 goals to finish second to Hull for the goal-scoring crown. Bob Pulford, with 28 goals, and Eddie Shack, with 26 tallies, were the other offensive stars for the Leafs. Johnny Bower registered the league's lowest goals-against average with a 2.25 mark, to solidify a shaky goaltending situation. The Leafs used five netminders over the course of the campaign, including Bruce Gamble, Al Smith, and Gary Smith.

In spite of a disastrous start, the Boston Bruins improved during the season. Boston had only seven wins at the season's halfway mark, but the young team gathered confidence as the schedule went on. The Bruins finished the campaign by going 14–19–3 to climb out of the cellar into fifth place with 21 wins and 48 points. Numerous problems still existed – the Bruins scored the fewest goals and allowed the most – but with veterans Bucyk, Stewart, and Oliver, plus young talent like McKenzie, Green, and Cheevers, there was optimism in the Bruins' camp.

Things were not much better in New York City, where the Rangers slumped into last place. After they recorded only five wins in their first twenty games, Emile Francis stepped behind the bench himself, replacing Red Sullivan. The Rangers didn't respond to the Cat either, crawling to the finish line with an 18–41–11 record. Rod Gilbert, one of the Blueshirts' most promising players, seriously injured his back after tripping over a piece of debris on the ice and missed 36 games after undergoing spinal-fusion surgery.

Two developments that were announced during the season served to restructure the NHL and change the way its teams were assembled. On February 9, the league announced expansion plans that would double the size of the NHL in 1967-68. Clarence Campbell, in his twentieth season as the NHL's president, announced that conditional franchises had been awarded to St. Louis, Minneapolis–St. Paul, Philadelphia, Los Angeles, San Francisco, and Pittsburgh. There was a concern in Canada that Vancouver had been neglected, but the NHL's Board of Governors explained that the Vancouver bid was unimpressive. The league also announced that it was discontinuing the sponsorship of junior teams by NHL clubs. In order to assure all teams an equal chance to recruit promising young players, a universal amateur draft was established for all eligible amateur players over the age of eighteen. This new draft arrangement would begin following the 1968-69 season, but all players currently signed to "C" forms and playing for NHL-sponsored teams would remain the property of those clubs.

For the third playoff season in a row, the Chicago Black Hawks and the Detroit Red Wings met in the semi-final round. The Black Hawks, blessed with firepower, tough defense, and solid goaltending, were expected to defeat the injury-riddled Red Wings, but Detroit showed surprising toughness and a timely scoring touch. Chicago won the first and third games by identical 2–1 scores, but Detroit took advantage of Chicago penalties to win the series. In the first nationally televised hockey game in the United States, the Red Wings embarrassed Chicago, 7–0, in game two, scoring four power-play goals. Detroit once again capitalized on Chicago miscues to tie the set with a 5–1 win in game four, adding three more power-play markers. Detroit moved into the finals with 5–3 and 3–2 triumphs in the next two matches, with veterans Norm Ullman, Dean Prentice, and Andy Bathgate leading the way. One of the unsung heroes for Detroit was Bryan Watson, who covered Bobby Hull like a blanket. Hull, the NHL's most gifted scorer, was limited to a pair of goals in the series, both earned when Watson wasn't on the ice.

In the other semi-final, the Montreal Canadiens easily disposed of the Toronto Maple Leafs in four straight games. The Leafs played well in the opening contest, but a late goal by Jean Béliveau gave the Habs a 4–3 decision. The result literally made Punch Imlach sick, and King Clancy took his place behind the Leafs' bench for game two, which was won, 2–0, by the Habs on the strength of two third-period markers. Montreal wrapped up the series with 5–2 and 4–1 come-from-behind victories to reach the finals for the second straight season.

Diminutive Roger Crozier was outstanding in the finals, particularly in the opening two games in the Montreal Forum, both won by the underdog Wings. Detroit's Paul Henderson scored the winner in a 3–2 decision in game one, before the Wings slammed home four third-period goals by four different marksmen to win the second contest, 5–2. The Red Wings' express was derailed when Crozier suffered a leg injury in game four, and even though he returned to action in game five, he couldn't stop the Montreal attack. The Canadiens won game three by a 4–2 count and took game four, 2–1, courtesy of a power-play marker scored by Ralph Backstrom with less than seven minutes left.

After a shaky performance by Crozier in the fifth meeting, in which he allowed five goals, the Habs opened a quick 2–0 advantage in game six. However, the Wings came back to force overtime on goals by Ullman and Floyd Smith. Just two minutes into the extra period, Dave Balon sent a cross-ice pass to Henri Richard as the Pocket Rocket was being muscled to the ice by a Detroit defender. The puck glanced off Richard's arm into the Detroit net to give the younger Richard his first Stanley Cup-winning goal. Roger Crozier, whose on-ice gymnastics had propelled the Wings into the finals, became the second player – and the first member of a losing team – to be awarded the Conn Smythe Trophy as playoff MVP. Other post-season award winners were Bobby Hull, who captured the Hart and Art Ross trophies, Jacques Laperrière, who won the Norris Trophy, and teammates Gump Worsley and Charlie Hodge, who shared the Vezina. Alex Delvecchio was awarded the Lady Byng, and rookie Brit Selby of the Maple Leafs won the Calder.

(Continued on p. 214)

BOBBY HULL BREAKS 50-GOAL BARRIER

The Black Hawks were held scoreless for eleven consecutive periods before Hull scored his record 51st goal.

**March 12, 1966
at Chicago Stadium
Chicago 4, New York 2**

FIRST PERIOD

No Scoring
PENALTIES – Stapleton CHI (hooking) 9:10.

SECOND PERIOD

1) NY Marshall 23 (Hicke) PPG 2:50
2) NY Hicke 7 (Ingarfield, Seiling) 13:08
PENALTIES – Wharram CHI (holding) :57; Fleming NY (highsticking), Mikita CHI (highsticking) 7:23; Howell NY (holding) 9:26.

THIRD PERIOD

3) CHI Maki 16 (Hull, Pilote) 2:57
4) CHI Hull 51 (Angotti, Hay) PPG 5:34
5) CHI Maki 17 (Hull, Esposito) 7:25
6) CHI Mohns 19 (Esposito, Pilote) 18:41
PENALTIES – Howell NY (slashing) 4:05; Angotti CHI (holding) 7:53; Brown NY (interference) 12:36.

SHOTS ON GOAL	1	2	3	T
NEW YORK	10	12	6	28
CHICAGO	13	11	9	33

GOALTENDERS		TIME	SA	GA	ENG	W/L
NY	Maniago	60:00	29	4	0	L
CHI	Hall	60:00	26	2	0	W

PP CONVERSIONS   NY 1/3   CHI 1/3

The Habs' Forgotten Dynasty

by Red Fisher

It has happened twenty-four times. The joyful noise. The babble of strange, as well as familiar, voices. The smiles that threatened to last forever. The happy exhilaration of winning. The pure joy of adults recapturing their boyhoods because another Stanley Cup had been won.

For the Montreal Canadiens, this scene has been repeated on twenty-four occasions. The first took place the year before the formation of the National Hockey League in 1917. The most recent occurred in 1993. Every one of these championships has been accompanied by piercing yelps from the open, happy mouths of players who earned the right to celebrate. More than any other statistic, it is this NHL-leading total of twenty-four Stanley Cup championships that tells the story of the Montreal Canadiens.

It's a story of hockey's most successful organization and of all of its glittering stars. Once, it was the blinding speed of a Howie Morenz. It was Joe Malone and Newsy Lalonde. It was the hot, black coals of Maurice Richard's eyes as he swept in on an opposing goaltender. It's the story of Georges Vezina and George Hainsworth and Bill Durnan. It's the cat-like quickness of Jacques Plante and Ken Dryden.

The first chapter of the Canadiens' Cup pursuit was written by players like Didier Pitre, Jack Laviolette, and Louis Berlinquette. Those were the names in 1916. Patrick Roy, Kirk Muller, and Vincent Damphousse are the names now.

The twenty-four Stanley Cup banners hanging from the roof of the Montreal Forum are the story of what hockey is all about. No team has sent as many of its players – thirty-nine – into the Hall of Fame. Ten of the organization's builders are there.

The Montreal Canadiens have been the speed and brilliance of Guy Lafleur, the grace of Jean Béliveau. They are Henri Richard with his record eleven Stanley Cup wins. They are the control of Doug Harvey, and the thunder of Ken Reardon and Larry Robinson on defense.

Has there ever been a dynasty to match those Canadiens teams of the last half of the 1950s, which won a record five Stanley Cups in a row, or the teams of the late 1970s that won four consecutive Cups? From one decade to another, the names and faces have changed, but the players rooted in excellence remain the same. One wavelet would leave, and another would gather and grow and burst like an exploding star on the game.

Hockey historians acknowledge – and they're right – that the teams of the late 1950s and 1970s are the organization's greatest. On the other hand, has there ever been a more under-rated dynasty than the teams that won two Stanley Cups in the mid-1960s as part of the six-team NHL? How strong was it? It stayed together to win two more in the expanded twelve-team league in 1968 and 1969. Only a six-game loss to the Toronto Maple Leafs in the 1967 finals prevented this Canadiens squad from matching the team that won five Cups in a row, beginning in 1956.

The inevitable end of the Habs' 1950s dynasty team wasn't apparent during the 1960 playoffs when the Canadiens won their fifth consecutive championship, conceding only 11 goals while winning eight consecutive games.

Could they add a sixth championship the following year, even though Maurice Richard had announced his retirement before the start of the 1960-61 season? In reality, the Rocket's departure after eighteen seasons

Henri Richard was the last of the Canadiens from the club's 1956-60 dynasty to retire, hanging up his skates following 1974-75. In twenty seasons, the "Pocket Rocket" won eleven Stanley Cup championships, the most by any player.

was management's idea. His 544 regular-season and 82 playoff goals included many of hockey's most memorable moments – and still do. But by then, the fire which had always sustained the Rocket was almost out. He was losing the battle of the bulge. The NHL's young bloods now could skate away from him, and he was increasingly hobbled by injuries.

Still, even without Richard, the Canadiens finished on top in 1960-61. Their 92 points were only two more than Toronto's total, but Bernie Geoffrion had led the NHL's point-getters with 95, including 50 goals. The

marvelous Béliveau finished second with 90 points, so there was ample reason to believe that the Canadiens were on track for a sixth consecutive Stanley Cup.

Instead, the Canadiens were eliminated in a six-game series with the Chicago Black Hawks, which included a triple-overtime 2–1 loss in game three. The cracks started to widen. It was time to go to work, time to rebuild.

The club that swept undefeated through the 1960 playoffs included Jacques Plante in goal, with Charlie Hodge as his backup. The defensemen were Doug Harvey, Tom Johnson, Bob Turner, Jean-Guy Talbot, and Albert Langlois. The forwards were Geoffrion, Ralph Backstrom, Bill Hicke, Richard, Dickie Moore, Claude Provost, Ab McDonald, Henri Richard, Marcel Bonin,

Jean Béliveau, whose offensive skills often overshadowed his defensive abilities, forechecks Chicago's Elmer "Moose" Vasko during the 1965 Stanley Cup finals.

Phil Goyette, Don Marshall, André Pronovost, and Béliveau. Frank Selke was the club's general manager and Toe Blake was its coach.

Four seasons later, only seven members of the 1959-60 team were still with the organization. Harvey, who was the best defenseman in Canadiens' history, had been dispatched to the New York Rangers after the 1961-62 season. Tom Johnson was gone, and so were Turner and Langlois. Up front, Geoffrion, Hicke, Moore, McDonald, Bonin, Goyette, Marshall, and Pronovost had departed. Plante, the best goaltender in Canadiens'

history, was gone, while general manager Frank Selke retired in 1964.

The constants, though, were coach Toe Blake, who was by far the best in hockey, Béliveau, and Henri Richard. Backup goaltender Hodge, defenseman Talbot, and forwards Backstrom and Provost were still there. With this nucleus, general manager Sam Pollock went to work.

It was Frank Selke who had started the rebuilding process in the early 1960s. He was convinced that his Canadiens had a capable NHL goaltender in Charlie Hodge, so he traded Jacques Plante to the New York Rangers as part of a six-player deal that brought Gump Worsley to Montreal in June 1963. Originally slated as

Hodge's backup, Worsley would eventually emerge as the Canadiens' number-one playoff goaltender of the 1960s.

Selke also sent Harvey to the Rangers and Johnson to the Boston Bruins. To replace them on defense he added Jean-Claude Tremblay, Terry Harper, and Jacques Laperrière, who won the Calder Trophy as the NHL's top rookie in 1963-64.

Selke was also convinced that one of the reasons for the Canadiens' consecutive semi-final series losses from 1961 to 1963 was a lack of toughness.

The answer: John Ferguson.

Fergie may not have been the toughest player ever to wear the *bleu, blanc, et rouge*, but he would surely be

Former Canadiens captain Hector "Toe" Blake coached the USHL's Houston Huskies and the Valleyfield Braves of the QHL before taking over the coaching reins of the Montreal Canadiens in 1955-56.

on everyone's shortlist. Until he joined the Canadiens for the start of the 1963-64 season, Ferguson seemed destined to a career in the minor leagues.

"There's this kid Ferguson," Selke told Floyd Curry, who had joined the Canadiens' front office after an eleven-season career with the team. "Check him out."

Curry went to scout Ferguson, who was then playing for the Cleveland Barons of the American Hockey League. What he saw astonished him: Ferguson shot the puck at a teammate named Terry Gray during the pre-game warm-up. Gray had made the mistake of taking a moment to exchange pleasantries with a player on the visiting team, and Ferguson had promptly fired the puck at Gray's head. Happily, he missed – but hit the mark with Curry.

"He was actually aiming at the guy's head," Curry cheerfully reported back to Selke.

"You sure?" asked Selke.

"So help me," said Curry.

Ferguson joined the Canadiens.

Defenseman Ted Harris was another addition. He was a big, raw-boned guy who was quite happy to play hard-nosed hockey. He, too, played his first games for the club in the 1963-64 season – and while the Canadiens were to go through a fourth consecutive campaign without a Stanley Cup, Frank Selke had remade the team, putting the right pieces in the right places. Among Selke's many moves, his best might have been grooming Sam Pollock as his successor.

The choice of Pollock as the Canadiens' new managing director in 1964-65 was by no means a foregone conclusion. Pollock, who had touched most of the bases with the organization as a junior and minor professional coach and manager was a strong candidate. Canadiens' vice-president and former All-Star defenseman Ken Reardon was another. In many ways, Reardon would have been an easy choice to make. He was well-known and respected, and his father-in-law, Senator Donat Raymond, had once owned the Canadiens. It was David Molson, the club's owner at that time, who made the final decision, and naming Pollock as manager was, perhaps, the best decision Molson ever made. Pollock's teams were to win nine Stanley Cups before he left for

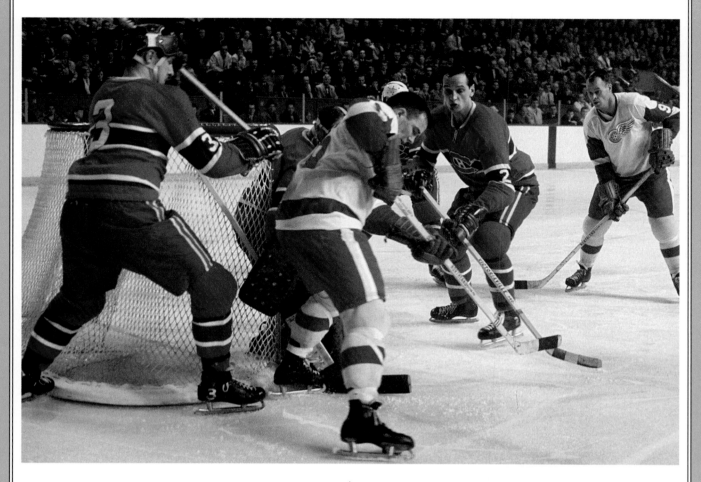

One of the enduring qualities of the Canadiens franchise has always been a strong defense corps. In the 1960s, J. C. Tremblay (3) and Jacques Laperrière (2) were the top guns on the Canadiens' blueline.

the corporate world after the 1977-78 season. He wasn't merely the best of hockey's general managers, before his time and since: he was the game's most successful. His favorite four-letter word was "work." He knew more about the opposition's strengths and weaknesses than anyone had a right to know. He wasn't merely a step ahead of his peers: he lapped them. He never made a trade he didn't like. He knew more about the young talent in his organization than any of his scouts. He was in control.

So there he was in his general manager's seat at the start of the 1964-65 season, armed with the toughness Selke had brought to the team. Wasting no time, Pollock made moves that brought talented new players to the Canadiens.

In December 1964, Pollock traded for Dick Duff, who had excelled with the Toronto Maple Leafs before being shipped to the New York Rangers. Yvan Cournoyer, who was to be an integral part of ten Canadiens Stanley

Cup teams, arrived. So did others who contributed to the team's chemistry. Pollock's strength and, by extension, his team's strength, was that, by dint of his hard work, almost all of his trades paid off. Only three of the players on the Canadiens' 1964-65 team that won the Stanley Cup were missing from the team that won again the following year.

In 1969, after Pollock's Canadiens won their fourth Stanley Cup in five seasons, their roster still included thirteen members of the 1965 Cup-winning team. And by the time the Pollock-era Canadiens had won their fourth Cup, Serge Savard and Jacques Lemaire, two players who would carry the team through the 1970s, had earned spots on the roster. Savard is now the Canadiens' managing director and Lemaire coaches the New Jersey

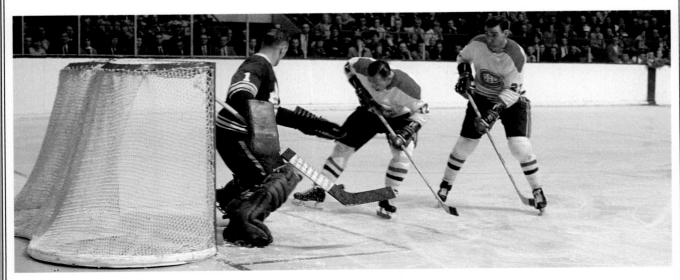

Devils, but it was as a rookie center in 1967-68 that Lemaire found himself playing an unlikely role in one of the major crises Pollock was to face during his Cup-filled years.

The controversy involved Henri Richard, whose thirteenth season with the Canadiens hadn't started well. After an early-season injury to Richard, Toe Blake was forced to press young Lemaire into service. He played well, and was still playing well when Richard was ready to return. Coach Blake was reluctant to bench a player who was doing his job, so Lemaire continued to feel the coach's tap on his back sending him over the boards. Meanwhile, Richard sat . . . and simmered.

With the Canadiens' next game less than an hour away, general manager Pollock coughed nervously, awaiting the start of a hastily convened press conference.

"Uh . . . I just want to announce that Henri Richard isn't here tonight," said Pollock. "We don't know why . . ."

"I'd rather pick garbage than sit on the bench," Richard told reporters the next day.

Pollock continued to support Blake's decision on whom to play. A week later, a contrite Richard returned. The proud Pocket Rocket learned that, while it's not much fun to sit on the bench, it's even less fun to stay away from the rink.

"I'll wait for my chance to play," he explained. "I still have a lot of years left."

How good were the Canadiens' teams of the mid-1960s?

After suffering four consecutive first-round playoff losses from 1961 to 1964, the Canadiens restructured their lineup, adding Yvan Cournoyer (12), who gave them speed and scoring punch, and John Ferguson (22), who provided size and strength.

Clearly, they weren't as strong or as deep as the dynasties of the 1950s and 1970s – if only because they didn't have a dominant goaltender like Jacques Plante or

A master scout with a master mind, "Silent Sam" Pollock was the architect of the Montreal Canadiens teams that ruled the hockey world from 1965 to 1979.

Along with Henri Richard and Toe Blake, Jean Béliveau provided the Canadiens of the mid-1960s with a direct link to the club's Cup dynasty of the previous decade. With 16 post-season points, Béliveau added the Conn Smythe Trophy to the Habs' Stanley Cup championship in 1965.

Ken Dryden in the nets. On defense, they had stars like Jacques Laperrière and J. C. Tremblay, but they didn't have a game-breaker like Doug Harvey or Larry Robinson. Up front, they had finish and firepower from Yvan Cournoyer, but they didn't have a superstar talent to compare to the Rocket or Guy Lafleur.

They did, however, have Jean Béliveau and Henri Richard still playing at the top of their games. The leadership and savvy of these two Hall-of-Fame players alone elevates the ranking of the mid-1960s Canadiens. Plus, they had a peerless coach in Toe Blake and the game's most gifted general manager in Sam Pollock.

All were there in 1966, when the Canadiens showed they were made of the right stuff.

The Habs had finished the season on top of the six-team standings with 90 points, eight more than the second-place Chicago Black Hawks – even though Bobby Hull and Stan Mikita had finished one–two in the league scoring race. The Canadiens drew Toronto

in the Stanley Cup semi-finals, and held the Maple Leafs to only six goals en route to a four-game series sweep. The Red Wings, fourth-place finishers with only 74 points, needed six games to eliminate the Hawks.

The Canadiens were heavy favorites to handle the Red Wings in the Stanley Cup finals, but a funny thing happened on the way to the Forum. The Canadiens were properly stunned when they fell, 3–2, to the Red Wings in game one. Imagine the reaction from players, management, and fans, then, when Detroit turned it up for a 5–2 victory in the second game.

As for the Red Wings, their celebrations started almost immediately. Newspaper photographs showed Bill Gadsby, Alex Delvecchio, and several others smoking big cigars and enjoying themselves at the racetrack the next day. Everybody was smiling broadly into the cameras for the very good reason that the underdog Wings held a two-game lead in the best-of-seven series, with the happy prospect of playing games three and four at home.

Two games later, the Wings' smiles were gone – mostly because an exercised Blake rolled the dice and put together an unlikely forward line of Richard flanked by journeyman forwards Dave Balon and Léon Rochefort. The Canadiens won their next two games, 4–2 and 2–1. They kept right on rolling, winning game five in Montreal, 5–1.

Two nights later, the teams were back in Detroit. A victory would provide the Canadiens with their second consecutive Stanley Cup, a loss would return the teams to Montreal for the seventh and deciding game. Blake kept the Balon–Richard–Rochefort line intact for game six, and, with the score tied, 2–2, sent the threesome over the boards early in overtime.

Two minutes of sudden death had ticked by when left-winger Balon raced for a puck in the Detroit corner of the rink. At the same time, Richard did what he had always done best: he headed for the net. Balon lofted a waist-high pass toward the crease, and the puck and Richard arrived in front of goaltender Roger Crozier at the same instant. A split-second later, the red light was on. The puck had struck Richard on the elbow and slipped into the net.

Montreal Canadiens

To many, it appeared that Richard had directed the puck past Crozier with his forearm. There was no signal from referee Frank Udvari, but behind the Canadiens' bench, Blake wasn't taking any chances.

"On the ice," he roared at his players. "Everybody on the ice."

So seconds later, once again, that joyful noise. The babble of strange, as well as familiar, voices. The smiles that threatened to last forever . . .

The 1965-66 Montreal Canadiens roster included three players – Henri Richard, Jean Béliveau, and Claude Provost – who were members of the team that won five Cup championships from 1956 to 1960. Provost, who was a prototypical defensive forward, played on nine Stanley Cup championship teams.

94 PTS.   77 PTS.   75 PTS.   72 PTS.   58 PTS.   44 PTS.

1966-67
Canada's Centennial Showdown:
Greybeard Leafs Upset Canadiens

A PAIR OF ANNIVERSARIES WERE IN THE SPOTLIGHT AS THE NATIONAL HOCKEY League's 1966-67 season got under way on October 19, 1966. Not only did the campaign mark the twenty-fifth and final season of the six-team NHL, it also coincided with the hundredth birthday of Canada's Confederation. On the ice, the highlight of 1966-67 was the appearance of Bobby Orr, Boston's remarkable rookie defenseman. Orr's instincts, skills, and speed would soon change the game.

Impending expansion meant that significant player movement was just around the corner, as the new franchises would fill their rosters with players selected from the six established clubs. Like many NHL and minor-league players, members of the Bruins had concerns about expansion and other issues related to salaries, pension benefits, and working conditions. Boston players met with lawyer Alan Eagleson on December 28 to form a permanent players' union. Eagleson, who had gained league-wide respect for negotiating an end to a players' strike in the American Hockey League and for securing a lucrative contract on behalf of Bobby Orr, agreed to help organize the union and promised to "quietly" visit every team and gather support. This session on December 28 would prove to be the inaugural meeting of the NHL Players' Association.

There was not much room for change on the roster of the Montreal Canadiens. The defending champions were content to enter the 1966-67 season with the same lineup, owing to the maturity of youngsters Cournoyer and Larose. Red Berenson was deemed to be expendable, and he was sent to the Rangers for Garry Peters, who had played briefly for the Habs in 1964-65, and Ted Taylor. Two youngsters who made their NHL debuts during the season, Serge Savard and Carol Vadnais, showed considerable promise.

The same deliberate, conservative route was taken in Chicago, where only minor adjustments were needed. Elmer Vasko retired after ten NHL seasons. His replacement, Ed Van Impe, was a rugged minor-league veteran, who led the WHL in penalty minutes twice during the early part of the decade. Denis DeJordy was promoted to serve as the backup to Glenn Hall for a second time. DeJordy had played for in St. Louis in the CPHL in 1965-66, appearing in all 70 games.

Police Escort

When a bus chartered to take the Canadiens from O'Hare Airport to Chicago Stadium for a game on February 26, 1967, did not show up, Chicago police transported the team and its equipment downtown, using an assortment of police vehicles, including a paddy wagon, two police cruisers, and a taxi.

While most experts dismissed the Toronto Maple Leafs as being too old and too slow, Punch Imlach was confident that "adding a couple of kids to some old pappies" would be enough to provide the city of Toronto with one more winning campaign. Brian Conacher, Jim Pappin, Pete Stemkowski, and Brit Selby were the kids, and the rest of the lineup were the old pappies. Even the Leafs' call-ups from their farm system were veterans. Dick Gamble, Aut Erickson, Larry Jeffrey, Milan Marcetta, and John Brenneman had all logged NHL ice time in previous seasons. Bruce Gamble, who played in eight games while filling in for injured incumbents Johnny Bower and Terry Sawchuk in 1965-66, was expected to share some of the goaltending duties.

There was similar concern in Detroit, where the Red Wings were also icing a veteran lineup. Paul Henderson and Bert Marshall were the only regulars under the age of twenty-five. Sid Abel, like his counterpart Punch Imlach, was optimistic that his charges could return to the Stanley Cup finals for a fourth time in five seasons. Other additions included defenseman Bob Wall, veteran forward Ted Hampson, and newcomers Peter Mahovlich and Bob Falkenberg.

Emile "The Cat" Francis would have to use each of his nine lives to revive the fortunes of the New York Rangers, who had missed the play-offs in seven of the previous eight years. It wouldn't take long for Francis to hit the jackpot. In the 1966 amateur draft, the Cat stole defenseman Brad Park out from under the nose of the Toronto Maple Leafs, who could have signed Park off the roster of one of their sponsored junior clubs, the Toronto Marlboros. The other three players Francis selected – Joey Johnston, Don Luce, and Jack Egers – were traded for more talent, including Gene Carr, Dave Balon, Jim Lorentz, and Wayne Connelly.

Francis decided to add veterans to the Rangers' roster. Forwards Red Berenson and Orland Kurtenbach were acquired, as was defenseman Al MacNeil, who came over from Chicago. One of Francis's most productive moves was drafting Bernie Geoffrion from the Montreal Canadiens. To everyone's surprise, Boom-Boom signed with New York and joined former teammates Don Marshall and Phil Goyette. Those three veterans, each sporting a handful of Stanley Cup rings, were to play a large role in reversing the fortunes of the franchise. It would be another nine years before New York missed the playoffs again.

The player who represented the future of the Boston Bruins arrived in 1966-67 after years of fan anticipation. Bobby Orr was depicted as the savior of the Bruins' franchise, but he would need a reliable core of supporting players before he could play the lead role. With that in mind, Milt Schmidt decided to step down as coach to concentrate on acquiring new talent. In the 1966 amateur draft of unsigned juniors, Schmidt selected Barry Gibbs, Garnet Bailey, Rick Smith, and Tom Webster, four players who went on to play a combined 39 seasons in the NHL. The Bruins

Led by twenty-seven-year-old rookie goalie Ed Giacomin (left), thirty-four-year old veteran defenseman Harry Howell (3) and coach Emile "The Cat" Francis, the New York Rangers made the playoffs for only the second time in nine seasons in 1966-67. The Rangers were a club on the rise and didn't miss the playoffs again until 1975-76.

Primarily known for his toughness, Montreal's John Ferguson was also a gifted offensive contributor who added 20 goals and 22 assists to the Habs' scoring totals during 1966-67. A deceptively fast skater who led the league with 177 penalty minutes, Ferguson had the ability to break into the clear, as he does here against Chicago's Denis DeJordy.

coaching job was assigned to Harry Sinden, a respected minor-league defenseman, who was captain of the Whitby Dunlops, winners of the Allan Cup in 1957 and the International Ice Hockey Federation World Championships in 1958. Sinden's first season in Boston would prove to be a difficult one. The Bruins were blessed with youth and had vast potential in goal and on defense, but inexperience kept the club off the winning side of the scoresheet in most games. Joe Watson joined Bobby Orr on defense, while forwards Jean-Paul Parisé and Ron Schock earned regular spots up front. However, other than some flashes of brilliance from Orr, the 1966-67 season was another disaster for the Bruins. Boston scored the fewest goals (182) and allowed the most (253), sliding back into sixth place with a 17–43–10 record. But shortly after the completion of the regular season, Milt Schmidt made a deal that would prove to be the revitalization of the franchise. He sent Jack Norris, Gilles Marotte, and Pit Martin to the Chicago Black Hawks for Phil Esposito, Ken Hodge, and Fred Stanfield. Bolstered by that trade and by some astute drafting and scouting, the Bruins have not missed the playoffs since Orr's first season in Boston.

An interesting script was being written in Chicago, where Stan Mikita won his third Art Ross Trophy in four seasons. That in itself was not a surprise. What was astonishing was that Mikita had completely altered his aggressive style of play by making a concerted effort to avoid the penalty box. Mikita, who had averaged over 100 minutes in penalties in each of his seven full seasons in the league, spent only 12 minutes in the penalty box during 1966-67. He also led the league with 62 assists and a record-tying 97 points. For a brief time, Mikita thought he had established a new NHL single-season points record, but an assist

Yvan Cournoyer (12) collected four points during a five-game debut with the Montreal Canadiens in 1963-64 and quickly proved that he possessed speed, strength, and finesse. Nicknamed the "Roadrunner," Cournoyer became the Canadiens' power-play specialist during 1966-67, scoring 20 of his 25 goals when the Habs held the man advantage.

originally credited to him was given to another player after the completion of the schedule.

Bobby Hull continued his onslaught on NHL goaltenders, becoming the only man to reach the 50-goal plateau three times, although he fell short of his NHL-record 54 goals, settling for 52. Bobby's brother Dennis Hull and Doug Mohns each chipped in with 25 goals, while Ken Wharram connected 31 times to finish third among league marksmen.

The Hawks, who established an NHL record by scoring 264 goals in the 70-game schedule, also had the toughest defense, allowing a league-low 170 goals. Most of the credit went to Glenn Hall and the "Big Three" of the Chicago defense, Pilote, Stapleton, and Jarrett, each of whom played all 70 games. One of the many highlights of the Hawks' superior

Loyal Bruins fans had been waiting for their team to reverse its fortunes since the late 1950s. When Robert Gordon Orr arrived at Boston Garden in 1966, the club's savior was finally delivered. After he scored his first NHL goal in a 3–2 loss to Montreal on October 23, 1966, the fans at the Garden rewarded him with a three-minute standing ovation. Orr went on to win the Calder Trophy as the NHL's top rookie and gained a spot on the NHL's Second All-Star Team.

Same Time, Same Station

CBC Radio, which had carried Saturday-night hockey games since the 1930s, discontinued its nationwide network coverage of the NHL in 1965-66. However, due to public demand, the Saturday-night radio games returned to the airwaves for the 1966-67 season.

season was a team-record 15-game unbeaten streak, a run that included 12 wins and three ties.

The struggle for the next three spots in the standings was an exciting clash between the Canadiens, the Maple Leafs, and the Rangers. Injuries played a major role in Montreal's failure to contest for top rank in the league. Jean-Guy Talbot was the only blueliner to complete the season injury free, as Laperrière, Harper, Harris, and J.C. Tremblay spent time on the shelf nursing minor aches and pains. Injuries also slowed down the Habs' offense. Yvan Cournoyer was the top marksman with 25 goals, of which 20 were scored on the power play. Béliveau, Duff, and Gilles Tremblay were all sidelined, but the Canadiens still finished second with a 32–25–13 record.

Similar problems plagued the Toronto Maple Leafs, whose season was marred by injuries, inconsistent play, and bickering between Punch Imlach and some of his players. Imlach's troops appeared sluggish most of the season, as Kelly, Mahovlich, Stanley, Baun, and Pronovost all missed action, leaving the Leafs in danger of missing the playoffs. In late January and early February, the team lost ten consecutive games in decisive fashion, nine of them by two or more goals. After a 2–1 victory over Detroit ended their winless streak at eleven games, Imlach was hospitalized for stress and exhaustion. His place behind the bench was taken by long-time Maple Leaf ambassador, King Clancy. The witty Irishman's good humor was just the tonic the Leafs needed, and the team went on a ten-game unbeaten streak to pull back into third place. Imlach returned to his duties on March 18, and the Leafs won six of their last nine games down the stretch to finish in third place, two points behind the Canadiens.

Paul Henderson had the night of a lifetime when he scored four goals in the Detroit Red Wings' 5–3 win over the New York Rangers on October 27, 1966. It was first time in his NHL career that he had scored three or more goals in a game.

Under the calm leadership of Emile Francis, the New York Rangers became the NHL's most-improved team. Francis, a former NHL goaltender, concentrated on improving team defense, and the Broadway Blues responded by allowing only 189 goals. Ed Giacomin, with able support from blueliners Harry Howell, Wayne Hillman, and Arnie Brown, led the NHL with 30 victories, while compiling a goals-against average of 2.61. This new dedication to team defense reduced the Rangers' offensive totals, but Rod Gilbert (28 goals) and Phil Goyette (61 points) put up impressive numbers. Bernie Geoffrion answered those critics who questioned his comeback with 17 goals and 25 assists in limited action, and he was a valuable voice on the bench and in the dressing room.

The revival of the Rangers franchise found the Detroit Red Wings stumbling into fifth place, a full 14 points behind the fourth-place New Yorkers. Weak defense was the major reason behind the Wings' demise, as the team allowed 241 goals, the second-highest total in the NHL. The situation became so serious that the Wings were forced to recall Doug Harvey from Pittsburgh, where he was attempting to work himself back into NHL shape. He showed up in Detroit twenty pounds overweight and lasted only two games before being dispatched back to the minors. Fine offensive seasons from Bruce MacGregor (28 goals), Paul Henderson (21 goals), and Norm Ullman (26 goals) only camouflaged the organization's lack of talent in the minor leagues. Andy Bathgate collected eight goals in 60 games, and his Hall-of-Fame career appeared to be coming to a close. With the prospect of losing players in the upcoming expansion draft, the future did not appear bright for Detroit, and the franchise went on to miss the playoffs in fifteen of the next seventeen seasons.

New York's first trip to the playoffs in six seasons was short lived, as the club had the misfortune to meet the defending Stanley Cup-champion Montreal Canadiens in the semi-finals. For the first 49 minutes of game one, the Rangers were in complete control, building a comfortable 4–1

The Name Game

The Detroit Red Wings experimented with placing players' names on the backs of their sweaters during 1966 pre-season games, but dropped the idea in the regular season. The practice became mandatory in 1978.

The 1966-67 Toronto Maple Leafs were dismissed as being too old and too slow to make the playoffs. However, coach Punch Imlach's team – a combination of hard-working role players, quickly maturing youngsters, and "a few old pappies" – combined to deliver Toronto's fourth Stanley Cup title of the 1960s.

lead. However, the Canadiens erupted for five goals in nine minutes to win the series opener, 6–4. The Habs then went on to sweep the Rangers in straight games to reach their third straight Stanley Cup final.

The other semi-final featured the powerhouse Chicago Black Hawks, tackling the "over-the-hill gang" of the Toronto Maple Leafs. The Hawks, with Hull, Mikita, and the league's most stubborn defense, were favored to win. Punch Imlach, however, had other ideas. He stressed to his players that for many of them, these were the last moments they would spend as members of the Toronto Maple Leafs. The team, which had been together for almost a decade, would be torn apart by the expansion draft. The Leafs, led by the sterling goaltending of Terry Sawchuk, responded

by eliminating the Black Hawks in six games. The key moment of the series came in game five, with the set tied at two games apiece. Terry Sawchuk replaced Johnny Bower after the first period, with the score even at 2–2, and stopped all 37 shots fired at him to enable the Leafs to squeeze out a 4–2 victory. Sawchuk continued his outstanding play in game six, as the Leafs downed the Hawks, 3–1, to guarantee an all-Canadian Stanley Cup final in Canada's Centennial year.

As part of Canada's Centennial celebration, the world's fair known as Expo '67, was being held in Montreal, so it was only fitting that the Stanley Cup finals began in that city. The Canadiens elected to start goaltender Rogie Vachon, a twenty-one-year-old who played 19 games during the season. Imlach, attempting to establish a psychological edge, called the rookie a "junior-B hack." It turned out Punch didn't need psychology, because he had a motivated veteran roster and a hard-working young line of Pete Stemkowski, Jim Pappin, and Brian Conacher. Terry Sawchuk, George Armstrong, and Allan Stanley were outstanding, and Pappin led all playoff scorers with seven goals and 15 points, as the Leafs ruined Montreal's party plans, needing six games to win their fourth Stanley Cup championship of the 1960s.

Jim Pappin compiled only 32 points during the 1966-67 regular season, but caught fire in the play-offs to lead all post-season scorers with 15 points in 12 games. Placed on a line with fellow youngbloods Pete Stemkowski and Brian Conacher, Pappin scored the Cup-winning goal for the Leafs when his cross-crease pass deflected off Montreal defenseman Terry Harper's skate and past goaltender Gump Worsley.

GREAT PERFORMANCE BY SAWCHUK IN GAME FIVE OF '67 SEMI-FINALS

Sawchuk stopped 37 shots in two periods of work, leading the Leafs to victory.

April 15, 1967
at Chicago Stadium
Toronto 4, Chicago 2

FIRST PERIOD

1) TOR Walton 2 (Stemkowski, Pappin) PPG 6:16
2) CHI Angotti 2 (Pilote) 9:31
3) CHI B. Hull 4 (Hay, Jarrett) 11:01
4) TOR Mahovlich 3 (Keon, Walton) PPG 14:14
PENALTIES – Horton TOR (interference) 2:36; D. Hull CHI (hooking) 5:05; Stemkowski TOR (highsticking), Van Impe CHI (highsticking) 9:09; Hodge CHI (hooking) 11:41; Hay CHI (hooking) 13:24; Pulford TOR (holding) 15:48; Pulford TOR (roughing), Nesterenko CHI (roughing) 19:28.

SECOND PERIOD

No Scoring
PENALTIES – Stanley TOR (charging) 3:19; Wharram CHI (slashing) 5:32; Pappin TOR (holding) 7:10; Pappin TOR (highsticking) 13:12; D. Hull CHI (holding) 17:03.

THIRD PERIOD

5) TOR Stemkowski 2 (Pulford, Pappin) 2:11
6) TOR Pappin 3 (Pulford, Horton) 17:14
PENALTIES – Stemkowski TOR (tripping) 4:23; Stemkowski TOR (tripping) 10:13; Angotti CHI (slashing) 13:54; Pulford TOR (highsticking), Mikita CHI (highsticking) 19:28.

SHOTS ON GOAL	1	2	3	T
TORONTO	7	9	15	31
CHICAGO	12	15	22	49

GOALTENDERS	TIME	SA	GA	ENG	W/L
TOR Bower	20:00	10	2	0	–
TOR Sawchuk	40:00	37	0	0	W
CHI DeJordy	60:00	27	4	0	L

PP CONVERSIONS   TOR 2/6   CHI 0/7

There were numerous heroes for the Leafs: Johnny Bower stopped 60 shots in a 3–2 double-overtime victory in game three, Dave Keon was easily the most effective forward on either team, and Terry Sawchuk closed the door on the Canadiens in games five and six when Johnny Bower was felled by a groin injury. Dave Keon was awarded the Conn Smythe Trophy as the playoff MVP, the only Leaf to have been so honored.

Stan Mikita made NHL history by becoming the first player to win the NHL's unofficial "Triple Crown," capturing the Hart, Art Ross, and Lady Byng trophies. Harry Howell received the Norris Trophy, which prompted him to say, "I'm glad I won it now, because there's a kid in Boston whose going to win it for the next ten years." The duo of Glenn Hall and Denis DeJordy shared the Vezina Trophy, and Bobby Orr, the "kid" Howell was referring to, won the Calder.

It was the last of the glory days for the Leafs, but just the beginning of a new period of prosperity for the Canadiens. When the Leafs' ownership troika of Harold Ballard, Stafford Smythe, and John Bassett found themselves short of cash in the mid-1960s, they sold their farm teams in Rochester and Victoria, losing forty-five players who had played or would eventually play in the NHL. This depleted the Leafs' talent pool, and the team struggled to repair the damage for two decades. On the other hand, the Montreal Canadiens were able to not only maintain their rich farm system, but to add to it. The Canadiens have won ten Stanley Cup titles in eleven visits to the championship final since the NHL's first expansion in 1967.

The twenty-five seasons of the six-team NHL are still regarded as a "golden era" for the game of hockey. Half of the goaltenders who are members of the Hockey Hall of Fame displayed their talents during this generation of greatness. Sixty-two players who performed their on-ice magic from 1942 to 1967 are now members of the Hall, as are eight linesman/referees and thirty-four executives, coaches, and builders of the game. Almost every one of the select group of NHLers who have played twenty or more seasons in the league played their hockey during this era. Since 1967, the NHL has grown from six teams, staffed almost exclusively by Canadian talent, to a twenty-six-team loop, featuring a talent base that brings together the finest athletes from every corner of the hockey-playing world. As the league expands its fan base and points toward further growth in the next century, the success and competitiveness of the six-team era remain the bedrock upon which today's game is built.

Many of the game's mega-stars – players like Richard, Howe, and Hull, who are the enduring icons of the sport – flourished in the six-team era. Today, more than a quarter-century after its end, their performances set the standards by which the greatest players of the modern game are still measured.

Notes on Contributors

Dan Diamond has been the NHL's consulting publisher since 1984. He produces the *NHL Official Guide & Record Book* along with guide books to each year's Stanley Cup Playoffs and NHL Entry Draft. He has written or edited numerous books about the history of the game.

Ralph Dinger is one of hockey's foremost photo researchers. He served as photo editor for *The Official NHL 75th Anniversary Book* and for *The Official NHL Stanley Cup Centennial Book*. He is managing editor of the *NHL Official Guide & Record Book*.

James Duplacey is the former curator of the Hockey Hall of Fame and Museum. He is the author of four Official NHL Quiz Books and of *Hockey Superstars: Great Goalies*, a children's book about NHL netminders from 1917 to the present day.

Milt Dunnell is one of Canada's most distinguished sports editors and writers, having covered hockey and a wide range of other sporting topics for the *Toronto Star* for more than half a century. He is a recipient of the Elmer Ferguson Memorial Award for journalistic excellence.

Donald R. Ellis joined the staff of the National Hockey League in Montreal after serving in the Canadian Armed Forces. He was named director of the league's Central Registry Bureau of Player Information in 1953 and held this post for thirty years.

Red Fisher is a member of the Hockey Hall of Fame's Player Selection Committee and a recipient of the Elmer Ferguson Memorial Award. A veteran hockey reporter with the Montreal *Gazette*, he is also the author of *Red Fisher: Hockey, Heroes, and Me*, published in 1994.

Trent Frayne is the author of numerous books, including *The Best of Times: Fifty Years of Canadian Sports*. He worked for the Toronto *Telegram*, the *Toronto Sun*, and the *Globe and Mail*, where his columns provided fresh perspectives on hockey and other sports. He currently writes a regular column for *Maclean's*.

Ira Gitler's enthusiasm for the New York Rangers spans the club's Stanley Cup victories in 1940 and 1994. He has written many features and articles, as well as the book *Ice Hockey A to Z*, published in 1978. He is also a highly regarded jazz historian and has recently completed work on a comprehensive jazz encyclopedia.

Bob Hesketh covered the Toronto Maple Leafs for the Toronto *Telegram* during the 1940s and 1950s. He won a National Newspaper Award in 1957 and, along with Jack Sullivan, co-wrote a history of the NHL that was first published in 1958. He began a distinguished on-air career with CFRB Radio in 1959.

Dan Moulton was given the Chicago Black Hawks' beat as one of his first assignments when he joined the Chicago *Tribune*'s sports department in the early 1950s. He chronicled the revamping of the hockey club, culminating in a Stanley Cup championship in 1961.

Francis Rosa is a former reporter and sports editor of the Boston *Globe*, covering the Boston Bruins from the six-team era through to the 1990s. He is a recipient of the Elmer Ferguson Memorial Award and serves on the Hockey Hall of Fame's Player Selection Committee.

Charles Wilkins is the co-author of a collection of biographies about stars of the six-team era entitled *After the Applause*. He also edited the best-selling adventure story, *Paddle to the Amazon*. His writing is regularly featured in *Canadian Geographic*.

Photo Credits

NHL RECORD BOOK

Years of Glory
1942-43 to 1966-67

Regular-Season Records

TEAM RECORDS

BEST WINNING PERCENTAGE, ONE SEASON:
.830 – Montreal Canadiens, 1943-44. 38w–5l–7t. 83pts in 50gp.
.800 – Montreal Canadiens, 1944-45. 38w–8l–4t. 80pts in 50gp.
.721 – Detroit Red Wings, 1950-51. 44w–13l–13t. 101pts in 70gp.

MOST POINTS, ONE SEASON:
101 – Detroit Red Wings, 1950-51. 44w–13l–13t. 70gp.
100 – Detroit Red Wings, 1951-52. 44w–14l–12t. 70gp.
   – Montreal Canadiens, 1955-56. 45w–15l–10t. 70gp.

MOST WINS, ONE SEASON:
45 – Montreal Canadiens, 1955-56. 70gp.
44 – Detroit Red Wings, 1950-51. 70gp.
   – Detroit Red Wings, 1951-52. 70gp.

FEWEST LOSSES, ONE SEASON:
 5 – Montreal Canadiens, 1943-44. 50gp.
 8 – Montreal Canadiens, 1944-45. 50gp.
 13 – Detroit Red Wings, 1950-51. 70gp.

WORST WINNING PERCENTAGE, ONE SEASON:
.170 – New York Rangers, 1943-44. 6w–39l–5t. 17pts in 50gp.
.221 – Chicago Black Hawks, 1953-54. 12w–51l–7t. 31pts in 70gp.
.257 – Chicago Black Hawks, 1950-51. 13w–47l–10t. 36pts in 70gp.

FEWEST POINTS, ONE SEASON:
 17 – New York Rangers, 1943-44. 6w–39l–5t. 50gp.
 30 – New York Rangers, 1942-43. 11w–31l–8t. 50gp.
 31 – Chicago Black Hawks, 1953-54. 12w–51l–7t. 70gp.

MOST LOSSES, ONE SEASON:
51 – Chicago Black Hawks, 1953-54. 70gp.
47 – Chicago Black Hawks, 1950-51. 70gp.
   – Boston Bruins, 1961-62. 70gp.

FEWEST WINS, ONE SEASON:
 6 – New York Rangers, 1943-44. 50gp.
 11 – New York Rangers, 1942-43. 50gp.
   – New York Rangers, 1944-45. 50gp.

MOST TIES, ONE SEASON:
 23 – Montreal Canadiens, 1962-63. 70gp.
 22 – Toronto Maple Leafs, 1954-55. 70gp.
 21 – Boston Bruins, 1954-55. 70gp.
   – New York Rangers, 1950-51. 70gp.

FEWEST TIES, ONE SEASON:
 4 – Toronto Maple Leafs, 1943-44. 50gp.
   – Boston Bruins, 1944-45. 50gp.
   – Montreal Canadiens, 1944-45. 50gp.
   – Toronto Maple Leafs, 1944-45. 50gp.
   – Chicago Black Hawks, 1946-47. 60gp.
   – Detroit Red Wings, 1966-67. 70gp.

LONGEST WINNING STREAK, ONE SEASON:
10 games – Montreal Canadiens, Feb. 17 to Mar. 11, 1944.

LONGEST UNDEFEATED STREAK, ONE SEASON:
18 games – Montreal Canadiens, Jan. 6 to Feb. 25, 1945. (16w–2t.)

LONGEST LOSING STREAK, ONE SEASON:
12 games – Chicago Black Hawks, Feb. 25 to Mar. 25, 1951.

LONGEST WINLESS STREAK, ONE SEASON:
21 games – New York Rangers, Jan. 23 to Mar. 19, 1944. (17l–4t.)
   – Chicago Black Hawks, Dec. 17, 1950, to Feb. 1, 1951.(18l–3t.)

MOST SHUTOUTS, ONE SEASON:
 13 – Toronto Maple Leafs, 1953-54. (Harry Lumley recorded all 13.)
   – Detroit Red Wings, 1953-54. (Terry Sawchuk recorded 12, Dave Gatherum 1.)

MOST GOALS, ONE SEASON:
 264 – Chicago Black Hawks, 1966–67. 70gp.
 259 – Montreal Canadiens, 1961–62. 70gp.
 258 – Montreal Canadiens, 1958–59. 70gp.

HIGHEST GOALS-PER-GAME AVERAGE, ONE SEASON:
4.68 – Montreal Canadiens, 1943-44. 234g in 50gp.
4.56 – Montreal Canadiens, 1944-45. 228g in 50gp.
4.46 – Boston Bruins, 1943-44. 223g in 50gp.

MOST GOALS AGAINST, ONE SEASON:
 310 – New York Rangers, 1943-44. 50gp.
 306 – Boston Bruins, 1961-62. 70gp.
 281 – Boston Bruins, 1962-63. 70gp.

HIGHEST GOALS-AGAINST-PER-GAME AVERAGE, ONE SEASON:
6.20 – New York Rangers, 1943-44. 310ga in 50gp.
5.36 – Boston Bruins, 1943-44. 268ga in 50gp.
5.06 – New York Rangers, 1942-43. 253ga in 50gp.

FEWEST GOALS, ONE SEASON:
 133 – New York Rangers, 1948-49. 60gp.
   – Chicago Black Hawks, 1953-54. 70gp.
 141 – Chicago Black Hawks, 1944-45. 50gp.

LOWEST GOALS-PER-GAME AVERAGE, ONE SEASON:

1.90 – Chicago Black Hawks, 1953-54. 133G in 70GP.
2.10 – Toronto Maple Leafs, 1954-55. 147G in 70GP.
  – Boston Bruins, 1955-56. 147G in 70GP.

FEWEST GOALS AGAINST, ONE SEASON:

109 – Montreal Canadiens, 1943-44. 50GP.
121 – Montreal Canadiens, 1944-45. 50GP.
124 – Detroit Red Wings, 1942-43. 50GP.

LOWEST GOALS-AGAINST-PER-GAME AVERAGE, ONE SEASON:

1.87 – Montreal Canadiens, 1955-56. 131GA in 70GP.
1.89 – Detroit Red Wings, 1953-54. 132GA in 70GP.
1.90 – Detroit Red Wings, 1951-52. 133GA in 70GP.
  – Detroit Red Wings, 1952-53. 133GA in 70GP.

MOST 40-OR-MORE-GOAL SCORERS, ONE SEASON:

2 – Montreal Canadiens, 1958-59. Jean Béliveau, 45; Dickie Moore, 41. 70GP.

MOST 30-OR-MORE-GOAL SCORERS, ONE SEASON:

3 – Detroit Red Wings, 1943-44. Carl Liscombe, 36; Mud Bruneteau, 35; Syd Howe, 32. 50GP.
  – Montreal Canadiens, 1954-55. Maurice Richard, 38; Bernie Geoffrion, 38; Jean Béliveau, 37. 70GP.
  – Montreal Canadiens, 1959-60. Jean Béliveau, 34; Henri Richard, 30; Bernie Geoffrion, 30. 70GP.
  – Montreal Canadiens, 1960-61. Bernie Geoffrion, 50; Dickie Moore, 35; Jean Béliveau, 32. 70GP.
  – Chicago Black Hawks, 1963-64. Bobby Hull, 43; Stan Mikita, 39; Ken Wharram, 39. 70GP.
  – Chicago Black Hawks, 1966-67. Bobby Hull, 52; Stan Mikita, 35; Ken Wharram, 31. 70GP.

MOST 20-OR-MORE-GOAL SCORERS, ONE SEASON:

7 – Montreal Canadiens, 1961-62. Claude Provost, 33; Gilles Tremblay, 32; Ralph Backstrom, 27; Bernie Geoffrion, 23; Henri Richard, 21; Bobby Rousseau, 21; Bill Hicke, 20. 70GP.

MOST GOALS, BOTH TEAMS, ONE GAME:

19 – Boston Bruins, New York Rangers, at Boston, March 4, 1944. Boston won 10–9.
  – Boston Bruins, Detroit Red Wings, at Detroit, March 16, 1944. Detroit won 10–9.

MOST GOALS, ONE TEAM, ONE GAME:

15 – Detroit Red Wings, at Detroit, January 23, 1944. Defeated New York Rangers 15–0.
14 – Boston Bruins, at Boston, January 21, 1945. Defeated New York Rangers 14–3.

MOST GOALS, BOTH TEAMS, ONE PERIOD:

10 – Toronto Maple Leafs, Detroit Red Wings, at Detroit, March 17, 1946, third period. Toronto scored six goals, Detroit scored four goals. Toronto won 11–7.

MOST GOALS, ONE TEAM, ONE PERIOD:

8 – Detroit Red Wings, at Detroit, January 23, 1944, third period. Defeated New York Rangers 15–0.

FASTEST TWO GOALS, ONE TEAM:

6 seconds – Montreal Canadiens, at Montreal, December 12, 1963, first period. Scorers were: Dave Balon at 0:58; Gilles Tremblay at 1:04. Defeated New York Rangers 6–4.

FASTEST TWO GOALS, BOTH TEAMS:

7 seconds – Chicago Black Hawks, Montreal Canadiens, at Montreal, March 20, 1948, third period. Scorers were: Bill Gadsby, Chicago, at 17:27; Maurice Richard, Montreal, at 17:34. Montreal won 7–4.

– New York Rangers, Toronto Maple Leafs, at New York, March 15, 1964, third period. Scorers were: Jim Neilson, New York, at 1:27; Tim Horton, Toronto, at 1:34. Toronto won 3–1.

FASTEST THREE GOALS, ONE TEAM:

21 seconds – Chicago Black Hawks, at New York, March 23, 1952, third period. Bill Mosienko scored all three goals, at 6:09, 6:20, and 6:30 of third period. Defeated New York Rangers 7–6.

FASTEST THREE GOALS, BOTH TEAMS:

18 seconds – Montreal Canadiens, New York Rangers, at Montreal, December 12, 1963, first period. Scorers were: Dave Balon, Montreal, at 0:58; Gilles Tremblay, Montreal, at 1:04; Camille Henry, New York, at 1:16. Montreal won 6–4.

FASTEST FOUR GOALS, ONE TEAM:

1:20 – Boston Bruins, at Boston, January 21, 1945, second period. Scorers were: Bill Thoms at 6:34; Frank Mario at 7:08 and 7:27; Ken Smith at 7:54. Defeated New York Rangers 14–3.

FASTEST FOUR GOALS, BOTH TEAMS:

1:05 – Montreal Canadiens, Toronto Maple Leafs, at Toronto, March 16, 1966, second period. Scorers were: Jean Béliveau, Montreal, at 5:00; Dave Keon, Toronto, at 5:21; Jean Béliveau, Montreal, at 5:43; Ralph Backstrom, Montreal, at 6:05. Montreal won 7–2.

INDIVIDUAL RECORDS

CAREER RECORDS

MOST SEASONS:

21 – Gordie Howe, Detroit, 1946-47 through 1966-67.
20 – Bill Gadsby, Chicago, New York, Detroit, 1946-47 through 1965-66.
  – Red Kelly, Detroit, Toronto, 1947-48 through 1966-67.

MOST GAMES:

1,398 – Gordie Howe, Detroit, 1946-47 through 1966-67.
1,316 – Red Kelly, Detroit, Toronto, 1947-48 through 1966-67.
1,248 – Bill Gadsby, Chicago, New York, Detroit, 1946-47 through 1965-66.

MOST GOALS:

649 – Gordie Howe, Detroit, 1946-47 through 1966-67.
544 – Maurice Richard, Montreal, 1942-43 through 1959-60.
399 – Jean Béliveau, Montreal, 1950-51, 1952-53 through 1966-67.
388 – Bernie Geoffrion, Montreal, New York, 1950-51 through 1963-64, 1966-67.

Cumulative NHL Regular-Season Standings 1942-43 to 1966-67

TEAM	GP	W	L	T	PTS	PTS/SEASON	%
Montreal	1640	855	493	292	2002	80.1	.610
Detroit	1640	784	572	284	1852	74.1	.565
Toronto	1640	725	623	292	1742	69.7	.531
Chicago	1640	594	779	267	1455	58.2	.444
Boston	1640	578	781	281	1437	57.5	.438
New York	1640	529	817	294	1352	54.1	.412

379 – Ted Lindsay, Detroit, Chicago, 1944-45 through 1959-60, 1964-65.
370 – Bobby Hull, Chicago, 1957-58 through 1966-67.
328 – Alex Delvecchio, Detroit, 1950-51 through 1966-67.
314 – Andy Bathgate, New York, Toronto, Detroit, 1952-53 through 1966-67.
294 – Norm Ullman, Detroit, 1955-56 through 1966-67.
281 – Red Kelly, Detroit, Toronto, 1947-48 through 1966-67.

HIGHEST GOALS-PER-GAME AVERAGE
(AMONG PLAYERS WITH 200 OR MORE GOALS):
.556 – Maurice Richard, Montreal, 544G in 978GP, 1942-43 through 1959-60.
.549 – Bobby Hull, Chicago, 370G in 674GP, 1957-58 through 1966-67.
.471 – Bernie Geoffrion, Montreal, New York, 388G in 824GP, 1950-51 through 1963-64, 1966-67.

MOST ASSISTS:
825 – Gordie Howe, Detroit, 1946-47 through 1966-67.
556 – Andy Bathgate, New York, Toronto, Detroit, 1952-53 through 1966-67.
545 – Jean Béliveau, Montreal, 1950-51, 1952-53 through 1966-67.
542 – Red Kelly, Detroit, Toronto, 1947-48 through 1966-67.
536 – Alex Delvecchio, Detroit, 1950-51 through 1966-67.
472 – Ted Lindsay, Detroit, Chicago, 1944-45 through 1959-60, 1964-65.
446 – Henri Richard, Montreal, 1955-56 through 1966-67.
437 – Bill Gadsby, Chicago, New York, Detroit, 1946-47 through 1966-67.
432 – Doug Harvey, Montreal, New York, Detroit, 1947-48 through 1963-64, 1966-67.
421 – Bert Olmstead, Chicago, Montreal, Toronto, 1948-49 through 1961-62.
   – Maurice Richard, Montreal, 1942-43 through 1959-60.

HIGHEST ASSISTS-PER-GAME AVERAGE
(AMONG PLAYERS WITH 300 OR MORE ASSISTS):
.672 – Stan Mikita, Chicago, 369A in 549GP, 1958-59 through 1966-67.
.634 – Elmer Lach, Montreal, 393A in 620GP, 1942-43 through 1953-54.
.631 – Jean Béliveau, Montreal, 545A in 864GP, 1950-51, 1952-53 through 1966-67.

MOST POINTS:
1,501 – Gordie Howe, Detroit, 1946-47 through 1966-67.
965 – Maurice Richard, Montreal, 1942-43 through 1959-60.
944 – Jean Béliveau, Montreal, 1950-51, 1952-53 through 1966-67.
870 – Andy Bathgate, New York, Toronto, Detroit, 1952-53 through 1966-67.
864 – Alex Delvecchio, Detroit, 1950-51 through 1966-67.
851 – Ted Lindsay, Detroit, Chicago, 1944-45 through 1959-60, 1964-65.
823 – Red Kelly, Detroit, Toronto, 1947-48 through 1966-67.
801 – Bernie Geoffrion, Montreal, New York, 1950-51 through 1963-64, 1966-67.
715 – Bobby Hull, Chicago, 1957-58 through 1966-67.
710 – Henri Richard, Montreal, 1955-56 through 1966-67.

HIGHEST POINTS-PER-GAME AVERAGE
(AMONG PLAYERS WITH 500 OR MORE POINTS):
1.093 – Jean Béliveau, Montreal, 944PTS in 864GP, 1950-51, 1952-53 through 1966-67.
1.074 – Gordie Howe, Detroit, 1,501PTS in 1398GP, 1946-47 through 1966-67.
1.064 – Stan Mikita, Chicago, 584PTS in 549GP, 1958-59 through 1966-67.

MOST THREE-OR-MORE-GOAL GAMES:
26 – Maurice Richard, Montreal, in 18 seasons. 23 three-goal games, 2 four-goal games, 1 five-goal game.
20 – Bobby Hull, Chicago, in 10 seasons. 16 three-goal games, 4 four-goal games.
15 – Bernie Geoffrion, in 15 seasons. 13 three-goal games, 1 four-goal game, 1 five-goal game.
   – Gordie Howe, in 21 seasons. 15 three-goal games.

MOST CONSECUTIVE GAMES:
630 – Andy Hebenton, New York, Boston. Nine complete 70-game seasons from 1955-56 to 1963-64.

MOST GAMES APPEARED IN BY A GOALTENDER:
914 – Terry Sawchuk, Detroit, Boston, Toronto, 1949-50 through 1966-67.
804 – Harry Lumley, Detroit, New York, Chicago, Toronto, Boston, 1943-44 through 1955-56, 1957-58 through 1959-60.
766 – Glenn Hall, Detroit, Chicago, 1952-53, 1954-55 through 1966-67.

MOST CONSECUTIVE COMPLETE GAMES BY A GOALTENDER:
502 – Glenn Hall, Detroit, Chicago. Seven complete 70-game seasons from 1955-56 to 1961-62 and first 12 games of 1962-63 season.

MOST SHUTOUTS BY A GOALTENDER:
100 – Terry Sawchuk, Detroit, Boston, Toronto, 1949-50 through 1966-67.
71 – Harry Lumley, Detroit, Chicago, Toronto, Boston, 1943-44 through 1955-56, 1957-58 through 1959-60.
68 – Glenn Hall, Detroit, Chicago, 1952-53, 1954-55 through 1966-67.

MOST 20-OR-MORE-GOAL SEASONS:
18 – Gordie Howe, Detroit, in 21 seasons.
14 – Maurice Richard, Montreal, in 18 seasons.
12 – Bernie Geoffrion, Montreal, New York, in 15 seasons.

MOST CONSECUTIVE 20-OR-MORE-GOAL SEASONS:
18 – Gordie Howe, Detroit, 1949-50 through 1966-67.
14 – Maurice Richard, Montreal, 1943-44 through 1956-57.
10 – Norm Ullman, Detroit, 1957-58 through 1966-67.

MOST 30-OR-MORE-GOAL SEASONS:
11 – Gordie Howe, Detroit, in 21 seasons.
9 – Maurice Richard, Montreal, in 18 seasons.
8 – Bobby Hull, Chicago, in 10 seasons.

MOST CONSECUTIVE 30-OR-MORE-GOAL SEASONS:
8 – Bobby Hull, Chicago, 1959-60 through 1966-67.
5 – Gordie Howe, Detroit, 1949-50 through 1953-54.
4 – Gordie Howe, Detroit, 1955-56 through 1958-59.
   – Maurice Richard, Montreal, 1953-54 through 1956-57.

MOST 40-OR-MORE-GOAL SEASONS:
4 – Maurice Richard, Montreal, in 18 seasons.
   – Gordie Howe, Detroit, in 21 seasons.
   – Bobby Hull, Chicago, in 10 seasons.

MOST CONSECUTIVE 40-OR-MORE-GOAL SEASONS:
3 – Gordie Howe, Detroit, 1950-51 through 1952-53.
2 – Maurice Richard, Montreal, 1949-50 through 1950-51.
   – Bobby Hull, Chicago, 1965-66 through 1966-67.

SINGLE-SEASON RECORDS

MOST GOALS, ONE SEASON:
54 – Bobby Hull, Chicago, 1965-66. 70-game schedule.
52 – Bobby Hull, Chicago, 1966-67. 70-game schedule.
50 – Maurice Richard, Montreal, 1944-45. 50-game schedule.
– Bernie Geoffrion, Montreal, 1960-61. 70-game schedule.
– Bobby Hull, Chicago, 1961-62. 70-game schedule.

HIGHEST GOALS-PER-GAME AVERAGE, ONE SEASON (AMONG PLAYERS WITH 20-OR-MORE GOALS):
1.000 – Maurice Richard, Montreal, 1944-45. 50G in 50GP.
.833 – Bill Cowley, Boston, 1943-44. 30G in 36GP.
.831 – Bobby Hull, Chicago, 1965-66. 54G in 65GP.

MOST ASSISTS, ONE SEASON:
62 – Stan Mikita, Chicago, 1966-67. 70-game schedule.
59 – Stan Mikita, Chicago, 1964-65. 70-game schedule.
58 – Jean Béliveau, Montreal, 1960-61. 70-game schedule.
– Andy Bathgate, New York, Toronto, 1963-64. 70-game schedule.

HIGHEST ASSISTS-PER-GAME AVERAGE, ONE SEASON (AMONG PLAYERS WITH 30-OR-MORE ASSISTS):
1.14 – Bill Cowley, Boston, 1943-44. 41A in 36GP.
1.08 – Elmer Lach, Montreal, 1944-45. 54A in 50GP.
1.00 – Elmer Lach, Montreal, 1943-44. 48A in 48GP.

MOST POINTS, ONE SEASON:
97 – Bobby Hull, Chicago, 1965-66. 70-game schedule.
– Stan Mikita, Chicago, 1966-67. 70-game schedule.
96 – Dickie Moore, Montreal, 1958-59. 70-game schedule.

HIGHEST POINTS-PER-GAME AVERAGE, ONE SEASON (AMONG PLAYERS WITH 50-OR-MORE POINTS):
1.97 – Bill Cowley, Boston, 1943-44. 71PTS in 36GP.
1.71 – Herb Cain, Boston, 1943-44. 82PTS in 48GP.
1.60 – Elmer Lach, Montreal, 1944-45. 80PTS in 50GP.

MOST SHUTOUTS, ONE SEASON:
13 – Harry Lumley, Toronto, 1953-54. 70-game schedule.
12 – Terry Sawchuk, Detroit, 1951-52. 70-game schedule.
– Terry Sawchuk, Detroit, 1953-54. 70-game schedule.
– Terry Sawchuk, Detroit, 1954-55. 70-game schedule.
– Glenn Hall, Detroit, 1955-56. 70-game schedule.

MOST WINS, ONE SEASON, BY A GOALTENDER:
44 – Terry Sawchuk, Detroit, 1950-51.
– Terry Sawchuk, Detroit, 1951-52.
42 – Jacques Plante, Montreal, 1955-56.
– Jacques Plante, Montreal, 1961-62.

LONGEST SHUTOUT SEQUENCE BY A GOALTENDER:
309:21 – Bill Durnan, Montreal. Shutout streak began after Chicago scored a goal at 16:15 of the first period on Feb. 24, 1949. Continued through four straight games on Feb. 26, Mar. 2, Mar. 5, and Mar. 6. Streak ended when Chicago scored a goal at 5:36 of the second period on Mar. 9, 1949.

MOST SHUTOUTS, ONE SEASON, BY A ROOKIE:
12 – Glenn Hall, Detroit, 1955-56. 70-game schedule.

MOST GOALS, ONE SEASON, BY A ROOKIE:
30 – Bernie Geoffrion, Montreal, 1951-52. 70-game schedule.

MOST ASSISTS, ONE SEASON, BY A ROOKIE:
40 – Gus Bodnar, Toronto, 1943-44. 50-game schedule.

MOST POINTS, ONE SEASON, BY A ROOKIE:
62 – Gus Bodnar, Toronto, 1943-44. 50-game schedule.

MOST POWERPLAY GOALS, ONE SEASON:
22 – Bobby Hull, Chicago, 1965-66. 70-game schedule.

MOST SHORTHANDED GOALS, ONE SEASON:
7 – Jerry Toppazzini, Boston, 1957-58. 70-game schedule.

LONGEST CONSECUTIVE POINT-SCORING STREAK, ONE SEASON:
22 games – Bronco Horvath, Boston, 1959-60. 16G–17A during streak.

LONGEST CONSECUTIVE GOAL-SCORING STREAK, ONE SEASON:
10 games – Andy Bathgate, New York, 1962-63. 11G during streak.

LONGEST CONSECUTIVE ASSIST-SCORING STREAK, ONE SEASON:
11 games – Jean Béliveau, Montreal, 1962-63. 13A during streak.

SINGLE-GAME RECORDS

MOST GOALS, ONE GAME:
6 – Syd Howe, Detroit, Feb. 3, 1944, at Detroit. Detroit 12, New York 2.
5 – Ray Getliffe, Montreal, Feb. 6, 1943, at Montreal. Montreal 8, Boston 3.
– Maurice Richard, Montreal, Dec. 28, 1944, at Montreal. Montreal 9, Detroit 1.
– Howie Meeker, Toronto, Jan. 8, 1947, at Toronto. Toronto 10, Chicago 4.
– Bernie Geoffrion, Montreal, Feb. 19, 1955, at Montreal. Montreal 10, New York 2.
– Bobby Rousseau, Montreal, Feb. 1, 1964, at Montreal. Montreal 9, Detroit 3.

MOST ASSISTS, ONE GAME:
7 – Billy Taylor, Detroit, March 16, 1947, at Chicago. Detroit 10, Chicago 6.
6 – Elmer Lach, Montreal, Feb. 6, 1943. Montreal 8, Boston 3.
– Walter "Babe" Pratt, Toronto, Jan. 8, 1944. Toronto 12, Boston 3.
– Don Grosso, Detroit, Feb. 3, 1944. Detroit 12, New York 2

MOST POINTS, ONE GAME:
> **8** – Maurice Richard, Montreal, Dec. 28, 1944, at Montreal, 5G–3A. Montreal 9, Detroit 1.
> – Bert Olmstead, Montreal, Jan. 9, 1954, at Montreal, 4G–4A. Montreal 12, Chicago 1.

MOST GOALS, ONE GAME, BY A PLAYER IN HIS FIRST NHL GAME:
> **3** – Alex Smart, Montreal, Jan. 14, 1943, at Montreal. Montreal 5, Chicago 1.

MOST GOALS, ONE GAME, BY A PLAYER IN HIS FIRST NHL SEASON:
> **5** – Howie Meeker, Toronto, Jan. 8, 1947, at Toronto. Toronto 10, Chicago 4.

MOST ASSISTS, ONE GAME, BY A PLAYER IN HIS FIRST NHL GAME:
> **4** – Earl "Dutch" Reibel, Detroit, Oct. 8, 1953, at Detroit. Detroit 4, New York 1.

MOST ASSISTS, ONE GAME, BY A PLAYER IN HIS FIRST NHL SEASON:
> **5** – Jim McFadden, Detroit, Nov. 23, 1947, at Chicago. Detroit 9, Chicago 3.

MOST POINTS, ONE GAME, BY A PLAYER IN HIS FIRST NHL GAME:
> **4** – Alex Smart, Montreal, Jan. 14, 1943, at Montreal. 3G–1A. Montreal 5, Chicago 1.
> – Earl "Dutch" Reibel, Detroit, Oct. 8, 1953, at Detroit. 4A. Detroit 4, New York 1.

MOST POINTS, ONE GAME, BY A PLAYER IN HIS FIRST NHL SEASON:
> **5** – Howie Meeker, Toronto, Jan. 8, 1947, at Toronto. 5G. Toronto 10, Chicago 4.
> – Jim McFadden, Detroit, Nov. 23, 1947, at Chicago. 5A. Detroit 9, Chicago 3.

MOST GOALS, ONE PERIOD:
> **4** – Max Bentley, Chicago, Jan. 28, 1943, at Chicago, third period. Chicago 10, New York 1.
> – Clint Smith, Chicago, March 4, 1945, at Chicago, third period. Chicago 6, Montreal 4.

MOST ASSISTS, ONE PERIOD:
> **4** – Buddy O'Connor, Montreal, Nov. 8, 1942, at Montreal, third period. Montreal 10, New York 4.
> – Doug Bentley, Chicago, Jan. 28, 1943, at Chicago, third period. Chicago 10, New York 1.
> – Joe Carveth, Detroit, Jan. 23, 1944, at Detroit, third period. Detroit 15, New York 0.
> – Phil Watson, Montreal, March 18, 1944, at Montreal, third period. Montreal 11, New York 2.
> – Bill Mosienko, Chicago, March 4, 1945, at Chicago, third period. Chicago 6, Montreal 4.
> – Jean-Claude Tremblay, Montreal, Dec. 29, 1962, at Montreal, second period. Montreal 5, Detroit 1.
> – Phil Goyette, New York, Oct. 20, 1963, at New York, first period. New York 5, Boston 1.

MOST POINTS, ONE PERIOD:
> **5** – Max Bentley, Chicago, Jan. 28, 1943, at Chicago, third period. 4G–1A. Chicago 10, New York 1.
> – Leo Labine, Boston, Nov. 28, 1954, at Boston, second period. 3G–2A. Boston 6, Detroit 2.

FASTEST GOAL BY A PLAYER IN HIS FIRST NHL GAME:
> **15 seconds** – Gus Bodnar, Toronto, Oct. 30, 1943, at Toronto. Toronto 5, New York 2.

FASTEST GOAL FROM START OF A GAME:
> **8 seconds** – Ted Kennedy, Toronto, Oct. 24, 1953, at Toronto. Boston 3, Toronto 2.

FASTEST GOAL FROM START OF A PERIOD:
> **4 seconds** – Claude Provost, Montreal, Nov. 9, 1957, at Montreal, second period. Montreal 4, Boston 2.

FASTEST THREE GOALS:
> **21 seconds** – Bill Mosienko, Chicago, March 23, 1952, at New York. Mosienko scored at 6:09, 6:20, and 6:30 of the third period. Chicago 7, New York 6.

FASTEST FOUR GOALS:
> **12:55** – Clint Smith, Chicago, March 4, 1945, at Chicago. Smith scored four goals between 4:31 and 17:26 of the third period. Chicago 6, Montreal 4.

Regular-Season Final Standings & Leading Scorers
1942-43 to 1966-67

1942-43

Team	GP	W	L	T	GF	GA	PTS
* Detroit	50	25	14	11	169	124	61
Boston	50	24	17	9	195	176	57
Toronto	50	22	19	9	198	159	53
Montreal	50	19	19	12	181	191	50
Chicago	50	17	18	15	179	180	49
New York	50	11	31	8	161	253	30

Leading Scorers

Player	Team	GP	G	A	PTS	PIM
Bentley, Doug	Chicago	50	33	40	73	18
Cowley, Bill	Boston	48	27	45	72	10
Bentley, Max	Chicago	47	26	44	70	2
Patrick, Lynn	New York	50	22	39	61	28
Carr, Lorne	Toronto	50	27	33	60	15
Taylor, Billy	Toronto	50	18	42	60	2
Hextall, Bryan	New York	50	27	32	59	28
Blake, Toe	Montreal	48	23	36	59	28
Lach, Elmer	Montreal	45	18	40	58	14
O'Connor, Buddy	Montreal	50	15	43	58	2

1943-44

Team	GP	W	L	T	GF	GA	PTS
* Montreal	50	38	5	7	234	109	83
Detroit	50	26	18	6	214	177	58
Toronto	50	23	23	4	214	174	50
Chicago	50	22	23	5	178	187	49
Boston	50	19	26	5	223	268	43
New York	50	6	39	5	162	310	17

Leading Scorers

Player	Team	GP	G	A	PTS	PIM
Cain, Herb	Boston	48	36	46	82	4
Bentley, Doug	Chicago	50	38	39	77	22
Carr, Lorne	Toronto	50	36	38	74	9
Liscombe, Carl	Detroit	50	36	37	73	17
Lach, Elmer	Montreal	48	24	48	72	23
Smith, Clint	Chicago	50	23	49	72	4
Cowley, Bill	Boston	36	30	41	71	12
Mosienko, Bill	Chicago	50	32	38	70	10
Jackson, Art	Boston	49	28	41	69	8
Bodnar, Gus	Toronto	50	22	40	62	18

* Stanley Cup winner.

1944-45

Team	GP	W	L	T	GF	GA	PTS
Montreal	50	38	8	4	228	121	80
Detroit	50	31	14	5	218	161	67
* Toronto	50	24	22	4	183	161	52
Boston	50	16	30	4	179	219	36
Chicago	50	13	30	7	141	194	33
New York	50	11	29	10	154	247	32

Leading Scorers

Player	Team	GP	G	A	PTS	PIM
Lach, Elmer	Montreal	50	26	54	80	37
Richard, Maurice	Montreal	50	50	23	73	36
Blake, Toe	Montreal	49	29	38	67	15
Cowley, Bill	Boston	49	25	40	65	2
Kennedy, Ted	Toronto	49	29	25	54	14
Mosienko, Bill	Chicago	50	28	26	54	0
Carveth, Joe	Detroit	50	26	28	54	6
DeMarco, Ab	New York	50	24	30	54	10
Smith, Clint	Chicago	50	23	31	54	0
Howe, Syd	Detroit	46	17	36	53	6

1945-46

Team	GP	W	L	T	GF	GA	PTS
* Montreal	50	28	17	5	172	134	61
Boston	50	24	18	8	167	156	56
Chicago	50	23	20	7	200	178	53
Detroit	50	20	20	10	146	159	50
Toronto	50	19	24	7	174	185	45
New York	50	13	28	9	144	191	35

Leading Scorers

Player	Team	GP	G	A	PTS	PIM
Bentley, Max	Chicago	47	31	30	61	6
Stewart, Gaye	Toronto	50	37	15	52	8
Blake, Toe	Montreal	50	29	21	50	2
Smith, Clint	Chicago	50	26	24	50	2
Richard, Maurice	Montreal	50	27	21	48	50
Mosienko, Bill	Chicago	40	18	30	48	12
DeMarco, Ab	New York	50	20	27	47	20
Lach, Elmer	Montreal	50	13	34	47	34
Kaleta, Alex	Chicago	49	19	27	46	17
Taylor, Billy	Toronto	48	23	18	41	14
Horeck, Pete	Chicago	50	20	21	41	34

1946-47

Team	GP	W	L	T	GF	GA	PTS
Montreal	60	34	16	10	189	138	78
* Toronto	60	31	19	10	209	172	72
Boston	60	26	23	11	190	175	63
Detroit	60	22	27	11	190	193	55
New York	60	22	32	6	167	186	50
Chicago	60	19	37	4	193	274	42

Leading Scorers

Player	Team	GP	G	A	PTS	PIM
Bentley, Max	Chicago	60	29	43	72	12
Richard, Maurice	Montreal	60	45	26	71	69
Taylor, Billy	Detroit	60	17	46	63	35
Schmidt, Milt	Boston	59	27	35	62	40
Kennedy, Ted	Toronto	60	28	32	60	27
Bentley, Doug	Chicago	52	21	34	55	18
Bauer, Bob	Boston	58	30	24	54	4
Conacher, Roy	Detroit	60	30	24	54	6
Mosienko, Bill	Chicago	59	25	27	52	2
Dumart, Woody	Boston	60	24	28	52	12

1947-48

Team	GP	W	L	T	GF	GA	PTS
* Toronto	60	32	15	13	182	143	77
Detroit	60	30	18	12	187	148	72
Boston	60	23	24	13	167	168	59
New York	60	21	26	13	176	201	55
Montreal	60	20	29	11	147	169	51
Chicago	60	20	34	6	195	225	46

Leading Scorers

Player	Team	GP	G	A	PTS	PIM
Lach, Elmer	Montreal	60	30	31	61	72
O'Connor, Buddy	New York	60	24	36	60	8
Bentley, Doug	Chicago	60	20	37	57	16
Stewart, Gaye	Tor., Chi.	61	27	29	56	83
Bentley, Max	Chi., Tor.	59	26	28	54	14
Poile, Bud	Tor., Chi.	58	25	29	54	17
Richard, Maurice	Montreal	53	28	25	53	89
Apps, Syl	Toronto	55	26	27	53	12
Lindsay, Ted	Detroit	60	33	19	52	95
Conacher, Roy	Chicago	52	22	27	49	4

1948-49

Team	GP	W	L	T	GF	GA	PTS
Detroit	60	34	19	7	195	145	75
Boston	60	29	23	8	178	163	66
Montreal	60	28	23	9	152	126	65
* Toronto	60	22	25	13	147	161	57
Chicago	60	21	31	8	173	211	50
New York	60	18	31	11	133	172	47

Leading Scorers

Player	Team	GP	G	A	PTS	PIM
Conacher, Roy	Chicago	60	26	42	68	8
Bentley, Doug	Chicago	58	23	43	66	38
Abel, Sid	Detroit	60	28	26	54	49
Lindsay, Ted	Detroit	50	26	28	54	97
Conacher, Jim	Det., Chi.	59	26	23	49	43
Ronty, Paul	Boston	60	20	29	49	11
Watson, Harry	Toronto	60	26	19	45	0
Reay, Billy	Montreal	60	22	23	45	33
Bodnar, Gus	Chicago	59	19	26	45	14
Peirson, John	Boston	59	22	21	43	45

1949-50

Team	GP	W	L	T	GF	GA	PTS
* Detroit	70	37	19	14	229	164	88
Montreal	70	29	22	19	172	150	77
Toronto	70	31	27	12	176	173	74
New York	70	28	31	11	170	189	67
Boston	70	22	32	16	198	228	60
Chicago	70	22	38	10	203	244	54

Leading Scorers

Player	Team	GP	G	A	PTS	PIM
Lindsay, Ted	Detroit	69	23	55	78	141
Abel, Sid	Detroit	69	34	35	69	46
Howe, Gordie	Detroit	70	35	33	68	69
Richard, Maurice	Montreal	70	43	22	65	114
Ronty, Paul	Boston	70	23	36	59	8
Conacher, Roy	Chicago	70	25	31	56	16
Bentley, Doug	Chicago	64	20	33	53	28
Peirson, John	Boston	57	27	25	52	49
Prystai, Metro	Chicago	65	29	22	51	31
Guidolin, Bep	Chicago	70	17	34	51	42

1950-51

Team	GP	W	L	T	GF	GA	PTS
Detroit	70	44	13	13	236	139	101
* Toronto	70	41	16	13	212	138	95
Montreal	70	25	30	15	173	184	65
Boston	70	22	30	18	178	197	62
New York	70	20	29	21	169	201	61
Chicago	70	13	47	10	171	280	36

Leading Scorers

Player	Team	GP	G	A	PTS	PIM
Howe, Gordie	Detroit	70	43	43	86	74
Richard, Maurice	Montreal	65	42	24	66	97
Bentley, Max	Toronto	67	21	41	62	34
Abel, Sid	Detroit	69	23	38	61	30
Schmidt, Milt	Boston	62	22	39	61	33
Kennedy, Ted	Toronto	63	18	43	61	32
Lindsay, Ted	Detroit	67	24	35	59	110
Sloan, Tod	Toronto	70	31	25	56	105
Kelly, Red	Detroit	70	17	37	54	24
Smith, Sid	Toronto	70	30	21	51	10
Gardner, Cal	Toronto	66	23	28	51	42

1951-52

Team	GP	W	L	T	GF	GA	PTS
* Detroit	70	44	14	12	215	133	100
Montreal	70	34	26	10	195	164	78
Toronto	70	29	25	16	168	157	74
Boston	70	25	29	16	162	176	66
New York	70	23	34	13	192	219	59
Chicago	70	17	44	9	158	241	43

Leading Scorers

Player	Team	GP	G	A	PTS	PIM
Howe, Gordie	Detroit	70	47	39	86	78
Lindsay, Ted	Detroit	70	30	39	69	123
Lach, Elmer	Montreal	70	15	50	65	36
Raleigh, Don	New York	70	19	42	61	14
Smith, Sid	Toronto	70	27	30	57	6
Geoffrion, Bernie	Montreal	67	30	24	54	66
Mosienko, Bill	Chicago	70	31	22	53	10
Abel, Sid	Detroit	62	17	36	53	32
Kennedy, Ted	Toronto	70	19	33	52	33
Schmidt, Milt	Boston	69	21	29	50	57
Peirson, John	Boston	68	20	30	50	30

1952-53

Team	GP	W	L	T	GF	GA	PTS
Detroit	70	36	16	18	222	133	90
* Montreal	70	28	23	19	155	148	75
Boston	70	28	29	13	152	172	69
Chicago	70	27	28	15	169	175	69
Toronto	70	27	30	13	156	167	67
New York	70	17	37	16	152	211	50

Leading Scorers

Player	Team	GP	G	A	PTS	PIM
Howe, Gordie	Detroit	70	49	46	95	57
Lindsay, Ted	Detroit	70	32	39	71	111
Richard, Maurice	Montreal	70	28	33	61	112
Hergesheimer, Wally	New York	70	30	29	59	10
Delvecchio, Alex	Detroit	70	16	43	59	28
Ronty, Paul	New York	70	16	38	54	20
Prystai, Metro	Detroit	70	16	34	50	12
Kelly, Red	Detroit	70	19	27	46	8
Olmstead, Bert	Montreal	69	17	28	45	83
Mackell, Fleming	Boston	65	27	17	44	63
McFadden, Jim	Chicago	70	23	21	44	29

1953-54

Team	GP	W	L	T	GF	GA	PTS
* Detroit	70	37	19	14	191	132	88
Montreal	70	35	24	11	195	141	81
Toronto	70	32	24	14	152	131	78
Boston	70	32	28	10	177	181	74
New York	70	29	31	10	161	182	68
Chicago	70	12	51	7	133	242	31

Leading Scorers

Player	Team	GP	G	A	PTS	PIM
Howe, Gordie	Detroit	70	33	48	81	109
Richard, Maurice	Montreal	70	37	30	67	112
Lindsay, Ted	Detroit	70	26	36	62	110
Geoffrion, Bernie	Montreal	54	29	25	54	87
Olmstead, Bert	Montreal	70	15	37	52	85
Kelly, Red	Detroit	62	16	33	49	18
Reibel, Earl	Detroit	69	15	33	48	18
Sandford, Ed	Boston	70	16	31	47	42
Mackell, Fleming	Boston	67	15	32	47	60
Mosdell, Ken	Montreal	67	22	24	46	64
Ronty, Paul	New York	70	13	33	46	18

1954-55

Team	GP	W	L	T	GF	GA	PTS
* Detroit	70	42	17	11	204	134	95
Montreal	70	41	18	11	228	157	93
Toronto	70	24	24	22	147	135	70
Boston	70	23	26	21	169	188	67
New York	70	17	35	18	150	210	52
Chicago	70	13	40	17	161	235	43

Leading Scorers

Player	Team	GP	G	A	PTS	PIM
Geoffrion, Bernie	Montreal	70	38	37	75	57
Richard, Maurice	Montreal	67	38	36	74	125
Béliveau, Jean	Montreal	70	37	36	73	58
Reibel, Earl	Detroit	70	25	41	66	15
Howe, Gordie	Detroit	64	29	33	62	68
Sullivan, George	Chicago	69	19	42	61	51
Olmstead, Bert	Montreal	70	10	48	58	103
Smith, Sid	Toronto	70	33	21	54	14
Mosdell, Ken	Montreal	70	22	32	54	82
Lewicki, Danny	New York	70	29	24	53	8

1955-56

Team	GP	W	L	T	GF	GA	PTS
* Montreal	70	45	15	10	222	131	100
Detroit	70	30	24	16	183	148	76
New York	70	32	28	10	204	203	74
Toronto	70	24	33	13	153	181	61
Boston	70	23	34	13	147	185	59
Chicago	70	19	39	12	155	216	50

Leading Scorers

Player	Team	GP	G	A	PTS	PIM
Béliveau, Jean	Montreal	70	47	41	88	143
Howe, Gordie	Detroit	70	38	41	79	100
Richard, Maurice	Montreal	70	38	33	71	89
Olmstead, Bert	Montreal	70	14	56	70	94
Sloan, Tod	Toronto	70	37	29	66	100
Bathgate, Andy	New York	70	19	47	66	59
Geoffrion, Bernie	Montreal	59	29	33	62	66
Reibel, Earl	Detroit	68	17	39	56	10
Delvecchio, Alex	Detroit	70	25	26	51	24
Creighton, Dave	New York	70	20	31	51	43
Gadsby, Bill	New York	70	9	42	51	84

1956-57

Team	GP	W	L	T	GF	GA	PTS
Detroit	70	38	20	12	198	157	88
* Montreal	70	35	23	12	210	155	82
Boston	70	34	24	12	195	174	80
New York	70	26	30	14	184	227	66
Toronto	70	21	34	15	174	192	57
Chicago	70	16	39	15	169	225	47

Leading Scorers

Player	Team	GP	G	A	PTS	PIM
Howe, Gordie	Detroit	70	44	45	89	72
Lindsay, Ted	Detroit	70	30	55	85	103
Béliveau, Jean	Montreal	69	33	51	84	105
Bathgate, Andy	New York	70	27	50	77	60
Litzenberger, Ed	Chicago	70	32	32	64	48
Richard, Maurice	Montreal	63	33	29	62	74
McKenney, Don	Boston	69	21	39	60	31
Moore, Dickie	Montreal	70	29	29	58	56
Richard, Henri	Montreal	63	18	36	54	71
Ullman, Norm	Detroit	64	16	36	52	47

1957-58

Team	GP	W	L	T	GF	GA	PTS
* Montreal	70	43	17	10	250	158	96
New York	70	32	25	13	195	188	77
Detroit	70	29	29	12	176	207	70
Boston	70	27	28	15	199	194	69
Chicago	70	24	39	7	163	202	55
Toronto	70	21	38	11	192	226	53

Leading Scorers

Player	Team	GP	G	A	PTS	PIM
Moore, Dickie	Montreal	70	36	48	84	65
Richard, Henri	Montreal	67	28	52	80	56
Bathgate, Andy	New York	65	30	48	78	42
Howe, Gordie	Detroit	64	33	44	77	40
Horvath, Bronco	Boston	67	30	36	66	71
Litzenberger, Ed	Chicago	70	32	30	62	63
Mackell, Fleming	Boston	70	20	40	60	72
Béliveau, Jean	Montreal	55	27	32	59	93
Delvecchio, Alex	Detroit	70	21	38	59	22
McKenney, Don	Boston	70	28	30	58	22

1958-59

Team	GP	W	L	T	GF	GA	PTS
* Montreal	70	39	18	13	258	158	91
Boston	70	32	29	9	205	215	73
Chicago	70	28	29	13	197	208	69
Toronto	70	27	32	11	189	201	65
New York	70	26	32	12	201	217	64
Detroit	70	25	37	8	167	218	58

Leading Scorers

Player	Team	GP	G	A	PTS	PIM
Moore, Dickie	Montreal	70	41	55	96	61
Béliveau, Jean	Montreal	64	45	46	91	67
Bathgate, Andy	New York	70	40	48	88	48
Howe, Gordie	Detroit	70	32	46	78	57
Litzenberger, Ed	Chicago	70	33	44	77	37
Geoffrion, Bernie	Montreal	59	22	44	66	30
Sullivan, Red	New York	70	21	42	63	56
Hebenton, Andy	New York	70	33	29	62	8
McKenney, Don	Boston	70	32	30	62	20
Sloan, Tod	Chicago	59	27	35	62	79

1959-60

Team	GP	W	L	T	GF	GA	PTS
* Montreal	70	40	18	12	255	178	92
Toronto	70	35	26	9	199	195	79
Chicago	70	28	29	13	191	180	69
Detroit	70	26	29	15	186	197	67
Boston	70	28	34	8	220	241	64
New York	70	17	38	15	187	247	49

Leading Scorers

Player	Team	GP	G	A	PTS	PIM
Hull, Bobby	Chicago	70	39	42	81	68
Horvath, Bronco	Boston	68	39	41	80	60
Béliveau, Jean	Montreal	60	34	40	74	57
Bathgate, Andy	New York	70	26	48	74	28
Richard, Henri	Montreal	70	30	43	73	66
Howe, Gordie	Detroit	70	28	45	73	46
Geoffrion, Bernie	Montreal	59	30	41	71	36
McKenney, Don	Boston	70	20	49	69	28
Stasiuk, Vic	Boston	69	29	39	68	121
Prentice, Dean	New York	70	32	34	66	43

1960-61

Team	GP	W	L	T	GF	GA	PTS
Montreal	70	41	19	10	254	188	92
Toronto	70	39	19	12	234	176	90
* Chicago	70	29	24	17	198	180	75
Detroit	70	25	29	16	195	215	66
New York	70	22	38	10	204	248	54
Boston	70	15	42	13	176	254	43

Leading Scorers

Player	Team	GP	G	A	PTS	PIM
Geoffrion, Bernie	Montreal	64	50	45	95	29
Béliveau, Jean	Montreal	69	32	58	90	57
Mahovlich, Frank	Toronto	70	48	36	84	131
Bathgate, Andy	New York	70	29	48	77	22
Howe, Gordie	Detroit	64	23	49	72	30
Ullman, Norm	Detroit	70	28	42	70	34
Kelly, Red	Toronto	64	20	50	70	12
Moore, Dickie	Montreal	57	35	34	69	62
Richard, Henri	Montreal	70	24	44	68	91
Delvecchio, Alex	Detroit	70	27	35	62	26

1961-62

Team	GP	W	L	T	GF	GA	PTS
Montreal	70	42	14	14	259	166	98
* Toronto	70	37	22	11	232	180	85
Chicago	70	31	26	13	217	186	75
New York	70	26	32	12	195	207	64
Detroit	70	23	33	14	184	219	60
Boston	70	15	47	8	177	306	38

Leading Scorers

Player	Team	GP	G	A	PTS	PIM
Hull, Bobby	Chicago	70	50	34	84	35
Bathgate, Andy	New York	70	28	56	84	44
Howe, Gordie	Detroit	70	33	44	77	54
Mikita, Stan	Chicago	70	25	52	77	97
Mahovlich, Frank	Toronto	70	33	38	71	87
Delvecchio, Alex	Detroit	70	26	43	69	18
Backstrom, Ralph	Montreal	66	27	38	65	29
Ullman, Norm	Detroit	70	26	38	64	54
Hay, Bill	Chicago	60	11	52	63	34
Provost, Claude	Montreal	70	33	29	62	22

1962-63

Team	GP	W	L	T	GF	GA	PTS
* Toronto	70	35	23	12	221	180	82
Chicago	70	32	21	17	194	178	81
Montreal	70	28	19	23	225	183	79
Detroit	70	32	25	13	200	194	77
New York	70	22	36	12	211	233	56
Boston	70	14	39	17	198	281	45

Leading Scorers

Player	Team	GP	G	A	PTS	PIM
Howe, Gordie	Detroit	70	38	48	86	100
Bathgate, Andy	New York	70	35	46	81	54
Mikita, Stan	Chicago	65	31	45	76	69
Mahovlich, Frank	Toronto	67	36	37	73	56
Richard, Henri	Montreal	67	23	50	73	57
Béliveau, Jean	Montreal	69	18	49	67	68
Bucyk, John	Boston	69	27	39	66	36
Delvecchio, Alex	Detroit	70	20	44	64	8
Hull, Bobby	Chicago	65	31	31	62	27
Oliver, Murray	Boston	65	22	40	62	38

1963-64

Team	GP	W	L	T	GF	GA	PTS
Montreal	70	36	21	13	209	167	85
Chicago	70	36	22	12	218	169	84
* Toronto	70	33	25	12	192	172	78
Detroit	70	30	29	11	191	204	71
New York	70	22	38	10	186	242	54
Boston	70	18	40	12	170	212	48

Leading Scorers

Player	Team	GP	G	A	PTS	PIM
Mikita, Stan	Chicago	70	39	50	89	146
Hull, Bobby	Chicago	70	43	44	87	50
Béliveau, Jean	Montreal	68	28	50	78	42
Bathgate, Andy	NYR, Tor.	71	19	58	77	34
Howe, Gordie	Detroit	69	26	47	73	70
Wharram, Ken	Chicago	70	39	32	71	18
Oliver, Murray	Boston	70	24	44	68	41
Goyette, Phil	New York	67	24	41	65	15
Gilbert, Rod	New York	70	24	40	64	62
Keon, Dave	Toronto	70	23	37	60	6

1964-65

Team	GP	W	L	T	GF	GA	PTS
Detroit	70	40	23	7	224	175	87
* Montreal	70	36	23	11	211	185	83
Chicago	70	34	28	8	224	176	76
Toronto	70	30	26	14	204	173	74
New York	70	20	38	12	179	246	52
Boston	70	21	43	6	166	253	48

Leading Scorers

Player	Team	GP	G	A	PTS	PIM
Mikita, Stan	Chicago	70	28	59	87	154
Ullman, Norm	Detroit	70	42	41	83	70
Howe, Gordie	Detroit	70	29	47	76	104
Hull, Bobby	Chicago	61	39	32	71	32
Delvecchio, Alex	Detroit	68	25	42	67	16
Provost, Claude	Montreal	70	27	37	64	28
Gilbert, Rod	New York	70	25	36	61	52
Pilote, Pierre	Chicago	68	14	45	59	162
Bucyk, John	Boston	68	26	29	55	24
Backstrom, Ralph	Montreal	70	25	30	55	41
Esposito, Phil	Chicago	70	23	32	55	44

1965-66

Team	GP	W	L	T	GF	GA	PTS
* Montreal	70	41	21	8	239	173	90
Chicago	70	37	25	8	240	187	82
Toronto	70	34	25	11	208	187	79
Detroit	70	31	27	12	221	194	74
Boston	70	21	43	6	174	275	48
New York	70	18	41	11	195	261	47

Leading Scorers

Player	Team	GP	G	A	PTS	PIM
Hull, Bobby	Chicago	65	54	43	97	70
Mikita, Stan	Chicago	68	30	48	78	58
Rousseau, Bobby	Montreal	70	30	48	78	20
Béliveau, Jean	Montreal	67	29	48	77	50
Howe, Gordie	Detroit	70	29	46	75	83
Ullman, Norm	Detroit	70	31	41	72	35
Delvecchio, Alex	Detroit	70	31	38	69	16
Nevin, Bob	New York	69	29	33	62	10
Richard, Henri	Montreal	62	22	39	61	47
Oliver, Murray	Boston	70	18	42	60	30

1966-67

Team	GP	W	L	T	GF	GA	PTS
Chicago	70	41	17	12	264	170	94
Montreal	70	32	25	13	202	188	77
* Toronto	70	32	27	11	204	211	75
New York	70	30	28	12	188	189	72
Detroit	70	27	39	4	212	241	58
Boston	70	17	43	10	182	253	44

Leading Scorers

Player	Team	GP	G	A	PTS	PIM
Mikita, Stan	Chicago	70	35	62	97	12
Hull, Bobby	Chicago	66	52	28	80	52
Ullman, Norm	Detroit	68	26	44	70	26
Wharram, Ken	Chicago	70	31	34	65	21
Howe, Gordie	Detroit	69	25	40	65	53
Rousseau, Bobby	Montreal	68	19	44	63	58
Esposito, Phil	Chicago	69	21	40	61	40
Goyette, Phil	New York	70	12	49	61	6
Mohns, Doug	Chicago	61	25	35	60	58
Richard, Henri	Montreal	65	21	34	55	28
Delvecchio, Alex	Detroit	70	17	38	55	10

Playoff Records
TEAM RECORDS

MOST STANLEY CUP CHAMPIONSHIPS:
10 – Montreal Canadiens (1944-46-53-56-57-58-59-60-65-66).
9 – Toronto Maple Leafs.
5 – Detroit Red Wings.

MOST FINAL-SERIES APPEARANCES:
16 – Montreal Canadiens.
13 – Detroit Red Wings.
11 – Toronto Maple Leafs.

MOST YEARS IN PLAYOFFS:
24 – Montreal Canadiens.
22 – Detroit Red Wings.
21 – Toronto Maple Leafs.

MOST CONSECUTIVE STANLEY CUP CHAMPIONSHIPS:
5 – Montreal Canadiens (1955-56 to 1959-60).

MOST CONSECUTIVE FINAL-SERIES APPEARANCES:
10 – Montreal Canadiens (1950-51 to 1959-60).

MOST CONSECUTIVE PLAYOFF APPEARANCES:
19 – Montreal Canadiens (1948-49 to 1966-67).
16 – Detroit Red Wings (1942-43 to 1957-58).

MOST GOALS, BOTH TEAMS, ONE GAME:
13 – Montreal Canadiens, Toronto Maple Leafs, at Montreal, March 29, 1945. Montreal 10, Toronto 3.

MOST GOALS, ONE TEAM, ONE GAME:
11 – Montreal Canadiens at Montreal, March 30, 1944. Montreal 11, Toronto 0.

MOST GOALS, BOTH TEAMS, ONE PERIOD:
7 – Montreal Canadiens, Toronto Maple Leafs, March 30, 1944, third period. Montreal scored all seven goals in 11–0 victory.
– Montreal Canadiens, New York Rangers, April 5, 1967, third period. Montreal scored five goals, New York scored two in Montreal's 5–4 victory.

MOST GOALS, ONE TEAM, ONE PERIOD:
7 – Montreal Canadiens at Montreal, March 30, 1944, against Toronto in 11–0 Montreal victory.

LONGEST OVERTIME:
70:18 – Toronto Maple Leafs at Detroit Red Wings, March 23/24, 1943. Toronto 3, Detroit 2. Jackie McLean scored, assisted by Bud Poile and Gaye Stewart, at 10:18 of the fourth overtime period, or 130 minutes and 18 seconds from the start of the game, which ended at 1:14 a.m. Detroit won SF series 4–2.

SHORTEST OVERTIME:
1:22 – Boston Bruins at Montreal Canadiens, April 16, 1953. Montreal 1, Boston Bruins 0. Elmer Lach scored, assisted by Maurice Richard. Montreal won F series 4–1.

MOST OVERTIME GAMES, ONE SERIES:
5 – Toronto Maple Leafs, Montreal Canadiens in 1951. Toronto defeated Montreal 4–1 in F series.

MOST OVERTIME GAMES, ONE PLAYOFF YEAR:
8 – 1951. Of the 17 games played, 8 went into overtime. Two in SF won 4–2 by the Montreal Canadiens over Detroit Red Wings, one in SF won 4–1 (with one tie) by the Toronto Maple Leafs over the Boston Bruins, and five in F series won 4–1 by the Toronto Maple Leafs over the Montreal Canadiens.

MOST CONSECUTIVE PLAYOFF-GAME VICTORIES:
11 – Montreal Canadiens. Streak began April 16, 1959, at Toronto, with 3–2 win in fourth game of F series, won by Montreal, 4–1, and ended March 23, 1961, when the Chicago Black Hawks defeated Montreal 4–3 in the second game of SF series. Included in streak were eight straight victories in 1960.

MOST CONSECUTIVE VICTORIES, ONE PLAYOFF YEAR:
8 – Detroit Red Wings in 1952. Detroit defeated Toronto 4–0 in SF and Montreal 4–0 in F.
– Montreal Canadiens in 1960. Montreal defeated Chicago 4–0 in SF and Toronto 4–0 in F.

MOST SHUTOUTS, ONE PLAYOFF YEAR, ALL TEAMS:
7 – 1950. Of 19GP, Toronto Maple Leafs had three, Detroit Red Wings had three, and the New York Rangers had one.

FEWEST SHUTOUTS, ONE PLAYOFF YEAR, ALL TEAMS:
0 – 1959. There were no shutouts in 18GP.

MOST SHUTOUTS, BOTH TEAMS, ONE SERIES:
5 – 1945 Final. Toronto Maple Leafs, Detroit Red Wings. Toronto had three shutouts, Detroit two. Toronto won series 4–3.
– 1950 Semi-final. Detroit Red Wings, Toronto Maple Leafs. Toronto had three shutouts, Detroit two. Detroit won series 4–3.

FASTEST TWO GOALS, BOTH TEAMS:
10 seconds – Toronto Maple Leafs, Montreal Canadiens, at Toronto, April 12, 1947. Vic Lynn of Toronto scored at 12:23 of second period, and Leo Gravelle of Montreal at 12:33. Toronto won game 4–2 and F series 4–2.

FASTEST TWO GOALS, ONE TEAM:
5 seconds – Detroit Red Wings, at Detroit, April 11, 1965, against Chicago. Norm Ullman scored at 17:35 and 17:40 of the second period. Detroit won game 4–2. Chicago won SF series 4–3.

FASTEST THREE GOALS, BOTH TEAMS:
38 seconds – Toronto Maple Leafs, Montreal Canadiens, at Toronto, April 13, 1965. Red Kelly of Toronto scored at 3:11 of first period, John Ferguson of Montreal at 3:32, and Ron Ellis of Toronto at 3:49. Montreal won game 4-3 in overtime and won SF series 4-2.

FASTEST THREE GOALS, ONE TEAM:
56 seconds – Montreal Canadiens at Detroit Red Wings, April 6, 1954. Dickie Moore scored at 15:03 of first period, Maurice Richard at 15:28, and again at 15:59. Montreal won game 3-1. Detroit won F series 4–3.

FASTEST FOUR GOALS, BOTH TEAMS:
1:39 – Toronto Maple Leafs, Montreal Canadiens, at Toronto, April 13, 1965. Dave Keon of Toronto at 2:10 of first period, Red Kelly of Toronto at 3:11, John Ferguson of Montreal at 3:32, and Ron Ellis of Toronto at 3:49. Montreal won game 4–3 in overtime and SF series 4-2.

FASTEST FOUR GOALS, ONE TEAM:
2:35 – Montreal Canadiens at Montreal, March 30, 1944, against Toronto. Toe Blake scored at 7:58 of third period, and again at 8:37; Maurice Richard at 9:17; Rey Getliffe at 10:33. Montreal won game 11–0 and SF series 4–1.

INDIVIDUAL RECORDS

MOST YEARS IN PLAYOFFS:
19 – Red Kelly, Detroit, Toronto (1947-48 to 1957-58; 1959-60 to 1966-67).
18 – Gordie Howe, Detroit.

MOST CONSECUTIVE YEARS IN PLAYOFFS:
14 – Bernie Geoffrion, Montreal (1950-51 to 1963-64).

MOST PLAYOFF GAMES:
164 – Red Kelly, Detroit, Toronto.
150 – Gordie Howe, Detroit.
134 – Marcel Pronovost, Detroit, Toronto.

MOST POINTS IN PLAYOFFS:
156 – Gordie Howe, Detroit, 65 goals, 91 assists.
128 – Jean Béliveau, Montreal, 61 goals, 67 assists.
126 – Maurice Richard, Montreal, 82 goals, 44 assists.

MOST GOALS IN PLAYOFFS:
82 – Maurice Richard, Montreal.
65 – Gordie Howe, Detroit.
61 – Jean Béliveau, Montreal.

MOST ASSISTS IN PLAYOFFS:
91 – Gordie Howe, Detroit.
67 – Jean Béliveau, Montreal.
   – Alex Delvecchio, Detroit.

MOST SHUTOUTS IN PLAYOFFS:
11 – Terry Sawchuk, Detroit, Toronto, in 13 playoff years.
10 – Jacques Plante, Montreal, in 11 playoff years (Plante also shared a shutout with Charlie Hodge, March 22, 1955.)

MOST PLAYOFF GAMES BY A GOALTENDER:
95 – Terry Sawchuk, Detroit, Toronto.
90 – Jacques Plante, Montreal.

MOST POINTS, ONE PLAYOFF YEAR:
21 – Stan Mikita, Chicago, in 1962. 6G and 15A in 12GP versus Montreal and Toronto.

MOST GOALS, ONE PLAYOFF YEAR:
12 – Maurice Richard, Montreal, in 9GP versus Toronto and Chicago in 1944.
   – Jean Béliveau, Montreal, in 10GP versus New York and Detroit in 1956.

MOST ASSISTS, ONE PLAYOFF YEAR:
15 – Stan Mikita, Chicago, in 1962, in 12GP versus Montreal and Toronto.

MOST POINTS BY A DEFENCEMAN, ONE PLAYOFF YEAR:
16 – Tim Horton, Toronto, in 1962. 3G and 13A in 12GP versus New York and Chicago.

MOST POINTS IN FINAL SERIES:
12 – Gordie Howe, Detroit, in 1955. 5G and 7A in 7GP versus Montreal.

MOST GOALS IN FINAL SERIES:
7 – Jean Béliveau, Montreal, in 1956, in 5GP versus Detroit.

MOST ASSISTS IN FINAL SERIES:
8 – Bert Olmstead, Montreal, in 1956, in 5GP versus Detroit.

MOST POINTS IN SEMI-FINAL SERIES:
14 – Fleming Mackell, Boston, in 1958. 4G and 10A in 6GP versus New York.

MOST GOALS IN SEMI-FINAL SERIES:
8 – Gordie Howe, Detroit, in 1949, in seven games versus Montreal.
   – Jerry Toppazzini, Boston, in 1958, in six games versus New York.
   – Bobby Hull, Chicago, in 1963, in five games versus Detroit.
   – Bobby Hull, Chicago, in 1965, in seven games versus Detroit.

MOST ASSISTS IN SEMI-FINAL SERIES:
10 – Fleming Mackell, Boston, in 1958, in six games versus New York.
   – Stan Mikita, Chicago, in 1962, in six games versus Montreal.

MOST SHUTOUTS, ONE PLAYOFF YEAR:
4 – Frank McCool, Toronto, in 1945, in 13 games versus Montreal and Detroit.
   – Terry Sawchuk, Detroit, in 1952, in eight games versus Toronto and Montreal.

MOST CONSECUTIVE SHUTOUTS:
3 – Frank McCool, Toronto, in F, 1945, won by Toronto 4–3 versus Detroit. McCool shutout Detroit 1-0, April 6; 2-0, April 8; 1-0, April 12.

LONGEST SHUTOUT SEQUENCE:
193:09 – Frank McCool, Toronto, in 1945. Streak started after Butch Bouchard scored for Montreal at 15:26 of the third period at Toronto, March 31, in sixth and final game of SF series. Streak ended at Toronto, April 14, when Flash Hollett scored for Detroit at 8:35 of first period of fourth game of F series.

MOST POINTS, ONE GAME:
6 – Dickie Moore, Montreal, March 25, 1954, at Montreal, in 8–1 victory over Boston. Moore had 2G, 4A.

MOST GOALS, ONE GAME:
5 – Maurice Richard, Montreal Canadiens, March 23, 1944, at Toronto in 5–1 victory over Toronto.

MOST ASSISTS, ONE GAME:
5 – Toe Blake, Montreal, March 23, 1944, at Toronto, in 5–1 victory over Toronto.
   – Maurice Richard, Montreal, March 27, 1956, at Montreal, in 7–0 victory over New York.
   – Bert Olmstead, Montreal, March 30, 1957, at Montreal, in 8–3 victory over New York.
   – Don McKenney, Boston, April 5, 1958, at Boston, in 8–2 victory over New York.

MOST POINTS, ONE PERIOD:
4 – Maurice Richard, Montreal, March 29, 1945, at Montreal, in third period of 10–3 victory over Toronto. Richard had 3G, 1A.
   – Dickie Moore, Montreal, March 25, 1954, at Montreal in first period of 8–1 victory over Boston. Moore had 2G, 2A.

MOST GOALS, ONE PERIOD:
3 – Maurice Richard, Montreal, March 23, 1944, at Montreal, in second period of 5–1 victory over Toronto.
   – Maurice Richard, Montreal, March 29, 1945, at Montreal, in third period of 10–3 victory over Toronto.
   – Ted Lindsay, Detroit, April 5, 1955, at Detroit, in second period of 7–1 victory over Montreal.
   – Maurice Richard, Montreal, April 6, 1957, at Montreal, in second period of 5–1 victory over Boston.

MOST ASSISTS, ONE PERIOD:

3 – Ten players: Toe Blake, 1944; Elmer Lach, 1944; Bobby Bauer, 1946; Jean Béliveau, 1954; Maurice Richard, 1956; Doug Harvey, 1957; Don McKenney, 1958; Dickie Moore, 1959; Henri Richard, 1960; and Alex Delvecchio, 1966.

FASTEST TWO GOALS:

5 seconds – Norm Ullman, Detroit, April 11, 1965, at Detroit, against Chicago goaltender Glenn Hall. Ullman scored at 17:35 and 17:40 of second period in 4–2 victory over Chicago.

FASTEST GOAL FROM START OF GAME AND PERIOD:

9 seconds – Gordie Howe, Detroit, April 1, 1954, at Detroit, against Toronto goaltender Harry Lumley. Detroit won game 4–3 in overtime.

– Ken Wharram, Chicago, April 13, 1967, at Toronto, against Toronto goaltender Terry Sawchuk. Chicago won game 4–3.

FASTEST TWO GOALS FROM START OF GAME AND PERIOD:

1:08 – Dick Duff, Toronto, April 9, 1963, at Toronto, against Detroit goaltender Terry Sawchuk. Duff scored at 0:49 and 1:08. Toronto won game 4–2.

MOST CONSECUTIVE GAMES SCORING GOALS:

8 – Maurice Richard, Montreal, twice. First streak started March 27, 1945, at Toronto, and ended April 2, 1946, at Montreal. Richard scored one goal in each of seven games and four in another. Second streak started April 5, 1951, at Detroit, and ended March 27, 1952, at Montreal. Richard scored one goal in each of seven games and two in another.

MOST GAME-WINNING GOALS:

18 – Maurice Richard, Montreal, in 15 playoff years.
14 – Bernie Geoffrion, Montreal, in 14 playoff years.
10 – Gordie Howe, Detroit, in 17 playoff years.

MOST OVERTIME GOALS:

6 – Maurice Richard, Montreal (1 in 1946, 3 in 1951, 1 in 1957, 1 in 1958)
2 – Seven players: Don Gallinger, 1943, 1946; Don Raleigh, 1950; Leo Reise, 1950; Elmer Lach, 1950, 1953; Ted Lindsay, 1954, 1956; Frank Mahovlich, 1959, 1960; Murray Balfour, 1961, 1964.

MOST OVERTIME GOALS, ONE PLAYOFF YEAR:

3 – Maurice Richard, Montreal, 1951. Richard scored two versus Detroit in SF, won by Montreal 4–2, and one versus Toronto in F, won by Toronto 4–1.

MOST OVERTIME GOALS, ONE PLAYOFF SERIES:

2 – Leo Reise, Detroit, versus Toronto, in 1950 SF series, won by Detroit 4–3. Reise scored at 20:38 of overtime on April 4, and 8:39 of overtime on April 9.

– Don Raleigh, New York, versus Detroit, in 1950 F series won by Detroit 4–3. Raleigh scored at 8:34 of overtime on April 18, and 1:38 of overtime on April 20.

– Maurice Richard, Montreal, versus Detroit in 1951 SF series, won by Montreal 4–2. Richard scored at 61:09 of overtime on March 27, and 42:20 of overtime on March 29.

MOST THREE-OR-MORE-GOAL GAMES:

7 – Maurice Richard, Montreal. Four three-goal games, two four-goal games, one five-goal game.
3 – Bernie Geoffrion, Montreal. Three goals in each.
3 – Norm Ullman, Detroit. Three goals in each.

Stanley Cup Standings
1943-67
(ranked by Cup wins)

Club	Years in Playoffs	Cup Wins	Series			Games			
			Series	W	L	GP	W	L	%
Montreal	24	10	40	26	14	215	130	85	.605
Toronto	21	9	32	20	12	*174	92	81	.532
Detroit	22	5	35	18	17	197	97	100	.492
Chicago	12	1	16	5	11	93	39	54	.419
Boston	14	0	19	5	14	*103	39	63	.383
New York	7	0	8	1	7	44	15	29	.341

* includes one tie in 1951 semi-finals.

Playoff Results and Regular-Season Finishes
1942-43 to 1966-67

Club	Times in Playoffs	Finals Reached	Cup Wins	First-Place Finish			Second-Place Finish			Third-Place Finish			Fourth-Place Finish		
				1st-Place Finishes	Finals Reached	Cup Wins	2nd-Place Finishes	Finals Reached	Cup Wins	3rd-Place Finishes	Finals Reached	Cup Wins	4th-Place Finishes	Finals Reached	Cup Wins
Montreal	24	16	10	12	8	7	8	7	3	3	1	0	1	0	0
Detroit	22	13	5	10	6	5	4	3	0	1	0	0	7	4	0
Toronto	21	11	9	2	2	2	5	4	3	10	3	3	4	2	1
Boston	14	5	0	0	0	0	4	2	0	4	2	0	6	1	0
Chicago	12	4	1	1	0	0	3	0	0	6	3	1	2	1	0
New York	7	1	0	0	0	0	1	0	0	1	0	0	5	1	0
Totals	**100**	**50**	**25**	**25**	**16**	**14**	**25**	**16**	**6**	**25**	**9**	**4**	**25**	**9**	**1**

Stanley Cup Winners, Finalists, Coaches, Captains, and Cup-Winning Goal Scorers
1942-43 to 1966-67

Year	Stanley Cup Winner	Finalist	Winning Coach	Winning Captain	Cup-Winning Goal Scorer
1942-43	Detroit Red Wings	Boston Bruins	Jack Adams	Sid Abel	Joe Carveth
1943-44	Montreal Canadiens	Chicago Black Hawks	Dick Irvin	Toe Blake	Toe Blake
1944-45	Toronto Maple Leafs	Detroit Red Wings	Hap Day	Bob Davidson	Babe Pratt
1945-46	Montreal Canadiens	Boston Bruins	Dick Irvin	Toe Blake	Toe Blake
1946-47	Toronto Maple Leafs	Montreal Canadiens	Hap Day	Syl Apps	Ted Kennedy
1947-48	Toronto Maple Leafs	Detroit Red Wings	Hap Day	Syl Apps	Harry Watson
1948-49	Toronto Maple Leafs	Detroit Red Wings	Hap Day	Ted Kennedy	Cal Gardner
1949-50	Detroit Red Wings	New York Rangers	Tommy Ivan	Sid Abel	Pete Babando
1950-51	Toronto Maple Leafs	Montreal Canadiens	Joe Primeau	Ted Kennedy	Bill Barilko
1951-52	Detroit Red Wings	Montreal Canadiens	Tommy Ivan	Sid Abel	Metro Prystai
1952-53	Montreal Canadiens	Boston Bruins	Dick Irvin	Butch Bouchard	Elmer Lach
1953-54	Detroit Red Wings	Montreal Canadiens	Tommy Ivan	Ted Lindsay	Tony Leswick
1954-55	Detroit Red Wings	Montreal Canadiens	Jimmy Skinner	Ted Lindsay	Gordie Howe
1955-56	Montreal Canadiens	Detroit Red Wings	Toe Blake	Butch Bouchard	Maurice Richard
1956-57	Montreal Canadiens	Boston Bruins	Toe Blake	Maurice Richard	Dickie Moore
1957-58	Montreal Canadiens	Boston Bruins	Toe Blake	Maurice Richard	Bernie Geoffrion
1958-59	Montreal Canadiens	Toronto Maple Leafs	Toe Blake	Maurice Richard	Marcel Bonin
1959-60	Montreal Canadiens	Toronto Maple Leafs	Toe Blake	Maurice Richard	Jean Béliveau
1960-61	Chicago Black Hawks	Detroit Red Wings	Rudy Pilous	Eddie Litzenberger	Ab McDonald
1961-62	Toronto Maple Leafs	Chicago Black Hawks	Punch Imlach	George Armstrong	Dick Duff
1962-63	Toronto Maple Leafs	Detroit Red Wings	Punch Imlach	George Armstrong	Eddie Shack
1963-64	Toronto Maple Leafs	Detroit Red Wings	Punch Imlach	George Armstrong	Andy Bathgate
1964-65	Montreal Canadiens	Chicago Black Hawks	Toe Blake	Jean Béliveau	Jean Béliveau
1965-66	Montreal Canadiens	Detroit Red Wings	Toe Blake	Jean Béliveau	Henri Richard
1966-67	Toronto Maple Leafs	Montreal Canadiens	Punch Imlach	George Armstrong	Jim Pappin

Playoff Game Results
1943 to 1967

1943

SEMI-FINALS

Mar. 21	Toronto	2	at	Detroit	4
Mar. 23	Toronto	3	at	Detroit	2 OT
Mar. 25	Detroit	4	at	Toronto	6
Mar. 27	Detroit	3	at	Toronto	6
Mar. 28	Toronto	2	at	Detroit	4
Mar. 30	Detroit	3	at	Toronto	2 OT

Detroit won series 4–2

Mar. 21	Montreal	4	at	Boston	5 OT
Mar. 23	Montreal	3	at	Boston	5
Mar. 25	Boston	3	at	Montreal	2 OT
Mar. 27	Boston	0	at	Montreal	4
Mar. 30	Montreal	4	at	Boston	5 OT

Boston won series 4–1

FINALS

Apr. 1	Boston	2	at	Detroit	6
Apr. 4	Boston	3	at	Detroit	4
Apr. 7	Detroit	4	at	Boston	0
Apr. 8	Detroit	2	at	Boston	0

Detroit won series 4–0

1944

SEMI-FINALS

Mar. 21	Toronto	3	at	Montreal	1
Mar. 23	Toronto	1	at	Montreal	5
Mar. 25	Montreal	2	at	Toronto	1
Mar. 28	Montreal	4	at	Toronto	1
Mar. 30	Toronto	0	at	Montreal	11

Montreal won series 4–1

Mar. 21	Chicago	2	at	Detroit	1
Mar. 23	Chicago	1	at	Detroit	4
Mar. 26	Detroit	0	at	Chicago	2
Mar. 28	Detroit	1	at	Chicago	7
Mar. 30	Chicago	5	at	Detroit	2

Chicago won series 4–1

FINALS

Apr. 4	Chicago	1	at	Montreal	5
Apr. 6	Montreal	3	at	Chicago	1
Apr. 9	Montreal	3	at	Chicago	2
Apr. 13	Chicago	4	at	Montreal	5 OT

Montreal won series 4–0

1945

SEMI-FINALS

Mar. 20	Toronto	1	at	Montreal	0
Mar. 22	Toronto	3	at	Montreal	2
Mar. 24	Montreal	4	at	Toronto	1
Mar. 27	Montreal	3	at	Toronto	4 OT
Mar. 29	Toronto	3	at	Montreal	10
Mar. 31	Montreal	2	at	Toronto	3

Toronto won series 4–2

Mar. 20	Boston	4	at	Detroit	3
Mar. 22	Boston	4	at	Detroit	2
Mar. 25	Detroit	3	at	Boston	2
Mar. 27	Detroit	3	at	Boston	2
Mar. 29	Boston	2	at	Detroit	3 OT
Apr. 1	Detroit	3	at	Boston	5
Apr. 3	Boston	3	at	Detroit	5

Detroit won series 4–3

FINALS

Apr. 6	Toronto	1	at	Detroit	0
Apr. 8	Toronto	2	at	Detroit	0
Apr. 12	Detroit	0	at	Toronto	1
Apr. 14	Detroit	5	at	Toronto	3
Apr. 19	Toronto	0	at	Detroit	2
Apr. 21	Detroit	1	at	Toronto	0 OT
Apr. 22	Toronto	2	at	Detroit	1

Toronto won series 4–3

1946

SEMI-FINALS

Mar. 19	Chicago	2	at	Montreal	6
Mar. 21	Chicago	1	at	Montreal	5
Mar. 24	Montreal	8	at	Chicago	2
Mar. 26	Montreal	7	at	Chicago	2

Montreal won series 4–0

Mar. 19	Detroit	1	at	Boston	3
Mar. 21	Detroit	3	at	Boston	0
Mar. 24	Boston	5	at	Detroit	2
Mar. 26	Boston	4	at	Detroit	1
Mar. 28	Detroit	3	at	Boston	4 OT

Boston won series 4–1

FINALS

Mar. 30	Boston	3	at	Montreal	4 OT
Apr. 2	Boston	2	at	Montreal	3 OT
Apr. 4	Montreal	4	at	Boston	2
Apr. 7	Montreal	2	at	Boston	3 OT
Apr. 9	Boston	3	at	Montreal	6

Montreal won series 4–1

1947

SEMI-FINALS

Mar. 25	Boston	1	at	Montreal	3
Mar. 27	Boston	1	at	Montreal	2 OT
Mar. 29	Montreal	2	at	Boston	4
Apr. 1	Montreal	5	at	Boston	1
Apr. 3	Boston	3	at	Montreal	4 OT

Montreal won series 4–1

Mar. 26	Detroit	2	at	Toronto	3 OT
Mar. 29	Detroit	9	at	Toronto	1
Apr. 1	Toronto	4	at	Detroit	1
Apr. 3	Toronto	4	at	Detroit	1
Apr. 5	Detroit	1	at	Toronto	6

Toronto won series 4–1

FINALS

Apr. 8	Toronto	0	at	Montreal	6
Apr. 10	Toronto	4	at	Montreal	0
Apr. 12	Montreal	2	at	Toronto	4
Apr. 15	Montreal	1	at	Toronto	2 OT
Apr. 17	Toronto	1	at	Montreal	3
Apr. 19	Montreal	1	at	Toronto	2

Toronto won series 4–2

1948

SEMI-FINALS

Mar. 24	Boston	4	at	Toronto	5 OT
Mar. 27	Boston	3	at	Toronto	5
Mar. 30	Toronto	5	at	Boston	1
Apr. 1	Toronto	2	at	Boston	3
Apr. 3	Boston	2	at	Toronto	3

Toronto won series 4–1

Mar. 24	New York	1	at	Detroit	2
Mar. 26	New York	2	at	Detroit	5
Mar. 28	Detroit	2	at	New York	3
Mar. 30	Detroit	1	at	New York	3
Apr. 1	New York	1	at	Detroit	3
Apr. 4	Detroit	4	at	New York	2

Detroit won series 4–2

FINALS

Apr. 7	Detroit	3	at	Toronto	5
Apr. 10	Detroit	2	at	Toronto	4
Apr. 11	Toronto	2	at	Detroit	0
Apr. 14	Toronto	7	at	Detroit	2

Toronto won series 4–0

1949

SEMI-FINALS
Mar. 22	Montreal	1	at	Detroit	2	OT
Mar. 24	Montreal	4	at	Detroit	3	OT
Mar. 26	Detroit	2	at	Montreal	3	
Mar. 29	Detroit	3	at	Montreal	1	
Mar. 31	Montreal	1	at	Detroit	3	
Apr. 2	Detroit	1	at	Montreal	3	
Apr. 5	Montreal	1	at	Detroit	3	

Detroit won series 4–3

Mar. 22	Toronto	3	at	Boston	0	
Mar. 24	Toronto	3	at	Boston	2	
Mar. 26	Boston	5	at	Toronto	4	OT
Mar. 29	Boston	1	at	Toronto	3	
Mar. 30	Toronto	3	at	Boston	2	

Toronto won series 4–1

FINALS
Apr. 8	Toronto	3	at	Detroit	2	OT
Apr. 10	Toronto	3	at	Detroit	1	
Apr. 13	Detroit	1	at	Toronto	3	
Apr. 16	Detroit	1	at	Toronto	3	

Toronto won series 4–0

1950

SEMI-FINALS
Mar. 28	Toronto	5	at	Detroit	0	
Mar. 30	Toronto	1	at	Detroit	3	
Apr. 1	Detroit	0	at	Toronto	2	
Apr. 4	Detroit	2	at	Toronto	1	OT
Apr. 6	Toronto	2	at	Detroit	0	
Apr. 8	Detroit	4	at	Toronto	0	
Apr. 9	Toronto	0	at	Detroit	1	OT

Detroit won series 4–3

Mar. 29	Montreal	1	at	New York	3	
Apr. 1	New York	3	at	Montreal	2	
Apr. 2	Montreal	1	at	New York	4	
Apr. 4	New York	2	at	Montreal	3	OT
Apr. 6	New York	3	at	Montreal	0	

New York won series 4–1

FINALS
Apr. 11	New York	1	at	Detroit	4	
Apr. 13	Detroit	1	at	New York*3		
Apr. 15	Detroit	4	at	New York*0		
Apr. 18	New York	4	at	Detroit	3	OT
Apr. 20	New York	2	at	Detroit	1	OT
Apr. 22	New York	4	at	Detroit	5	
Apr. 23	New York	3	at	Detroit	4	OT

* played in Toronto

Detroit won series 4–3

1951

SEMI-FINALS
Mar. 27	Montreal	3	at	Detroit	2	OT
Mar. 29	Montreal	1	at	Detroit	0	OT
Mar. 31	Detroit	2	at	Montreal	0	
Apr. 3	Detroit	4	at	Montreal	1	
Apr. 5	Montreal	5	at	Detroit	2	
Apr. 7	Detroit	2	at	Montreal	3	

Montreal won series 4–2

Mar. 28	Boston	2	at	Toronto	0	
Mar. 31	Boston	1	at	Toronto	1	OT*
Apr. 1	Toronto	3	at	Boston	0	
Apr. 3	Toronto	3	at	Boston	1	
Apr. 7	Boston	1	at	Toronto	4	
Apr. 8	Toronto	6	at	Boston	0	

* game ended after one overtime period due to curfew.

Toronto won series 4–1

FINALS
Apr. 11	Montreal	2	at	Toronto	3	OT
Apr. 14	Montreal	3	at	Toronto	2	OT
Apr. 17	Toronto	2	at	Montreal	1	OT
Apr. 19	Toronto	3	at	Montreal	2	OT
Apr. 21	Montreal	2	at	Toronto	3	OT

Toronto won series 4–1

1952

SEMI-FINALS
Mar. 25	Toronto	0	at	Detroit	3	
Mar. 27	Toronto	0	at	Detroit	1	
Mar. 29	Detroit	6	at	Toronto	2	
Apr. 1	Detroit	3	at	Toronto	1	

Detroit won series 4–0

Mar. 25	Boston	1	at	Montreal	5	
Mar. 27	Boston	0	at	Montreal	4	
Mar. 30	Montreal	1	at	Boston	4	
Apr. 1	Montreal	2	at	Boston	3	
Apr. 3	Boston	1	at	Montreal	0	
Apr. 6	Montreal	3	at	Boston	2	OT
Apr. 8	Boston	1	at	Montreal	3	

Montreal won series 4–3

FINALS
Apr. 10	Detroit	3	at	Montreal	1	
Apr. 12	Detroit	2	at	Montreal	1	
Apr. 13	Montreal	0	at	Detroit	3	
Apr. 15	Montreal	0	at	Detroit	3	

Detroit won series 4–0

1953

SEMI-FINALS
Mar. 24	Boston	0	at	Detroit	7	
Mar. 26	Boston	5	at	Detroit	3	
Mar. 29	Detroit	1	at	Boston	2	OT
Mar. 31	Detroit	2	at	Boston	6	
Apr. 2	Boston	4	at	Detroit	6	
Apr. 5	Detroit	2	at	Boston	4	

Boston won series 4–2

Mar. 24	Chicago	1	at	Montreal	3	
Mar. 26	Chicago	3	at	Montreal	4	
Mar. 29	Montreal	1	at	Chicago	2	OT
Mar. 31	Montreal	1	at	Chicago	3	
Apr. 2	Chicago	4	at	Montreal	2	
Apr. 4	Montreal	3	at	Chicago	0	
Apr. 7	Chicago	1	at	Montreal	4	

Montreal won series 4–3

FINALS
Apr. 9	Boston	2	at	Montreal	4	
Apr. 11	Boston	4	at	Montreal	1	
Apr. 12	Montreal	3	at	Boston	0	
Apr. 14	Montreal	7	at	Boston	3	
Apr. 16	Boston	0	at	Montreal	1	OT

Montreal won series 4–1

1954

SEMI-FINALS
Mar. 23	Toronto	0	at	Detroit	5	
Mar. 25	Toronto	3	at	Detroit	1	
Mar. 27	Detroit	3	at	Toronto	1	
Mar. 30	Detroit	2	at	Toronto	1	
Apr. 1	Toronto	3	at	Detroit	4	OT

Detroit won series 4–1

Mar. 23	Boston	0	at	Montreal	2	
Mar. 25	Boston	1	at	Montreal	8	
Mar. 28	Montreal	4	at	Boston	3	
Mar. 30	Montreal	2	at	Boston	0	

Montreal won series 4–0

FINALS
Apr. 4	Montreal	1	at	Detroit	3	
Apr. 6	Montreal	3	at	Detroit	1	
Apr. 8	Detroit	5	at	Montreal	2	
Apr. 10	Detroit	2	at	Montreal	0	
Apr. 11	Montreal	1	at	Detroit	0	OT
Apr. 13	Detroit	1	at	Montreal	4	
Apr. 16	Montreal	1	at	Detroit	2	OT

Detroit won series 4–3

1955

SEMI-FINALS

Mar. 22	Toronto	4	at Detroit	7	
Mar. 24	Toronto	1	at Detroit	2	
Mar. 26	Detroit	2	at Toronto	1	
Mar. 29	Detroit	3	at Toronto	0	

Detroit won series 4–0

Mar. 22	Boston	0	at Montreal	2	
Mar. 24	Boston	1	at Montreal	3	
Mar. 27	Montreal	2	at Boston	4	
Mar. 29	Montreal	4	at Boston	3	OT
Mar. 31	Boston	1	at Montreal	5	

Montreal won series 4–1

FINALS

Apr. 3	Montreal	2	at Detroit	4	
Apr. 5	Montreal	1	at Detroit	7	
Apr. 7	Detroit	2	at Montreal	4	
Apr. 9	Detroit	3	at Montreal	5	
Apr. 10	Montreal	1	at Detroit	5	
Apr. 12	Detroit	3	at Montreal	6	
Apr. 14	Montreal	1	at Detroit	3	

Detroit won series 4–3

1956

SEMI-FINALS

Mar. 20	New York	1	at Montreal	7	
Mar. 22	New York	4	at Montreal	2	
Mar. 24	Montreal	3	at New York	1	
Mar. 25	Montreal	5	at New York	3	
Mar. 27	New York	0	at Montreal	7	

Montreal won series 4–1

Mar. 20	Toronto	2	at Detroit	3	
Mar. 22	Toronto	1	at Detroit	3	
Mar. 24	Detroit	5	at Toronto	4	OT
Mar. 27	Detroit	0	at Toronto	2	
Mar. 29	Toronto	1	at Detroit	3	

Detroit won series 4–1

FINALS

Mar. 31	Detroit	4	at Montreal	6	
Apr. 3	Detroit	1	at Montreal	5	
Apr. 5	Montreal	1	at Detroit	3	
Apr. 8	Montreal	3	at Detroit	0	
Apr. 10	Detroit	1	at Montreal	3	

Montreal won series 4–1

1957

SEMI-FINALS

Mar. 26	Boston	3	at Detroit	1	
Mar. 28	Boston	2	at Detroit	7	
Mar. 31	Detroit	3	at Boston	4	
Apr. 2	Detroit	0	at Boston	2	
Apr. 4	Boston	4	at Detroit	3	

Boston won series 4–1

Mar. 26	Montreal	4	at New York	1	
Mar. 28	Montreal	3	at New York	4	OT
Mar. 30	New York	3	at Montreal	8	
Apr. 2	New York	1	at Montreal	3	
Apr. 4	New York	3	at Montreal	4	OT

Montreal won series 4–1

FINALS

Apr. 6	Boston	1	at Montreal	5	
Apr. 9	Boston	0	at Montreal	1	
Apr. 11	Montreal	4	at Boston	2	
Apr. 14	Montreal	0	at Boston	2	
Apr. 16	Boston	1	at Montreal	5	

Montreal won series 4–1

1958

SEMI-FINALS

Mar. 25	Detroit	1	at Montreal	8	
Mar. 27	Detroit	1	at Montreal	5	
Mar. 30	Montreal	2	at Detroit	1	OT
Apr. 1	Montreal	4	at Detroit	3	

Montreal won series 4–0

Mar. 25	Boston	3	at New York	5	
Mar. 27	Boston	4	at New York	3	OT
Mar. 29	New York	0	at Boston	5	
Apr. 1	New York	5	at Boston	2	
Apr. 3	New York	1	at Boston	6	
Apr. 5	New York	2	at Boston	8	

Boston won series 4–2

FINALS

Apr. 8	Boston	1	at Montreal	2	
Apr. 10	Boston	5	at Montreal	2	
Apr. 13	Montreal	3	at Boston	0	
Apr. 15	Montreal	1	at Boston	3	
Apr. 17	Boston	2	at Montreal	3	OT
Apr. 20	Montreal	5	at Boston	3	

Montreal won series 4–2

1959

SEMI-FINALS

Mar. 24	Chicago	2	at Montreal	4	
Mar. 26	Chicago	1	at Montreal	5	
Mar. 28	Montreal	2	at Chicago	4	
Mar. 31	Montreal	1	at Chicago	3	
Apr. 2	Chicago	2	at Montreal	4	
Apr. 4	Montreal	5	at Chicago	4	

Montreal won series 4–2

Mar. 24	Toronto	1	at Boston	5	
Mar. 26	Toronto	2	at Boston	4	
Mar. 28	Boston	2	at Toronto	3	OT
Mar. 31	Boston	2	at Toronto	3	OT
Apr. 2	Toronto	4	at Boston	1	
Apr. 4	Boston	5	at Toronto	4	
Apr. 7	Toronto	3	at Boston	2	

Toronto won series 4–3

FINALS

Apr. 9	Toronto	3	at Montreal	5	
Apr. 11	Toronto	1	at Montreal	3	
Apr. 14	Montreal	2	at Toronto	3	OT
Apr. 16	Montreal	3	at Toronto	2	
Apr. 18	Toronto	3	at Montreal	5	

Montreal won series 4–1

1960

SEMI-FINALS

Mar. 24	Chicago	3	at Montreal	4	
Mar. 26	Chicago	3	at Montreal	4	OT
Mar. 29	Montreal	4	at Chicago	0	
Mar. 31	Montreal	2	at Chicago	0	

Montreal won series 4–0

Mar. 23	Detroit	2	at Toronto	1	
Mar. 26	Detroit	2	at Toronto	4	
Mar. 27	Toronto	5	at Detroit	4	OT
Mar. 29	Toronto	1	at Detroit	2	OT
Apr. 2	Detroit	4	at Toronto	5	
Apr. 3	Toronto	4	at Detroit	2	

Toronto won series 4–2

FINALS

Apr. 7	Toronto	2	at Montreal	4	
Apr. 9	Toronto	1	at Montreal	2	
Apr. 12	Montreal	5	at Toronto	2	
Apr. 14	Montreal	4	at Toronto	0	

Montreal won series 4–0

1961

SEMI-FINALS

Mar. 21	Chicago	2	at Montreal	6	
Mar. 23	Chicago	4	at Montreal	3	
Mar. 26	Montreal	1	at Chicago	2	OT
Mar. 28	Montreal	5	at Chicago	2	
Apr. 1	Chicago	3	at Montreal	0	
Apr. 4	Montreal	0	at Chicago	3	

Chicago won series 4–2

Mar. 22	Detroit	2	at Toronto	3	OT
Mar. 25	Detroit	4	at Toronto	2	
Mar. 26	Toronto	0	at Detroit	2	
Mar. 28	Toronto	1	at Detroit	4	
Apr. 1	Detroit	3	at Toronto	2	

Detroit won series 4–1

FINALS

Apr. 6	Detroit	2	at Chicago	3	
Apr. 8	Chicago	1	at Detroit	3	
Apr. 10	Detroit	1	at Chicago	3	
Apr. 12	Chicago	1	at Detroit	2	
Apr. 14	Detroit	3	at Chicago	6	
Apr. 16	Chicago	5	at Detroit	1	

Chicago won series 4–2

1962

SEMI-FINALS

Mar. 27	Chicago	1	at	Montreal	2
Mar. 29	Chicago	3	at	Montreal	4
Apr. 1	Montreal	1	at	Chicago	4
Apr. 3	Montreal	3	at	Chicago	5
Apr. 5	Chicago	4	at	Montreal	3
Apr. 8	Montreal	0	at	Chicago	2

Chicago won series 4–2

Mar. 27	New York	2	at	Toronto	4
Mar. 29	New York	1	at	Toronto	2
Apr. 1	Toronto	4	at	New York	5
Apr. 3	Toronto	2	at	New York	4
Apr. 5	New York	2	at	Toronto	3 OT
Apr. 7	New York	1	at	Toronto	7

Toronto won series 4–2

FINALS

Apr. 10	Chicago	1	at	Toronto	4
Apr. 12	Chicago	2	at	Toronto	3
Apr. 15	Toronto	0	at	Chicago	3
Apr. 17	Toronto	1	at	Chicago	4
Apr. 19	Chicago	4	at	Toronto	8
Apr. 22	Toronto	2	at	Chicago	1

Toronto won series 4–2

1963

SEMI-FINALS

Mar. 26	Montreal	1	at	Toronto	3
Mar. 28	Montreal	2	at	Toronto	3
Mar. 30	Toronto	2	at	Montreal	0
Apr. 2	Toronto	1	at	Montreal	3
Apr. 4	Montreal	0	at	Toronto	5

Toronto won series 4–1

Mar. 26	Detroit	4	at	Chicago	5
Mar. 28	Detroit	2	at	Chicago	5
Mar. 31	Chicago	2	at	Detroit	4
Apr. 2	Chicago	1	at	Detroit	4
Apr. 4	Detroit	4	at	Chicago	2
Apr. 7	Chicago	4	at	Detroit	7

Detroit won series 4–2

FINALS

Apr. 9	Detroit	2	at	Toronto	4
Apr. 11	Detroit	2	at	Toronto	4
Apr. 14	Toronto	2	at	Detroit	3
Apr. 16	Toronto	4	at	Detroit	2
Apr. 18	Detroit	1	at	Toronto	3

Toronto won series 4–1

1964

SEMI-FINALS

Mar. 26	Toronto	0	at	Montreal	2
Mar. 28	Toronto	2	at	Montreal	1
Mar. 31	Montreal	3	at	Toronto	2
Apr. 2	Montreal	3	at	Toronto	5
Apr. 4	Toronto	2	at	Montreal	4
Apr. 7	Montreal	0	at	Toronto	3
Apr. 9	Toronto	3	at	Montreal	1

Toronto won series 4–3

Mar. 26	Detroit	1	at	Chicago	4
Mar. 29	Detroit	5	at	Chicago	4
Mar. 31	Chicago	0	at	Detroit	3
Apr. 2	Chicago	3	at	Detroit	2 OT
Apr. 5	Detroit	2	at	Chicago	3
Apr. 7	Chicago	2	at	Detroit	7
Apr. 9	Detroit	4	at	Chicago	2

Detroit won series 4–3

FINALS

Apr. 11	Detroit	2	at	Toronto	3
Apr. 14	Detroit	4	at	Toronto	3 OT
Apr. 16	Toronto	3	at	Detroit	4
Apr. 18	Toronto	4	at	Detroit	2
Apr. 21	Detroit	2	at	Toronto	1
Apr. 23	Toronto	4	at	Detroit	3 OT
Apr. 25	Detroit	0	at	Toronto	4

Toronto won series 4–3

1965

SEMI-FINALS

Apr. 1	Chicago	3	at	Detroit	4
Apr. 4	Chicago	3	at	Detroit	6
Apr. 6	Detroit	2	at	Chicago	5
Apr. 8	Detroit	1	at	Chicago	2
Apr. 11	Chicago	2	at	Detroit	4
Apr. 13	Detroit	0	at	Chicago	4
Apr. 15	Chicago	4	at	Detroit	2

Chicago won series 4–3

Apr. 1	Toronto	2	at	Montreal	3
Apr. 3	Toronto	1	at	Montreal	3
Apr. 6	Montreal	2	at	Toronto	3 OT
Apr. 8	Montreal	3	at	Toronto	4
Apr. 10	Toronto	1	at	Montreal	3
Apr. 13	Montreal	4	at	Toronto	3 OT

Montreal won series 4–2

FINALS

Apr. 17	Chicago	2	at	Montreal	3
Apr. 20	Chicago	0	at	Montreal	2
Apr. 22	Montreal	1	at	Chicago	3
Apr. 25	Montreal	1	at	Chicago	5
Apr. 27	Chicago	0	at	Montreal	6
Apr. 29	Montreal	1	at	Chicago	2
May 1	Chicago	0	at	Montreal	4

Montreal won series 4–3

1966

SEMI-FINALS

Apr. 7	Toronto	3	at	Montreal	4
Apr. 9	Toronto	0	at	Montreal	2
Apr. 12	Montreal	5	at	Toronto	2
Apr. 14	Montreal	4	at	Toronto	1

Montreal won series 4–2

Apr. 7	Detroit	1	at	Chicago	2
Apr. 10	Detroit	7	at	Chicago	0
Apr. 12	Chicago	2	at	Detroit	1
Apr. 14	Chicago	1	at	Detroit	5
Apr. 17	Detroit	5	at	Chicago	3
Apr. 19	Chicago	2	at	Detroit	3

Detroit won series 4–2

FINALS

Apr. 24	Detroit	3	at	Montreal	2
Apr. 26	Detroit	5	at	Montreal	2
Apr. 28	Montreal	4	at	Detroit	2
May 1	Montreal	2	at	Detroit	1
May 3	Detroit	1	at	Montreal	5
May 5	Montreal	3	at	Detroit	2 OT

Montreal won series 4–2

1967

SEMI-FINALS

Apr. 6	Toronto	2	at	Chicago	5
Apr. 9	Toronto	3	at	Chicago	1
Apr. 11	Chicago	1	at	Toronto	3
Apr. 13	Chicago	4	at	Toronto	3
Apr. 15	Toronto	4	at	Chicago	2
Apr. 18	Chicago	1	at	Toronto	3

Toronto won series 4–2

Apr. 6	New York	4	at	Montreal	6
Apr. 8	New York	1	at	Montreal	3
Apr. 11	Montreal	3	at	New York	2
Apr. 13	Montreal	2	at	New York	1 OT

Montreal won series 4–0

FINALS

Apr. 20	Toronto	2	at	Montreal	6
Apr. 22	Toronto	3	at	Montreal	0
Apr. 25	Montreal	2	at	Toronto	3 OT
Apr. 27	Montreal	6	at	Toronto	3
Apr. 29	Toronto	4	at	Montreal	1
May 2	Montreal	1	at	Toronto	3

Toronto won series 4–2

Index

Page numbers in italics refer to photographs.

Overleaf: Although Terry Sawchuk (right) robbed Yvan Cournoyer and his Montreal Canadiens teammates during the 1967 Stanley Cup finals, Cournoyer would go on to enjoy another eight Stanley Cup victories in his Hall-of-Fame career. For Sawchuk, arguably the game's greatest goaltender, the 1967 championship that brought the curtain down on the six-team era, was his final glimpse of glory. For the rest of his career, he was steadily on the move, playing with Los Angeles, Detroit, and the New York Rangers during the next three seasons before his untimely death in the summer of 1970.